Timing of Behavior

Timing of Behavior

Neural, Psychological, and·Computational
Perspectives

---

edited by David A. Rosenbaum and Charles E. Collyer

A Bradford Book
The MIT Press
Cambridge, Massachusetts
London, England

© 1998 Massachusetts Institute of Technology

This book was set in Palatino on the Monotype "Prism Plus" PostScript Imagesetter by Asco Trade Typesetting Ltd., Hong Kong and was printed and bound in the United States of America.

Library of Congress Cataloging-in-Publication Data

Timing of behavior : neural, psychological, and computational / David
   A. Rosenbaum and Charles E. Collyer, editors.
      p.   cm.
   "A Bradford book."
   Includes bibliographical references and index.
   ISBN 0-262-18188-6 (alk. paper)
   1. Movement, Psychology of. 2. Perceptual-motor processes.
3. Neuropsychology. I. Rosenbaum, David A. II. Collyer, Charles E.
BF295.T56   1998
152.3—dc21   97-37189
                                                      CIP

To Our Parents

Contents

Foreword

In recent years there has been considerable growth in interest in timing aspects of human behavior in the brain and behavioral sciences. In bringing together the work of a number of leading researchers, this book is a welcome addition to the literature. The editors, both of whom have a long-standing professional interest in the area, are to be congratulated on their efforts.

There are empirical chapters providing interesting and novel accounts of a variety of tasks ranging from locomotion to finger tapping with timing requirements that may be implicit or explicit. There are theoretical chapters providing quantitative models that include topics as diverse as eyeblink conditioning and posture during gait. There are chapters concerned with neuroanatomical bases of timing behavior. And although the majority of chapters focus on motor output, there are chapters addressing perceptual issues.

All in all, this book will be valuable to workers in the field seeking an up-to-date reference source and to newcomers and students interested in learning about the ideas and methods of this lively and dynamic field of growing importance in the study of human behavior.

Alan M. Wing
MRC Applied Psychology Unit, Cambridge, and
Centre for Sensory Motor Neuroscience, Birmingham University

Preface

All of us marvel at the skills of athletes and musicians as they demonstrate the levels to which humans can ascend in the timing of behavior. But these feats merely illustrate a broader range of capabilities shown in everyday life. Picking up a cup and bringing it to one's lips, opening a door for an elderly friend, tapping one's foot in time with music all reveal how we temporally organize our behavior. In cases where there is damage to the nervous system, the ability to time behavior can break down, and we become aware, sometimes painfully so, of the many things that must go right for timing not to go crazily wrong.

This volume assembles research from several teams of investigators who have studied the timing of behavior from different perspectives—the neural perspective, the psychological perspective, and the computational perspective. All of these perspectives are equally important, in our judgment. Viewing timing only from a neural perspective leaves out the psychological functions being served and the computations being performed. Viewing timing from a purely psychological perspective omits the biological substrates that make behavior possible and excludes the abstract or formal properties being evinced behaviorally. Finally, viewing timing from a purely computational perspective leaves out the richness of actual behavior, the complexity of neural machinery, and the impact that behavioral and neural constraints can have on the computations. To show the rich interconnections among all these approaches, we have assembled in one place works representing all three traditions.

What also brought this work together was a series of meetings that began over a breakfast in New Orleans at the November 1990 meeting of the Psychonomics Society. At that breakfast, Charles Collyer, David Rosenbaum, Jonathan Vaughan, and Daniel Willingham, all of whom were then working in the greater New England area, agreed that it was silly to talk about common research interests only at a gathering more than a thousand miles from our geographical center. We resolved to get together in New England, and did so soon thereafter, in January 1991 in Amherst, Massachusetts. The meeting was lively but informal. It amounted to the breakfast group and a few others sitting around a table for a few hours telling each other what we were working on. Very much with tongue-in-cheek, we declared that this was the first meeting of New England Sequencing and Timing, or NEST for short. The NEST acronym was appealing because we shared the view, held by virtually everyone working in this field, that timing relies on hierarchically nested structures and processes.

That first NEST meeting was so much fun that we resolved to hold another meeting the following year. To that meeting we invited more people, used a transparency machine rather than just a blackboard, made arrangements with a food service, and so on. Despite the grandiosity of the second NEST meeting, it was still a success. The tradition of meeting once a year has continued; the first five meetings were held in Amherst, organized by David Rosenbaum, when he was still at the University of Massachusetts. After his departure for Penn State in the summer of 1994, the organizing chores went to Charles Collyer, who has hosted the succeeding meetings in Providence.

With the "changing of the guard" after the fifth NEST meeting, it occurred to us that it might be useful to invite speakers from the first five meetings to write up their work for publication in a single volume that would represent, in effect, "the Best of NEST." After several steps, this book has materialized. For such a transformation to occur, many people and situations must allow the necessary work to transpire. We are grateful to the authors, not only for their chapters, but also for their anonymous (and usually tough) reviewing of the chapters of the other contributors. We are also grateful to the following funding sources for aid that made it possible for the editors to do the work represented here: the National Science Foundation (grants BNS 90-08665 and DBS 93-08671/ SBR-9496290 to David Rosenbaum, and grants BNS 9110158 and BNS94 21243 to Charles Collyer and his colleagues); the Research and Graduate Studies Office of Pennsylvania State University (to David Rosenbaum); the University of Rhode Island (grant NSS2-S07-RR07086-14 to Charles Collyer); and the National Institutes of Health (NIMH Research Scientist Development Award KO2 MH00977 to David Rosenbaum). In addition, we thank MIT Press for their support throughout this process. Finally, we thank those with whom we live for their daily support (Judith Kroll, Nora and Sarah Kroll-Rosenbaum, whose patience was tried by David Rosenbaum, and Pam Zappardino, whose patience was tried by Charles Collyer).

Part I

Neural Perspectives

Chapter 1

Predictive Timing under Temporal Uncertainty: The Time Derivative Model of the Conditioned Response

John W. Moore, June-Seek Choi, and Darlene H. Brunzell

Abstract

Classical conditioning procedures instill knowledge about the temporal relationships between conditioned stimuli, which are regarded both as predictive signals and triggers for action, and the unconditioned stimulus (US), the event to be timed. This knowledge is expressed in the temporal features of the conditioned response (CR), which can be viewed as prediction about the imminence of the US. The peak amplitude of the CR typically coincides with the timing of the unconditioned stimulus. A simple connectionist network based on Sutton and Barto's (1990) Time Derivative (TD) Model of Pavlovian Reinforcement provides a mechanism that can account for and simulate virtually all known aspects of conditioned response timing in a variety of protocols. This chapter describes extensions of the model to predictive timing under temporal uncertainty. The model is expressed in terms of equations that operate in real time according to Hebbian competitive learning rules. The unfolding of time from the onsets and offsets of events such as conditioned stimuli is represented by the propagation of activity along a sequence of time-tagged elements. The model can be aligned with anatomical circuits of the cerebellum and brainstem that are essential for learning and performance of eyeblink conditioned responses. The eyeblink conditioned response is a simple skeletal response in that lid movement can be expressed as a scalar quantity. For the purposes of this chapter, the form of this response is portrayed as an index of an actor's expectation of the timing of the target event. Hence, this chapter uses eyeblink conditioning as a model system for understanding the acquisition and expression of knowledge for timing and action at behavioral, computational, and physiological levels.

1.1 Introduction

Imagine a task in which an actor is required to predict not only the timing of some target event but also the degree of certainty or confidence that the prediction is correct. In its simplest form, the actor is presented with a signal or cue that initiates the timing. This cue is followed some fixed time later by the to-be-predicted (target) event. The actor's prediction of the target at each point in time is expressed as a scalar quantity. Performance is assessed by the degree to which the peak or maximum of the prediction coincides with the onset of the target. The simplest variation of this task is one in which the actor predicts the offset of the timing cue.

In this form, the task reduces to duration prediction or judgment. Whenever the target event is distinct from the timing cue, the task is analogous to classical Pavlovian conditioning. The onset of the timing cue can be regarded as a conditioned stimulus (CS) and the target event can be regarded as an unconditioned stimulus (US). The TD model of the CR, the main focus of this chapter, can be applied to duration prediction by regarding the offset of the timing cue as the target event.

If the actor responds to the timing cue at full strength with the shortest possible reaction time, then performance would be assessed as being rather poor because the prediction lacks precision. Furthermore, the longer the timing interval, the poorer the performance would be. Performance would be assessed more favorably were the actor to delay responding (predicting) until precisely the time when the target occurs and then respond with a step-impulse of maximum amplitude. Because of inertia and delays in effector systems, however, the actor may need to begin responding before the target event occurs, so that the prediction response can rise smoothly to a maximum that coincides with onset of the target.

Although too much anticipation can spoil prediction accuracy, some anticipation can be a desirable feature of a timing device or controller. For example, foreknowledge allows an actor to marshal whatever resources are needed for an imminent target event or perturbation. Because prediction of the moment-by-moment likelihood of the target is a scalar quantity, experimental tests of theories of prediction in the domain of action must rely on actions such as the eyeblink that can be expressed as a scalar (i.e., single degree of freedom) quantity. Because of its rich literature and ties with core issues of learning theory, eyeblink conditioning has become the focus of work on predictive timing and prediction be several groups of investigators (Gabriel and Moore, 1990).

Sutton and Barto (1990) developed a computational model based on TD learning that is capable of generating basic features of predictive timing in the context of classical conditioning.[1] This chapter shows how TD learning can be extended to predictive timing under temporal uncertainty. Here, temporal uncertainty refers to procedures in which the timing of the target event, the US, with respect to the CS varies randomly from trial to trial.

As in the case of other models of conditioned response timing (e.g., Desmond and Moore, 1988), implementation of the TD models assumes that time is represented as an ordered sequence of time-tagged components or elements. The core assumption is that a CS event initiates a cascade of activation such that one component excites that next, with some delay. The target event might occur at any point in the cascade. When it does occur, a connection is established between elements of the cascade and the target. Thus, a nominal CS is simply an event that triggers a cascade of activation among hypothetical components that are the actual CSs at the level of the nervous system. A neural network representation of time-tagged CS components and their connections to representations of the target and action generators are described later.

1.2 The TD Model of the Conditioned Response

Before stating the TD model in mathematical form, let us introduce some notation and key assumptions.

1. The symbol X refers to the strength or weight of a cue such as a CS. In the TD model each time step after the initiation of the CS cascade is regarded as a separate stimulus. (The TD model treats time, t, as a discrete variable.) We refer to such stimuli as serial component CSs. In this role (as a time-tagged serial component), X is given a subscript that denotes its ordinal position in the cascade: X_1 denotes the first serial componet CS, X_2 denotes the second serial component CS, and so forth. On the first time step X_1 has a positive real value (typically assumed to equal 1.0 in simulations), and X_2 equals 0. On the second time step, X_2 is activated to a level that is typically assumed to equal 1.0, and X_1 reverts to 0 because it is no longer active. On the next time step, X_3 is activated, and X_2 reverts to 0.

2. CS triggered cascades, which result in the activation of successive serial components, do not last indefinitely. There is a limit on how many serial components can be activated by a nominal CS event. For any learning to occur, however, this limit must span the interval between the onset of the cascade and the target.

3. The salience of a CS refers its *associability*, not its ability to control behavior, although the two features are often correlated. One CS is more salient then another if it lends itself more readily to association with the US. Salience is partially determined by a CS's intensity, but salience can also depend on attentional factors that are themselves subject to cognitive processes such as set and vigilance. The Greek letter α, introduced later on, is a parameter that specifies a CS's salience. The variant of the TD model presented here assumes that all serial components of a CS cascade are equally salient.

4. The symbol $\overline{X}_i$ represents the decaying trace of the ith serial component CS. This trace is referred to as the CS's *eligibility* for changing the weight of its connection to the target event. $\overline{X}_i$ is not a stimulating trace because it does not evoke a response. Its role is to allow a serial component CS to participate in computations of connection weights even though it is no longer active (see Sutton and Barto, 1981, 1990; Desmond, 1990).

5. The symbol V_i (associative value) refers to the strength or weight of the connection between the ith serial component CS and the target, but it is equally correct to think of it as the connection between the CS and the conditioned (prediction) response.

6. Because V_i is a function of time, the notation $V_i(t)$ denotes the value of V_i at time t, where t denotes the time step after onset of the CS cascade.

7. The symbol $Y(t)$ refers to the strength or magnitude of the response at time t. In conditioning, Y reflects the effects of contiguous pairing of a CS and US, $Y(t)$ is equal to $X(t) \times V(t)$. In the TD model, $V(t)$ is estimated by $V(t-1)$ because $V(t)$ is not immediately available, and $X(t) \times V(t-1)$ is therefore an estimate of $Y(t)$. This estimate is attenuated (discounted) by the factor γ, a parameter of the model.

8. The symbol $\dot{Y}$ (Y-dot), the first time derivative of Y, represents the change in the value of Y from one time step to the next: $\dot{Y} = Y(t) - Y(t-1)$.

9. The Greek letter Δ refers to a change in a variable such as V from one time-step to the next. Hence, $\Delta V_i(t)$ refers to the change in the connection between the ith serial component CS and the target event computed on time step t. Computation of $\Delta V_i(t)$ requires $\dot{Y}(t)$. Because the TD model treats time as discrete, $\dot{Y}$ is computed using connection weights from the preceding time step $t-1$. This is made explicit in the formal statement of the model given next.

10. The Greek letters α, β, γ, are δ are parameters in equations describing the TD model. The purpose of parameters not previously mentioned will be described later.

1.3 Formal Statement of the TD Model

The TD model is a member of a class of computational models that Sutton and Barto (1990) refer to as $\dot{Y}$ or time-derivative theories of reinforcement learning. Such theories take the form of equation 1.1, which specifies the moment-by-moment changes in associative value, V_i, the weight of the connection between CS_i, the ith of a potential set of CSs, and the US.

$$\Delta V_i = \beta \dot{Y} \times \alpha_i \overline{X}_i \tag{1.1}$$

As with Hebbian learning rules generally, changes in associative value, ΔV_i for CS_i, are computed as the product of two factors. The coefficents α_i and β are rate parameters ($0 < \alpha_i, \beta \leq 1$). Coefficient α_i is the salience of the ith serial component CS. The factor $\overline{X}_i$ represents the eligibility of the connection between CS_i and the US for modification. Eligibility is a weighted average of previous and current levels of activation of CS_i. The other factor, $\dot{Y}$, represents *reinforcement*. Reinforcement in time-derivative models is a function of the difference (time derivative) between the response or output at time t, $Y(t)$, and the response or output at some previous time, $Y(t - \Delta t)$ (equation 1.2).

$$\dot{Y} = Y(t) - Y(t - \Delta t) \tag{1.2}$$

with time treated as a discrete variable, $\dot{Y} = Y(t) - Y(t - 1)$, as noted previously.

Any system or device that would implement a time-derivative learning rule must be capable of monitoring the actor's output on both current and immediately preceding time steps. Later on, we discuss how this might be accomplished within the cerebellum, the putative site of learning in classical eyeblink conditioning.

Sutton and Barto (1990) reviewed evidence showing how their TD model is superior to other computational theories of classical conditioning, because it encompasses problematic phenomema such as the form of CS–US interval functions and higher-order conditioning. CS–US interval functions are empirically derived relationships between conditioning performance and the CS–US interval employed in training. Higher-order conditioning refers to conditioning derived from the pairing a novel stimulus with a previously established CS. In addition, the TD model can describe the appropriate timing and topography of eyeblink CRs, provided the CS–US interval is segmented into a sequence of time-tagged elements. Each of these elements develops its own associative value with training. Sutton and Barto (1990) have referred to this representation of the CS as a complete serial compound (CSC).[2]

The following equation expresses the TD learning rule for classical conditioning.

$$\Delta V_i(t) = \beta[\lambda(t) + \gamma Y(t) - Y(t - 1)] \times \alpha \overline{X}_i(t) \tag{1.3}$$

where

$$Y(t) = \sum_j V_j(t) X_j(t). \tag{1.4}$$

In equation 1.3, the Y-dot factor of equation 1.2 becomes $\lambda(t) + \gamma Y(t) - Y(t - 1)$; $\lambda(t)$ represents the strength of the US at time t. As in equation 1.1, α and β are rate parameters. Notice that we have dropped the subscript from α, so that $\alpha_i = \alpha$ for all serial component CSs.

In equation 1.4, the subscript j includes all serial component CSs, and $X_j(t)$ indicates the on-off status of the jth component at time t; $Y(t)$ corresponds to CR amplitude at time t; and $\overline{X}_i(t)$ is the eligibility of the ith CS component for modification at time t, given by the following expression.[3]

$$\overline{X}_i(t+1) = \overline{X}_i(t) + \delta[X_i(t) - \overline{X}_i(t)], \tag{1.5}$$

where $0 < \delta \leq 1$.

A key feature of the TD model is the parameter γ ($0 < \gamma \leq 1$). This parameter determines the rate of increase of CR amplitude, $Y(t)$, as the US becomes increasely imminent. With the CSC representation of CSs, the TD model generates realistic portraits of CRs. Realistic CRs resemble goal gradients in that CR amplitude increases progressively to the onset of the US. The behavior of the model with variations in γ is illustrated in figure 1.1, which is presented later.

Parameter γ is referred to as the *discount* parameter in applications of the TD learning rule. γ is applied to $Y(t)$ in equation 1.3 because $Y(t)$ is actually an estimate or prediction. On time step t, $Y(t)$ is not known with certainty until after the fact, although $Y(t)$ can be estimated by the sum of products of the form $X_j(t) \times V_j(t-1)$. That is, the connection weights from the preceding time step are used to estimate the value of $V(t)$ for the current time step. γ can be regarded as the penalty for using $V_j(t-1)$ instead of the true connection weight, $V_j(t)$. To reiterate the point, $V_j(t)$ does not become known until time step $t+1$.

Basically, equation 1.3 says that the connection between the ith serial component CS and the US is modified to the extent that there exists a discrepancy (algebraic difference) between the value of the US, $\lambda(t)$, plus the predicted output $Y(t)$ discounted or attenuated by γ, and the output on the preceding time step, $Y(t-1)$. Equation 1.4 states that output is the algebraic sum of weighted input. Equation 1.5 states that $\overline{X}$ declines geometrically at a rate determined by δ. The larger the value of δ, the faster the decline. A low value of δ implies that connections between serial component CSs and the US remain eligible for modification for several time steps.

Simulation Form of the TD Model

For technical reasons, equations 1.3 through 1.5 are not readily applicable for simulations. For simulations, it is necessary to decompose $Y(t)$ into its constituent parts, $X(t)$ and $V(t)$. Although it is straightforward to substitute $X(t-1) \times V(t-1)$ for $Y(t-1)$ for the preceding time step, for the current time step (t) the simulation must use the value of V from the preceding time step. As discussed previously, $V(t-1)$ is multiplied by $X(t)$ in order to obtain $Y(t)$. This makes sense because, as a conditioned response, $Y(t)$ reflects prior experience. It is also essential (to ensure convergence) that the sums of products of X and V not be negative. The notation $\lfloor \sum XV \rfloor$ specifies this constraint: If this quantity is less than 0, it is set equal to 0. (See Sutton and Barto, 1990, p. 533). These two constraints have been incorporated into equation 1.6, the simulation form of equation 1.3.

$$\Delta V_i(t) = \beta \left\{ \lambda(t) + \gamma \left[\sum_j X_j(t) V_j(t-1) \right] \right.$$

$$\left. - \left[\sum_j X_j(t-1) V_j(t-1) \right] \right\} \times \alpha \overline{X}_i(t). \qquad (1.6)$$

Equation 1.6 emphasizes the fact that changes in the strength of connections between serial components CS and the US are functions of their level of activation.

1.4 Simulations of CR Timing by the TD Model

Figure 1.1 shows a family of CR waveforms with different values of γ and δ. The figure shows that CR amplitude depends primarily on γ: The smaller the value of γ, the lower the peak value of CR amplitude, $Y(t)$. Lower values of γ also increase the positive acceleration of CR amplitude, $\Delta \dot{Y}(t)$, without compromising the accuracy of $Y(t)$'s prediction of the timing of the US.

In simulations, $X_j(t)$ takes on values of 1 (when activated) or 0 (when not activated), with activation lasting for one time-step (10 ms in the simulations). Under these circumstances response topography depends only on the model's other parameters and on constraints on the effector system.[4] In the case of classically conditioned eyelid movements, the eyelids are normally open. In this position, CR amplitude has a value of 0. A fully developed CR is one in which the eyelid's position moves from open to completely closed. Yet, no matter how strong the prediction that the US will occur, the eyelids can only close so far. This constraint implies that the progressive closure of the lids in the course of CR production can saturate before the US's anticipated time of occurrence. In addition, these constraints on eyelid position render it impossible for negative predictions of the US to be expressed directly in eyelid movement. By negative prediction, we mean predictions that the US will not occur at some time when it would otherwise be anticipated. No matter how strong the prediction that the US will not occur, the eyelids can only open so far and no farther.

Simulating Predictive Timing under Uncertainty

Consider now a variation of the predictive timing task discussed in section 1.1 in which the timing of the target event varies from one occasion or trial

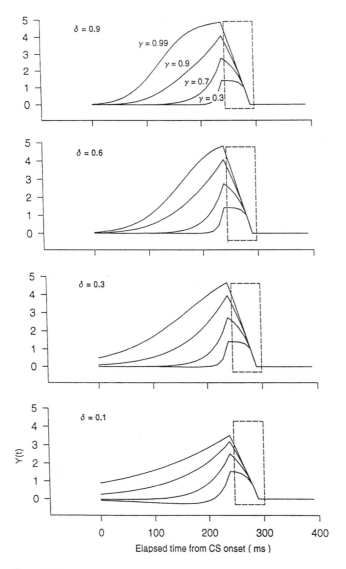

Figure 1.1
Simulated CRs, $Y(t)$, after 200 trials as a function of γ and δ. Time-steps in this and other simulations are 10 ms, $\alpha = 0.05$, $\beta = 1.0$, and $\lambda = 1.0$. The rectangle in each panel indicates the duration of the US, which is 50 ms. Note that CR timing and amplitude are determined primarily by the discount factor, γ.

to the next. Here, a trial is the inititation of a CS cascade, and uncertainty arises from random variation in the timing of the target event, the US. That is, target timing from one trial to the next is a random variable.

Predictions of target timing, reflected in CR topography, will clearly be affected by the probability distribution of target times. Simulations were confined to the case where the target occurs at one of three times after onset of the CS. In order to connect with data presented in the next section, these times are 300, 500, and 700 ms, each CS–US interval occurring equally often and randomly over a sequence of trials.

1.5 Prediction Strategies and CR Topography

There are a number of prediction strategies that might be adopted by an actor. Predictions generated by TD learning are based on the actor's experience with the timing cue and target, although the actor might expect that target timing can change abruptly and without warning. The actor might then generate predictions based on the possibility that the target will occur at some unprecedented time or that the target will occur more than once. Although exogenous to the model, processes that produce such expectancies could alter the parameters of the model or the structure of timing. With the appropriate parametric alterations and timing structure, the TD model can simulate any of a number of prediction strategies.

The TD model does not state *how* a given prediction strategy is selected.[5] Nor does the model specify *why* a strategy is selected, although its consequences (values and costs) would be relevant considerations. These topics are beyond the scope of this chapter. The TD model provides the means or mechanisms for *implementing* a strategy through a combination of parameter setting and structuring of the timing mechanism.

Fail-Safe Predicting

One prediction strategy would be to respond with a maximal prediction response before the first possible target time and to sustain this prediction until the target event occurs or the trial terminates. This is a *fail-safe* strategy in that the actor's response is appropriate for all possible times that the target *might* occur. In the example, the prediction response would begin before the earliest possible target time, 300 milliseconds in the example. It would then plateau to a maximum at that point in time, as illustrated in figure 1.2. The TD model simulates this type of response by assuming that the target event, the US, occupies every time-step between 300 ms, and some later time-step beyond the maximum possible target time of 700 ms.

A fail-safe strategy makes sense if there is a lot of inertial or resistive force to be overcome by the effector system in moving from its starting

200 trials

$\alpha = 0.05$ $\beta = 1.0$ $\gamma = 0.99$ $\delta = 0.99$ $\lambda = 1.0$

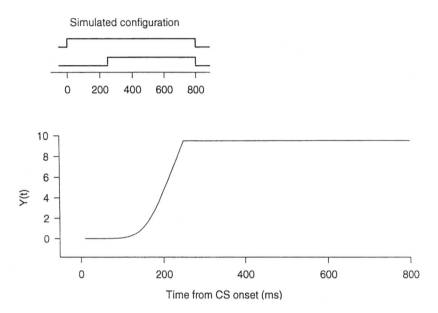

Simulated configuration

Figure 1.2
Simulated fail-safe prediction response under temporal uncertainty.

position to its maximum displacement and back again. Fail-safe prediction also makes sense if the costs of error are low or if the actor believes that the past is not a reliable guide to the present, that is, that target timing or number of occurrences per trial might change without warning. Fail-safe prediction involves considerable error, as the target is predicted with minimal precision.

Hedging
A second strategy would have the actor respond maximally to each of the three possible target times it has experienced on previous occasions, as illustrated in figure 1.3. The TD model simulates this type of response through any of a variety of parametric adjustments that produce large-amplitude waveforms, such as inflating the value of λ or selecting a large value of the discount factor, γ (see figure 1.1).

This is a *hedging* strategy in that the actor's predictions are appropriate for the possibility that the target might appear at any one, or indeed all, of the three target times. Instead of making one prediction, the actor

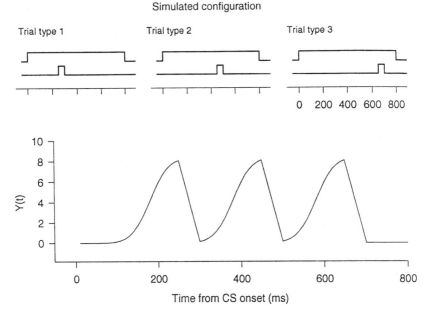

Figure 1.3
Simulated hedging prediction under temporal uncertainty.

makes three, one for each target time. Unlike a fail-safe strategy, a hedging strategy ensures that the target event is predicted with accuracy (a "hit" in the vernacular of signal detection theory), but at the cost of "false alarms." Hedging makes sense if the costs of moving from baseline and back again are negligible and the penalties for false alarms are low.

Proportionate Hedging
A third strategy would be to partition costs of predictions equally among the three target times, as with the hedging strategy, but with less than maximal amplitude. This is illustrated in figure 1.4. The TD model simulates this prediction strategy without parametric adjustments.

We call this strategy *proportionate hedging* because the actor's predictions are proportionate to the percentage of times the target occurs at each of the three CS–US intervals. This strategy makes sense when the costs of full-fledged false alarms outweigh the benefits of hits.

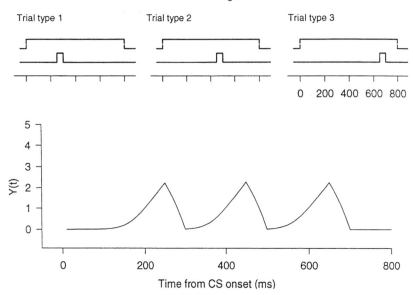

500 total trials
$\alpha = 0.02$ $\beta = 1.0$ $\gamma = 0.99$ $\delta = 0.99$ $\lambda = 1.67$

Simulated configuration

Trial type 1   Trial type 2   Trial type 3

0   200   400   600   800

Y(t)

Time from CS onset (ms)

Figure 1.4
Simulated proportionate hedging prediction under temporal uncertainty.

Conditional Expectation

A fourth strategy would be one based on conditional expectations of target timing, as illustrated in figure 1.5. The TD model simulates this strategy only with additional assumptions about the structure of timing. These additional assumptions are spelled out later on.

Using a *conditional expectation* strategy, the actor's predictions reflect the fact that the probability of the target occurring at later times increases if it has not occurred at earlier times. This strategy makes sense if both the costs of false alarms and the benefits of hits are high. The conditional expectation strategy is a reasoned compromise between the hedging and proportionate hedging strategies.

All of the aforementioned prediction strategies are feedforward actions triggered by the CS. As shown by figures 1.2 through 1.5, they can all be generated by the TD model of the CR, using different parameters or assumptions about the structure of timing. The next section presents data bearing on predictive timing strategies expressed by CR topography.

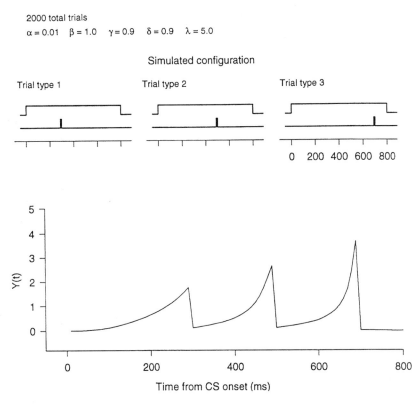

2000 total trials

$\alpha = 0.01$ $\beta = 1.0$ $\gamma = 0.9$ $\delta = 0.9$ $\lambda = 5.0$

Simulated configuration

Figure 1.5
Simulated conditional expectation prediction under temporal uncertainty.

1.6 CR Topography Under Predictive Uncertainty

We trained eight rabbits to make conditioned eyelid movements under temporal uncertainty. The CS was a compound stimulus consisting of a tone and light. It lasted 800 milliseconds. The US was a 50-ms train of pulses from a direct current (DC) source applied to the periocular region of the right eye by steel sutures. The US was applied at either 300, 500, or 700 ms following CS onset. Because the time of the US was selected randomly, its timing from trial to trial was uncertain. Rabbits were not cued as to whether the US would occur at 300, 500, or 700 ms. The interval between CS presentations was 30 to 40 seconds, and there were 60 such trials per day for 10 days. Movements of the right superior eyelid were recorded with a low torque potentiometer.

We examined the waveforms depicting eyelid movement for each rabbit for the subset of trials on which the US occurred at 700 ms. These

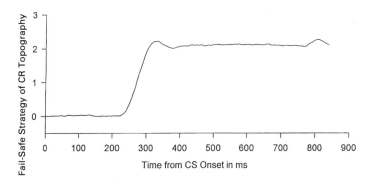

Figure 1.6
Eyeblink conditioned response consistent with a fail-safe prediction strategy.

trials provided waveforms that covered the entire interval of uncertainty without contamination by the reflexive response to the US occurring earlier in the interval.

The data revealed that half the animals ($n = 4$) developed a fail-safe stategy and the remainder ($n = 4$) developed a conditional expectation strategy. Response patterns that reflect hedging strategies were not observed. (We have observed hedging when the number of possible times of US occurrences number two instead of three and the separation is 400 milliseconds instead of the 200-ms separation employed in this study.)

Figure 1.6 shows a single trial record from a typical fail-safe responder (Subject 11, Day 4, Trail 14). The CR begins just after 200 msec has elapsed from CS onset and peaks quickly at 300 milliseconds. This peak is largely sustained through the remaining duration of the trial.[6]

Figure 1.7 shows a single trial record from an animal employing a conditional expectation strategy (Subject 3, Day 4, Trial 45). Although the timing of the succession of peaks of increasing amplitude does not match the actual times that the US might occur, one nevertheless gets the impression that the increasing likelihood of the eye shock as the CS unfolds controls this animal's CR topography. By the end of training, all eight rabbits responded with a fail-safe strategy, likely indicating saturation of the effector system for all (in terms of the TD model) serial component CSs.

The conditional expectation strategy is interesting because it contradicts expectations from experiments in which the CS–US interval remains constant throughout training. Such studies show that relatively brief intervals are more favorable for conditioning those of greater duration (Desmond, 1990; Desmond and Moore, 1988; Sutton and Barto, 1990).

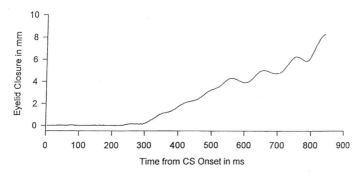

Figure 1.7
Eyeblink conditioned response consistent with a conditional expectation strategy.

For the rabbit eyeblink preparation, this "optimal interval" is on the order of 250 ms and declines progressively with longer intervals. From this perspective, response peaks should first appear at 300, then 500, and finally 700 ms. A reversal of this sequence implied by the conditional expectation strategy was therefore a surprising observation.

The strategies for predictive timing and CR topography discussed previously and illustrated in figures 1.2 through 1.7 have a cognitive flavor, in that they can be implemented as rule-based actions. For example, the fail-safe strategy of conditioned eyelid movement follows from the rule: *Close eye quickly and keep it closed until probability of US is minimal.* Indeed, the response topography shown in figure 1.6 is what researchers in this field traditionally call a voluntary response (Coleman and Webster, 1988). It is equally clear that this strategy can also be implemented by low-level processes involving a combination of interval-optimality and generalization to other intervals sufficient to produce saturation of the effector system. Similarly, the conditional expectation strategy follows from the rule: *Close eye progressively as the conditional probability of the US increases to maximum.* Is there a low-level mechanism consistent with the TD model for implementing this rule? The next section develops ideas that underly such a mechanism.

1.7 Structure of Timing

This section reviews assumptions about the structure of timing that underly application of the TD model to predictive uncertainty. This structure allows the model to simulate the conditional expectation strategy.

1. Elapsed time (duration) from the onset of a timing cue or CS can be segmented into a sequence of time-tagged elements or units. Previously, we referred to these units as serial components, in discussing the TD model. Let CS_{on_i} be the ith element of the onset-triggered timing cascade. The subscript *on* distinguishes this element from the ith element of an offset triggered cascade, discussed below. These time-tagged units, when activated, provide input to effector systems that generate timing predictions. The TD model assumes that connections between these elements and the effector systems are modifiable, according to the basic equations of TD learning.

2. The TD model does not specify the real-time that elapses between activation of successive elements of a timing cascade. The "temporal grain" or segmentation rate is simply a parameter of the simulation. The segmentation rate can depend on processes outside the learning device that depend on the state of the system. Thus, the TD model does not specify the number of time-tagged elements that constitute a given elapsed time. Nor does it specify the speed of propagated activation along the cascade. These factors have testable consequences, but the model does not explicitly take them into account. In order to implement the model, the learning device need only differentiate between its output at two successive time steps (equation 1.2).

3. Stimulus offset can trigger a timing cascade. The offset cascade involves *different elements* from those involved in an onset cascade. Introducing notation, CS_{off_i} designates the ith element of an offset cascade, which distinguishes it from the ith element of the corresponding onset cascade, CS_{on_i}. Although the two cascades compete for associative value, they are otherwise independent. It is important to appreciate that onset cascades can persist after offset of the triggering stimulus. Therefore, the output of offset elements summate with onset elements to determine the magnitude of the actor's prediction responses. Desmond and Moore (1991a) demonstrated the validity of this assumption in a study of classically conditioned eyeblinks in rabbits following a trace conditioning procedure.

4. Salient events such as CS onsets and offsets initiate (trigger) cascades of activation, thereby marking the onset of the to-be-timed interval. The likelihood and degree of activation depend on a host of variables, including physical and psychophysical factors and the state of the actor. The degree to which a cue or complex of cues is adequate for timing is basically an empirical question that can be assessed in the actor's performance.

5. Timing elements are activated sequentially, such that an element active at time t will activate its next-in-line neighbor at some later

time $t + 1$. This is the *delay line* assumption, but the notion can be extended to arrays (Desmond, 1990). If these elements are neurons (or strings of neurons), then the delay between activation of element CS_i and element CS_{i+1} represents neuronal processes of recruitment, propagation, and transmission. These processes run forward in time, which simply means that activation of element CS_i can directly activate element CS_{i+1} (with a delay) but not element CS_{i-1}.

6. Different timing cues or CSs are capable of triggering different onset and offset cascades. These timing cascades summate to determine the amplitude of the actor's prediction response. There is good evidence that this summation in fact occurs in rabbit eyeblink conditioning (e.g., Kehoe, Graham-Clarke, and Schreurs, 1989).[7]

7. Any element in an onset-triggered timing cascade can potentially initiate another timing cascade through a branching process we shall refer to as *marking*. Branching (or marking) can occur at any point along a timing cascade. Thus, activation of the *i*th element of a cascade might trigger the activation of another, independent cascade, as well as activation of the next-in-line element of the original cascade. By incorporating *marking*, as in marking time, the TD model can generate the conditional expectation strategy simulated in figure 1.5. The next section develops this idea further.

Marking

Marking is a mechanism that can initiate a separate cascade of serial component CSs that parallels the cascade triggered by the nominal CS or its offset. The basic idea is that serial components that have been active at the same time the US occurs can acquire the ability to evoke an additional set of serial component CSs that contribute to the form of the prediction response.

Suppressing the distinction between onset and offset cascades for the time being, it should be clear at this juncture that a timing cue or CS triggers a cascade by activating element CS_1, the first element of the cascade. Its level of activation, X_1, increases within a computational cycle or time-step from some below-threshold value (typically 0 in simulations) to an above-threshold value (typically 1.0 in simulations). Activation of CS_1 activates the next element in the sequence CS_2, with some delay equal to the assumed temporal grain or segmentation rate. In marking, we assume that activation of any element of the cascade, CS_i, can, *in principle*, cause the activation of another cascade that proceeds from that point in time in parallel with activation of the remaining elements of the original cascade of serial component CSs. Input elements of marking cascades do not compete for associative value with those from CS onset or offset cascades or from other marking cascades.

Under what circumstances does marking occur? We suggest that marking is an acquired property of the timing structure that follows a simple *delta* learning rule. Let μ_i denote the weight of a connection from CS_i to M_{i_1}, the first element of the marking cascade activated by CS_i. Increments in μ_i are given by the following equation:

$$\Delta\mu_i = \eta(\lambda - \mu_i) \times X_i, \tag{1.7}$$

where $0 < \eta \leq 1.0$ is a rate parameter. Parameter μ_i is the likelihood (up to the maximum value, $\lambda \leq 1.0$) that activation of element CS_i will trigger a marking cascade; X_i denotes the level of activation of the marker, CS_i; and λ, donated by the target or US, is the asymptotic likelihood of marking. In sum, marking develops whenever the target event occurs contiguously with activation of an element. If the target is a US, then the likelihood of marking increases asymptotically to λ as a function of repeated occurrences of the US that are contiguous with activation of the marker.

It is necessary to make explicit what happens when element CS_i is activated but the target or US does not occur contiguously. In keeping with assumptions of related delta learning rules, we shall assume that this causes a down-regulation of μ_i according to the following equation.

$$\Delta\mu_i = -\theta\mu_i \times X_i, \tag{1.8}$$

where $0 < \theta \ll \eta$.

Let us now consider what happens when more than one element of a timing cascade branches through marking. We assume that each branch consists of a sequence of unique elements. That is, the element M_{i_k} is not the same as the element M_{k_i}. The former is the kth element of a marking cascade triggered by CS_i; the latter is the ith element of a separate marking cascade triggered by CS_k. The output of these elements, M_{i_k} and M_{k_i}, summates with elements of the original CS-onset and CS-offset cascades to determine the actor's response. Extending the notation, offset elements as well as onset elements can participate in marking. CS_{on_i} denotes the ith element of an onset-triggered cascade. Element CS_{off_j} denotes the jth element of an offset-triggered cascade, and $M_{on_{i_k}}$ denotes the kth element of a marking cascade triggered by the ith element of an onset cascade and $M_{off_{k_l}}$ denote the lth element of a marking cascade triggered by kth element of an offset cascade.

Consider now the implications of the marking mechanism for predictive timing under temporal uncertainty. In our example, we imagine a timing cue or CS that signals that the target or US might occur at any one of three intervals, 300, 500, or 700 ms after onset of the cue. Whenever the target occurs at 300 ms, the contiguously activated element, here designated CS_{300}, acquires some capacity to trigger a marking cascade. With a sufficient number of such coincidental events, the likelihood that this will happen saturates (asymptotically) to the value λ, the magnitude or intensity of the target, i.e., $\mu_{300} \doteq \lambda$. The first element of the marking cascade is designated M_{300_1} using notation developed in the preceding paragraph. When the target or US occurs at 500 ms, another marking cascade develops. That is triggered by CS_{500} and the first element of its marking cascade is M_{500_1}.

To mitigate combinatorial explosion, we assume that marking cascades can only branch from elements of CS-triggered cascades. That is, CS_{500} can initiate marking when the target occurs contiguously with its activation, but element $M_{300_{200}}$, which can also be contiguously activated when the target occurs at 500 ms, does not spawn marking. Furthermore, elements of this cascade, the first element of which is M_{500_1} in our notation, are *not* also elements of the first marking cascade, the one triggered by CS_{300}. That is, M_{500_1} is different from $M_{300_{200}}$ because they exist on different timing cascades. Extending this principle, when the target or US occurs at 700 ms, a third marking branch develops. This timing cascade is triggered by CS_{700}, and its first element is denoted M_{700_1}. It is different from elements $M_{300_{400}}$ and $M_{500_{200}}$ because it exists on a separate timing cascade.

The basic idea in marking should now be clear. Each element of a CS-triggered timing cascade, be it onset or offset, has the capacity to mark the beginning of another cascade operating in parallel. The mechanism of marking is contiguous activation arising from the timing cascade and the target event. Whenever target timing is uncertain (stochastic), the contribution of marking elements to the prediction response is proportional to the probabilities that their first elements have acquired the capacity to trigger cascades. Because more marking cascades would be recruited as time elapses, the number of elements contributing to the actor's prediction increases across the CS–US interval. And because the output of timing elements are assumed to summate to determine output of the system, the scheme predicts larger prediction responses as elapsed time unfolds. If the probability distribution of target times is uniform across the CS–US interval, our assumptions of the structure of timing leads to the prediction that the response increases linearly across the interval. If, as in our original example, the target occurs equally often at the three interval of 300, 500, and 700 ms, then the prediction response will have three peaks, one for each target time, but they would be successively larger. That is, the response would correspond to a conditional expectation strategy, as illustrated in figures 1.5 and 1.7.

Connectivity of Elements
We have discussed two types of connections of the elements of a timing cascade. These are afferent projections from one element to the next in

line, $CS_i \rightarrow CS_{i+1}$, and projections that can activate additional cascades acting in parallel through marking, $CS_i \rightarrow M_{i_1}$, $CS_{i+k} \rightarrow M_{i+k_1}$, and so forth. Because of branching of a timing cascade through marking, it is also evident that elements receive afferent connection from the target or US. It is important to realize that input from the target serves only to promote marking, as given by equations 1.7 and 1.8, and the strength of the connection between the timing element and the response, as given by equations 1.3 through 1.5. It does not affect the element's activation of the next-in-line element. In order to realize this assumption in the brain, it is necessary to view a timing element as a multicellular ensemble.

Before considering the possible neuronal organization of a timing element, there are other types of connections that must be considered. Foremost of these are inputs that deliver $\dot{Y}$ information. Together with the target or US, $\dot{Y}$ determines the strength of the connection between the element and the response (equations 1.1–1.3). It does not affect the element's activation of the next-in-line element. Another possible input to a timing element would come from one of the brain's oscillators. This input would not affect the strengths of connections, but it would influence the temporal coherence of the timing cascade of which the element is a member. Oscillation pulses can entrain timing cascades, determining the inter-element activation rate and the degree to which delays in transmission from one element to the next are correlated. Such entrainment would affect timing accuracy and consistency.

Timing Accuracy
Although the TD model is deterministic, the structure of timing need not be, and therefore timing predictions are subject to error that arises from stochastic processes. The delay in the spread of activation from one timing element to the next is a random variable with some mean and variance. It might be reasonable to assume that the same distribution applies to the delay between any two successive elements and that this distribution remains stationary. Under these circumstances, the mean elapsed time from the onset of a timing cue or CS to the peak prediction would be equal to the mean inter-element delay in activation multiplied by the number of elements in the cascade. If the distributions governing activation delay for each of the elements are independent, then the variance of the peak predictions would be given by the sum of the variances of the elements of the cascade. This implies that the coefficient of variation (standard deviation/mean) would decrease as the timing interval increases. Such an observation would be at odds with the Weberian property (coefficient of variation is constant) that holds for many timing tasks (Wearden, 1994). This is likely not the case, however, as the spreading activation of elements would be correlated, particularly under entrainment

from oscillators. Covariation among the inter-element activation delays would contribute to peak variance, perhaps enough to maintain a constant coefficient of variation. This covariation can be estimated as the proportion of variance in peak timing that cannot be accounted for under the independence assumption.

Neuronal Realization of Timing Elements

Each element of a timing cascade should be regarded as an ensemble of neuronal elements. The various connections discussed in the preceding sections would influence different parts of the ensemble. Because the cerebellum has been characterized as a prediction device (Maill, et al., 1993) and is the primary neural substrate of classical eyeblink conditioning (Rosenfield and Moore, 1995), it is here that we shall speculate about the anatomical basis of timing and implementation of the TD model.

1.8 Implementation of TD Learning in the Cerebellum

TD learning can be implemented in the cerebellum by aligning known anatomical ingredients with elements of the learning rule. In TD learning, we assume that each computational time step after the onset or offset of a CS is represented by an anatomically distinct input to the cerebellum. We have suggested that the onset of a CS initiates a spreading pattern of activation among neurons tied to whatever sense modality is involved. This spreading of activation, possibly under entrainment from an oscillator, would sequentially engage pontine nuclear cells, which are the primary source of cerebellar mossy fibers and their associated granule cells. Under this assumption, timing elements would consist of an ensemble that includes pontine nuclear cells, mossy fibers, granule cells, parallel fibers, and influences from intrinsic cerebellar neurons such as Golgi cells. Entrainment by oscillators would likely occur at the level of the pontine nuclei, as these are the nexus of neural influences from the lemniscal systems, midbrain, and forebrain (Wells, Hardiman, and Yeo, 1989).

This implementation scheme relies on evidence from rabbit eyeblink conditioning that CR topography is formed in cerebellar cortex through converging contiguous action of parallel fiber and climbing fiber input to Purkinje cells. This action produces synaptic changes known as long term depression (LTD). Mechanisms of LTD in the cerebellum have been spelled out in recent articles (Eilers, Augustine, and Konnerth, 1995; Ghosh and Greenberg, 1995; Kano et al., 1992; Konnerth, Dreesen, and Augustine, 1992).

Figure 1.8, adapted from Rosenfield and Moore (1995), summarizes the neural circuits that are likely involved in rabbit eyeblink conditioning. The figure shows that CS information ascends to granule cells in the cerebellar

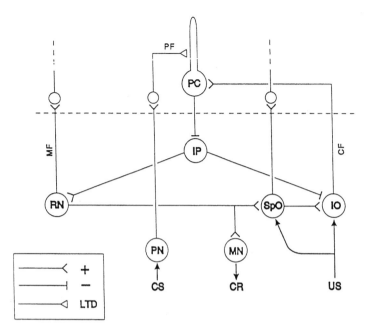

Figure 1.8
Cerebellar and brain stem circuits underlying eyeblink conditioning (after Rosenfield and Moore, 1995). MF, mossy fibers; PF, parallel fibers; PC, Purkinje cell; RN, red nucleus; IP, interpositus nucleus; SpO, spinal trigeminal nucleus pars oralis; CF, climbing fiber; IO, inferior olivary nucleus; PN, pontine nucleus; MN, motoneurons; LTD, long-term depression; CS, conditioned stimulus; CR, conditioned response; US, unconditioned stimulus.

cortex (Larsell's lobule H-VI) via mossy fibers originating in the pontine nuclei (PN). Information about the US ascends to cerebellar cortex by two routes, mossy fiber (MF) projections from the sensory trigeminal complex, spinal oralis (SpO) in the figure, and climbing fiber (CF) projections from the inferior olive (IO). A CR is generated within deep cerebellar nucleus interpositus (IP), where the CR is formed by modulation from Purkinje cells (PCs). A full-blown CR is expressed as an increased rate of firing among IP neurons (e.g., Berthier and Moore, 1990; Berthier, Barto, and Moore, 1991). This activity is projected to the contralateral red nucleus (RN). From RN, activity is projected to motoneurons (MN) that innervate the peripheral musculature controlling the position and movements of the eyelids and eyeball (Desmond and Moore, 1991a). The RN also projects to SpO, giving rise to CR-related activity among these neurons (Richards, Ricciardi, and Moore, 1991).

Figure 1.8 depicts an inhibitory projection from IP to IO. The consequence of this arrangement is that olivary signals to PCs are suppressed

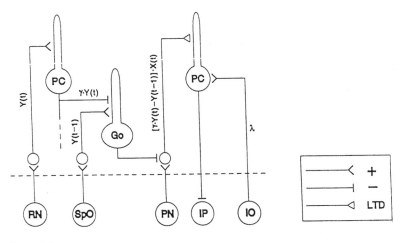

Figure 1.9
Neural circuits implementing $\gamma Y(t)$ and other variables of the TD learning rule. (See figure 1.8 for key to abbreviations.)

when the CR-representation within IP is robust. This anatomical feature suggests that climbing fibers are only excited when the US occurs *and* the CR is weak or absent. The TD model with the CSC representation regards the CR as a response that anticipates the US. Hence, according to the model, there should be no CR representation within IP if a climbing-fiber reponse to the US is to occur. If there is, through variations in timing, for example, the climbing-fiber signal triggered by the US would be suppressed. Such occasions would be tantamount to extinction trials.

The TD learning rule is implemented by a combination of two reinforcement components. The first is donated by the US, λ in the model's learning rule. The implementation scheme assumes that λ can be aligned with climbing-fiber activation of PCs, which functions to produce LTD among coactive parallel fiber (PF) synapses, as depicted in the figure. The second reinforcement operator is donated by the $\dot{Y}(t)$ terms in the learning rule, $\gamma Y(t) - Y(t-1)$.

Figure 1.9 shows circuit elements, not shown in figure 1.8, for implementing the $\dot{Y}(t)$ component of the learning rule. These components include the projections to cerebellar cortex from the RN and SpO indicated in figure 1.8. We hypothesize that the RN projection carries information about $Y(t)$ to cerebellar cortex as efference copy. Parallel fibers project this information to PCs that have collaterals to a set of Golgi cells (Go). Because these projections are inhibitory (Ito, 1984), these PCs invert the efference signal from the RN. In addition, the interpositioning of the PCs between the RN and Golgi cells attenuates the signal and implements the TD model's discount factor, γ.

Because Golgi cells are inhibitory on granule cells, the consequence of their inhibition by PCs receiving efference from the RN would be to disinhibit activity of granule cells. In other words, because granule cells relay CS-information from the PN to PCs involved in LTD and CR generation, disinhibition of granule cells by Golgi cells enhances the information flow from active CS components. Mathematically, the implementation scheme assumes that the variables X_j in equation 1.4 activate granule cells. Parallel fibers arising from these granule cells trigger output, and they affect connection weights thought to reside at PF/PC synapses in proportion to $\dot{Y}(t) \times X_j$.

In this scheme, PCs driven by projections from the RN would increase their firing rate so as to mimic the representation of the CR as it passes through the RN enroute to MN and SpO. Berthier and Moore (1986) recorded from several H-VI PCs with CR-mimicking increases in firing. Because increases in firing during a CS are incompatible with CR formation through LTD, it is likely that these PCs were inhibiting motor programs incompatible with CR generation, for example, eyelid and eyeball musculature that would lead to eyelid opening instead of eyelid closure. Here we are suggesting an additional function of these PCs, that of projecting inverted and discounted CR efference from the RN to Golgi cells.

The implementation scheme assumes that the Golgi cells that receive the inverted efference from the RN also receive a direct, noninverted, excitatory projection from SpO. This projection carries information about the CR at time $t - \Delta t$. Therefore, the Golgi cell in figure 1.9 fires at a rate determined by the differential between two inputs: $\gamma Y(t)$ donated by the RN and $Y(t - \Delta t)$ donated by SpO. Hence, Golgi cells act as $\dot{Y}(t)$ detectors. In terms of equation 1.3, $Y(t)$ is transmitted to cerebellar granule cells by the RN, and $Y(t - 1)$ is transmitted to granule cells from SpO. The RN input engages PCs that inhibit Golgi cells responsible for gating inputs from CSs to PCs. Efference from SpO engages the same Golgi cells directly. Because Golgi cells are inhibitory on granule cells, the bigger the RN input relative to SpO input, the bigger the signal from serial component CSs active at that time, be they from onset, offset, or marking cascades. Enhanced throughput from active CS elements in the granular layer would lead to local recruitment of other active PFs that synapse on PCs involved in LTD and CR generation.

In this way, the Golgi cells which implement $\dot{Y}(t)$ reinforce and maintain the down-regulated state of active PF/PC synapses subject to LTD. Parallel fiber/PC synapses that are activated by a CS element are downregulated by the contiguous US-triggered activation of climbing fiber input from the inferior olive. As elements earlier in the sequence of component CSs become capable of evoking an output that anticipates the US, inhibition is released from IP cells and a CR ensues. As mentioned previously, activity within IP might inhibit climbing-fiber inputs triggered by the US. Although this inhibition of IO would constitute an extinction trial, the down-regulation of these synapses is maintained, and still earlier CS-elements are recruited, by PFs carrying $\dot{Y} \times X_j$ to LTD-PCs, as indicated in figure 1.9.

In a single-unit recording study, Desmond and Moore (1991a) observed an average lead-time of 36 ms from the onset RN cells with highly CR-related firing patterns and the peripherally observed CR. The average lead-time of SpO cells with CR-related activity was 20 ms. Therefore, the time difference in CR-related efference arising from the two structures is probably on the order of 15 to 20 ms. This difference spans one 10-millisecond time-step used in our simulations with the TD model. This temporal difference is consistent with a conduction velocity of 2 meters per second for the 10-mm trajectory of unmyelinated axons from the RN to rostral portions of SpO. The 10-millisecond grain also ensures high-fidelity resolution of fast transients. The fastest transients in eyeblink conditioning occur during unconditioned responses (URs). At its fastest, the eyelids require 80 milliseconds to move from completely open to completely closed, with a peak velocity of approximately 4 to 5 mm per 20 ms.

Efference from SpO neurons recorded among H-VI PCs would tend to lag behind the peripherially observed CR, if it arises from more caudal portions of the structure. Berthier and Moore (1986) observed a continuum of lead and lag times among PCs that increased their firing to the CS. Purkinje cells that receive projections from SpO (not shown in the figure) would be expected to increase their firing, but with a lag relative to those receiving projections from the RN. It makes sense that the proportion of CR-leading PCs observed by Berthier and Moore (1986) matched the number of CR-lagging PCs, because these two populations would merely be reflecting CR efference from two temporal vantage points.

Figure 1.10 is an expanded version of figure 1.9 showing three sets of granule cells associated with three serial component CSs. These components include those arising from CS onset and offset, as well as those that might arise from marking processes. The degree to which information from any of these serial component CSs reaches the PCs to which they project is determined by Golgi cells firing in relation to $\dot{Y}(t)$, as just described. Figure 1.1 shows that, depending on γ, TD-simulated CRs are positively accelerating in time up to the occurrence of the US, so $\dot{Y}(t)$ increases progressively over the CS–US interval. Therefore, those PF/PC synapses activated near the time of the climbing fiber signal from the US would have the greatest impact in establishing and maintaining LTD of PF/PC synapses that ensure the appropriate form and timing of CRs.

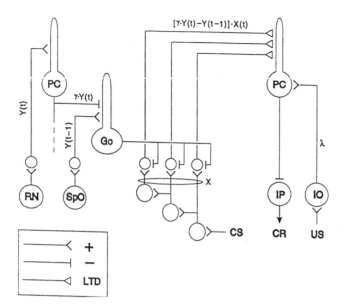

Figure 1.10
The complete TD implementation scheme showing three sequentially activated CS components, representing both onset and offset cascades in the manner of Desmond and Moore's
(1988) VET model. (See figure 1.8 for key to abbreviations.)

Implications of the Implementation
The implementation scheme has several testable implications. One that
has already been mentioned is that there are two types of CR-related
firing patterns among PCs. One type is associated with LTD. These PCs
decrease their firing rate in anticipation of the US. The other type (the
majority) is not associated with LTD. Instead of decreasing their rate of
firing, activity during the CS–US interval increases. We maintain that this
latter pattern of firing reflects CR efference. Because this efference cannot
arise from proprioceptors, which are largely absent in muscles controlling
the eyeblink, and since the axons of motoneuons innervating these muscles do not possess recurrent collaterals, this efference must arise from
premotor centers. The RN and SpO are the prime candidates. We suggest
that one function of this efference is to activate Golgi cells that modulate
information flow through the granule cells. Another function is to excite
PCs that ultimately control muscles that, if engaged, would preclude or
interfere with CR performance, such as those that would produce eye
opening or saccadic movements.
   The implementation scheme also requires that Golgi cells that modulate
information flow from serial component CSs fire in relation to *changes* in

eyelid position, that is, they fire in relation to $\dot{Y}$. This property of Golgi cell firing patterns has been reported by van Kan, Gibson, and Houk (1993), in a study of monkey limb movements, and Edgley and Lidierth (1987), in a study of cat locomotion.

A third implication of the implementation scheme concerns the effects of inactivation of the RN through the use of pharmacolgical agents or cryo-static probes. Although inactivation of the RN would cause a temporary interruption of information flow that results in a conditioned response, it would not prevent learning of the primary association between components of the CS and the US. This association would procede with little disruption because the pontine nuclei and the IO would still be able to convey CS and US information to cerebellar cortex. Evidence for this proposition comes from a study of rabbit eyeblink conditioning by Clark and Lavond (1993). They demonstrated that inactivation of the RN by cooling did not prevent learning, as CR magnitude recovered immediately upon reactivation of the RN.

However, inactivation of the RN would interrupt efference about the position of the eyelid at times t and $t - \Delta t$ from the RN and SpO. Thus, $\dot{Y}$ would not be available to cerebellar cortex. According to the TD model, $\dot{Y}$ allows for increments of predictive associations in the absence of the US, as would occur in second-order conditioning (Kehoe, Feyer, and Moses, 1981). This being the case, inactivation of the RN would interfere with second-order conditioning. Animals trained simultaneously in first- and second-order conditioning with the RN inactivated, would be expected to show first-order learning, as in the Clark and Lavond (1993) study, but little or no second-order learning.[8]

Interpretations of $\dot{Y}$: Efference or Afference
Equation 1.3 emphasizes interpretations of $\dot{Y}$ as efference, but it is equally correct to interpret changes in connection weights in terms of afference, as discussed earlier in connection with equation 1.6. A recent study by Ramnani, Hardiman, and Yeo (1995) suggests that the efference inter-pretation of $\dot{Y}$ is correct. They showed that reversible inactivation of IP by muscimol application prevents extinction of the CR. CS-alone trials that would normally lead to a gradual elimination of the CR, instead had no effect whatsoever. When tested later, after the muscimol blockade had been removed, the previously established CR was at full strength. It did extinguish with continuing presentation of CS-alone trials. This finding is consistent with the efference interpretation of the model because inactiva-tion of IP eliminates the CR and therefore prevents efference from the RN and SpO from affecting prior learning. It is clear from equation 1.3 that connection weights cannot change if both $Y(y)$ and $Y(t-1)$ are 0. In constrast, under an afference interpretation of equation 1.3, inactivation of

IP would not prevent CS information from ascending to cerebellar cortex, where extinction would proceed normally, as this information arises from the PN and bypasses IP enroute to H-VI.

Prediction Strategies and the Cerebellar Implementation
The anatomical and physiological relationships reviewed in the preceding sections do not exhaust all of the potentially important circuits and factors that are likely involved in predictive timing by the cerebellar system (see Ito, 1984; Rosenfield and Moore, 1995). These other influences could be important for implementing specific prediction strategies. Before considering some of these options, it should be clear that the cerebellum need not participate in any of them. The fail-safe strategy, for example, resembles a voluntary response (Coleman and Webster, 1988). Such a response could come about through the direct action of cerebral motor cortex on motoneurons, bypassing the cerebellum altogether. The same is true of the other prediction strategies reviewed previously. But there is no evidence that cerebral motor cortex is involved in eyeblink conditioning. Specifically, CR timing and topography are normal following aspiration of this part of the brain, although learning-dependent timing of conditioned eyeblink responses is disrupted by lesions of the cerebellar cortex (Perrett, Ruiz, and Mauk, 1993).

Within the context of the cerebellum, a fail-safe strategy can be implemented in any of number of ways. Perhaps the most straightforward from the standpoint of the TD model would be to assume that timing uncertainty promotes a marking cascade that is directed to the inferior olive, a putative site of representation of the US (figure 1.8). In fail-safe mode, this marking provokes olivary neurons to oscilliate in such a way as to saturate the system and prevent return to baseline until after the trial terminates (e.g., Yarom, 1989).

A hedging strategy would not involve this sort of marking-derived prolonged activation of the inferior olive, and there would be no prolonged saturation of Purkinje cells. The degree of hedging would depend on the value of the discount parameter of the TD model, γ, and this could be controlled through of aminergic modulation of Purkinje cells, as discussed by Ito (1984, p. 60). For example, a high state of noradrenergic "arousal" would inhibit Purkinje cells and this would decrease the value of $\dot{\gamma}$ computed by Golgi cells. Assuming no other effects, this attenuation of γ would lower response amplitude (see figure 1.1), as in proportionate hedging. Removing the aminergic modulation would have the opposite effect on γ and response amplitude.

A conditional expectation strategy requires the recruitment of additional timing elements through marking. This marking involves interactions with the US that occur in precerebellar neurons, and brain stem reticular formation would seem to be a likely candidate, on anatomical and physiological grounds (Richards, Ricciardi, and Moore, 1991).

Entrainment of Timing and the Cerebellar System

Previously, we speculated that timing cascades might have the capacity to become entrained by one of the brains oscillators. The inferior olive is an oscillator, with a normal rhythm of 10 Hz. Because the primary projection of the inferior olive is to Purkinje cells, the entrainment of timing elements could well occur at this level, but a more plausible scenario would be entrainment by oscillations within catecholamine systems that engage brainstem reticular formation neurons and ultimately the pontine nuclei.

1.9 Summary and Conclusions

This chapter considered how the TD theory of reinforcement learning, which lies at the heart of promising applications in adaptive control in both real and artificial systems, might be adapted to training protocols in which behavior is controlled by cascades of activation of time-tagged serial elements. The TD model with the CSC assumption generates appropriate CR waveforms in simple protocols, but it can also be extended to predictive timing under temporal uncertainty.

The chapter also suggests an implementation scheme for TD learning within the cerebellum. The implementation draws on neurobiological evidence regarding how LTD is established, reinforced, and maintained among Purkinje cells that form the CR. The implementation incorporates recent anatomical findings, reviewed by Rosenfield and Moore (1995), that allow these Purkinje cells to receive both components of the TD model's reinforcement operator, one component donated by the US and another component donated by $\dot{Y}(t) = Y(t) - Y(t - \Delta t)$. The implementation scheme lays the foundation for network simulations at the cellular level.

The entire exercise reinforces the synergy that has enlightened and invigorated behavioral and neurobiological studies of reinforcement learning. In particular, the TD model appears to be the most comprehensive rendering of classical conditioning that has been proposed to date, and as such it provides a framework for novel insights about sequencing and timing behavior.

Notes

1. TD methods have been used with considerable success in training connectionist networks (e.g., Barto, 1995; Barto, Sutton, and Anderson, 1983; Sutton, 1992).
2. This representation resembles the approach to conditioned response timing and topography employed by Desmond and Moore's VET model (Desmond, 1990; Desmond and

Moore, 1988, 1991a, 1991b; Moore, 1991, 1992; Moore and Desmond, 1992; Moore, Desmond, and Berthier, 1989). VET is an acronym for the process of mapping associative *value* onto action based on *expectancies* about *timing*. The main advantage of the TD model over the VET model is that it generates higher-order associative connections, such as those underlying secondary reinforcement, a feature of $\dot{Y}$ models that is lacking in the VET model. The timing structure employed in the VET model is here extended to the TD model. The TD model with the CSC representation of time has been applied to action selection based on the dopamine reward system (Schultz, Dayan, and Montague, 1997).

3. The values of $V_j(t)$ in equation 1.4 are understood to be the latest available. They are updated after the output has occurred. Therefore, these weights technically are computed at the end of the preceding time step, $t - 1$.

4. In general, CR topography depends on the physical characteristics of CSs and their serial components. These characteristics, such as acoustic frequency and intensity, can be captured by the variables $X_j(t)$ in equations 1.4 through 1.6, as suggested by Kehoe, et al. (1995), but these complexities are suppressed here.

5. We use the expression "strategy selection" to facilitate communication. We do not assume, nor do we rule out, the contribution of cognitive processes. Strategies may reflect high level top-down control, low level bottom-up control, or a combination of both.

6. There is no special significance in the fact that the maximum eyelid movement in figure 1.6 is just over 2 mm, as individual rabbits vary in the maximum blink they can produce.

7. Although this assumption does not imply an unmanageable "combinatorial explosion" in complexity, it again begs the question of what processes contribute to stimulus salience and how stimulus components cohere to become timing cues.

8. Mechanisms for establishing second-order conditioning are not known. A TD implementation based on LTD assumes that PF inputs arising from second-order serial components express LTD even though the US is withheld. Hartell (1996) presents evidence supportive of this assumption.

References

Barto, A. G. (1995). Adaptic critics and the basal ganglia. In J. C. Houk, J. L. Davis, D. C. Beiser (eds.), *Models of information processing in the basal ganglia* (pp. 215–232). Cambridge, MA: MIT Press.

Barto, A. G., Sutton, R. S., & Anderson, C. W. (1983). Neuronlike elements that can solve difficult control problems. *IEEE Transactions on Systems, Man, and Cybernetics, SMC-13,* 834–846.

Berthier, N. E., Barto, A. G., & Moore, J. W. (1991). Linear systems analysis of the relationship between firing of deep cerebellar neurons and the classically conditioned nictitating membrane response in rabbits. *Biological Cybernetics, 65,* 99–105.

Berthier, N. E., & Moore, J. W. (1986). Cerebellar Purkinje cell activity related to the classically conditioned nictitating membrane response. *Experimental Brain Research, 63,* 341–350.

Berthier, N. E., & Moore, J. W. (1990). Activity of deep cerebellar nuclear cells during classical conditioning of nictitating membrane extension in rabbits. *Experimental Brain Research, 83,* 44–54.

Clark, R. E., & Lavond, D. G. (1993). Reversible lesions of the red nucleus during acquisition and retention of a classically conditioned behavior in rabbits. *Behavioral Neuroscience, 107,* 264–270.

Coleman, S. R., & Webster, S. (1988). The problem of volition and the conditioned reflex. Part II. Voluntary-responding subjects, 1950–1980. *Behaviorism, 16,* 17–49.

Desmond, J. E. (1990). Temporally adaptive responses in neural models: The stimulus trace. In M. Gabriel & J. Moore (eds.), *Learning and computational neuroscience: Foundations of adaptive networks* (pp. 421–461). Cambridge, MA: MIT Press.

Desmond, J. E., & Moore, J. W. (1988). Adaptive timing in neural networks: The conditioned response. *Biological Cybernetics, 58*, 405–415.

Desmond, J. E., & Moore, J. W. (1991a). Activity of red nucleus neurons during the classically conditioned rabbit nictitating membrane response. *Neuroscience Research, 10,* 260–279.

Desmond, J. E., & Moore, J. W. (1991b). Altering the synchrony of stimulus trace processes: tests of a neural-network model. *Biological Cybernetics, 65,* 161–169.

Edgley, S. A., & Lidierth, M. (1987). Discharges of cerebellar Golgi cells during locomotion in cats. *Journal of Physiology, London, 392,* 315–332.

Eilers, J., Augustine, G. J., & Konnerth, A. (1995). Subthreshold synaptic Ca^{2+} signalling in fine dendrites and spines of cerebellar Purkinje neurons. *Nature, 373,* 155–158.

Gabriel, M., & Moore, J. (eds.) (1990). *Learning and computational neuroscience: Foundations of adaptive networks.* Cambridge, MA: MIT Press.

Ghosh, A., & Greenberg, M. E. (1995). Calcium signaling in neurons: Molecular mechanisms and cellular consequences. *Science, 268,* 239–247.

Hartell, N. A. (1996). Strong activation of parallel fibers produces localized calcium transients and a form of LTD that spreads to distant synapses. *Neuron, 16,* 601–610.

Ito, M. (1984). *The cerebellum and neural control.* New York: Raven Press.

Kano, M., Rexhausen, U., Dreesen, J., & Konnerth, A. (1992). Synaptic excitation produces a long-lasting rebound potentiation of inhibitory synaptic signals in cerebellar Purkinje cells. *Nature, 356,* 601–604.

Kehoe, E. J., Feyer, A. M., & Moses, J. L. (1981). Second-order conditioning of the rabbit's nictitating membrane response as a function of the CS2–CS1 and CS1–US intervals. *Animal Learning & Behavior, 9,* 304–315.

Kehoe, E. J., Graham-Clarke, P., & Schreurs, B. G., (1989). Temporal patterns of the rabbit's nictitating membrane response to compound and component stimuli under mixed CS–US intervals. *Behavioral Neuroscience, 103,* 283–295.

Kehoe, E. J., Schreurs, B. G., Macrae, M., & Gormezano, I. (1995). Effects of modulating tone frequency, intensity, and duration on the classically conditioned rabbit nictitating membrane response. *Psychobiology, 23,* 103–115.

Konnerth, A., Dressen, J., Augustine, G. T. (1992). Brief dendritic signals initiate long-lasting synaptic degression in cerebellar Purkinje cells. *Proceedings of the National Academy of Science USA, 89,* 7051–7055.

Maill, R. C., Weir, D. J., Wolpert, D. M., & Stein, J. F. (1993). Is the cerebellum a Smith Predictor? *Journal of Motor Behavior, 25,* 203–216.

Moore, J. W. (1991). Implementing connectionist algorithms for classical conditioning in the brain. In M. L. Commons, S. Grossberg, & J. E. R. Staddon (eds.), *Neural Network Models of Conditioning and Action* (pp. 181–191). Hillsdale, NJ: Lawrence Erlbaum Associates.

Moore, J. W. (1992). A mechanism for timing conditioned responses. In F. Macar, V. Pouthas, & W. J. Friedman (eds.), *Time, Action and Cognition* (pp. 229–238). Dordrecht, The Netherlands: Kluwer Academic Publishers.

Moore, J. W., & Desmond, J. E. (1992). A cerebellar neural network implementation of a temporally adaptive conditioned response. In I. Gormezano & E. A. Wasserman (eds.), *Learning and memory: The behavioral and biological substrates* (pp. 347–368). Hillsdale, NJ: Lawrence Erlbaum Associates.

Moore, J. W., Desmond, J. E., & Berthier, N. E. (1989). Adaptively timed conditioned responses and the cerebellum: A neural network approach. *Biological Cybernetics, 62,* 17–28.

Perrett, S. P., Ruiz, B. P., & Mauk, M. D. (1993). Cerebellar cortex lesions disrupt learning-dependent timing of conditioned eyelid responses. *Journal of Neuroscience, 13*, 1708–1718.

Ramnani, N., Hardiman, M. J., & Yeo, C. H. (1995). Temporary inactivation of the cerebellum prevents the extinction of conditioned nictitating membrane responses. *Society for Neuroscience Abstracts, 21*, 1222.

Richards, W. G., Ricciardi, T. N., & Moore, J. W. (1991). Activity of spinal trigeminal pars oralis and adjacent reticular formation units during differential conditioning of the rabbit nictitating membrane response. *Behavioural Brain Research, 44*, 195–204.

Rosenfield, M. E., & Moore, J. W. (1995). Connections to cerebellar cortex (Larsell's HVI) in the rabbit: A WGA-HRP study with implications for classical eyeblink conditioning. *Behavioral Neuroscience, 109*, 1106–1118.

Schultz, W. P., Dayan, P., & Montague, P. R. (1997). A neural substrate of prediction and reward. *Science, 275*, 1593–1599.

Sutton, R. S. (1992). Guest Editor: Special issue on reinforcement learning. *Machine Learning, 8*, 1–171.

Sutton, R. S., & Barto, A. G. (1981). Toward a modern theory of adaptive networks: Expectation and prediction. *Psychological Review, 73*, 135–170.

Sutton, R. S., & Barto, A. G. (1990). Time-derivative models of Pavlovian reinforcement. In M. Gabriel & J. Moore (eds.), *Learning and computational neuroscience: Foundations of adaptive networks* (pp. 497–537). Cambridge, MA: MIT Press.

van Kan, P. L. E., Gibson, A. R., & Houk, J. C. (1993). Movement-related inputs to intermediate cerebellum of the monkey. *Journal of Neurophysiology, 69*, 74–94.

Wearden J. (1994). Prescriptions for models of biopsychological time. In M. Oaksford & G. D. A. Brown (eds.), *Neurodynamics and psychology* (pp. 215–236). San Diego: Academic Press.

Wells, G. R., Hardiman, M. J., & Yeo, C. H. (1989). Visual projections to the pontine nuclei of the rabbit: Orthograde and retrograde tracing studies with WGA-HRP. *Journal of Comparative Neurology, 279*, 629–652.

Yarom, Y. (1989). Oscillatory behavior of olivary neurons. In P. Strata (eds.), *The olivocerebellar system in motor control* (pp. 209–220). Berlin: Springer-Verlag.

Chapter 2

Sequencing and Timing Operations of the Basal Ganglia

Deborah L. Harrington and Kathleen Y. Haaland

Abstract

This chapter examines the cognitive-motor functions of the basal ganglia, which continue to be debated. The intricate neuroanatomy and neurophysiology of the basal ganglia have guided many speculations about its possible role(s) in higher-level cognitive operations, which are involved in learning and controlling movements. In fact, it has been suggested that this system may mediate multiple processes, because corticostriatal inputs are integrated at various levels, each of which may perform different computations. One question has centered around whether the basal ganglia and its connecting neural pathways are involved in motor programming. Studies are reviewed here in which different issues pertaining to this question have been investigated, typically by using Parkinson's disease as a human model of basal ganglia dysfunction. We hypothesize that the basal ganglia play a role in the forward planning of sequential movements. This hypothesis then is contrasted with other competing proposals. The remainder of the chapter is devoted to an appraisal of another line of research, which investigates whether explicit timing operations are regulated by the basal ganglia.

2.1 Introduction

Over the last decade scientists have come to recognize that the basal ganglia serve behavioral functions beyond those suggested by the classic extrapyramidal motor symptoms of basal ganglia abnormalities (e.g., tremor, rigidity, bradykinesia, dyskinesia) such as those seen in Parkinson's disease (PD) or Huntington's disease (HD). It is now clear from human and animal models of basal ganglia function that this system also plays a key role in the higher-level control of movements. Hence, it is fitting that the focus of this chapter be on the role of the basal ganglia in the sequencing and the timing of movements in normal and abnormal populations.

The chapter begins with a summary of the neuroanatomy and neurophysiology of the basal ganglia and its pathways. This summary sets the stage for considering hypotheses about basal ganglia function. We then briefly review key findings from early research that provide the foundation for contemporary investigations that bear on these hypotheses. Next we turn to a study from our laboratory that investigated several hypotheses about the role of the basal ganglia in the cognitive control of motor sequencing. This research suggests that the basal ganglia are critical for regulating the forward planning of sequential movements. The presentation of this study leads to a discussion of preliminary findings from another experiment in which the aforementioned planning hypothesis was tested against other hypotheses of basal ganglia dysfunction. Though the findings from this latter study appear to confirm the planning hypothesis, we argue that the hypothesis may not explain all aspects of cognitive-motor dysfunction in individuals with basal ganglia abnormalities. Other lines of research suggest that the basal ganglia play a central role in the processing of temporal information. Here we draw the distinction between programmed control, in which timing is an emergent property of other operations (e.g., computing the serial order of a sequence), and explicit timing in which a mechanism computes time. We then describe a study in our laboratory that investigated the role of the basal ganglia in explicit timing within the context of an influential model where the mechanism for the computation of time is hypothesized to be a central neural clock or pacemaker. The results of this study are consistent with a role for the basal ganglia in explicit timing. Throughout the chapter we will briefly mention relevant empirical findings that are drawn from studies of individuals with damage to other areas of the brain to illustrate that cognitive-motor dysfunction in PD is not simply due to the generalized effects of brain damage.

2.2 Neuroanatomy and Neurophysiology of the Basal Ganglia

The basal ganglia are nuclei in the forebrain that include the striatum (i.e., putamen and caudate nucleus), the globus pallidus, the amygdala, the substantia nigra, and the subthalamic nucleus. They have extensive connections with the thalamus, cortex, and the midbrain structures, which include the substantia nigra. Although the basal ganglia have no direct pathways to the spinal cord, traditionally its behavioral functions have been ascribed to the motor system, largely because basal ganglia abnormalities are manifested in a wide variety of disordered body movements including bradykinesia (slowness of movement), akinesia (poverty of movement), tremor (abnormal oscillation), rigidity (stiffness of muscle during passive stretch), or dyskinetic movements such as chorea (involuntary rapid, jerky movement). It is now clear that basal ganglia abnormalities are also associated with cognitive deficits, though the nature of these impairments continues to be disputed.

It is not surprising that the behavioral functions of the basal ganglia remain controversial given the complex neuroanatomical interconnections of this brain region. The striatum receives input from most of the cortex.

This cortical input is topographically organized and although it is distributed broadly throughout the striatum, the projections from homologous body part representations overlap (e.g., for a review, see Graybiel and Kimura, 1995). One intriguing possibility is that this input is distributed to multiple sites within the striatum for different computations before it is sent to output sites. Importantly, it now appears that coordination of these computations occurs in several distinct pathways or circuits that project back to the cortex. Specifically, the output from the basal ganglia is confined largely to areas of the frontal lobe by means of at least five neuroanatomically separate, nonoverlapping basal ganglia-thalamocortical circuits (e.g., Alexander, DeLong, and Strick, 1986; Middleton and Strick, 1997). The frontal lobe projection sites that have been identified include the supplementary motor area (SMA), frontal eye fields (FEF), dorsolateral prefrontal cortex (DPC), lateral orbitofrontal cortex (LOC), and anterior cingulate (AC) area. The putamen projects to the SMA and this has been designated the "motor circuit" because it appears to be specialized for planning movements. The "complex circuit" consists of various sites in the caudate nucleus that project to distinct areas in the prefrontal cortex, forming the FEF, DPC, LOC, and AC circuits. The function of the FEF circuit (i.e., oculomotor control) is best understood perhaps because it has been studied most extensively, whereas the functions of the other complex circuits have not been resolved. Each circuit receives multiple corticostriatal inputs that are partially overlapping and integrated at various levels as they interconnect separate regions of the striatum, the globus pallidus, the thalamus, and the frontal lobes. There are also subsidiary basal ganglia circuits that receive topographically organized cortical input. One of these subsidiary circuits is the nigrostriatal pathway, which includes the substantia nigra. In PD, the loss of dopaminergic neurons in the substantia nigra alters the neurochemical balance of these pathways and so disrupts their operations.

These intricate afferent and efferent circuits illustrate the potential functional complexity of the basal ganglia. In addition, a variety of neurotransmitters and neuropeptides modulate these pathways. Though a detailed discussion of this topic is not possible here (e.g., for a review, see Alexander and Crutcher, 1990; Graybiel, 1990), each basal ganglia-thalamocortical circuit contains a direct and an indirect GABA-mediated pathway, which have opposing excitatory and inhibitory effects on the thalamus. Furthermore, dopaminergic input from the substantia nigra to the striatum also appears to have inhibitory and excitatory effects on the indirect and direct pathways, respectively, although, the functional significance of the opposing effects on the striatal output pathways is unknown. In addition, little is known about how other neurotransmitter systems, such as acetylcholine, affect striatal functions.

How does this neuroanatomical and neurophysiological organization guide hypotheses about the cognitive-motor computations of the basal ganglia? One speculation is that while each circuit may be devoted to the computation of a specific function (e.g., motor planning, eye movements), the basal ganglia may engage in multiple operations that differ depending on the level of the circuit (i.e., striatum, pallidum, substantia nigra, thalamus, cortex) (Alexander, DeLong, and Strick, 1986). Second, because the basal ganglia receive cortical input from most areas of the brain, it may be situated to perform higher-level computations that integrate multiple sources of afferent information and to modify ongoing action plans. Moreover, the aforementioned excitatory and inhibitory pathways raise the possibility that the basal ganglia serve the dual purpose of selecting cognitive-motor patterns that are activated at the cortical level while also suppressing conflicting patterns (Alexander and Crutcher, 1990). Proposals consistent with these properties will be discussed in the next section, which analyzes the role of the basal ganglia in specific aspects of sequencing actions. As a final observation, the basal ganglia are in a strategic position to regulate the spatial and temporal coordination of converging cortical inputs. This is consistent with the possibility that the basal ganglia play a key role in timing, discussed in the final section of this chapter.

2.3 Cognitive-Motor Functions of the Basal Ganglia

Early descriptions of the clinical symptomatology of PD were enormously valuable in furnishing clues about the possible role(s) of the basal ganglia in cognitive and motor behavior. Descriptions of cognitive slowing or bradyphrenia suggested that conceptions of the basal ganglia as a motor system were far too restrictive and raised the possibility that nonmotoric aspects of behavior also were diminished in PD. Additionally, the observation that PD produced difficulties in initiating skilled movements such as walking, and that visual cues (e.g., tape on the floor) helped compensate for this deficit, led to the proposal that the basal ganglia played a key role in programming entire series of actions.

Before reviewing investigations into this issue, the concept of motor programming should be clarified as referring throughout this chapter to an internal representation of an action plan. There have been many critiques of the term "motor program," in part because it is vague and does not stipulate explicit mechanisms. Furthermore, the analogy to computer programs in which serial, algorithmic modes of processing are carried out may well be incompatible with the organization of neurobiological systems (e.g., Alexander, DeLong, and Crutcher, 1992). Despite these objections, the motor program concept has stimulated numerous explorations into specific mechanisms that give rise to coordinated patterns of movement.

The term also provides a useful metaphor for characterizing functional states of the central nervous system that permit the preparation of an action and the on-line control of behavior. It is in this sense that we will apply the concept of the motor program in this chapter.

The search for the functional role of the basal ganglia has been dominated by inquiries into whether it is crucial for motor programming. One approach to this problem was to determine if PD patients can use predictable information to guide movements. The rationale was that the ability to employ predictive strategies is indicative of intact motor programming. Some studies reported that motor programming was intact in PD because these patients could normally track a predictable, visual target, although visual cues were available during tracking to guide the production of movements, which could have minimized the necessity for preplanning (Bloxham, Mindel, and Frith, 1984; Day, Dick, and Marsden, 1984). In fact, Flowers (1978) reported that PD patients were impaired in tracking a predictable target when the target path briefly disappeared or jumped to a different spatial location. This suggests that the availability of visual information to guide forthcoming movements is crucial for PD patients, even when the movement path is predictable, because an advance plan of action has not been formulated so that the movement can be carried out using open-loop control. This hypothesis was reaffirmed by Stern and colleagues (1984) in a task in which subjects traced predictable patterns with and without deleted segments. Here, PD patients showed deficits primarily in the former condition, which was consistent with the conclusions of Flowers.

Still another approach to this issue was to examine whether basal ganglia abnormalities disrupt the ability to make optimal use of advance information to prepare for forthcoming movements. Some researchers reported that PD impaired the ability to use advance information to select and initiate movements (Bloxham, Mindel, and Frith 1984; Sheridan, Flowers, and Hurrell, 1987; Pullman et al., 1988), but others found no such deficit (Rafal et al., 1984; Rafal et al., 1987; Stelmach, Worringham, and Strand, 1986). These discrepant results were probably due to methodological differences among the studies. For example, abnormal planning in PD is not always seen when subjects are highly practiced (Stelmach, Worringham, and Strand, 1986) or when the same response is repeated on successive trials (Rafal et al., 1984). Variations in practice or in the number of response repetitions could have produced different outcomes.

We recently tested this speculation in a rotary pursuit learning task in which subjects participated in one of two conditions that differed in terms of their programming demands (Haaland et al., 1997). Learning was normal in PD when the same rotation speed was repeated over successive trials. In this condition, subjects ostensibly utilized the same motor program from trial to trial, though they likely altered some movement parameters to optimize learning. In contrast, learning was disrupted in PD when the rotation speed was randomly presented and therefore, a new motor plan had to be constructed from trial to trial. These findings suggest that the basal ganglia abnormalities manifested in PD do not entirely disrupt the ability to carry out simple forms of programming. Instead, these abnormalities appear to undermine the ability to carry out more complex computations during motor learning.

2.4 The Role of the Basal Ganglia in Programming Sequences

The vast cortical input into the basal ganglia from cortical motor and association areas would seem to position this system for programming sequential behaviors. What specific aspects of programming are regulated by the basal ganglia when such a program must be constructed? We conducted a study to explore several hypotheses about this (Harrington and Haaland, 1991b). First, we tested the controversial issue of whether basal ganglia abnormalities disrupted the ability to use advance information about the identity of a movement sequence to improve preparatory reaction time (RT). If this were the case, preparatory RT should not improve as much for PD patients as for controls when they are given more time to plan the sequence. A second objective was to determine whether basal ganglia abnormalities disrupted the ability to program a series of movements, in which case we predicted that preparatory RT would not increase as much with sequence length (i.e., the number of movements) in PD patients as compared to controls.

Methods

Twenty-four patients with PD and 20 neurologically intact control subjects were studied; for a detailed subject description see Harrington and Haaland (1991b). The experimental task required subjects to execute sequences of hand postures using the apparatus depicted in figure 2.1. The apparatus was interfaced with a computer and contained 15 manipulanda (i.e., 5 plates, 5 recessed buttons, 5 handle bars). Hand postures consisted of plate (P) responses that required contact with the side of the hand, button (B) responses that required contact with the index finger, and handlebar (H) responses which required a grasp around the bar from underneath. Subjects wore gloves equipped with metal contacts to computerize the recording of responses. Subjects always moved from the left to the right across the face of the apparatus, and to change hand postures they moved to the right diagonally (up or down) to the next manipulandum. Figure 2.1 shows that a hand-posture sequence was displayed on a 3 by 5 grid using a pictorial representation of the manipulanda. The bottom of this

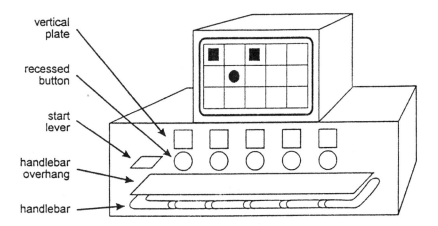

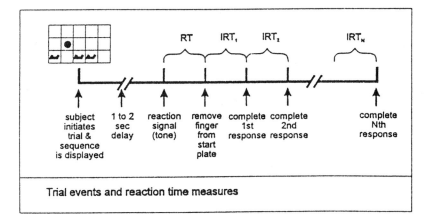

Figure 2.1

Diagram of the hand-posture sequencing apparatus, the trial events and the reaction time measures. The apparatus contains 15 manipulanda. At the top is a row of 5 plates, in the middle a row of 5 recessed buttons, and at the bottom a row of 5 handlebars. To the left of the manipulanda is a start plate. A monitor displays the stimulus sequence which depicts the type of manipulanda associated with a response and its spatial location on the apparatus. The reaction time measures include: (1) Preparatory reaction time (RT), (2) Interresponse time (IRT) for each hand posture, and total movement time (MT) which is the sum of all IRTs.

figure illustrates the trial events that began with the subject resting his or her index finger on the start plate, whereupon the sequence immediately appeared on the monitor. After a random delay of 250 ms or 2000 ms, a tone signaled the subject to begin responding, and upon completion of the last response the visual display turned off. Figure 2.1 also shows the measures of time obtained in each trial. For purposes of our discussion, we will focus on preparatory RT, which was measured from the onset of the imperative signal (i.e., the tone) until the subject lifted his or her index finger from the start plate.

Two types of sequences were presented; these varied in length from one to five hand postures. Repetitive sequences contained repetitions of the same hand posture. Heterogeneous sequences were constructed so that the first two responses required a change in hand posture and for sequences exceeding three postures, the remaining postures consisted of a repetition of the first one (e.g., PB, PBP, PBPP, and PBPPP, where P indicates contact with the manipulandum using the side of the hand and B indicates contact using the index finger).

Results and Discussion
Figure 2.2 displays the preparatory RTs for repetitive and heterogeneous sequences as a function of sequence length and the delay interval prior

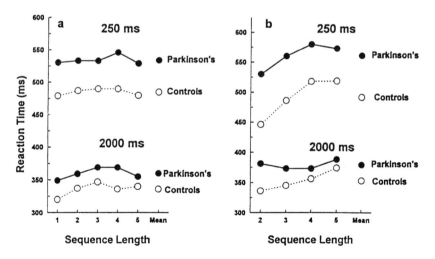

Figure 2.2
Mean preparatory reaction times (RTs) for repetitive (a) and heterogeneous (b) hand-posture sequences. RTs are displayed as a function of sequence length and the delay interval prior to the imperative stimulus (i.e., 250 ms and 2000 ms). The data graphed on the right side of the abscissa depict the mean preparatory RTs averaged across the sequence lengths.

to the imperative signal. The mean preparatory RT, averaged across the sequence lengths, is also graphed. First, there were no group differences in the duration of the preparatory RT interval for either type of sequence. It is also clear from this figure that preparatory RTs in the PD group benefited from the longer delay interval as much as in the control group, and this was true for both sequence types. Hence, we rejected the hypothesis that basal ganglia abnormalities disrupt the ability to use advance information about movements to improve preplanning. This conclusion is also consistent with other recent examinations of this issue (Jennings, 1995; Willingham et al., 1995).

Figure 2.2a shows that prior to movement, PD patients programmed sequences of repetitive hand-postures similarly to controls, irrespective of the length of the delay interval prior to the imperative signal. In both groups, sequence length had only a small effect on RTs such that preparation for a single hand-posture was slightly faster than preparation for repetitions of the same posture. Though linear sequence length effects have been reported for repetitive responses in control subjects (i.e., Stelmach, Worringham, and Strand, 1987), we have consistently shown that variations in the number of hand postures have little or no effect on preparatory RT, perhaps because subjects tend to organize repetitive sequences into a single grouping. These findings may be due in part to the spatial cues from the apparatus, which permitted the terminal response to be programmed in the same amount of time, irrespective of the sequence length. In any case, PD patients appear to accomplish this level of programming normally.

In contrast, PD patients did not show normal programming of heterogeneous sequences. Figure 2.2b shows that preparatory RT increased with sequence length for both groups, presumably because a motor plan must be constructed for each response in the sequence. Though preparatory RT was not significantly longer in the PD group, the sequence length X group interaction $[F(1, 123) = 3.4, p < .025]$ indicated that sequence length had less of an effect on preparatory RT in the PD group, irrespective of the delay interval. Figure 2.2b shows that the PD group displayed some forward planning, but they apparently did not construct a motor program for the entire hand-posture sequence. This outcome is consistent with other findings (Jennings, 1995; Stelmach, Worringham, and Strand, 1987). Importantly, these deficits were not eliminated when subjects had more time to prepare. The slope of the preparatory RT function decreased with the duration of the delay interval for all subjects, indicating that more of the sequence was programmed (e.g., Klapp, 1995), although similar reductions in the slope were found for both groups. Moreover, the programming impairments that were found in the PD group for heterogeneous sequences negatively affected the actual performance of the hand-posture sequences. Though a detailed appraisal of the inter-response time (IRT) and movement time (MT) data cannot be presented here (see Harrington and Haaland, 1991b), impairments in MT were increasingly apparent in the PD group as sequence length increased. Most importantly, this was more the case for heterogeneous than repetitive sequences. Analyses of the IRT data further suggested that this result was due partially to the significant impairment (i.e., longer IRTs) observed in the PD group when making hand-posture transitions, which were required for heterogeneous, but not repetitive, hand-posture sequences. The latter finding raises the possibility that basal ganglia dysfunction disrupts the ability to switch among motor sets or programs, although the IRT results also could be explained by a failure of PD patients to construct a program for all hand-postures in heterogeneous sequences, as suggested by their preparatory RT patterns.

Before addressing these issues further, a comment is in order about the specificity of the above findings to basal ganglia damage. It is possible that a disruption in any process (e.g., attention, retrieval, visuospatial analysis) might produce programming deficits of the kind described here, but programming deficits are not universally caused by deficits of any kind. We reported that subjects with right hemisphere damage due to stroke demonstrated normal programming (i.e., a normal sequence length effect on preparatory RT slope) and execution of repetitive and heterogeneous hand-posture sequences, despite the significant visuospatial deficits shown by such patients (Harrington and Haaland, 1991a). In addition, individuals with left-hemisphere damage due to stroke also showed normal programming of these sequences, despite encoding and response selection deficits as well as problems of grouping or parsing sequential responses into higher-order chunks (Harrington and Haaland, 1992). Thus, the ability to develop a motor plan is not necessarily disrupted by brain damage. As an aside, we were somewhat surprised at the time by the absence of forward planning deficits in subjects with left-hemisphere damage given the specialized role of the left hemisphere for the representation of movements (e.g., Kimura, 1982; Haaland and Harrington, 1990; Kim et al., 1993). In hindsight, this finding makes far more sense given recent developments that strongly implicate basal ganglia-thalamocortical pathways in planning operations.

2.5 The Role of the Basal Ganglia in Programming and Switching

Recently, we conducted a preliminary investigation designed to distinguish between the advance programming and the motor program switching hypotheses of basal ganglia function. Support for the hypothesis that the basal ganglia regulate switching comes from studies showing that individuals with PD have difficulty switching between different movements within a sequence, each of which presumably requires a different motor program (e.g., Benecke et al., 1987; Harrington and Haaland, 1991b), and shifting conceptual set on various neuropsychological tests (e.g., Cools et al., 1984; Flowers and Robertson, 1985; Lees and Smith, 1983; Raskin, Borod, and Tweedy, 1992). Proponents of the basal ganglia-switching hypothesis generally maintain that diminished switching competency is due to dysfunction in the frontal-cortical circuits because this deficit is especially pronounced in individuals with primary damage to the prefrontal lobes. Frontal lobe dysfunction in PD is attributed to the depletion of dopamine and other neurotransmitters throughout the prefrontal circuits and frontal cortex, as evidenced by frontal cortical atrophy (e.g., Lichter et al., 1988) and reduced regional cerebral blood flow (rCBF) (e.g., Rascol et al., 1992). Despite the evidence for a reduction in frontal lobe functioning, however, other plausible alternative explanations for the set shifting or switching deficits in PD include deficits in response selection, planning, or generalized slowing in cognitive-motor processing.

A Test of the Programming and Switching Hypotheses
In the following preliminary study we set out to test between the programming and switching hypotheses of basal ganglia function within a single experiment. A two-choice RT (CRT) paradigm was designed in which PD and control subjects memorized two sequences, each consisting of three key-press responses. Each sequence was associated with a unique stimulus cue (X or O) that served as the imperative stimulus designating the sequence to be executed. Although it is possible to plan parameters of the choice set that are known before the imperative stimulus, uncertain response characteristics must be programmed upon the onset of the imperative stimulus. Hence, CRT represents stimulus identification (i.e., imperative stimulus), response selection, programming, and execution processes. In this study, we were concerned primarily with programming and switching processes. Therefore we manipulated the structural relationship between the two sequences in the choice set in order to investigate the effect of increasing the number of superordinate programs that were constructed for a particular choice set.

Table 2.1 displays the two sets of sequence pairs, one of which was selected randomly for each subject. A set consisted of four different sequences, each of which was presented within the context of a congruent or an incongruent sequence pair. Congruent pairs shared the same structural arrangement among the responses, but had different initial responses. Incongruent sequences contained different structures and different initial responses.

Table 2.1
Sequence pairs in the choice reaction time task

	Congruent Choice Set		Incongruent Choice Set	
Set 1	IIM	RRM	IIM	RMM
	IMM	RMM	IMM	RRM
Set 2	MMR	IIR	MMR	IRR
	MRR	IRR	MRR	IIR

Note: I, M, and R correspond to index, middle, and ring finger.

In neurologically intact individuals the time required to choose between congruent sequences is faster than between incongruent sequences (Rosenbaum, Inhoff, and Gordon, 1984). This is because with congruent pairs, although the identity of the response is unknown prior to the target stimulus, the superordinate structure (i.e., spatiotemporal organization of responses) of both sequences is similar. In contrast, for incongruent pairs the identity of the response and the structure are unknown prior to the target stimulus. Thus, the programming requirements during CRT are greater for sequence pairs that have an incongruent structural arrangement.

We hypothesized that if the basal ganglia regulate preprogramming, the difference between the congruent and the incongruent CRT (i.e., choice context effect) should be reduced in PD. This is because the structure of congruent choice pairs is the same, so only the parameters of the individual responses need to be programmed after the onset of the imperative stimulus. In contrast, incongruent sequence pairs have different structures, so both the superordinate plan and the response parameters need to be programmed upon the onset of the imperative stimulus. Hence, any difficulty in PD with generating multiple motor plans could disrupt the development of different hierarchical structures, one for each sequence in the incongruent choice set. Alternatively, if the basal ganglia regulate switching among motor sets, but programming is normal, only CRT for the incongruent choice set should be longer in the PD group relative to the controls. Here the underlying assumption is that the two sequences remain active in a short-term buffer where they are rehearsed. Thus, if the target cue specifies a sequence that is not active, the subject must shift to the alternate sequence. In this line of thinking, switching deficits should cause problems mostly in the incongruent condition because prior to the imperative stimulus there is uncertainty about which of the two competing superordinate structures will be activated. In contrast, switching operations presumably are not required in the congruent condition because both sequences in the choice set are governed by the same superordinate structure, which is known in advance of the reaction signal, so that only the response parameters (i.e., fingers) need to be selected.

Thirty-five individuals with PD and 31 control subjects performed the CRT task using their right hand. Keypresses were executed on a computer key board. Four blocks of trials were presented, in which the order of the two congruent and the two incongruent choice sets was randomized across subjects. Prior to each experimental block, practice trials were given in which subjects memorized the choice set and the stimulus cue (X or O) associated with each sequence. A trial began with the presentation of a warning signal consisting of a start box centered on the screen and a 50 ms tone. The box remained on the screen for 1 s and then, after a variable delay of 500, 750, or 1000 ms, the stimulus cue was presented. Once criterion performance on the practice trials was attained (i.e., 4 consecutively correct trials for each sequence), 30 experimental trials followed; these consisted of 15 random presentations of each sequence. CRT latency for the first response was recorded from the onset of the stimulus cue to the completion of the first keypress, and latency for the second and the third keypresses was measured from the end of a prior keypress to the completion of the next one. Error trials included wrong responses, extra responses, first keypress latencies longer than 2 s, and second or third keypress latencies longer than 1200 ms.

First we analyzed the number of trials to criterion during the practice trials using an analysis of variance (ANOVA) with repeated measures with group as the between-subjects factor and choice context (congruent, incongruent) as the within-subjects factor. The main finding was a group X context interaction $[F(1, 64) = 4.07, p < .05]$, which showed that the PD group had more difficulty than the control group in learning incongruent choice sets (Mean = 29, SD = 20.7 for the PD group; Mean = 19.7, SD = 9.2 for the control group) than congruent choice sets (Mean = 16.3, SD = 8.9 for the PD group; Mean = 13.6, SD = 5.6 for the control group).

Figure 2.3 displays the results from the experimental trials. These data suggest that the pattern of RTs differed between the groups, but only for the first keypress. This observation was confirmed by the significant group X context X keypress interaction $[F(2, 128) = 5.86, p < .01]$ and the simple effects analyses in which group interacted with context only for the first response $[F(1, 64) = 5.95, p < .02]$. Here, context had a greater effect on the CRTs in the control group than in the PD group, although both groups showed a significant context effect, replicating the finding of Rosenbaum, Inhoff, and Gordon (1984) for neurologically intact subjects, and extending the finding to PD patients. There were no group differences in the latency of the first response, irrespective of the choice set context. As for the second and third keypresses, latencies did not differ

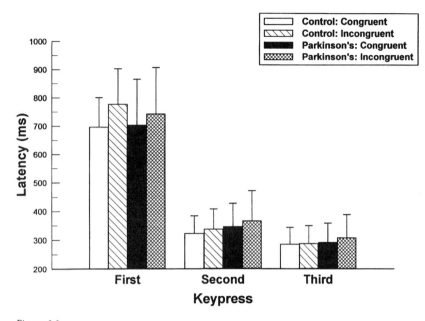

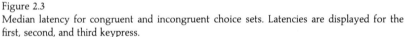

Figure 2.3
Median latency for congruent and incongruent choice sets. Latencies are displayed for the first, second, and third keypress.

between the groups. Although the choice context continued to exert a significant effect on these latter keypresses, the magnitude of the effect was small and similar for both groups.

The reduced context effect in the PD group for the first keypress confirmed the hypothesis that the basal ganglia regulates programming. These results are intriguing because they suggest that the PD group did not program different superordinate structures for the incongruent choice sets. In contrast, there was no evidence to corroborate the switching hypothesis that would have predicted an exaggerated context effect in the PD group. It was also notable that the findings were inconsistent with response selection or execution explanations of basal ganglia dysfunction. These proposals would have predicted elevated CRTs in the PD group for both choice contexts, which was not found.

Up to this point it appears that, despite the depressed context effect in the PD group, overall performance was not impaired in terms of keypress latencies. In fact, the performance of very short sequences may not be substantially improved by developing higher-level representations since it is possible to execute such sequences on a response-by-response basis. Nonetheless, programming deficits in the PD group were manifested by a lower rate of accurate responses (90% and 85% correct trials for congruent and incongruent choice sets, respectively) than in the control group (96% and 92% correct trials for congruent and incongruent choice sets, respectively), although this was the case irrespective of choice set. Accuracy was compromised significantly more for incongruent than congruent choice sets in both groups, consistent with the premise that incongruent choice sets place greater demands on programming processes than do congruent choice sets.

The above studies are consistent with other reports of programming deficits in PD under conditions in which two motor programs must be developed and carried out either concurrently or in rapid succession (Benecke et al., 1987; Haaland et al., 1997; Malapani et al., 1994). In PD it appears that there may be a problem in loading or maintaining more than one program into a motor buffer. This forward planning deficit is also consistent with animal studies showing sequence-specific activity in the striatum (e.g., Aldridge et al., 1993; Kermadi and Joseph, 1995; Kimura, 1990) and functional imaging studies in neurologically intact humans implicating the basal ganglia in sequence learning (e.g., Seitz et al., 1990).

One intriguing speculation is that deficits in forward planning may be due to a reduction in attentional control (e.g., Bennett et al., 1995; Malapani et al., 1994) or working memory (e.g., Brown and Marsden, 1991) because these processes have been associated with frontal lobe functioning, which can be diminished in PD. Although this hypothesis has some merit and is consistent with our main findings, the role of the basal ganglia in attentional control remains controversial. More research is need that directly tests this proposal against competing alternative explanations. It will be important to investigate the specific aspects of attentional control (e.g., spatial versus nonspatial attention, focused versus divided attention, switching versus maintenance of attention) that may be mediated by the basal ganglia, as well as the possibility that other neural systems (e.g., parietal or frontal areas of the cortex) play a more primary role in regulating these mechanisms.

2.6 The Basal Ganglia as a Regulator of Timing

Up to this point we have proposed that the basal ganglia play a critical role in the anticipatory planning of sequences. The question arises as to whether this can entirely explain all the sequence production problems that have been observed in PD and other basal ganglia disorders. One could argue that this is unlikely for at least two reasons. First, disorders of the basal ganglia vary in their symptomatology because the underlying neurophysiological processes differ and, as a consequence, the functioning of certain pathways is selectively altered more than others, at least in earlier stages of degenerative disorders such as PD or HD. Second, recall that others have proposed that the basal ganglia-thalamocortical system regulates multiple processes because the corticostriatal inputs are integrated at various levels (i.e., striatum, globus pallidus, thalamus), each of which may perform different computations. For these reasons, it is important to explore other key aspects of sequence production, such as timing.

Rapid, fluent movements are fundamental to the production of skilled actions, and this observation suggests that one feature of the motor program is the control of fast-paced timing operations. Although some forms of timing may be an emergent property of other processes (e.g., computation of serial order, manual interactions), many complex actions, such as playing a musical instrument or hitting a tennis ball, require precise control over timing and so may be represented explicitly in the motor program. The possibility that the basal ganglia could be involved in regulating explicit timing operations has received support in studies of unmedicated PD patients, pharmacological manipulations of dopamine and other neurotransmitters, and animal studies of timing. Before turning to this work, let us first review the theoretical framework that has guided some influential investigations in this area.

Most investigations of psychological time in humans have been concerned with time intervals of greater than 1 sec, in which case judgments of the passage of time are probably more susceptible to the effects of strategic processing and other nontemporal factors than are judgments of shorter intervals. Here we are interested in timing competency for much shorter intervals because they are more likely to be involved in the planning and control of skilled actions. The scope of this review will be restricted to studies that have examined timing competency under conditions in which subjects must consciously reproduce intervals of a constant duration. In these studies, subjects tap with their index finger in synchrony to a series of fast-paced tones, after which the tones stop and the subjects continue to tap at the same pace. Timing competency is assessed when the tone is absent because it is during this period that subjects must maintain an internal representation of the target interval duration.

One early observation made with this procedure was that adjacent interresponse intervals were negatively correlated so that, for example, if one interresponse interval was short, the next one was long. This phenomenon could reflect a feedback mechanism that compensates for the production of intervals that are either too long or too short. An additional finding was that nonadjacent intervals were uncorrelated. These results were accommodated by a model of Wing and Kristofferson (1973) according to which the total variability of interresponse intervals can be partitioned into two independent sources. One source of variance is the clock component, which ostensibly reflects a central timekeeping operation; the other source is the motor delay component, which reflects the variability due to response implementation processes. The chapter of Collyer and Church describes in more detail the decomposition of these sources of variability. Briefly, the total variability (I) of the interresponse interval (IRI) is equal to the additive variability of the clock (C) and motor delay (MD) sources. This is expressed as $\text{var}(I) = \text{var}(C) + 2\,\text{var}(MD)$. According to this model, the clock produces a pulse when the target interval passes and this activates the motor implementation process. The motor delay component is doubled because each IRI includes two implementation processes, one that produces the first response and the other that produces the second response. For a discussion of the model's assumptions, see Wing and Kristofferson (1973) and Wing (1980). Empirical tests of this model have shown that only the variance in the clock component increases with the mean duration of the interval (Wing, 1980; for exceptions to this finding, see Wing and Kristofferson, 1973), because the variability in the pulses from the internal pacemaker or clock accumulates the more it pulsates. The clock and motor delay components also appear to have some functional specificity, as some experimental manipulations affect one component but not the other (e.g., Sergent, Hellige, and Cherry, 1993).

This theoretical framework drove the first single case study of motor timing in PD (Wing, Keele, and Margolin, 1984). In this study, elevated interresponse variability in a medicated PD patient was attributed to a deficient central timekeeper because only the clock component was found to be impaired in the paced-finger tapping task. Group studies of PD patients have shown that the clock and motor delay components of motor timing are impaired in patients who are withdrawn from medication (O'Boyle, Freeman, and Cody, 1996; Pastor et al., 1992). Though the study of unmedicated patients can offer a more sensitive analysis of basal ganglia dysfunction, elevations in both sources of variability in unmedicated PD patients may confound the interpretation of the clock component because it is derived directly from the motor delay variance (i.e., $\text{var}[C] = \text{var}[I] - 2\,\text{var}[MD]$). For this reason, it is more preferable to study medicated PD patients because motor delay variability is normal (Ivry and Keele, 1989; O'Boyle, Freeman, and Cody, 1996), despite the fact that medication does not restore normal dopaminergic functioning, and other neurotransmitters are also depleted (Jankovic and Marsden, 1988). Discrepant results have been reported in medicated PD patients with one study showing impaired motor timing (i.e., abnormal clock variability) (O'Boyle, Freeman, and Cody, 1996) and two other studies reporting normal motor timing (Duchek, Balota, and Ferraro, 1994; Ivry and Keele, 1989).

Time perception has received less attention in PD, but because perceptual timing tasks have no motor requirements, performance may be more of a pure reflection of explicit timing than in motor timing tasks. Only two studies have investigated time perception in PD and conflicting results have been reported. Artieda and colleagues (1992) reported that time perception was disrupted in PD patients who were withdrawn from medication, when they were tested for their ability to discriminate two stimuli that were separated by small intervals of time. In contrast, Ivry and Keele (1989) found that medicated PD patients were normal in their judgments of the relative duration of two tone intervals. There could be several reasons for these incongruous findings, including the use of different tasks that may vary in their dependence on time perception mechanisms or differences in the medication status of patients.

There have been no further attempts to examine the role of the basal ganglia in explicit timing, which is surprising given the controversial nature of the published findings. Moreover, only one study has investigated both perceptual and motor timing in the same group of PD patients (Ivry and Keele, 1989), which is important because the same mechanism(s) used for timing movements may also be used for perceptual timing (Keele et al., 1985; Ivry and Keele, 1989; Rosenbaum and Patashnik, 1980). If this is the case, both forms of timing should be diminished in individuals who have damage to a neural system that is critical for carrying out explicit timing operations. Recently, however, we investigated the role of the basal ganglia in both perceptual and motor timing (Harrington, Haaland, and Hermanowicz, 1998). We predicted that if the basal ganglia controls motor timing processes, individuals with PD should show greater variability in the clock component of paced-finger tapping than normal controls. Similarly, if the basal ganglia controls time perception processes, PD patients should show less perceptual acuity for discriminating small differences in interval durations than control subjects. Alternatively, if the basal ganglia controls both forms of timing, PD patients should be impaired on both tasks relative to normal control subjects.

Methods
Thirty-four PD patients who were tested during their normal medication cycle and 24 neurologically intact control subjects were studied in two conditions of a paced-finger tapping task and a perceptual timing task. In the paced-finger tapping tasks, subjects used their right index finger to tap in synchrony to a series of 20 tones (induction phase), after which the tone stopped and subjects continued to tap at the same pace for 22 responses (continuation phase). In one condition the tones were separated by a 300-ms interval and in the other by 600 ms. We studied paced-finger tapping at two intervals to assess timing competency across more than

one interval. Only the data from the continuation phase were analyzed. The mean IRI was computed as a measure of the extent to which subjects achieved the target interval. The Wing and Kristofferson (1973) model was applied to the IRI data to obtain estimates of the clock and motor implementation sources of variance

In the perceptual timing tasks, subjects judged the relative duration of two tone pairs. A standard tone pair was presented and followed 1 second later by a comparison tone pair. Subjects indicated by pressing a key whether the interval between the comparison tone pair was longer or shorter than the standard. In one condition the interval between the two tones in the standard pair was always 300 msec and in the other it was 600 msec. Ten practice trials were presented, followed by 50 experimental trials (i.e., 25 judgments each for the upper and lower thresholds) and the parameter estimation by sequential testing (PEST) procedure was used to derive a difference threshold (see Ivry and Keele, 1989). This threshold is an index of perceptual acuity and reflects the smallest difference in time between two intervals that an individual can discriminate. Subjects also performed a frequency perception task which controlled for the auditory processing requirements of both timing tasks. This task used similar procedures as for the duration perception task except the tones in the standard and the comparison tone pairs was fixed at 550 msec. The frequency of the standard tones was always 1000 Hz and the comparison tones consisted of higher or lower frequencies so that subjects judged whether the pitch of the second tone pair was higher or lower than the standard pair. A difference threshold was derived in the same way as for the duration perception task.

Results and Discussion

Table 2.2 shows the findings. First, note that in the paced-finger tapping task the mean tapping pace in both groups was very close to the target interval, though the PD group tapped at a slightly faster pace than the control group at both target intervals $[F(1, 54) = 4.25, p < .05]$. The finding of principal interest was that the total variability in paced-finger tapping was greater in the PD group than in the control group, irrespective of the target interval $[F(1, 54) = 5.60, p < .025]$. This finding was due entirely to the clock source of variability, which was greater in the PD group than in the control group $[F(1, 54) = 8.25, p < .01]$. No impairment was found in the motor delay variability. These results were consistent with the findings from the duration perception task which are also given in table 2.2. Judgments of duration were less accurate in the PD group than in the control group $[F(1, 54) = 10.84, p < .01]$ for both interval conditions. Table 2.2 indicates as well that there were no group differences in frequency perception, so that performance on the two timing

Table 2.2
Timing and frequency perception performance

	Parkinson's Group	Control Group
Finger Tapping (ms)[a]		
300 ms interval		
Interresponse interval	320.6 (15.2)	325.9 (14.7)
Total variability	34.1 (21.3)	26.7 (15.3)
Clock variability	27.0 (20.5)	19.5 (14.1)
Motor delay variability	13.7 (6.8)	12.3 (6.6)
600 ms interval		
Interresponse interval	604.5 (21.7)	617.9 (16.4)
Total variability	53.3 (33.0)	36.7 (12.8)
Clock variability	42.4 (26.6)	27.8 (13.5)
Motor delay variability	20.9 (16.7)	15.7 (5.6)
Duration Perception (ms)[b]		
300 ms interval	52.5 (30.8)	35.4 (20.4)
600 ms interval	80.6 (33.1)	53.8 (24.1)
Frequency Perception (Hz)[b]	9.9 (6.0)	7.5 (6.8)

Note: Tabled values are means with standard deviations in parentheses.
[a] Measures of variability are expressed as standard deviations.
[b] Tabled values are difference thresholds that are calculated by subtracting the upper and lower thresholds and then dividing this quantity by 2.

tasks could not be attributed to potential group differences in basic auditory processing abilities.

This pattern of results is similar to previous findings in patients with cerebellar atrophy or focal lesions (Ivry and Keele, 1989; Ivry, Keele, and Diener, 1988) and suggests that explicit timing is mediated by the basal ganglia-thalamocortical pathways. These results are also consistent with other reports of motor and perceptual timing deficits in unmedicated and medicated PD patients (Artieda et al., 1992; Pastor et al., 1992; O'Boyle, Freeman, and Cody, 1996), but contradict the findings of others (Duchek, Balota, and Ferraro, 1994; Ivry and Keele, 1989). The reasons for the discrepancies are not readily apparent, especially with respect to the pace-finger tapping task in which the majority of the studies have shown elevated clock variability.

Still, other alternative explanations for these results should be entertained, including the possibility that the perceptual and motor timing deficits in PD are secondary to another more primary deficit, which has an additive effect on variability by delaying the completion of a computation that is required for the timekeeping operation to be implemented. This argument was put forth by Ivry and Keele (1989) to explain the elevated clock variance in PD patients who were tested on their affected limb. They suggested that the basal ganglia may be responsible for the computation of a motor parameter, such as force, that is disrupted in PD. However, studies of neuronal firing rates and regional cerebral blood flow (rCBR) activation suggest that the basal ganglia do not support the computation of movement parameters such as force, amplitude, and velocity (i.e., for a review see Brooks, 1995). Most importantly, this proposal does not account for the PD group's impairment in duration perception, which has been viewed as strong evidence for the role of a neural system in explicit timing operations (Ivry and Keele, 1989), since time perception is not confounded by motor factors.

Our finding of perceptual timing deficits in PD is consistent with pharmacological manipulations of timekeeping mechanisms in animals, in which dopaminergic drugs have been shown to alter the internal clock speed (Meck, 1986) whereas cholinergic drugs modify nontemporal aspects (i.e., memory) of duration perception (Meck and Church, 1987). Recordings of cell activity in primates also have linked timing operations to the dopaminergic nigrostriatal inputs (for a review, see Graybiel and Kimura, 1995). In these studies, striatal interneurons have been found to increase their synaptic strength through classical conditioning, in which timing appears essential. It is also noteworthy that after classical conditioning, the conditioned stimulus (CS) appeared to evoke a temporally coordinated firing of striatal interneurons in widely separated sites within the striatum. Furthermore, a reduction in conditioned responses (CRs) was reported with the infusion of MPTP (n-methyl 4 phenyl 1236-tetrahydropyridine), which is toxic to cells of the substantia nigra and, subsequently, the CRs were not regained even after extended retraining. Recently, others have reported that the timing of CRs is abnormal in HD, despite the normal acquisition of the CR (Woodruff-Pak and Papka, 1996).

The research just discussed provides converging evidence for the view that the basal ganglia play a fundamental role in the control of timing. It is important, nevertheless, to consider the fact that depletion of dopaminergic neurons in the substantia nigra also alters the normal functioning of dopaminergic-dependent prefrontal cortical areas (Rascol et al., 1992; Jenkins et al., 1992; Jenkins et al., 1994). This raises the possibility that timing deficits in PD or MPTP-induced parkinsonism could reflect a breakdown in the pathways that link the basal ganglia with areas of the frontal cortex. A recent study of perceptual timing using positron emission tomography (PET) does not support this speculation, however (Jueptner et al., 1995). In this study, rCBF in various areas of the frontal lobe was not specifically related to time perception in neurologically intact individuals. Rather, time perception performance was associated with increased rCBF in the putamen, thalamus, superior portions of the vermis, and cerebellar hemispheres, which suggests explicit timing operations are supported by distributed neural systems.

Before concluding this section, it is important to comment briefly on the influential claim of Ivry and Keele that the cerebellum regulates central timekeeping operations. There are several reasons to question this conclusion given the *existing* empirical findings. One limitation is that the bulk of the data that supports this view is based largely on patients with cerebellar atrophy, which is rarely focal and typically involves the cerebral cortex. Similarly, acute cerebellar stroke commonly has broader effects on the central nervous system due to the effects of edema. In fact, rCBF is reduced in other areas of the brain in patients with cerebellar degeneration (Wessel et al., 1995), and focal cerebellar damage produces a broad range of cognitive impairments (e.g., Bracke-Tolkmitt et al., 1989; Wallesch and Horn, 1990; Akshoomoff and Courchesne, 1994), some of which have been more associated with functions of the cerebral cortex. Other empirical findings are also inconsistent with the proposal that the cerebellum regulates both motor and perceptual timing. In particular, elevated clock variance in chronic cerebellar stroke patients is found in the affected limb, despite normal perceptual timing (Ivry, Keele, and Diener, 1988). This finding is puzzling because if perceptual timing were intact, normal motor timing would be expected, given the claim that both forms of timing share the same timekeeping mechanism (Ivry and Keele, 1989; Ivry, Keele, and Diener, 1988). Alternatively, these findings may suggest that different timekeeping mechanisms underlie motor and perceptual timing, and the cerebellum supports only motor timing operations. Hence, the dissociation between perceptual and motor timing competency in chronic cerebellar stroke patients, who are more likely to show focal deficits, calls for additional investigations into the role of this system in timing. Timing operations may be a distributed process, dependent of the functioning of more than one neural system, but more compelling empirical demonstrations are needed to support the role of the cerebellum in this process.

2.7 *Concluding Remarks*

In this chapter we stressed the potential role of the basal ganglia and its pathways in two aspects of cognitive-motor control. First, we reported on a line of research in PD that associates the basal ganglia with the forward planning of sequences. It still is debatable whether these findings represent a fundamental deficit in programming sequential behaviors or depict more general operations such as attentional control or working memory.

These latter proposals seem to implicate the basal ganglia only *indirectly*, because of its interconnections with neural systems that have been associated more directly with attentional control (i.e., right hemisphere, especially the parietal cortex) and working memory (i.e., dorsolateral prefrontal cortex) functions. Second, we presented some new data in PD that implicate the basal ganglia in explicit timing operations. This proposal is still controversial, but it is noteworthy that research in animals and functional imaging studies of neurologically intact humans corroborate or are consistent with this hypothesis. We anticipate that this issue will be resolved only with the use of more analytic studies that separate timing from the confounding effects of other cognitive operations, such as attention and memory.

Our proposals are but a few that have been put forth to explain diminished learning or sequencing with basal ganglia damage in humans and animals (e.g., for a review see Graybiel, 1995). It may turn out that many of these proposals are essentially talking about the same functional mechanism. Nonetheless, it is reasonable to consider that the basal ganglia engage in multiple computational functions, given its neuroanatomy and physiology and the array of clinical symptoms seen in basal ganglia disorders. Progress continues to be made in uncovering the system's complex neuroanatomy and physiology (Graybiel, 1995; Middleton and Strick, 1997) and, no doubt, these developments will continue to play an important role in constraining and guiding hypotheses about the behavioral function of the basal ganglia.

Acknowledgments

This research was supported by a grant from the Department of Veterans Affairs to the two authors. We are grateful to Laura Anderson for her research assistance in the preparation of this manuscript.

References

Akshoomoff, N. A., & Courchesne, E. (1994). ERP evidence for a shifting attention deficit in patients with damage to the cerebellum. *Journal of Cognitive Neurosciences, 6*, 388–399.

Aldridge, J. W., Berridge, K. C., Herman, M., & Zimmer, L. (1993). Neuronal coding of serial order: syntax of grooming in the neostriatum. *Psychological Science, 4*, 391–395.

Alexander, G. E., & Crutcher, M. D. (1990). Functional architecture of basal ganglia circuits: Neural substrates of parallel processing. *Trends in Neuroscience, 13*, 266–271.

Alexander, G. E., DeLong, M. R., & Crutcher, M. D. (1992). Do cortical and basal ganglionic motor areas use "motor programs" to control movement? *Behavioral and Brain Sciences, 15*, 656–665.

Alexander, G. E., DeLong, M. R., & Strick, P. L. (1986). Parallel organization of functionally segregated circuits linking basal ganglia and cortex. *Annual Review of Neurosciences, 9*, 357–381.

Artieda, J., Pastor, M. A., Lacruz, F., & Obeso, J. A. (1992). Temporal discrimination is abnormal in Parkinson's disease. *Brain, 115*, 199–210.

Benecke, R., Rothwell, J. C., Dick, J. P. R., Day, B. L., & Marsden, C. D. (1987). Disturbance of sequential movements in patients with Parkinson's disease. *Brain, 110*, 361–379.

Bennett, K. M. B., Waterman, C., Scarpa, M., & Castiello, U. (1995). Covert visuospatial attentional mechanisms in Parkinson's disease. *Brain, 118*, 153–166.

Bloxham, C. A., Mindel, T. A., & Frith, C. D. (1984). Initiation and execution of predictable and unpredictable movements in Parkinson's disease. *Brain, 107*, 371–384.

Bracke-Tolkmitt, R., Linden, A., Canavan, A. G. M., Rockstroh, B., Scholz, E., Wessel, K., & Diener, H. C. (1989). The cerebellum contributes to mental skills. *Behavioral Neurosciences, 103*, 442–446.

Brooks, D. J. (1995). The role of the basal ganglia in motor control: Contributions from PET. *Journal of the Neurological Sciences, 128*, 1–13.

Brown, R. G., & Marsden, C. D. (1991). Dual task performance and processing resources in normal subjects and patients with Parkinson's disease. *Brain, 114*, 215–231.

Cools, A. R., van den Bercken, J. H. L., Horstink, M. W. I., van Spaendonck, K. P. M., & Berger, H. J. C. (1984). Cognitive and motor shifting aptitude disorder in Parkinson's disease. *Journal of Neurology, Neurosurgery and Psychiatry, 47*, 443–453.

Day, B. L., Dick, J. P. R., & Marsden, C. D. (1984). Patients with Parkinson's disease can employ a predictive motor strategy. *Journal of Neurology, Neurosurgery, and Psychiatry, 47*, 1299–1306.

Duchek, J. M., Balota, D. A., & Ferraro, F. R. (1994). Component analysis of a rhythmic finger tapping task in individuals with senile dementia of the Alzheimer type and in individuals with Parkinson's disease. *Neuropsychology, 8*, 218–226.

Flowers, K. A. (1978). Lack of prediction in the motor behaviour of parkinsonism. *Brain, 101*, 35–52.

Flowers, K. A., & Robertson, C. (1985). The effect of Parkinson's disease on the ability to maintain a mental set. *Journal of Neurology, Neurosurgery and Psychiatry, 48*, 517–529.

Graybiel, A. M. (1990). Neurotransmitters and neuromodulators in the basal ganglia. *Trends in Neurosciences, 13*, 244–254.

Graybiel, A. M. (1995). Building action repertoires: memory and learning functions of the basal ganglia. *Current Opinion in Neurobiology, 5*, 733–741.

Graybiel, A. M., & Kimura, M. (1995). Adaptive neural networks in the basal ganglia. In J. C. Houk, J. L. Davis, & D. G. Beiser (eds.), *Models of information processing in the basal ganglia* (pp. 103–116). Cambridge, MA: MIT Press.

Haaland, K. Y., & Harrington, D. L. (1990). Complex movement behavior: Toward understanding cortical and subcortical interactions in regulating control processes. In G. E. Hammond (ed.), *Cerebral control of speech and limb movements* (pp. 169–200). New York: North-Holland.

Haaland, K. Y., Harrington, D. L., O'Brien, S, & Hermanowicz, N. (1997). Cognitive-motor learning in Parkinson's disease. *Neuropsychology, 11*, 1–8.

Harrington, D. L., & Haaland, K. Y. (1991a). Hemispheric specialization for motor sequencing: Abnormalities in levels of programming. *Neuropsychologia, 29*, 147–163.

Harrington, D. L., & Haaland, K. Y. (1991b). Sequencing in Parkinson's disease: Abnormalities in programming and controlling movement. *Brain, 114*, 99–115.

Harrington, D. L., & Haaland, K. Y. (1992). Motor sequencing with left hemisphere damage: Are some cognitive deficits specific to limb apraxia? *Brain, 115*, 857–874.

Harrington, D. L., Haaland, K. Y., & Hermanowicz, N. (1998). Temporal processing in the basal ganglia. *Neuropsychology, 12*, 3–12.

Ivry, R. B., & Keele, S. W. (1989). Timing functions of the cerebellum. *Journal of Cognitive Neurosciences, 1*, 136–152.

Ivry, R. B., Keele, S. W., & Diener, H. C. (1988). Dissociation of the lateral and medial cerebellum in movement timing and movement execution. *Experimental Brain Research, 73,* 167–180.

Jankovic, J., & Marsden, C. D. (1988). Therapeutic strategies in Parkinson's disease. In J. Jankovic & E. Tolosa (eds.), *Parkinson's disease and movement disorders* (pp. 95–119). Baltimore, MD: Urban and Schwarzenberg.

Jenkins, I. H., Fernandez, W., Playford, E. D., Lees, A. J., Frackowiak, R. S. J., Passingham, R. E., & Brooks, D. J. (1992). Impaired activation of the supplementary motor area in Parkinson's disease is reversed when akinesia is treated with apomorphine. *Annuals of Neurology, 32,* 749–757.

Jenkins, I. H., Jahanshahi, M., Brown, R., Frackowiak, R. S. J., Marsden, C. D., Passingham, R. E., & Brooks, D. J. (1994). Impaired activation of mesial frontal cortex during self-paced movements in Parkinson's disease. *Neurology, 44 (Supplement 2),* A352.

Jennings, P. J. (1995). Evidence of incomplete motor programming in Parkinson's disease. *Journal of Motor Behavior, 27,* 310–324.

Jueptner, M., Rijntes, M., Weiller, C., Faiss, J. H., Timmann, D., Mueller, S. P., & Diener, H. C. (1995). Localization of a cerebellar timing process using PET. *Neurology, 45,* 1540–1545.

Keele, S. W., Pokorny, R. A., Corcos, D. M., & Ivry, R. (1985). Do perception and motor production share common timing mechanisms: A correlational analysis. *Acta Psychologica, 60,* 173–191.

Kermadi, I., & Joseph, J. P. (1995). Activity in the caudate nucleus of monkey during spatial sequencing. *Journal of Neurophysiology, 74,* 911–933.

Kim, S., Ashe, J., Hendrich, K., Ellermann, J. M., Merkle, H., Ugurbil, K., & Georgopoulos, A. P. (1993). Functional magnetic resonance imaging of motor cortex: Hemispheric asymmetry and handedness. *Science, 261,* 615–617.

Kimura, D. (1982). Left-hemisphere control of oral and brachial movements and their relation to communication. *Philosophical Transactions of the Royal Society of London, B298,* 135–149.

Kimura, M. (1990). Behaviorally contingent property of movement-related activity in the primate putamen. *Journal of Neurophysiology, 63,* 1277–1296.

Klapp, S. T. (1995). Motor response programming during simple and choice reaction time: The role of practice. *Journal of Experimental Psychology: Human Perception and Performance, 21,* 1015–1027.

Lees, A. J., & Smith, E. (1983). Cognitive deficits in the early stages of Parkinson's disease. *Brain, 106,* 257–270.

Lichter, D. G., Corbett, A. J., Fitzgibbon, G. M., Davidson, O. R., Hope, J. K. A., Goddard, G. V., Sharples, K. J., & Pollock, M. (1988). Cognitive and motor dysfunction in Parkinson's disease. *Archives of Neurology, 45,* 854–860.

Malapani, C., Pillon, B., Dubois, B., & Agid, Y. (1994). Impaired simultaneous cognitive task performance in Parkinson's disease: A dopamine-related dysfunction. *Neurology, 44,* 319–326.

Meck, W. H. (1986). Affinity for the dopamine D2 receptor predicts neuroleptic potency in decreasing the speed of an internal clock. *Pharmacology, Biochemistry and Behavior, 25,* 1185–1189.

Meck, W. H., & Church, R. M. (1987). Cholinergic modulation of the content of temporal memory. *Behavioral Neurosciences, 101,* 457–464.

Middleton, F. A., & Strick, P. L. (1997). New concepts about the organization of basal ganglia output. In J. A. Obeso, M. DeLong, C. Ohye, & C. D. Marsden (eds.), *Advances in neurology, Vol. 74, Basal ganglia and new surgical treatment of Parkinson's disease.* Philadedphia: Lippincott-Ravin.

O'Boyle, D. J., Freeman, J. S., & Cody, F. W. J. (1996). The accuracy and precision of timing of self-paced, repetitive movements in subjects with Parkinson's disease. *Brain, 119,* 51–70.

Pastor, M. A., Artieda, J., Hahanshahi, M., & Obeso, J. A. (1992). Performance of repetitive wrist movements in Parkinson's disease. *Brain, 115,* 875–891.

Pullman, S. L., Watts, R. L., Juncos, J. L., Chase, T. N., & Sanes, J. N. (1988). Dopaminergic effects on simple and choice reaction time performance in Parkinson's disease. *Neurology, 38,* 249–254.

Rafal, R. D., Inhoff, A. W., Friedman, J. H., & Bernstein, E. (1987). Programming and execution of sequential movements in Parkinson's disease. *Journal of Neurology, Neurosurgery and Psychiatry, 50,* 1267–1273.

Rafal, R. D., Posner, M. I., Walker, J. A., & Friedrich, F. J. (1984). Cognition and the basal ganglia: Separating mental and motor components of performance in Parkinson's disease. *Brain, 107,* 1083–1094.

Rascol, O., Sabatini, U., Chollet, F., Celsis, P., Montastruc, J.-L., Marc-Vergnes, J.-P., & Rascol, A. (1992). Supplementary and primary sensory motor area activity in Parkinson's disease. Regional cerebral blood flow changes during finger movements and effects of apomorphine. *Archives of neurology, 49,* 144–148.

Raskin, S. A., Borod, J. C., & Tweedy, J. R. (1992). Set-shifting and spatial orientation in patients with Parkinson's disease. *Journal of Clinical and Experimental Neuropsychology, 14,* 801–821.

Rosenbaum, D. A., Inhoff, A. W., & Gordon, A. M. (1984). Choosing between movement sequences: A hierarchical editor model. *Journal of Experimental Psychology: General, 113,* 372–393.

Rosenbaum, D. A., & Patashnik, O. (1980). A mental clock setting process revealed by reaction times. In G. Stelmach & J. Requin (eds.), *Tutorials in motor behavior* (pp. 487–499). New York: North-Holland.

Seitz, R. J., Roland, P. E., Bohm, C., Greitz, T., & Stone-Elander, S. (1990). Motor learning in man: A positron emission tomographic study. *NeuroReport, 1,* 57–66.

Sergent, V., Hellige, J. B., & Cherry, B. (1993). Effects of responding hand and concurrent verbal processing on time-keeping and motor-implementation processes. *Brain and Cognition, 23,* 243–262.

Sheridan, M. R., Flowers, K. A., & Hurrell, J. (1987). Programming and execution of movement in Parkinson's disease. *Brain, 110,* 1247–1271.

Stelmach, G. E., Worringham, C. J., & Strand, E. A. (1986). Movement preparation in Parkinson's disease: The use of advance information. *Brain, 109,* 1179–1194.

Stelmach, G. E., Worringham, C. J., & Strand, E. A. (1987). The programming and execution of sequences in Parkinson's disease. *International Journal of Neuroscience, 36,* 55–65.

Stern, Y., Mayeus, R., & Rosen, J. (1984). Contribution of perceptual motor dysfunction to construction and tracing disturbances in Parkinson's disease. *Journal of Neurology, Neurosurgery, and Psychiatry, 47,* 983–989.

Wallesch, C.-W., & Horn, A. (1990). Long-term effects of cerebellar pathology on cognitive functions. *Brain and Cognition, 14,* 19–25.

Wessel, K., Zeffiro, T., Lou, J. S., Toro, C., & Hallett, M. (1995). Regional cerebral blood flow during a self-paced sequential finger opposition task in patients with cerebellar degeneration. *Brain, 118,* 379–393.

Willingham, D. B., Koreshetz, W. J., Treadwell, J. R., & Bennett, J. P. (1995). Comparison of Huntington's and Parkinson's disease patients' use of advance information. *Neuropsychology, 9,* 39–46.

Wing, A. M. (1980). The long and short of timing in response sequences. In G. Stelmach & J. Requin (eds.), *Tutorials in motor behavior* (pp. 469–486). New York: North-Holland.

Wing, A. M., Keele, S. W., & Margolin, D. I. (1984). Motor disorder and the timing of repetitive movements. In J. Gibbon & L. Allen (eds.), *Annuals of the New York Academy of Sciences, 423,* 183–192.

Wing, A. M., & Kristofferson, A. B. (1973). Response delays and the timing of discrete motor responses. *Perception and Psychophysics, 14,* 5–12.

Woodruff-Pak, D. S., & Papka, M. (1996). Huntington's disease and eyeblink classical conditioning: Normal learning but abnormal timing. *Journal of the International Neuropsychological Society, 2,* 323–334.

Chapter 3

Interresponse Intervals in Continuation Tapping

Charles E. Collyer and Russell M. Church

Abstract

Continuation tapping is one of the classic paradigms in the study of human timing. A subject listens to a train of stimuli and attempts to continue this pattern by finger tapping after the stimuli have ended. In this chapter we review the quantitative characteristics of this behavior for the case of isochronous (constant-rate) stimuli. Five main results are (a) the approximate accuracy of the mean interresponse interval; (b) a systematic pattern of departures from completely accurate interresponse intervals, known as the oscillator signature; (c) the proportional increase in the standard deviation with increasing interstimulus interval; (d) the negative autocorrelation between adjacent interresponse intervals, along with zero autocorrelations between non-adjacent interresponse intervals; and (e) the frequency distribution of interresponse intervals, which is more peaked than a normal distribution. We show that the Wing-Kristofferson theory, the conventional information-processing version of scalar timing theory and a connectionist version of scalar timing theory can account for different aspects of these results. Then we present a general model obtained by combining these explanations. Of special interest to us is the potential of theories such as the connectionist scalar timing model and the general model, which posit multiple oscillators, to apply across two or more orders of magnitude of time.

3.1 Introduction

A psychology of time, treating the various ways in which time is perceived and in which behavior is temporally organized, could potentially concern itself with several orders of magnitude of time, as suggested by the "temporal spectrum" shown in figure 3.1. The physiological, behavioral, and developmental phenomena of psychology can to some extent be sorted by how long it takes events to occur. Psychologists have studied temporal phenomena over about 12 orders of magnitude, from 10^{-2} to 10^9 seconds. In most regions of the temporal spectrum, however, theoretical questions regarding time are either not the primary focus of research, or remain to be formulated. Research efforts with a consciously temporal emphasis historically have been concentrated in three ranges: (a) approximately 0.01 to 10.0 seconds, the range where we can be said to "perceive" time and where we plan and execute the timing of many "here and now"

Order of Magnitude	More Familiar Time Interval	Phenomena
10^{-4}	0.1 milliseconds	– Chemical reactions
10^{-3}	1 millisecond	– Neural and sensory action
10^{-2}	10 milliseconds	
10^{-1}	100 milliseconds	– Time perception and motor timing
10^{0}	1 second	
10^{1}	10 seconds	– Temporal learning and cognitive processing
10^{2}	Minute $= 0.6 \times 100$ seconds	
10^{3}	Hour $= 3.6 \times 1,000$ seconds	– Social interactions
10^{4}	Day $= 8.6 \times 10,000$ seconds	– Circadian rhythms
10^{5}	Week $= 6.0 \times 100,000$ seconds	– Schedules and projects
10^{6}	Month $= 2.6 \times 1$ million seconds	– Circalunar rhythms
10^{7}	Year $= 3.2 \times 10$ million seconds	– Education and training
10^{8}	Decade $= 3.2 \times 100$ million seconds	– Development
10^{9}	1000 months $= 2.6 \times 1$ billion seconds	– Human lifespan
10^{10}	Millenium $= 3.2 \times 10$ billion seconds	– Cultural history
10^{11}	Last ice age ended $\sim 10,000$ years ago	– Recent earth history
10^{12}	First *H. sapiens sapiens* $\sim 100,000$ years ago	– Evolutionary history

Figure 3.1
The "temporal spectrum." This logarithmic scale represents the wide range of time intervals over which important psychological processes occur.

actions; (b) a range of seconds to minutes where investigators, especially students of animal behavior, have studied the effect of temporal variables on performance; and (c) the circadian range of about 23 to 25 hours, where several physiological and psychological cycles naturally entrain to the cycle of day and night and can continue at a relatively fixed period in the absence of entraining stimuli.

This chapter fits into the first of these three traditions. We present data on the perception and production of time intervals in the range of 0.1 to 1.0 seconds. We hold the broader context of the temporal spectrum in mind, however, and eventually suggest a theoretical approach to time perception and time production that may be able to span several orders of magnitude of psychological time.

3.2 Continuation Tapping

Consider this simple task: A person listens to a series of brief tones presented at a steady rate and begins to tap a finger in synchrony with them, one tap to each tone. The tones are then turned off, and the person continues to tap, attempting to maintain the original steady rate. The recorded behavior that occurs after the tones have ended is referred to as continuation tapping.

The continuation tapping task was pioneered over a century ago by L. T. Stevens (1886). Stevens used a metronome to set the target rate. He recorded Morse-key taps on moving paper. Variations on the continuation task have been used to study various aspects of timed performance by Bartlett and Bartlett (1959), Wing and Kristofferson (1973a, 1973b), Vorberg and Hambuch (1978), Nagasaki and Nagasaki (1982), Hary and Moore (1985, 1987), and others.

In this chapter we ask several questions about the interresponse intervals (IRIs) in continuation tapping, that is, the time intervals between successive taps. Does the sequence of IRIs have internal structure, and if so, what kind? Is the resulting distribution of IRIs normal, or does it follow some other probability law? Is there a lawful relationship between the rate of tapping and the variability of the IRIs? How accurately does the central tendency of IRIs reproduce the interstimulus interval (ISI) that defines the original steady rate of the tones? In particular, are some ISIs reproduced more accurately than others?

Each of these questions will draw our attention to a different aspect of IRI data, and will invite a choice between alternative theoretical possibilities. We will show how answers to these questions constrain ideas about the kind of mechanism that could perform continuation tapping. At the end of the chapter we will present a model that satisfies these empirical constraints.

Let us begin with a concrete example of continuation tapping. Figure 3.2 shows the successive IRIs produced on one trial. The subject heard a series of 12 metronome-like sounds presented at an interstimulus interval (ISI) of 600 ms. She began tapping while the sounds could still be heard, and continued tapping after the twelfth sound, until a signal was presented to indicate the end of the trial. Twenty-eight taps occurred between the last pacer sound and the termination signal, which defined 27 IRIs, the data points in figure 3.2. The median of these values was 587.5 ms (mean 591.5), and the semi-interquartile range was 7.2 ms (standard deviation 16.6).[1]

The median was about 2% shorter than the target ISI and the semi-interquartile range was about 1% of ISI. In percentage terms, both accuracy and precision were quite impressive. This is a task people are good at. A goal of timing research is to explicate the mechanisms that permit such good performance.

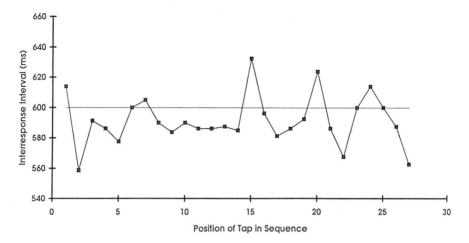

Figure 3.2
A sequence of interresponse intervals (IRIs) from one trial on which the interstimulus interval (ISI) was 600 ms. Each data point represents one IRI: the time from the beginning of one tap to the next.

3.3 The Fine Structure of IRI Sequences: The Wing-Kristofferson Model

Is the series of IRIs shown in figure 3.2 simply a sample of 27 independent values drawn from a distribution with a certain mean and variance? If so, we would describe it as unstructured. Alternatively, is the series of IRIs structured by a clock-like periodic process? Wing and Kristofferson (1973a, 1973b) showed that continuation IRIs exhibit the kind of structure predicted by a model in which taps are initiated by the ticks of a clock.

Figure 3.3 shows the two-process model of Wing and Kristofferson. At the top of the diagram, a clock or timer produces a series of pulses, $p(i)$, defining clock intervals denoted $c(i)$. We can think of the average value of the c_i's as the subject's internal representation of ISI. Each pulse initiates a tap, denoted $r(i)$, with a variable motor delay, denoted $m(i)$, occurring between pulse and tap. The model thus views the time between two successive taps, $IRI(i)$, as composed of a clock interval adjusted for the current and the preceding motor delays:

$$IRI(i) = c(i) + m(i) - m(i-1), \qquad i > 1. \tag{3.1}$$

Because an IRI is influenced in opposite ways by adjacent motor delays, a given motor delay will have opposite effects on $IRI(i)$ and $IRI(i+1)$. Because of this property, and with simplifying independence assumptions, the model predicts a negative correlation between adjacent IRIs.

Wing and Kristofferson and other investigators confirmed this prediction in a number of studies. A very readable description of the model and

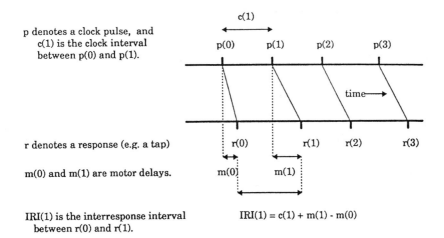

p denotes a clock pulse, and
    c(1) is the clock interval
    between p(0) and p(1).

r denotes a response (e.g. a tap)

m(0) and m(1) are motor delays.

IRI(1) is the interresponse interval
    between r(0) and r(1).

$$IRI(1) = c(1) + m(1) - m(0)$$

Figure 3.3
The two-process model of Wing and Kristofferson. A clock process generates a series of pulses at intervals that approximate the interstimulus interval. Each pulse triggers a tap response after a variable motor delay. The model leads to a theoretical expression for interresponse intervals (IRI), and to estimates of clock and motor variability. (Sketch based on Wing, Keele, and Margolin, 1984.)

tests of it can be found in Wing (1980). In the terminology of time-series analysis (e.g., Glass, Willson, and Gottman, 1975), the Wing-Kristofferson model is a first-order moving average model.

Another prediction of the two-process model is that the variance of IRI will be composed of independent timer and motor variance components, as follows:

$$Var(IRI) = Var(c) + 2Var(m), \qquad (3.2)$$

where $Var(c)$ is timer variance and $Var(m)$ is motor variance. The variance of IRI can be estimated from the data. An estimate of $Var(m)$ can be obtained by calculating the covariance between adjacent IRIs. This value is predicted to satisfy the following equality:[2]

$$Cov[IRI(i), IRI(i+1)] = -Var(m). \qquad (3.3)$$

$Var(c)$ can then be obtained by solving these equations. The estimation procedure allows a separation of timer and motor variability.

A number of studies have examined differential effects of various conditions on these two types of variability (e.g. Wing, Keele, and Margolin, 1984; Ivry and Keele, 1989). Wing (1973) showed that as ISI increased, timer variance increased, but motor variance remained relatively low and constant. Figure 3.4 shows this pair of findings. The different behavior of

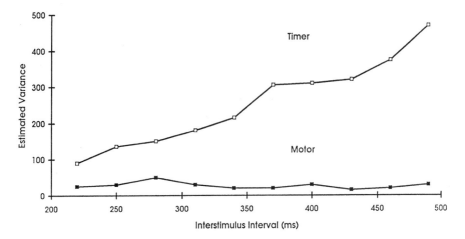

Figure 3.4
Estimates of timer and motor variance as a function of ISI. Estimates were based on the
Wing-Kristofferson two-process model using data consisting of 50 trials at each ISI from
each of four subjects (data from Wing, 1973, experiment 2).

the two variance estimates with changing ISI adds further empirical support for the two processes proposed by the model.

3.4 Which Measure of Variability Grows Linearly with Duration?

A specific technique for separating different aspects of performance can be
expected to appeal to scientists, who are always eager to make analytic
progress. The additivity and separability of variance components suggested by the Wing-Kristofferson model also has the general effect of
emphasizing variance itself as an important quantity. Other models, however, point toward the standard deviation of produced time intervals as
the measure most directly addressed by predictions about the variability
of performance. Let us consider the *variance versus standard deviation* issue
in the analysis of continuation IRIs.

The variability of time intervals increases with their duration, across a
wide variety of tasks and situations. Several models of timing and time
perception provide specific predictions about the form of this relationship.
The two most familiar predictions are: (a) that variance increases linearly
with duration (McGill, 1962; McGill and Gibbon, 1965; Creelman, 1962;
Wing, 1980); and (b) that the standard deviation increases linearly with
duration (Gibbon, 1977, 1991; Gibbon, Church, and Meck, 1984; Ivry and
Hazeltine, 1995). It is instructive to consider each of these predictions in
some detail and then to place continuation IRI data into this context.

Wing (1980) noted that a linear increase of timer variance with interval mean (see figure 3.4) would be consistent with a stochastic count mechanism in which time is measured by the number of independent events (such as neurons firing) during specified conditions. Such a mechanism has the property that the count variance increases linearly with the mean count. Wing observed that the roughly linear growth of timer variance might be taken as support for a stochastic count mechanism for the generation of the clock intervals required in the two-process model. We would then expect a linear dependence of Var(IRI) on ISI. It is possible, however, that the appearance of linearity over a small range of ISIs is misleading. These data may be more consistent with another generalization that follows from an alternative account of timing, to which we turn next.

As formulated by John Gibbon and his colleagues (Gibbon, 1977, 1991; Gibbon, Church, and Meck, 1984), scalar timing theory provides an example of a theory that can predict linear dependence of both the mean and the standard deviation of behaviorally produced time intervals on the corresponding stimulus-defined durations. It is an information-processing model in which there are three major components: a clock, a memory, and a comparator. In the continuation tapping task there are two phases: the phase in which the person attempts to tap in synchrony with the tone, and the phase in which the person attempts to continue to tap at the same intertap interval in the absence of tones. According to scalar timing theory, the ISI is represented in memory as a distribution of remembered examples of the ISI values that have been presented. The perceived current time since the last tap is represented as the value of the clock, which is an accumulation of pulses from a pacemaker. To decide when to make the next response, the person puts in working memory a sample of a single remembered example from memory and compares it to the perceived current time. Responding occurs when the perceived current time is sufficiently close to the sampled value from memory. A ratio measure of closeness is used, $(a - m)/m$, where a is the perceived current time and m is the remembered value. A tap response is made when this ratio is less than some threshold, such as 10%.

Quantitative fits of this model to data are possible. Gibbon (1991) identified a number of sources of variability in the model that lead to the expectation that the standard deviation of time intervals will be linearly related to the mean. For symmetrical distributions, the semi-interquartile range, SIQR, (but not its square) is proportional to the standard deviation, and the median is equal to the mean; thus scalar timing theory also leads to the expectation that SIQR will be linearly related to the mean or median interval.

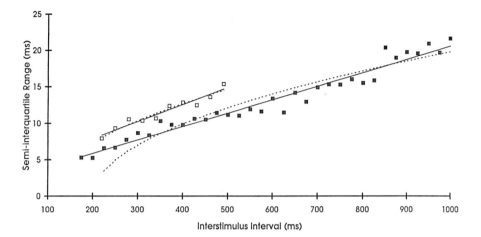

Figure 3.5
Semi-interquartile range is approximately a linear function of ISI. (The data series ranging from 175 ms to 1000 ms is from Collyer, Boatright-Horowitz, and Hooper, 1997.) Standard deviation is proportional to semi-interquartile range, and so would also be described by a linear function. If the alternative hypothesis—that variance is linear—were correct, the data points would follow a negatively accelerated curve. The series of data points from ISI = 220 to 490 show semi-interquartile ranges estimated from the variances used to obtain the timer and motor variance components of figure 3.4. Two smooth functions are shown for each set of data, corresponding to the "linear standard deviation" and "linear variance" hypotheses. It can be seen that the smaller set of data is about equally consistent with both hypotheses. Table 3.1 shows that the "linear standard deviation" hypothesis fits the data a little better for both sets of data.

Figure 3.5 shows that there is a linear relationship between the semi-interquartile range of IRI and ISI, to a very good approximation. Given the approximate linearity of mean IRI and ISI, the relationship shown in figure 3.5 confirms the expectations of scalar timing theory quite well. In contrast, the best-fitting function based on the alternative hypothesis that variance or $SIQR^2$ is linearly related, is not confirmed. Wing's data for the range of ISI from 220 to 490 ms are also plotted in figure 3.5 for comparison. Seen in this context, the data that suggested linearity of variance do not violate the scalar timing prediction of linearity of the standard deviation. Table 3.1 provides the statistical comparison of the two hypotheses in terms of parameter estimates for the linear regression of SIQR on ISI, and the linear regression of $SIQR^2$ on ISI. Using either set of data, SIQR gives a higher goodness-of-fit index. Note further that regression using the squared measure leads to a negative intercept estimate in both sets of data, which is inconsistent with a simple stochastic count mechanism (cf. Ivry and Hazeltine, 1995).

Table 3.1
Regression analyses of two variability measures, semi-interquartile range (SIQR) and SIQR squared, on ISI

	Data of Wing (1973)		Data of Collyer et al. (1997)	
	SIQR	SIQR Squared	SIQR	SIQR Squared
Slope	.023	.541	.018	.493
Intercept	3.22	−54.87	2.16	−99.03
Pearson r	.97	.96	.98	.95
r squared	.94	.92	.96	.90

SIQR gives a better and more interpretable fit for both the Wing (1973) and Collyer et al. (1997) data sets.

To summarize, there are two views on how the variability of time intervals might increase with duration. One view, based on the idea of representing time as a count of independent random events, leads to the expectation that the variance will increase linearly with duration. The other view, exemplified by scalar timing theory, leads to the expectation that the standard deviation will increase linearly with duration. Continuation tapping data are more consistent with scalar timing theory. As shown by figure 3.5, however, a large range of ISIs is needed to clearly discriminate between these predictions using goodness of fit. The finding that standard deviation seems more nearly linear than does variance challenges the idea of timing based on stochastic count processes. We are led to ask, then, whether another type of timing mechanism might be incorporated into the Wing-Kristofferson model.

3.5 The Form of the IRI Distribution

One of the strengths of the Wing-Kristoferson model is that its predictions do not require any particular distribution form for the interval between successive clock pulses or for the distribution of motor delays. It simply requires that clock pulses are independent of each other, that motor delays are independent of each other, that clock pulses are independent of motor delays, and that the response to one clock pulse occurs before the response to the next clock pulse.

Scalar timing theory makes explicit assumptions regarding the distribution of clock pulses, memory storage constants, thresholds, and other parameters to fit results from temporal perception and production experiments, but these particular assumptions are not essential to the theory; that is, they could be changed without changing any other features of the theory. Thus, it does not make any strong predictions about the form of the IRI distribution either.

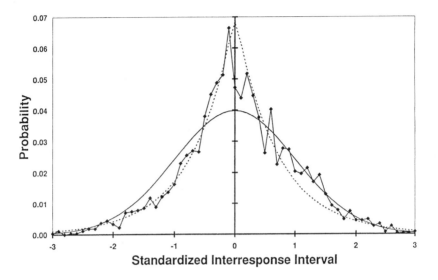

Figure 3.6
Frequency distribution of standardized intertap intervals of one subject (data from Collyer, Boatright-Horowitz, and Hooper, 1997). Each IRI was converted to a standardized score by subtracting the mean IRI of the trial and dividing by the standard deviation obtained on that trial. The two smooth functions are a standardized normal distribution and a standardized Laplace distribution. The distribution of IRIs is certainly more peaked than the normal distribution.

As described previously, the central tendency of the intertap interval is approximately veridical, and the standard deviation is proportional to the interstimulus interval. Thus, as required by scalar timing theory, the coefficient of variation (the ratio of the standard deviation to the mean) is approximately constant. If the deviations from the mean were due to a large number of independent factors, equally likely to produce IRIs longer or shorter than the ISI, the form of the resulting IRI distribution would be approximately normal. In fact, the distribution has been found to be more peaked than a normal distribution (Church, Broadbent, and Gibbon, 1992). This is also seen in figure 3.6.

The data in figure 3.6 were calculated as follows: On each trial at a particular ISI, the 27 IRI values were expressed as standard scores, that is, the ISI was subtracted from the mean of the IRIs on that trial, and these 27 differences were each divided by the standard deviation of the IRIs on that trial. This was done for each of three trials at each of the 34 ISI conditions. The distribution of these standardized values is shown in figure 3.6. The mean of 0 represents the trial mean, and the standard deviation is slightly less than 1.0 because of the use of trial means and standard deviations rather than the population values.

How might a markedly peaked distribution arise? If the independent motor delays following each timer pulse were distributed as exponential decay functions, then the time between successive responses would be distributed as a Laplace distribution. The Laplace distribution, like the empirical distribution shown in figure 3.6, is more peaked than the normal. The empirical distribution form may be somewhat more complicated than this, reflecting variability in both the clock and the motor processes (Church, Broadbent, and Gibbon, 1992), and it may be slightly asymmetrical with rightward skew. The Laplace hypothesis seems plausible, however, and can be simulated easily.

To summarize, the Wing-Kristofferson model and scalar timing theory are open to further specification by modeling the distribution of IRIs. The form of the distribution of IRIs can be used to limit the range of possible mechanisms for the timer process of the Wing-Kristofferson model, and scalar timing theory would be tolerant of such a restriction. Figure 3.6 suggests that the Laplace distribution gives a better approximation than the normal distribution. This in turn suggests that the (not directly observable) distribution of motor delays following a clock pulse resembles an exponential decay function.

3.6 Accuracy of Reproduction: The Oscillator Signature

Continuation tapping is a type of copying task; the subject's finger taps are supposed to reproduce the timing of the stimulus sounds. Accurate reproduction would be obtained if the central tendency of each IRI distribution matched the ISI of the stimulus sounds. In this section we will examine IRI data over a wide range of ISI conditions, at two levels of description. We will see that, at a relatively gross level, the central tendency of IRI does match ISI closely. At this level, there is good copying. At the level of residuals (the small discrepancies between IRI and ISI), however, there are systematic as well as random errors in the reproduction of time intervals. A complete theory of continuation tapping will have to account for these systematic departures from perfect copying.

Figure 3.7 shows median IRI as a function of ISI. It can be seen that the data come very close to the identity function, IRI = ISI, which would represent perfect reproduction of time intervals. Simple linear regression yields the prediction equation IRI = 0.988 ISI + 3.650, with 99.9% of the variance in IRI accounted for by ISI.

A linear function that is very close to the identity function seems to account for experiment-wide variability in IRI extremely well. Why go any further? Figure 3.8 shows a second level of description for these data. In this figure IRI has been expressed as a percentage of ISI; thus, perfect reproduction would be 100%, larger values would signify tapping that is

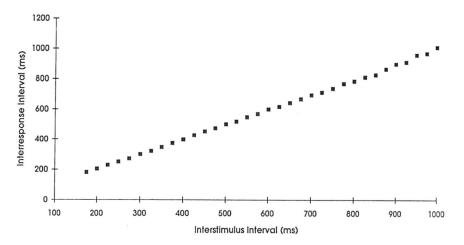

Figure 3.7
Interresponse intervals (IRI) as a function of interstimulus interval (ISI). Data was averaged over seven subjects (Collyer, Boatright-Horowitz, and Hooper, in press). The global linearity of this function is not surprising, as continuation tapping is a copying task and human subjects perform with good accuracy and precision; however, see figure 3.8.

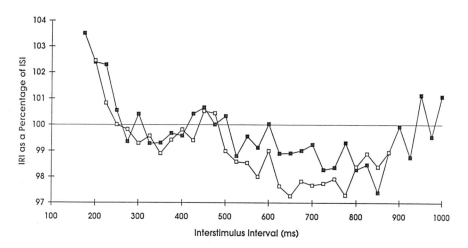

Figure 3.8
Expressing IRI as a percentage of ISI emphasizes the small inaccuracies present in continuation tapping. These inaccuracies are not completely random, but follow a characteristic nonlinear pattern we have called the oscillator signature. Two averaged oscillator signatures are shown here, one from a group of 16 subjects (Collyer, Broadbent, and Church, 1994) spanning the range 200 to 875 ms, and the other from a group of 7 subjects (Collyer, Boatright-Horowitz, and Hooper, 1997), spanning 175 to 1000 ms. The correlation between the two functions over the range where they overlap is +.78, suggesting that group averages can reliably reveal a "prototypical" oscillator signature.

too slow, and smaller values would signify tapping too fast. The data are close to 100%, generally within a few percent, but exhibit a systematic wave-like pattern that is sometimes above 100% and sometimes below.

The pattern seen in figure 3.8, which we have called the oscillator signature, has been replicated in three of our studies (Collyer, Broadbent, and Church, 1992, 1994; Collyer, Boatright-Horowitz, and Hooper, 1997) and a study from another laboratory has found a corresponding result in the production of musical tempos (Collier and Collier, 1994). It is a surprising pattern, because earlier findings and theory gave no reason to expect any departures from 100% except for random error. Why should there be a wave-like pattern of reproduction errors?

One possibility is that the oscillator signature is further evidence for a clock-like timing mechanism, that its form gives clues about imperfections in time-keeping that characterize this mechanism. Another possibility is that these reproduction errors arise from the biomechanical action of finger-tapping, and are unrelated to central timing functions. We carried out a comparison of finger-flexion and wrist-flexion tapping conditions to test the biomechanical hypothesis (Collyer, Broadbent, and Church, 1992). Similar oscillator signatures were obtained under the two different modes of tapping, suggesting that the oscillator signature originates in a part of the nervous system that is common to the finger and wrist. This result encouraged us to think of the pattern of reproduction errors as a reflection of how subjects represent and control time intervals.

Are there stable individual differences in the oscillator signature? Collyer, Broadbent, and Church (1992) demonstrated highly correlated within-subject replications of the oscillator signature, and lower correlations between subjects. The stability of one subject's oscillator signature over several months was reported by Collyer, Broadbent, and Church (1994). Thus, we think of the oscillator signature as an individual characteristic. The specific origins of between-subject variation may become better known through studies of practice effects, musical training, age, and group differences.

Despite these individual differences, is there a "typical" oscillator signature that might be found by averaging? Figure 3.8 provides an answer to this question. Two sets of data are shown, one from our 1994 study and one from a recently completed replication. Although no subjects served in both studies, and although both groups included individual variations, the two averaged oscillator signatures are visually similar, and are highly correlated. This result suggests that there is a "prototypical" oscillator signature. Over the range of ISIs shown (175–1000 ms), the signature has a W-like shape, with a maximum at very short ISIs, a trough around 325 ms, a local peak around 450 ms, another trough around 700 ms, and a rise, apparently toward another peak, at the longest ISIs.

What is the significance of the oscillator signature's shape? Presumably the local peaks and troughs arise from the way the nervous system represents ISIs and controls the production of IRIs. Peaks and troughs could reflect resistance to entrainment of local clocks characterized by natural periods. In the simplest case, trying to tap out intervals shorter than the natural period would result in IRIs that were a little too long, and trying to produce intervals longer than the natural period would result in IRIs that were a little too short. Under this conception, a portion of the oscillator signature where the function crosses 100% with negative local slope, locates an ISI equal to a natural period. If the oscillator signature consisted of one monotonic line segment crossing 100% at only one point, we would be led to think of a single oscillator with a natural period at the crossing ISI. The actual oscillator signature, with its W shape, leads us to think instead that the timing system has two or more natural periods. (Compare this interpretation of the oscillator signature to the one provided by Rosenbaum in his chapter on the Broadcast Theory of timing in this volume. Briefly, broadcast theory attributes these inaccuracies in timing to a preference for producing low-variance but slightly inaccurate intervals at some rates of tapping.)

We do have one reservation about the foregoing discussion. The location of negative-slope zero crossings may not be a reliable way to identify natural periods. For one thing, if a subject's entire oscillator signature were above or below 100% (that is, if the subject's tapping were uniformly too slow or too fast), there would be no *crossings*. Such overall biases are certainly part of a subject's timing performance, but like *response biases* in signal detection, they challenge the adequacy of any account couched simply in terms of accuracy. Collyer, Broadbent, and Church (1994) cautioned that the form of the oscillator signature could be interpreted differently under different mappings of real time onto psychological time. A natural period might be located at the ISI where the negative local slope begins, at the value where it ends, or in the middle of such a subrange. It is, however, more difficult to imagine a natural period in the middle of a subrange where the local slope is positive.

To summarize, although continuation tapping is quite accurate, there are systematic as well as random errors in subjects' reproduction of time intervals. The systematic errors, captured in the oscillator signature, provide a further constraint on possible models.

3.7 A Multiple Oscillator Version of Scalar Timing

Any model of timing must be able to represent perceived current time and remembered target time. For the perception of current time, the information-processing version of scalar timing theory (Gibbon, Church, and Meck, 1984) uses the sum of the number of pulses emitted by a pacemaker in a given amount of physical time; for the reference memory of the target time it uses a distribution of remembered numbers of pulses; for the working memory of the target time it uses a single sample from that distribution; and for a comparison of perceived to remembered time it uses a ratio rule. A connectionist version of scalar timing theory developed by Church and Broadbent (1990) uses different representations for the perceived current time, for working and reference memory, and for comparison of perceived to remembered time. A vector of the current half-phases[3] of several oscillators represents the perceived current time; this feature of the connectionist model draws on the work of Gallistel (1990). The working memory and reference memory are modeled as autoassociation matrices, following a proposal by Anderson and colleagues (1977). The similarity of perceived to remembered time is measured by the cosine of the angle between the corresponding vectors, and this measure is compared to a threshold to determine when to respond.

The essential similarities and differences between the information-processing and connectionist versions are shown in figure 3.9. Both contain representations of clock, memory, and decision processes, but the two versions differ in how these components are conceptualized. The top panel shows that, in the information processing model, the number of pulses in the accumulator (a) is equal to the pulse rate (lambda) times the physical time (t); the number in the accumulator is transferred to working memory; the elements in reference memory (r) are equal to the the number of pulses in the accumulator at the time of reinforcement times a memory constant (k^*) that might differ from 1.0; and the decision to respond is made based on a thresholded comparison between the number of pulses in the accumulator and the number of pulses in reference memory using a ratio rule. A response occurs when the ratio is below some threshold.

The bottom panel outlines the connectionist model. The condition of the status indicators (a vector of of 0s and 1s) depends upon the current half-phases of a bank of oscillators. (The oscillators and status indicators used for storage are not assumed to be identical to those used for retrieval.) Working memory is a matrix—the outer product of the storage vector with its transpose. Reference memory is also a matrix—a linear combination of the weights presently in reference memory with the weights in working memory. The decision to respond is made based on a thresholded comparison between an input vector (f) based upon the current representation of time, and an output vector (g, the product of the memory matrix and input vector) based on the remembered representation of reinforced time. The similarity comparison measure (the cosine) is a correlation that varies from -1 to $+1$; a response occurs when this value exceeds some threshold.

Information Processing

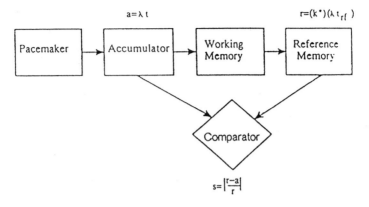

Connectionist

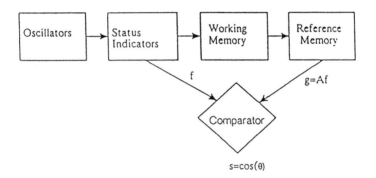

Figure 3.9
Two versions of scalar timing theory: The well-known information-processing version (top panel) and the more recent connectionist version (bottom panel) of Church and Broadbent (1990).

The connectionist model was first developed to determine whether a connectionist approach could capture aspects of the data that are well described by the information processing model of timing. It was found to produce three important features of such data: (a) the mean output time was approximately equal to the input time; (b) the standard deviation of the output time was approximately proportional to the mean input time; and (c) the distribution of output times was approximately the same at all mean times if the times were scaled as a percentage of the mean input time (the superposition result). Shortly after the oscillator signature result was observed in human tapping data, we found that the multiple oscillator connectionist model also captured the essential features of this result (Collyer, Broadbent, and Church, 1994).

This connectionist model of timing, as described by Church and Broadbent (1990), can be directly applied to the continuation tapping task. When the brief tones are presented at a regular interstimulus interval, the person develops a reference memory for the interval as follows: At the end of one interstimulus interval, the status indicators are filled with the half-phase of the oscillators as a perceptual representation of the ISI, the auto-association matrix is calculated as a working memory representation of this interval, the reference memory representation of the interstimulus interval is updated, and the oscillators are reset. With this identification of variables, performance in continuation tapping can be simulated. The original model provides a qualitative fit to three of the observed results of continuation tapping: (a) the mean interresponse interval is approximately equal to the mean interstimulus interval, based on the simulations described by Church and Broadbent (1990); (b) the standard deviation of the interresponse interval is approximately proportional to the mean interstimulus interval, also based on these same simulations; and (c) the mean interresponse interval is not exactly a constant proportion of the interstimulus interval: there are small, systematic departures from linearity that are related to the interval. We regarded this last finding as an important, novel result. When the original model was being developed we appreciated that it produced local irregularities in the representation of time, and these were regarded as a problem to be overcome. The method of obtaining a smoother representation of time was to introduce variability, and we argued that some degree of variability was essential for accurate time perception (Church and Broadbent, 1991). Later, when we discovered the oscillator signature in continuation tapping (Collyer, Broadbent, and Church, 1992, 1994) we recognized that this fact was a natural outcome of the connectionist model of timing.

The original connectionist model did not provide a qualitative fit to two of the observed results of continuation tapping. (1) It did not produce the characteristic autocorrelation pattern in which the autocorrelation at lag 1 varies between 0 and $-.5$, and at all higher lags approximates 0, and (2) It did not produce the typical distribution of interresponse intervals that is more peaked than a normal distribution. But, following the analysis of Wing and Kristofferson (1973a, 1973b) along with the distributional assumptions of Church, Broadbent, and Gibbon (1992), these facts are readily incorporated. The idea is as follows: The time of the output of the connectionist model is not the time of an overt response, but rather the time of an internal representation defining a time interval. In the terms of the Wing-Kristofferson model, the connectionist model outputs clock pulses rather than overt taps. Following each internal representation, there is a motor delay that is an exponential decay function. Because this motor delay is relatively short, it was inconsequential in our previous simulations of performance in intervals in the tens of seconds, but it is a relevant factor in continuation tapping in the range of hundreds of milliseconds.

The specific model used for the simulations in this chapter can be obtained from the authors. For these simulations, we decided to use the programming application MatLab because, by using vectors and matrices as the primitive elements, it provides a succinct but readable way to implement the connectionist model.

The MatLab simulation of the general model contains four sections: initialization, synchronization, continuation, and output. In initialization the conditions of the experiment are described, the parameters of the model are set, and various structures are initialized. In the synchronization section, the actual interstimulus interval is transformed into a perceived interstimulus interval, passed into working memory and added to reference memory. In the continuation section, the perceived time is combined with the reference memory to obtain a remembered time that can be compared with a representation of the perceived time. When the similarity exceeds the threshold, a response is generated after a random exponential delay. (The plotting of the similarity measure as a function of time was used for figure 3.10.) The output section generates various lists and statistics of the interresponse intervals.

The decision to initiate a response depends upon the time at which the similarity between perceived and remembered time exceeds a threshold value. Figure 3.10 provides a representative instance in which there is an overall increase and then decrease in the similarity function, with multiple steps. If the threshold were set at .9, a response would have been initiated at about .25 s.

The simulated results (shown in figures 3.11 to 3.14) are based on 3 trials at ISIs varying from 175 to 1000 ms, at intervals of 25 ms. The standard deviation of clock speed, as a proportion of period, was set at .15; the threshold for criterion similarity for a response was set at .9; the ratio of clock speed in retrieval to clock speed in storage was set at .7, and the mean waiting time from a decision to respond until a response was set at 50 ms. (The use of a differential clock speed for storage and retrieval compensated for the fact that the leading edge of the similarity function was used to initiate a response, rather than the center of the highest area of the similarity function. It is possible that this ratio is a variable controlled by the subject to achieve maximum correspondence between perceived and remembered time.)

The scalar properties of the simulated data are shown in figure 3.11. The mean IRI is approximately equal to the ISI, and the standard devia-

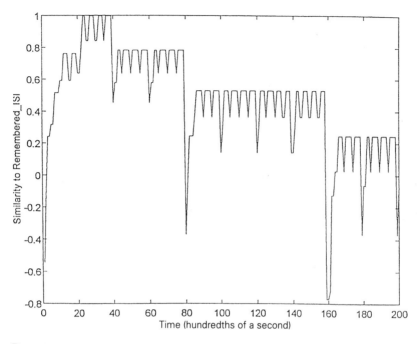

Figure 3.10
Similarity of times (0 to 2 seconds) to the remembered time of the interstimulus interval. Illustrates how the Church-Broadbent and the general multiple oscillator models compute the time of a tap.

tion of the IRI is approximately proportional to the ISI. The coefficient of variation begins high and gradually descends to a relatively constant value. The constancy is consistent with Weber's Law, and the initial decrease is consistent with a generalized Weber's Law, which allows for some latent period before the clock is started. With the connectionist model, this added assumption may not be necessary.

The simulation of the oscillator signature is shown in figure 3.12. The central tendency of IRI is not a constant 100% of ISI except for random error. Over the range of 175 to 1000 ms, there are local areas that are greater or less than 100 percent.

The simulation of the autocorrelations at lags 1 to 5 are shown in figure 3.13. Lag 1 refers to adjacent intervals, and higher lags refer to correspondingly greater separations within the series of IRIs. The characteristic pattern of a negative autocorrelation at lag 1 and zero autocorrelation at higher lags was observed. The magnitude of the negative lag 1 autocorrelation is a measure of random motor variability under the Wing-Kristofferson model, and the zero autocorrelations at higher lags are

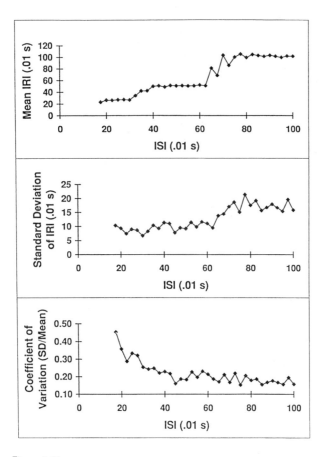

Figure 3.11
Simulated results. Mean interresponse interval as a function of interstimulus interval (top panel); Standard deviation of interresponse interval as a function of interstimulus interval (middle panel); and coefficient of variation of interresponse interval as a function of interstimulus interval (bottom panel). Data generated by the general model of continuation tapping.

consistent with the independence of separated intervals implied by that model. The addition of the motor delay to the original connectionist model produces the same result for the same reason.

The distribution of standardized intertap intervals from the simulated results is shown in figure 3.14. They were calculated in the same way that the data were calculated for figure 3.6. The distribution of simulated IRIs was more peaked than a normal distribution, although less than a Laplace. It also was slightly asymmetrical with a rightward skew.

The conclusion we reach based on these simulations is that a general connectionist model incorporating a multiple-oscillator representation of

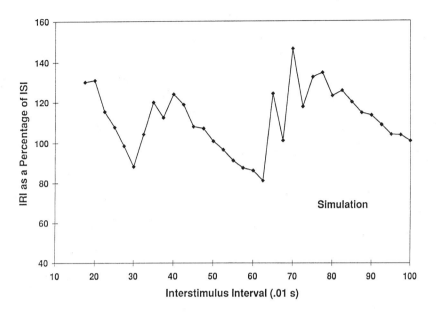

Figure 3.12
Simulated results. An oscillator signature shown as the ratio of mean interresponse interval to interstimulus interval (times 100) as a function of interstimulus interval. Data generated by the general model of continuation tapping.

time, scalar timing operations to define clock pulses, and random motor delays between pulses and responses produces the five main results of studies of continuation tapping: (a) the approximate accuracy of the mean or the median, (b) the proportional increase in the standard deviation or the SIQR with increasing ISI, (c) the oscillator signature, (d) the auto-correlation function, and (e) the form of the frequency distribution of IRIs. With an extensive data set based upon reliable data, it would be feasible to attempt to make some adjustments to this model to provide a quantitative fit to these five results. This modeling approach provides one depiction of a mechanism for timing in the range of 175 to 1000 ms, and it is possible that similar mechanisms are used at other time ranges as well.

3.8 The Temporal Spectrum Revisited

A general problem for living organisms is the tradeoff between sensitivity (the ability to respond differentially to small stimulus differences) and range of operation (the ability to respond effectively across many stimulus values). High sensitivity and a wide range are both desirable features,

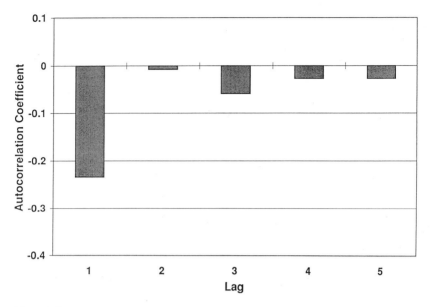

Figure 3.13
Simulated results. Autocorrelation function for sequences of interresponse intervals generated by the general model of continuation tapping.

because they promote adaptiveness, but a single mechanism rarely possesses both to the degree required by nature. Often, nature's solution to this problem is to employ more than one mechanism to carry out a function. Pitch perception is subserved by place and frequency coding; the visible spectrum is spanned by the spectral sensitivity curves of three (or more in some species) photopigments; sound localization depends on interaural time differences at some frequencies, and intensity differences at others; and so on (Geldard, 1972). We think that the broad range of time intervals that are important in perception and action require a clock that is an ensemble of "clocks," each providing a temporal reference for part of the temporal spectrum. This idea is embodied in the multiple-oscillator connectionist model of Church and Broadbent (1991), and in the more general model described here for continuation tapping data.

The empirical sign of multiple mechanisms is often a function with characteristic nonlinearity or irregularity. An example is the rod or cone break after about 7 minutes of dark adaptation, where the detection threshold asymptotes briefly as the cones reach full adaptation, and then continues to fall as this behavioral measure comes to be controlled by the still-adapting rods. Another example is the discrimination function for visible wavelengths, which shows local peaks at color category boundaries

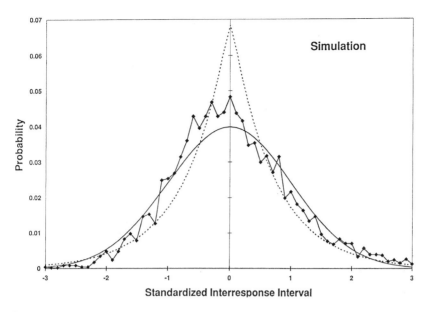

Figure 3.14
Simulated results. Distribution of interresponse intervals generated by the general model.

and troughs within the categories red, yellow, green, and blue. We think that the nonlinear oscillator signature described by Collyer, Broadbent, and Church (1992, 1994) is analogous to these and other "signatures" of underlying processes that have multiple components.

Thus, there are both a priori and empirical reasons to believe that time is represented and controlled by multiple periodic processes in living organisms. The temporal spectrum encompasses many orders of magnitude of time, a range so large that different mechanisms in different subranges would likely be needed to achieve adequate sensitivity in all of them. The oscillator signature suggests that the range from 175 ms to 1000 ms is divided into at least two subranges. The multiple-oscillator connectionist models implement timing by an ensemble of oscillators, with oscillators operating in different temporal ranges, and generate both an oscillator signature and the more global scalar properties seen in human tapping data. These models are worthy of further attention.

Acknowledgments

Support for the work described in the chapter was provided by National Science Foundation Grants BNS9109638 to the University of Rhode Island and BNS9110158 and SBR9421243 to Brown University. Support was also provided by Grant NSS2-S07-RR07086-14 to the University of Rhode Island from the National Center for Research Resources.

Notes

1. We prefer the nonparametric descriptives, median for central tendency and semi-interquartile range for variability, because they are less sensitive to occasional outliers than are the mean and standard deviation. For symmetrical distributions, the median is equal to the mean, and the semi-interquartile range of a normal distribution is about 2/3 of the standard deviation. The semi-interquartile range also has historical interest in psychophysics for its role in estimating difference thresholds.

2. In general the covariance of two variables X and Y is defined as follows:

$$\mathrm{Cov}(X, Y) = E(X - \mu_x)(Y - \mu_y) = E(XY) - \mu_x\mu_y$$

where E denotes expected value and μ_x and μ_y are the population means of the two variables. A positive value of covariance indicates that corresponding deviations tend to have the same sign; a negative value indicates that opposite signs predominate. A covariance of zero indicates a balance of same and opposite signs, as would occur if the two variables were independent of each other. Covariance is estimated from data by calculating a sum of deviation crossproducts and dividing this sum by $N - 1$, the degrees of freedom for a list of N paired values. The familiar correlation coefficient is defined in terms of the covariance as follows:

$$r_{xy} = \frac{\mathrm{cov}(X, Y)}{\sqrt{\mathrm{Var}(X)\mathrm{Var}(Y)}}.$$

3. An example of "half-phase" coding is the familiar use of "A.M." to denote the half of the 24-hour day before noon, and "P.M." for the half after noon. A vector of phase fractions can be used to specify times if the elements of the vector represent "oscillators" or recurring time intervals that include the desired precision. For example, the time 12.31 P.M. could be represented as the vector (pm, 1, 2, 1) using the convention that, in order, "P.M." denotes after noon, 1 means during the first hour (first twelfth) of that half day, 2 means during the second half of that hour, and 1 means near the first minute (first thirtieth) of that half hour. Although this example uses an awkward mix of codes, it illustrates that time can be coded in vector form, and that half-phase is one choice of precision in describing the state of an oscillator.

References

Anderson, J. A., Silverstein, J. W., Ritz, S. A., & Jones, R. S. (1977). Distinctive features, categorical perception, and probability learning: Some applications of a neural model. *Psychological Review, 84*, 413–451.

Bartlett, N., & Bartlett, S. (1959). Synchronization of a motor response with an anticipated sensory event. *Psychological Review, 66*, 203–218.

Church, R. M., & Broadbent, H. A. (1990). Alternative representations of time, number, and rate. *Cognition, 37*, 55–81.

Church, R. M., & Broadbent, H. A. (1991). A connectionist model of timing. In M. L. Commons, S. Grossberg, & J. E. R. Staddon (eds.), *Quantitative models of behavior: Neural networks and conditioning* (pp. 225–240). Hillsdale, NJ: Erlbaum.

Church, R. M., Broadbent, H. A., & Gibbon, J. (1992). Biological and psychological description of an internal clock. In I. A. Gormezano & E. A. Wasserman (eds.), *Learning and memory: The behavioral and biological substrates* (pp. 105–127). Hillsdale NJ: Erlbaum.

Collier, G. L., & Collier, J. L. (1994). An exploration of the use of tempo in jazz. *Music Perception, 11,* 219–242.

Collyer, C. E., Boatright-Horowitz, S., & Hooper, S. (1997). A motor timing experiment implemented using a musical instrument digital interface (MIDI) approach. *Behavior Research Methods, Instruments, and Computers, 29,* 346–352.

Collyer, C. E., Broadbent, H. A., & Church, R. M. (1992). Categorical time production: Evidence for discrete timing in motor control. *Perception and Psychophysics, 51,* 134–144.

Collyer, C. E., Broadbent, H. A., & Church, R. M. (1994). Preferred rates of repetitive tapping and categorical time production. *Perception and Psychophysics, 55,* 443–453.

Creelman, C. D. (1962). Human discrimination of auditory duration. *Journal of the Acoustical Society of America, 34,* 582–593.

Gallistel, C. R. (1990). *The organization of learning.* Cambridge: MIT Press.

Geldard, F. A. (1972). *The human senses.* 2d ed. New York: Wiley.

Gibbon, J. (1977). Scalar expectancy theory and Weber's Law in animal timing. *Psychological Review, 84,* 279–325.

Gibbon, J. (1991). Origins of scalar timing. *Learning and Motivation 22,* 3–38.

Gibbon, J., Church, R. M., & Meck, W. H. (1984). scalar timing in memory. In J. Gibbon and L. G. Allan (eds.), *Timing and time perception* (Annals of the New York Academy of Sciences, Vol. 423, pp. 52–77). New York: New York Academy of Sciences.

Glass, G. V., Willson, V. L., & Gottman, J. M. (1975). *Design and analysis of time-series experiments.* Boulder: Colorado Associated University Press.

Hary, D., & Moore, G. P. (1985). Temporal tracking and synchronization strategies. *Human Neurobiology, 4,* 73–77.

Hary, D., and Moore, G. P. (1987). Synchronizing human movement with an external clock source. *Biological Cybernetics, 56,* 305–311.

Ivry, R., and Hazeltine, R. E. (1995). Perception and production of temporal intervals across a range of durations: Evidence for a common timing mechanism. *Journal of Experimental Psychology: Human Perception and Performance, 21,* 3–18.

Ivry, R., and Keele, S. W. (1989). Timing functions of the cerebellum. *Journal of Cognitive Neuroscience, 1,* 136–152.

McGill, W. J. (1962). Random fluctuations of response rate. *Psychometrica, 27,* 3–17.

McGill, W. J., & Gibbon, J. (1965). The general-gamma distribution and reaction times. *Journal of Mathematical Psychology, 2,* 1–18.

Nagasaki, H., & Nagasaki, N. (1982). Rhythm formation and its disturbances: A study based on periodic response of a motor output system. *Journal of Human Ergology, 11,* 127–142.

Stevens, L. T. (1886). On the time sense. *Mind, 11,* 393–404.

Vorberg, D. and Hambuch, R. (1978). On the temporal control of rhythmic performance. In J. Requin (ed.). *Attention and performance VII* (pp. 535–555). Hillsdale, NJ: Erlbaum.

Wing, A. M. (1973). *The timing of interresponse intervals by human subjects.* Doctoral dissertation, McMaster University, Hamilton, Ontario.

Wing, A. M. (1980). The long and short of timing in response sequences. In G. E. Stelmach and J. Requin (eds.). *Tutorials in motor behavior* (pp. 469–486). Amsterdam: North-Holland, 469–486.

Wing, A. M., Keele, S. W., and Margolin, D. I. (1984). Motor disorder and the timing of repetitive movements. In J. Gibbon and L. G. Allan (eds.), *Timing and time perception* (Annals of the New York Academy of Sciences, Vol. 423, pp. 183–192). New York: New York Academy of Sciences.

Wing, A. M. and Kristofferson, A. B. (1973a). Response delays and the timing of discrete motor responses. *Perception and Psychophysics, 14,* 5–12.

Wing, A. M. and Kristofferson, A. B. (1973b). The timing of inter-response intervals. *Perception and Psychophysics, 13,* 455–460.

Chapter 4

Touching Surfaces for Control, Not Support

John J. Jeka

Abstract

Sensory information through light touch contact of the hand with surrounding objects and surfaces is often spontaneously recruited by patient and elderly populations with poor balance control. Contact with the environment through touch of the hand has also been shown to profoundly influence body movements and sense of body orientation. Such observations suggest that touch contact may provide spatial information about body orientation that subjects use to enhance postural stability. Recent findings have shown that touch of the fingertip to a stationary surface at force levels far below those adequate to provide physical support can enhance the perception of body orientation and stabilize postural control. Analysis of the relationship between the body sway motion and the pattern of force at the fingertip indicate that subjects use slight changes in contact force at the fingertip to gain sensory cues about the direction of body sway, allowing for the attenuation of sway. Moreover, a moving somatosensory reference leads to entrainment of the entire body to the frequency of the moving surface. The movement of contact forces across the skin surface of remote extremities provides orientation cues about movement of the body and signals muscular activation for corrections of body sway.

4.1 Introduction

It has been estimated that the viscolelastic properties of the human musculoskeletal system are capable of maintaining upright stance within $\pm 1°$ of body sway around the ankles (El'ner, Popov, and Gurfinkel, 1972; Nashner, 1976). Beyond this narrow range, human upright stance would be impossible without the numerous sensory inputs that provide information about orientation and lead to patterns of muscular activity that stabilize body sway. Fortunately, the sources from which we derive our sense of spatial orientation are multiple, including visual, auditory, vestibular, and somatosensory (for reviews see Horak and MacPherson, 1995; Howard, 1986; Nashner, 1981). These numerous sources of information allow for the maintenance of upright stance within a wide variety of physiological and environmental conditions.

This flexibility is particularly important when considering rehabilitative methods for patients with sensory-motor disorders or injuries, as the interaction of the multiple sensory influences on human postural control becomes most apparent when sensory input is lost. Multiple inputs allow for the maintenance of upright stance even with an impairment, but the range and flexibility of performance is often degraded. For example, a primary source of sensory information about upright orientation stems from the sense of contact of the feet to the supporting surface and orientation around the ankle joints (Nashner, 1981). Experimental studies with normal subjects which translate the base of support to study the recovery from postural perturbations have identified a continuum of compensatory strategies that maintain the body's center of mass over the base of support (Horak and Nashner, 1986). Subjects respond to small or slow translations of the support surface with an *ankle strategy*, in which sway occurs primarily around the ankle joint with minimal changes around the knee and hip joint. When ankle torques are not large enough to counteract center of mass movements, due to short support surfaces (Horak, Nashner, and Diener, 1990) or fast translations (Kuo and Zajac, 1993), healthy individuals respond with a *hip strategy*, in which antiphase motions of the hip and knee quickly restore the center of mass over the base of support. Patients with bilateral vestibular loss compensate for support surface translations with an ankle strategy when their feet are in contact with the full length of the support surface, but on a surface that is shorter than the length of the feet, vestibular patients lose equilibrium almost immediately after a perturbation, rather than changing to the hip strategy. Such observations are not confined to the laboratory. Patients with vestibular loss commonly have no difficulty walking on hard support surfaces, but report discomfort maintaining normal equilibrium on a "spongy" surface (e.g., grass), which disrupts the interpretation of somatosensory information at the feet and severely hampers their range of functional mobility.

These examples illustrate the complex interactions that can occur between multiple sensory inputs affecting the perception of body orientation. No input acts alone and the loss of one sensory input can disrupt the information derived from sensory channels that are still intact. Reliance on multiple sensory inputs may be viewed as an opportunity to develop rehabilitative techniques and methods that take advantage of the sensory complexity inherent in postural control. Therapies and assistive devices that provide alternate forms of sensory information may compensate for the loss of sensory information due to injury, neurological disorder, or aging, and may provide long-term restitution of function.

One such form of alternate sensory information that is often spontaneously recruited by patient and elderly populations is light touch contact of a surface through the hands and fingertips. Clinicians often observe patients with balance disorders using light touch of surrounding objects and surfaces to stabilize themselves while standing and walking. Touch contact with an assistive device such as a cane is used extensively by the elderly and blind, but canes are considered assistive primarily in terms of exploration of the environment or physical support (Farmer, 1980). Recent studies (reviewed later) investigating light touch contact with the finger-tip while standing show that the basis of the improved balance with light touch contact is not mechanical. Light touch contact provides somato-sensory information about body orientation that is used to initiate appropriate muscular activity to stabilize upright posture and locomotion.

Touch Cues and Body Orientation
Touch information is most extensively studied in manual motor activities (Solomon and Turvey, 1988; Johansson, 1991) and in the cognitive exploration of objects (Gordon, 1978; Klatzky, Lederman, and Reed, 1987). Studies of body orientation illusions produced by conflicting sensory inputs suggest that touch and pressure cues from any part of the body provide sensory cues that influence apparent body orientation much more profoundly and systematically than earlier believed (Gurfinkel and Levik, 1993; Lackner, 1981, 1992). In a study by Brandt, Büchele, and Arnold (1977), subjects sitting in the dark in the middle of a rotating optokinetic drum produced the sensation of body rotation by pressing the palm to the wall of the moving drum and allowing the arm to rotate with the drum. The sensation of body rotation was accompanied by eye movements normally associated with body rotation, so-called arthrokinetic nystagmus. Lackner and DiZio (1984) demonstrated similar perceived illusions of self rotation and nystagmus when subjects lowered their feet to touch a rotating floor within an optokinetic drum. The perception of self-rotation was augmented when subjects received passive tactile stimulation from a circular railing that was rigidly attached to the rotating drum.

Gurfinkel and Levik (1991, 1993) suggested that tactile contact with a rigid object induces a transition from perception of body orientation in a body-centered reference system to a reference system connected to the external environment. They showed that grasping a rigid ground-based handle during trunk rotation suppressed the cervico-ocular illusion, the sensation of head rotation in space when the trunk is rotated at slow speeds while the head is held still. Subjects grasping a handle not only perceived the true situation, trunk rotation in space with a stationary head, but the nystagmus normally associated with the cervico-ocular illusion was significantly reduced. Interestingly, when the handle was compliant rather than rigid, neither the cervico-ocular illusion nor the corresponding nystagmus were diminished.

Tendon vibration studies have also revealed a role for touch contact on body orientation. Lackner and Levine (1978) showed that when the Achilles tendon of a blindfolded, restrained standing subject is vibrated externally, illusory forward body tilting centered around the ankles is reported. If provided with contact cues through a bite block, however, the pivot point of tilt changes and the same vibration leads instead to illusory forward tilt centered around the head. Such illusions are reported despite no change in stimulation to the otolith receptors and semicircular canals, which are considered the primary influence on the perception of postural upright (Benson, 1982; Howard, 1986).

These examples illustrate that touch and pressure cues signal more than the shape and texture of surrounding surfaces. Somatosensory information derived from contact with surfaces is intimately linked with body configuration and capable of inducing dramatic "perceptual remappings" of whole-body orientation. Consequently, it is not surprising that patients and elderly individuals with poor balance control spontaneously seek light touch contact with surrounding objects and surfaces. Touch cues provide meaningful alternative sensory information about upright orientation for postural control when typical sensory inputs are disrupted.

Touch Cues and Postural Equilibrium
Intuitively, we conceive of contact with a stable surface, such as leaning against a wall with the hand and arm, as providing postural stabilization through passive physical forces. Contact forces on the stable surface counteract movements of the body's center of mass which diminish the need for leg and trunk muscular forces to maintain postural equilibrium. However, touch contact does not have to be physically supportive to influence postural control. Marsden, Merton, and Morton (1972, 1981) showed that contact forces as small as 7.5 grams applied to the left thumb of a standing subject resulted in postural responses similar to those observed with loads of 300 grams or more. Stribley and colleagues (1974) investigated the role of fingertip contact in stabilizing unilateral stance by instructing subjects to lightly touch support rails with their fingertips. The results showed that contact with the hand rails led to significant reduction in body sway. The actual forces applied to the support rails were not measured, however, making it impossible to judge whether touch contact was providing mechanical support or not.

Experimental studies have also shown that contact with an object influences the timing of local stretch reflexes involved in postural control. Cordo and Nashner (1982) found that when standing subjects pulled on a handle in response to an auditory stimulus, postural muscles in the leg contracted to maintain equilibrium before electromyographic (EMG) activity was observed in the arm. In contrast, if a subject's shoulder was braced to prevent forward movement, no leg muscle activity was observed when the subject's arm was displaced. Such modulation of reflex circuits is thought to be generated by postural set, namely, by descending influences acting on spinal neurons in a feedforward manner. Such studies suggest that touch contact may not provide physical support of the musculo-skeletal frame, but instead influences perception of body orientation.

A recent series of investigations has focused more directly on the properties of contact cues that aid postural equilibrium in darkness (Holden, Ventura, and Lackner, 1994; Jeka and Lackner, 1994, 1995). The paradigm allows the study of contact with a surface while standing with only light touch, that is, without biomechanical support of the body. The results show that somatosensory cues derived from contact of a single fingertip with a stationary surface have a remarkable stabilizing effect on the balance of healthy individuals standing in darkness. Even at levels of applied force far below those necessary to provide physical stabilization of the body, body sway is attenuated with fingertip contact. Analysis of the relationship between the body sway and the pattern of applied forces at the fingertip indicates that subjects use slight changes in contact force to gain sensory cues about the direction of body sway that allows them to attenuate sway (Jeka and Lackner, 1994, 1995). The following is a summary of the evidence, which illustrates how somatosensory cues from fingertip contact provide stabilizing information for human postural control.

4.2 Experimental Results

Touch contact of a fingertip on a stable surface reduces postural sway in subjects standing on one foot (Holden, Ventura, and Lackner, 1994) and in a heel-to-toe stance (Jeka and Lackner, 1994, 1995). Figure 4.1 shows a subject in a heel-to-toe stance on a force platform touching a device used to measure the forces applied by the tip of the right index finger. The touch apparatus consisted of a horizontal metal bar attached to a metal stand, parallel to the sagittal plane of the subject. The subject placed his or her right index finger on the middle of the bar while strain gauges mounted on the metal bar transduced the forces applied by the fingertip. The subject was required to stand in three ways: (1) without touching the bar (arms by side), (2) while touching the bar only lightly, that is, with less than 1 Newton of force (^{a}100 grams), or (3) while applying as much force to the touch bar as desired (force contact condition). All three conditions were performed both with eyes open and with eyes closed. In the light touch condition, if 1 Newton of force was exceeded, an auditory alarm went off, indicating that the subject should apply less force without losing contact with the surface. The light touch condition was very easy to perform. After just one practice trial to get a "feel" for the threshold force, subjects rarely set off the alarm (<5% of the light touch trials in all the experiments).

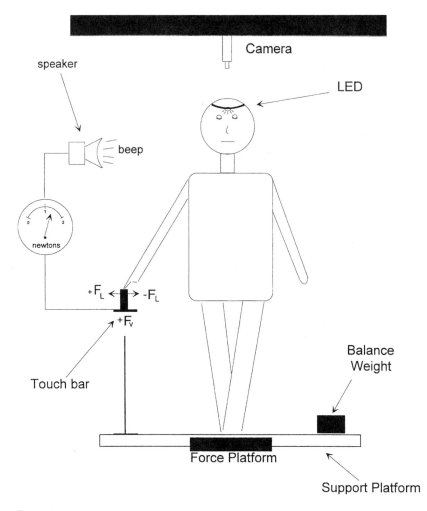

Figure 4.1
Subject depicted in a heel-to-toe stance on the force platform in a touch contact condition with her right index fingertip on the touch bar positioned at waist-level. For the sake of illustration, the subject is shown exceeding a typical threshold force of 1 N and the alarm is sounding. In actual experiments, this occurred in less than 5% of all touch contact trials. In the force contact conditions, the auditory alarm was turned off and the subject could apply as much force as desired. In the no contact conditions, the subject's arms hung passively by her side.

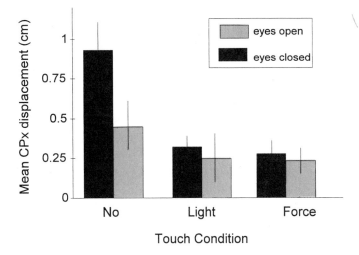

Figure 4.2
Mean medial-lateral center of pressure (CPx) displacement collapsed across subjects for each experimental condition. CPx displacement was highest in the no contact–eyes closed condition and lowest with any form of fingertip contact. (Error bars: standard error).

The primary measure of postural stability was mean center of pressure displacement in the medial-lateral direction (CPX). Figure 4.2 shows the combined results from five subjects. Mean CPx displacement was highest in the no-touch/eyes-closed condition and significantly reduced in all other conditions ($p < .01$). This indicates that touch and force contact lowered body sway equivalently, with or without vision present, despite mean force levels which were over 10 times greater with force contact ([a]400 grams) than with only touch contact ([a]40 grams). In a model designed to study the reduction in body sway due to passive mechanical forces at the fingertip (Holden et al., 1994), contact forces of 40 grams predicted a 2 to 3% reduction of sway. Touch contact reduced sway by 50 to 60% in all subjects, however, suggesting that light touch contact is providing much more than passive support of the body.

Temporal Relationships
Having established that body sway was reduced equivalently by light touch contact and force contact of the touch bar, the next question was whether different temporal relationships between body sway and contact force were observed with different levels of applied force. When a person leans on the touch bar for physical support of the body (i.e., force contact), we expect applied force levels to increase as the body sways toward the contact surface and to decrease as the body sways away from the

contact surface. In other words, body sway and contact force should be approximately in-phase. When fingertip contact forces are restricted to <1 Newton, contact forces cannot vary freely with body sway without exceeding the threshold. The subject must somehow control the forces to remain below 1 Newton as the body sways to and from the bar. Thus, a different temporal relationship between contact forces and body sway is expected with light touch contact versus force contact.

A consistently different temporal pattern between body sway and contact force was observed in all five subjects. Figure 4.3a and b shows the time series and respective correlations between CPx and lateral fingertip contact force (FL), along with the respective time lags where maximum correlations were found in a typical force contact (figure 4.3a) and light touch contact (figure 4.3b) trial. Correlations between CPx displacement and FL were highest with force contact (^{a}0.9), with very small time lags between the two signals (<50 ms). The small time lags show that lateral contact force was in-phase with body sway in the force contact condition; subjects were essentially leaning on the contact surface through their finger for support. A very different temporal relationship was observed with light touch contact, however; lateral contact force (FL) led body sway by ^{a}300 ms. This suggests that as subjects swayed toward the touch bar with only light touch, contact forces initially increased, but as the body continued to lean toward the bar, contact forces decreased so as not to trigger the alarm threshold. This feedforward temporal relationship was consistently maintained throughout the trial. The small applied forces used with light touch contact along with the feedforward temporal relationship suggest that subjects used slight force changes at the fingertip to trigger musculature remote from the fingertip to arrest sway toward the touch bar. The small touch contact forces were not large enough to arrest sway. The point is that the additional stabilization provided by touch contact was due to body orientation information derived from a sensorimotor relationship. Forces generated by musculature remote from the fingertip (legs, trunk, etc.) were guided by sensory information provided by cutaneous receptors in the fingertip (Johansson, 1991; Srinivasan, Whitehouse, and LaMotte, 1990) and proprioceptive information about arm position (e.g., Burgess et al., 1982). Potential neurophysiological mechanisms are discussed in more detail later in this chapter.

Fingertip Contact with a Lubricated Surface
In a follow-up experiment, the friction of the contact surface was reduced by covering it with a lubricant. A slippery contact surface renders shear forces on the finger mechanically less effective to counteract body sway. This means that with physically supportive fingertip forces on a slippery surface, subjects may: (1) sway more than with contact on a rough surface;

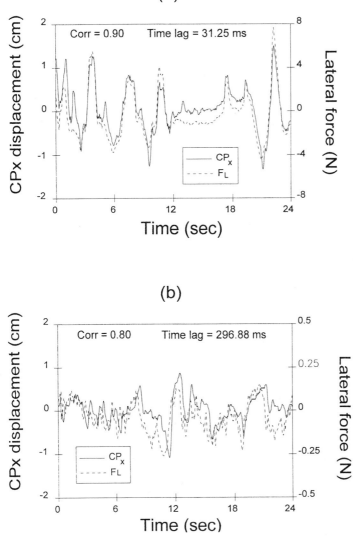

Figure 4.3
Overlaid time series of medial-lateral center of pressure (CPx) displacement (solid line) and lateral fingertip force (dotted line) in the: (a) eyes open–force contact condition and (b) eyes open–light touch contact condition. Individual correlations and time delays for each trial are shown.

or (2) use a coordinative strategy more indicative of "touch contact," in which fingertip contact force changes lead body sway by about 200–300 ms. In contrast, contact surface characteristics were not expected to influence postural stability with light touch contact of the finger, because sensory information from the fingertip is available through cutaneous and proprioceptive inputs. Consequently, sway amplitude or the timing relationships between fingertip forces and body sway were not predicted to be affected by a rough or slippery contact surface in the light touch case.

Figure 4.4 shows 3-sec sections of representative time series of CPX displacement and lateral force from each condition of the rough-slippery experiment with respective correlations and time lags below each time series. The time lags between contact force and body sway were equivalent in the rough and slippery light touch contact conditions, averaging 200 to 300 ms, but the time lags between contact forces and body sway were different in the rough and slippery conditions with force contact. Time lags changed from an in-phase relationship with force contact on a rough surface (<100 ms) to a 200 to 300 ms time lag with force contact on a slippery surface (Jeka and Lackner, 1995). The time lag in the slippery surface–force contact condition was equivalent to that observed in the light touch conditions. The slippery surface adds a constraint: Too much contact force will overcome the low static friction and the finger will slip off the touch bar. Thus, the nervous system implements a similar anticipatory strategy used with light touch contact. The slippery surface had no effect with light touch contact, providing further support for the view that sensorimotor cues, not physical support, play the crucial role for sway reduction with light touch. Moreover, these results suggest that sensory touch cues are inherently more flexible than physically supportive contact forces in adapting to different conditions to provide postural stabilization. This insight may be important for the design of assistive devices and therapies for patients with poor balance control.

Muscular Activity

In the rough-slippery surface experiment, electromyographic activity in the peroneal muscles was measured to determine whether activity in these muscles changed with different contact cues. These muscles are located on the lateral side of the lower leg and are particularly important in stabilizing lateral body sway. EMG amplitude was approximately 40% lower with force contact than with touch contact, indicating that the peroneal muscles played a smaller role in the force contact condition than with light touch contact. Correlations between CPx displacement and EMG activity in each leg demonstrated that EMG activity led changes in CPx displacement by [a]150 ms in each condition. This means that with light touch contact, changes in lateral contact force began [a]150 ms ahead of

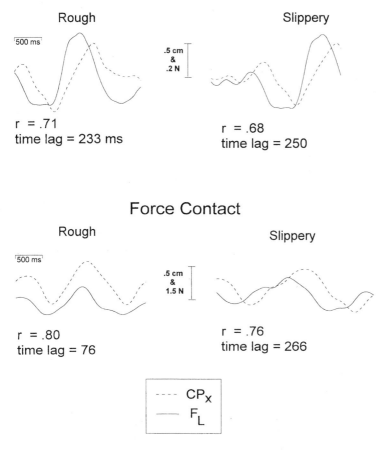

Figure 4.4
Overlaid time series segments (3 s) of medial-lateral center of pressure (CPX) displacement and lateral fingertip contact force (FL). The CPX–FL correlation was highest and had the shortest time lag with fingertip force contact on a rough surface. With force contact on a slippery surface, the CPX–FL correlation and time lag were equivalent to the touch contact conditions.

correlated changes in EMG activity, enough time for a stabilizing long-loop reflex to be initiated (Diener and Dichgans, 1986) or for conscious anticipatory innervations to be employed. By contrast, in the force contact conditions, leg muscle EMG activity was approximately in-phase with CPX displacement, indicating that the contact forces were not precuing a particular muscle activity pattern. The fact that muscle activation patterns appropriate to reduce postural sway were triggered by touch contact indicates that light touch contact cues provide information about body orientation that are as effective as physically supportive contact forces in stabilizing upright stance.

4.3 Neurophysiological Mechanisms

What are the neurophysiological mechanisms that permit light touch contact to provide information about body orientation? The receptors of the index fingerpad are well suited to provide information about the position and configuration of the finger in relation to the touch bar. For example, cutaneous receptors are known to discharge in relation to joint angle (Hullinger et al., 1979; Knibestöl, 1975) so that finger joint movement can, in relation to other information about arm position, provide information about body sway. Slowly adapting (SA) cutaneous receptors, which are primarily responsible for tactual form and roughness perception through the distribution of forces across the skin surface (Johnson and Hsiao, 1992), may also provide information about body sway with light touch contact through skin surface deformation (i.e., vertical or normal forces) or through "skin stretch" (i.e., horizontal or shear forces). Srinivasan, Whitehouse, and LaMotte (1990) measured detection thresholds for movement of a polished glass plate across the fingerpads. At levels of contact force equivalent to those in our light touch contact conditions ([a]20 g), when the plate was moved only enough to stretch the skin, its direction of motion was identified accurately more than 90% of the time. Subjects in our touch contact conditions thus can use the direction of index finger skin stretch and skin surface deformation to identify the direction of body sway movements.

An interesting observation in support of this sensorimotor interpretation can be found in the studies of Johansson and colleagues (for review, see Johansson, 1991). In these "precision grip" studies, small objects are lifted with the thumb and index finger. One such study implementing single unit recordings of cutaneous fibers found maximal afferent activity at approximately 35 to 50 grams of load (vertical) force (Westling and Johansson, 1987). Interestingly, this is the same range of contact force subjects spontaneously adopted in the touch contact conditions, even though up to 100 grams of force was allowed. This suggests that subjects adjusted their applied contact force to levels where neurophysiological sensitivity was greatest to provide the highest resolution of contact force changes and consequently, enhanced control of body sway.

Consistent with our results with a lubricated surface, sensitivity to the frictional characteristics of an object have been demonstrated in "precision grip" studies (Johansson and Westling, 1984). While holding an object between the thumb and index finger, subjects control grip forces so that the "slip ratio" (i.e., normal force/shear force) is just above that necessary to avoid slip. This slip ratio is immediately and automatically updated when objects with different frictional characteristics are gripped. Localized anesthetization of the finger abolishes the automatic updating of the slip ratio and subjects apply far more force than necessary to hold an object, regardless of frictional properties (Johansson and Westling, 1984). Rapidly adapting (RA) cutaneous fibers, which have high spatial acuity and sensitivity to local vibration, are thought to be responsible for the detection of localized movement between the skin and a surface (Johnson and Hsiao, 1992). Subjects in the rough-slippery experiment showed extreme sensitivity to "slip" during force contact of the fingertip with the lubricated surface, suggesting that rapidly adapting (RA) fibers are likely signaling localized slips between fingertip and surface.

When contact forces are too small to mechanically counteract body sway, sensory activity at the fingertip must be interrelated with proprioceptive information about the ongoing configuration of the arm and body to activate postural muscles for body sway attenuation. There is much evidence to suggest that muscle spindles could provide these signals. Muscle spindle signals interpreted in relation to motor commands are the primary source of information for the position sense representation of the body and about body orientation relative to the support surface (Lackner, 1988; Matthews, 1988). When muscle spindle activity levels are manipulated artificially (e.g., by muscle vibration), changes in apparent orientation of the vibrated limb are evoked. For example, applied vibration to muscles of an arm that is prevented from moving produce a false signal of limb extension (Goodwin, McCloskey, and Matthews, 1972; Lackner and Levine, 1978).

In summary, present knowledge of neurophysiological mechanisms suggests that, in our light touch paradigm, force changes at the fingertip that are correlated with position sense signals may represent ongoing body orientation, allowing for anticipatory corrections to reduce sway to a minimum.

4.4 Timing and Perception-Action Coupling

Recent evidence illustrated that if the surface that subjects are touching moves rhythmically, postural sway is driven by the moving somatosensory cues (Jeka, Schöner and Lackner, 1994; Jeka et al., 1997). This method is similar to the "moving room" paradigm that has been used to demonstrate the influence of an oscillating visual environment on human postural sway (Berthoz et al., 1979; Lee and Lishman, 1975; van Asten, Gielen, and Denier van der Gon, 1988; Soechting and Berthoz 1979). These studies of visually driven postural sway found a steadily decreasing amplitude of body sway with increasing phase lags at stimulus frequencies greater than 0.2 to 0.3 Hz, which is considered the *natural* or eigen-frequency of sway. The decreasing amplitude response (or gain) along with increasing phase lags suggested that the postural control system is passively driven by sensory information. Dijkstra, Schöner, and Gielen (1994) have shown adaptive increases in gain by varying the distance to a constant amplitude oscillating visual display. Postural sway amplitude closely matched the amplitude of the visual motion, even though the visual angle subtended by movement of the visual display decreased with increasing distance from the display. Quantitative modeling revealed that not only coupling strength to visual input changed with increasing distance, but the system decreased its own damping to become more sensitive to the visual stimulus (Giese et al., 1996). The differences in amplitude response observed between earlier and more recent moving room studies may be due to the amplitude of the visual stimulus, which more closely matched the typical sway amplitudes observed with upright stance in the Dijkstra et al. (1994) study. Precise matching of sensory and sway amplitude may result in stronger coupling than previously observed and therefore may allow adaptive mechanisms to unfold.

In terms of the somatosensory information provided by a moving contact surface, changing position and force at the fingertip can no longer be attributed to body sway alone. Rather than reducing sway as with a stationary touch bar, body sway couples to the moving touch bar, resulting in a 50 to 100% increase in sway amplitude at a frequency equivalent to that of the touch bar. Interestingly, at the low frequencies (0.1–0.5 Hz) and amplitude (4 mm peak-to-peak) of touch bar movement, the majority of subjects never perceive that the touch bar is moving. During the moving bar trials, they often attribute their increase in sway amplitude to a *sponginess* of the floor, suggesting that somatosensory information at the fingertip is processed and interpreted centrally with regard to the expectations of the subject that the bar is stationary. The "somatosensory moving room" provides an interesting paradigm to explore how somatosensory receptors, which are distributed throughout the body surface and musculature, process differential stimuli at various locations for an overall sense of body orientation. Moreover, considering the similarity of results when postural sway is driven by either visual or somatosensory information, the notion of coupling may provide a crucial conceptual link to decipher the multisensory nature of postural control.

4.5 Summary

A series of studies on postural control with light touch contact of the fingertip has demonstrated that somatosensory cues are a powerful orientation reference for improved control of upright stance. Not only are somatosensory cues from the fingertip and arm capable of triggering postural musculature to stabilize body sway, but a moving somatosensory reference leads to entrainment of the entire body to the frequency of touch bar movement. The movement of contact forces across the skin surface of remote extremities provides orientation cues about movement of the body and signals muscular activation for corrections of body sway. The small applied forces are not capable of physically moving the body. The fact that they have such pronounced effects on balance and orientation indicates how rich is the sensory nature of the information we derive from the surfaces upon which we stand, lean and touch. Understanding how such somatosensory information is integrated with other sources of sensory information for postural control is the challenge that lies ahead.

Acknowledgments

The author was supported by a NIH postdoctoral fellowship 1 F32 NS09025-02, NASA grant NAG9-515, and by a Graduate Research Board Award at the University of Maryland.

References

Benson, A. J. (1982). The vestibular sensory system. In H. B. Barlow & J. D. Mollon (eds.), *The senses*. (pp. 333–368). New York: Cambridge University Press.

Berthoz, A., Lacour, M., Soechting, J. F., & Vidal, P. P. (1979). The role of vision in the control of posture during linear motion. *Progress in Brain Research, 50*, 197–209.

Brandt, T., Büchele, W., & Arnold, F. (1977). Arthrokinetic nystagmus and ego-motion sensation. *Experimental Brain Research, 30*, 331–338.

Burgess, P. R., Wei, J. Y., Clark, F. J., & Simon, J. (1982). Signaling of kinesthetic information by peripheral sensory receptors. *Annual Review Neuroscience, 5*, 171–187.

Cordo, P. J., & Nashner, L. M. (1982). Properties of postural adjustments associated with rapid arm movements. *Journal of Neurophysiology, 47*, 287–302.

Diener, H. C., & Dichgans, J. (1986). Long loop reflexes and posture. In W. Bles & T. Brandt (eds.), *Disorders of Posture and Gait*. (pp. 41–51). New York: Elsevier Science.

Dijkstra, T. M. H., Schöner, G., Giese, M. A., & Gielen, C. C. A. M. (1994). Frequency dependence of the action-perception cycle for postural control in a moving visual environment: Relative phase dynamics. *Biological Cybernetics, 71*, 489–501.

Dijkstra, T. M. H., Schöner, G., & Gielen, C. C. A. M. (1994). Temporal stability of the action-perception cycle for postural control in a moving visual environment. *Experimental Brain Research, 97*, 477–486.

El'ner, A. M., Popov, K. E., & Gurfinkel, V. S. (1972). Changes in stretch reflex system concerned with the control of postural activity of human muscle. *Agressologie, 13D*, 19–23.

Farmer, L. W. (1980). Mobility devices. In R. L. Welsh & B. B. Blasch (eds.), Foundations of Orientation and Mobility. (pp. 357–412). New York: American Foundation for the Blind.

Giese, M. A., Dijkstra, T. M. H., Schöner, G., & Gielen, C. C. A. M. (1996). Identification of the state space dynamics of the action-perception cycle for visually induced postural sway. Biological Cybernetics, 74, 427–441.

Goodwin, G. M., McCloskey, D. I., & Matthews, P. B. C. (1972). Proprioceptive illusions induced by muscle vibration: contribution to perception by muscle spindles? Science, 175, 1382–1384.

Gordon, G. (1978). Active touch. The mechanism of recognition of objects by manipulation: A multi-disciplinary approach. Oxford: Pergamon.

Gurfinkel, V. S., & Levik, Y. S. (1991). Perceptual and automatic aspects of the postural body scheme. In J. Paillard (ed.), Brain and space. (pp. 147–162). Oxford: Oxford University.

Gurfinkel, V. S., & Levik, Y. S. (1993). The suppression of cervico-ocular response by the haptokinetic information about the contact with a rigid, immobile object. Experimental Brain Research, 95, 339–342.

Holden, M., Ventura, J., & Lackner, J. R. (1994). Stabilization of posture by precision contact of the index finger. Journal of Vestibular Research, 4, 285–301.

Horak, F. B., & Macpherson, J. M. (1995). Postural orientation and equilibrium. In J. Shepard & L. Rowell (eds.), Handbook of physiology (pp. 252–292). New York: Oxford University.

Horak, F. B., & Nashner, L. M. (1986). Central programming of postural movements: Adaptation to altered support-surface configurations. Journal of Neurophysiology, 55(6), 1369–1381.

Horak, F. B., Nashner, L. M., & Diener, H. C. (1990). Postural strategies associated with somatosensory and vestibular loss. Experimental Brain Research, 82, 167–177.

Howard, I. P. (1986). The perception of posture, self motion and the visual vertical. In K. R. Boff, L. Kaufmann, & J. P. Thomas (eds.), Handbook of perception and human performance, Vol. 1, Sensory processes and perception (pp. 18-1–18-62). New York: John Wiley.

Hullinger, M., Nordh, E., Thelin, A.-E., & Vallbo, Å. B. (1979). The responses of afferent fibres from the glabrous skin of the hand during voluntary finger movements in man. Journal of Physiology, 291, 233–249.

Jeka, J. J., & Lackner, J. R. (1994). Fingertip contact influences human postural control. Experimental Brain Research, 100, 495–502.

Jeka, J. J., & Lackner, J. R. (1995). The role of haptic cues from rough and slippery surfaces in human postural control. Experimental Brain Research, 103, 267–276.

Jeka, J. J., Schöner, G. S., Dijkstra, T. M. H., Ribeiro, P. & Lackner, J. R. (1997). Coupling of fingertip somatosensory information to head and body sway. Experimental Brain Research, 113, 475–483.

Jeka, J. J., Schöner, G. S., & Lackner, J. R. (1994). Entrainment of postural sway to sinusoidal haptic cues. Society for Neuroscience Abstracts, 20, 336.

Johansson, R. S. (1991). How is grasping modified by somatosensory input? In D. R. Humphrey & H.-J. Freund (eds.), Motor control: Concepts and issues (pp. 331–355). New York: John Wiley & Sons.

Johansson, R. S., & Westling, G. (1984). Roles of glabrous skin receptors and sensorimotor memory in automatic control of precision grip when lifting rougher or more slippery objects. Experimental Brain Research, 56, 550–564.

Johnson, K. O., & Hsiao, S. S. (1992). Neural mechanisms of tactual form and texture perception. Annual Revue Neuroscience, 15, 227–250.

Klatzky, R. L., Lederman, S., & Reed, C. (1987). There's more to touch than meets the eye: The salience of object attributes for haptics with and without vision. Journal of Experimental Psychology: General, 116, 356–369.

Knibestöl, M. (1975). Stimulus-response functions of slowly adapting mechanoreceptors in the human glabrous skin area. *Journal of Physiology, 245,* 63–80.

Kuo, A. D., & Zajac, F. E. 1993. Human standing posture: multi-joint movement strategies based on biomechanical constraints. *Progress in Brain Research, 97,* 349–358.

Lackner, J. R. (1981). Some contributions of touch, pressure, and kinesthesis to human spatial orientation and oculomotor control. *Acta Astronautica, 8,* 825–830.

Lackner, J. R. (1988). Some proprioceptive influences on the perceptual representation of body shape and orientation. *Brain, 111,* 281–297.

Lackner, J. R. (1992). Multimodal and motor influences on orientation: Implications for adapting to weightless and virtual environments. *Journal of Vestibular Research, 2,* 307–322.

Lackner, J. R., & DiZio, P. (1984). Some efferent and somatosensory influences on body orientation and oculomotor control. In R. Wooten & L. Spillman (eds.), *Sensory experience, adaption and perception* (pp. 281–301). New Jersey: Erlbaum.

Lackner, J. R., & Levine, M. S. (1978). Visual direction depends on the operation of spatial constancy mechanisms: The oculobrachial illusion. *Neuroscience Letters, 7,* 207–212.

Lee, D. N., & Lishman, J. R. (1975). Visual proprioceptive control of stance. *Journal of Human Movement Studies, 1,* 87–95.

Marsden, C. D., Merton, P. A., & Morton, H. B. (1972). Servo action in human voluntary movement. *Nature, 238,* 140–143.

Marsden, C. D., Merton, P. A., & Morton, H. B. (1981). Human postural responses. *Brain, 104,* 513–534.

Matthews, P. B. C. (1988). Proprioceptors and their contribution to somatosensory mapping: complex messages require complex processing. *Canadian Journal of Physiological Pharmacology, 66,* 430–438.

Nashner, L. M. (1976). Adapting reflexes controlling the human posture. *Experimental Brain Research, 26,* 59–72.

Nashner, L. M. (1981). Analysis of stance posture in humans. In A. Towe & E. Luschei (eds.), *Handbook of behavioral neurobiology,* Vol. 5, *Motor coordination.* (pp. 527–565). New York: Plenum Press.

Soechting, J., & Berthoz, A. (1979). Dynamic role of vision in the control of posture in man. *Experimental Brain Research, 36,* 551–561.

Solomon, H. Y. & Turvey, M. T., (1988) Haptically perceiving the distances reachable with hand-held objects. *Journal of Experimental Psychology: Human Perception and Performance, 14,* 404–427.

Srinivasan, M. A., Whitehouse, J. M., & LaMotte, R. H. (1990). Tactile detection of slip: Surface microgeometry and peripheral neural codes. *Journal of Neurophysiology, 63(6),* 1323–1332.

Stribley, R. F., Albers, J. W., Tourtelotte, W. W., & Cockrell, J. L. (1974). A quatitative study of human stance in normal subjects. *Archives of Physical Medicine and Rehabilitation. 55,* 74–80.

Van Asten, N. J. C., Gielen, C. C. A. M., & Denier van der Gon, J. J. (1988). Postural adjustments induced by simulated motion of differently structured environments. *Experimental Brain Research, 73,* 371–383.

Westling, G., & Johansson, R. S. (1987). Responses in glabrous skin mechanorceptors during precision grip in humans. *Experimental Brain Research, 66,* 128–140.

Part II
Psychological Perspectives

Chapter 5

The Perception of Segmentation in Sequences: Local Information Provides the Building Blocks for Global Structure

Steven M. Boker and Michael Kubovy

Abstract

We propose that sequences of auditory events may be thought of as being partitioned according to boundaries constructed at times of maximum surprise. A strong version of this hypothesis states that this same mechanism for segmentation of sequences should hold in different modalities and at widely varying time scales, from events measured in years to events measured in milliseconds. One way of quantifying surprise is via information theoretic predictions. The results of an experiment are presented that test the plausibility of the local information segmentation hypothesis using simple repeating auditory rhythmic sequences. Local estimators of information content within an auditory sequence are used to construct predictors of perceived segmentation. These predictors are fit to results of the experiment by using a structural equation model and are compared to the run and gap principles of Garner (1974). The information theoretic model is found to be a significantly better predictor of the experimental results than the run and gap model.

5.1 Introduction

To understand the perception and representation of time, we must understand the organization of temporal events. The simplest event is an impulse, an instantaneous burst of activity preceded and followed by intervals of no activity. A train of impulses manifests the purest organization in time, an organization entirely determined by the relationship of the intervals between the impulses; its organization is purely that of relative durations. For this reason, psychologists interested in the perception and representation of time have turned to sequences of impulses as the most elemental temporal stimuli. The work presented here uses simple repeating sequences of auditory impulses to examine the way that people segment a continuous stream of auditory input into the perception of an auditory object: a rhythm.

We propose that temporal distance in auditory perception can be quantified using a metric derived from information theory (Shannon and

Weaver, 1949). When two events share a great deal of information, then after perceiving the first event we are not particularly surprised by the second event. When two events share little information between them, we are surprised by the second event and the first event and second are likely to be perceived as a segmentation boundary in time. The experiments presented here use the perception of segmentation in simple auditory rhythms to test this proposition.

Perception of Isochronous Sequences

Garner and his colleagues asked subjects who were presented with a variety of visual and auditory cyclic temporal patterns to indicate which element started the pattern (Royer and Garner, 1966; Garner and Gottwald, 1968; Garner, 1974). Royer and Garner (1966) began by presenting isochronous auditory sequences selected from the set of all the patterns of length eight, excluding those that were reducible to shorter cycles (such as *ABAAABAA* or *ABABABAB*) or could be derived from each other merely by changing a pattern's starting point. In the first experiment all the intervals were filled with an *A* or a *B* tone. This turned out to be a more complicated paradigm than necessary, and once Garner and Gottwald (1968) began to use a filled-not-filled interval paradigm, they discovered that subjects reported having perceived a segmentation that had a simple structure.

Garner and his colleagues found that the subjects' response latency was correlated with the variance of their choices, and so they proposed that each pattern had a difficulty level that was correlated with its organizational ambiguity. They proposed that two principles govern the organization of single-pitch, uniform intensity cyclic sequences: the run principle and the gap principle. According to the run principle, a cyclic sequence will appear to begin at the beginning of the longest run of filled intervals. According to the gap principle, a pattern will appear to end at the completion of the longest gap of unfilled intervals. The strength of the prediction made by the run or gap principle is proportional to the length of the longest run or gap.

In some patterns the run and the gap principles coincide, predicting the same perceived starting point to a pattern, and in others they are in conflict, predicting different starting points. When they are in conflict, the stronger of the two principles (as defined by the relative length of the longest run and the longest gap) dominates the other (Garner and Gottwald, 1968).

We performed an experiment that involved the measurement of segmentation in cyclic rhythmic stimuli. We had subjects listen to cyclic rhythms and we asked them to tap a key each time they perceived the pattern to begin. We measured the velocity and timing of these responses and used them as dependent variables to test two models: (1) a model based on the run and gap principles and (2) a model that made predictions of segmentation based on information theory.

5.2 Information Theory and Boundary Segmentation

Shannon and Weaver (1949) formulated a measure of the information contained in a communication, a measure that can be thought of as an extension of Boltzmann's entropy to mixtures of molecules. If x_i is the ith letter in an N letter alphabet and x_i is transmitted with probability $p(x_i)$, then on the average, the information transmitted by one letter is

$$I = -\sum_{i=1}^{N} p(x_i) \log_2 p(x_i),$$

where the Shannon entropy, I, is information measured in bits.

Garner and Hake (1951), Attneave (1954) and others noted the similarity between the formulation of Shannon entropy and Fechner's psychophysical function

$$R = a_i \log S,$$

where S is magnitude of a stimulus, R is the magnitude of a response and a_i is a constant for individual i. These researchers measured the amount of information contained in stimuli by measuring the responses of subjects perceiving the stimuli. Barlow (1961) proposed that information was extracted from the environment by a process of "reduction of redundancy." Redundancy can be thought of as the amount of information shared between features of a stimulus. As two features share more information, the presence of one of the features becomes more redundant. Barlow suggested that as information from the environment is transmitted from a perceptual organ through the nervous system, at each stage redundant information is extracted and discarded. Thus the perceptual signal is reduced to the minimum required to efficiently transmit the information from the environment to the brain.

Now suppose that the events comprising a stimulus consist of cyclical patterns of auditory pulses. If a perceptual system can find a way to combine these events so as to minimize the amount of information, then the system has succeeded in reducing the redundancy in the auditory signal. The resultant perception will be that of a rhythm. By measuring the information shared between possible combinations of the auditory pulses, we can make probabilistic predictions about how these elements are likely to be combined in the perception of a rhythmic stream.

Redundancy can be stated in terms of a ratio of entropies (Barlow, 1961), and has been explored by Redlich (1993) as an active mechanism in visual perception. Redlich proposed a measure of redundancy that we have adapted to rhythmic stimuli.

Consider a measure M to be a cyclic pattern of length v consisting of the ordered set $M = \{m_1, m_2, m_3, \ldots, m_v\}$. Each element m_i in the measure can take on a value of 1 if that element is sounded or 0 if that element is not sounded. We will call these elements beats, and beats with a value of 1 we will call notes. Thus we have an "alphabet" consisting of the set of notes $N = \{n_0, n_1\}$ where $n_0 = 0$ and $n_1 = 1$. Given a random element drawn from M we can calculate $p(n)$, the probability that a note n will occur, as the number of total occurrences of the note n within the measure M divided by the length of the measure v.

We define a feature x of size s within a measure M of length v to be a contiguous ordered subset of the cyclic ordered set M in which the element m_v is considered to be followed by the element m1. The set $X^{(s)}$ will be defined to be all of the possible features of size s. Since in our case each feature x is composed of s notes from the set N where the elements of N are 0 and 1, then the set $X^{(s)}$ must map to the binary numbers of length s bits. For instance suppose that $s = 2$. Then the set of features of size 2 would consist of $X^{(2)} = \{\{0, 0\}, \{0, 1\}, \{1, 0\}, \{1, 1\}\}$.

We can now define the probability $p(x)$ that a feature x of size s occurs at a random position i in the measure M to be

$$p(x) = t/T, \tag{5.1}$$

where t denotes the total occurrences of the feature x within the measure M starting at position i and T denotes the total possible unique features of size s in the cyclic ordered set M starting at a position i. The total possible unique features of size s within a cyclic ordered set M of length v is calculated as $T = kv/s$ where k is the smallest integer that will result in T being an integer. For example, if the length of the measure M is $v = 4$ and the size of the feature x is $s_x = 2$, then there are only two possible unique features of size 2 in the ordered set M starting at some arbitrary point i in the set. However for the same measure M of length $v = 4$, if the size of the feature x is $s_x = 3$, then there are four possible unique features of size 3 starting at an arbitrary point i in the set (see figure 5.1).

We can now calculate R_c, the total redundancy in the cyclic pattern due to correlations between the notes as

$$R_c = 1 - \frac{H(x)/\bar{s}}{H(N)}, \tag{5.2}$$

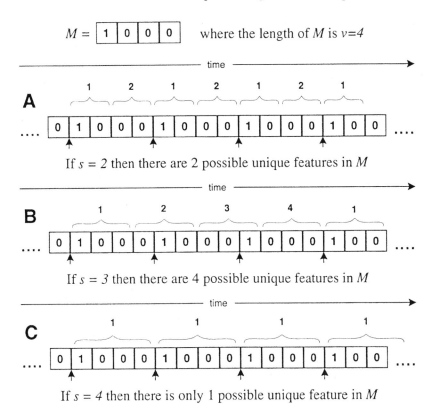

Figure 5.1
Total unique features of size s in a cyclic measure M of length v = 4 calculated by finding the smallest number of measures for which the feature size is an integral divisor. (A) s = 2, (B) s = 3, (C) s = 4.

where $H(N)$ is the entropy in the original notes,

$$H(N) = -\sum_{n \in N} p(n) \log_2 p(n);$$ (5.3)

and $H(X)/S$ is the entropy per beat of a repeated rhythmic pattern, where

$$H(X) = -\sum_{x \in X} p(x) \log_2 p(x);$$ (5.4)

and s is the average of the lengths of the derived features sx

$$s = \sum_{x \in X} p(x) s_x.$$ (5.5)

To understand segmentation, we must calculate local information content rather than global redundancy (which does not distinguish between

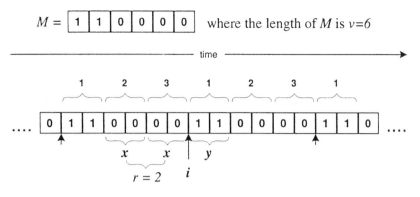

Figure 5.2
Cyclic measure M of length v = 6 with three possible unique features of size s = 2. There are two repetitions of the feature x = {0,0} immediately prior to the position i. Thus in this case the number of successive repetitions of a feature x of size 2 immediately prior to position i will be calculated as r = 2. In this example the feature x does not reoccur after the point i, instead the feature y = {1,1} occurs.

different starting points for the pattern). Suppose we have a measure M of length v and a set of features X of size s as defined previously. We now wish to calculate the local information at position i within the measure M given features of size s. Let r be the number of successive repetitions of a feature x of size s immediately prior to position i as shown in figure 5.2. We calculate the local information at position i if feature x does reoccur immediately following position i as

$$L_s(x) = \frac{H(x)}{H(!x)}$$

$$= \frac{-r/(r+1)\log_2(r/(r+1))}{-1/(r+1)\log_2(1/(r+1))}$$

$$= \frac{r\log_2(1/(r+1))}{\log_2(r/(r+1))};$$

$$(5.6)$$

where $!x$ stands for all of the features excluding x. On the other hand, if x does not occur immediately following position i then the local information is calculated as

$$L_s(x) = \frac{H(!x)}{H(x)}$$

$$= \frac{\log_2(1/(r+1))}{\log_2(r/(r+1))}.$$

$$(5.7)$$

In this way, we can calculate a value for the local "surprise," which is generated immediately following position i within the measure M.

For each beat in a stimulus, we can calculate the local information for features of different lengths. We have chosen to calculate local information for features of 1 beat, 2 beats, and 3 beats in length: $L_1(x)$, $L_2(x)$, and $L_3(x)$. Thus we calculate three variables that will contribute to a prediction of segmentation at every beat in a stimulus. The probability that a subject will segment a pattern at beat x is a positive function of the magnitude of these variables at beat x. Note that this method of prediction does not just generate one predicted segmentation point. It generates a probability of segmentation for every beat in the sequence; many beats may have a low probability while more than one may have a high probability.

5.3 Methods

To examine the perception of structure within auditory sequences, we performed a psychophysical experiment in which subjects listened to a cyclic rhythm (Boker, 1994; Boker and Kubovy, 1998). We asked the subjects to indicate where in the sequence they heard the "beginning" of the cycle. In this way we examined a large set of stimuli comprising a variety of temporal structures. We calculated predictions based on Garner's run and gap principles for each of the stimuli and fit them to the subjects' responses using Structural Equation Modeling (Bollen, 1989). We also calculated a second set of predictions based on information theory for each of the stimuli and fit them to the subjects' responses. After studying the results of these analyses, we performed a replication of the experiment to cross-validate the results.

For experiment 1 we recruited 11 subjects who completed the procedure presented below on five separate occasions of measurement. For experiment 2 we recruited 28 subjects; each completed the experimental procedure once. Subjects were selected from a pool of college student volunteers so that half of the subjects in each experiment reported having more than four years of formal training in playing a musical instrument, whereas the remaining subjects reported no such training.

On each trial, we presented the subjects with one cyclic pattern and asked them to indicate the perceived starting point of the pattern. They did so by striking a key on a synthesizer keyboard in synchrony with the perceived starting point. We asked them to continue to strike the key at the perceived beginning of each cycle (not necessarily occurring at the same point in the cycle) until they had settled on a stable starting point. They then pressed a mouse button to end the trial.

Each stimulus was a cyclic repetition of a fixed number of beats: equal intervals of time that could either be silent or begin with a percussive sound. Thus a stimulus could be represented by a binary number where each binary digit represents a beat: a zero representing silence and a one representing sound. The set of stimuli for Experiment 1 consisted of all of the unique rhythmic patterns of length 8 or less, 115 patterns in all. The set of rhythmic stimuli in Experiment 2 consisted of a random sample of 115 stimuli drawn half from the unique patterns of length 8 or less and half from the unique patterns of length 12.

We used two methods to minimize the likelihood that subjects would associate the first beat of the stimulus with the perceived beginning of the cycle: (1) We began each trial at a very fast tempo (10 ms per beat) and within 2 seconds we slowed it to a steady beat length of 250 ms, and (2) the stimulus was started at a random point in the cycle.

The percussive sound we used was a synthesized musical cowbell produced by a wavetable synthesis module (Roland MT-32 MIDI) and delivered to the subjects binaurally via headphones (Sennheiser HD-414-SL). The subjects responded by striking a key on a Kawai K5 Digital Synthesizer keyboard. We measured three variables for each keypress: (1) the time of response in milliseconds relative to the beginning of the presentation of the stimulus; (2) the time of response in milliseconds relative to the beginning of current repetition of the pattern as represented internally by the computer software; and (3) the velocity of the response as an integer between 1 and 127.

5.4 Models

Run-Gap Predictions

We used a latent variable structural Equation model to test the goodness of fit of Garner's "run-gap" heuristic predictions to the data gathered from the two experiments. Figure 5.3 shows a path model of Garner's run-gap heuristics. The predictor variables are run, the length of subsequent run, and gap, the length of the previous gap. The latent variable is S, the perceived structure of the rhythmic pattern. The measured outcome variables are RB, the response within the beat; A, the accuracy of the response; and V, the velocity of the response.

We constructed the run variable as follows: if the current stimulus beat value is 1 and the previous stimulus beat value is 0, then run = 1 + (the number of stimulus beats following the current stimulus beat before another stimulus beat with a value of 0 is encountered). We constructed the gap variable similarly: if the current stimulus beat value is 1 and the previous stimulus beat value is 0, then gap = 1 + (the number of stimulus

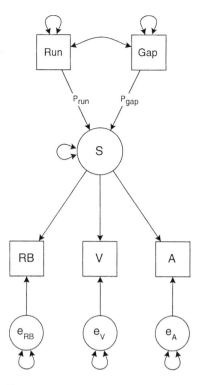

Figure 5.3
Path diagram showing a structural equation model of Garner's basic run-gap theory. Single-headed arrows are regression coefficients and double-headed arrows are variances. *Run*, is the length of subsequent run, *Gap* is the length of the previous gap, *S* is the latent perceived structure of the rhythmic pattern, *RB* is the response within the beat, *A* is the accuracy of the response and *V* is the velocity of the response. e_{RB}, e_{RB} and e_{RB} are the residuals remaining after prediction. P_{run} and P_{gap} are the regression coefficients by which the *Run* and *Gap* variables predict the perceived structure *S*.

beats preceding the current stimulus beat before a stimulus beat with a value of 1 is encountered).

We coded the outcome variables as follows. If a keypress occurred within 0.5 beat of the onset of the current stimulus beat, then we coded RB as 1, otherwise as 0. If RB was 1, we coded the MIDI velocity of the keypress (range 1–127) as *V*. If RB was 1, we coded *A* as

$$A = 1 - \frac{2|t_k - t_b|}{b},\tag{5.8}$$

where t_k is the elapsed time to the keypress, t_b is the elapsed time to the onset of the stimulus beat, and b is the duration of the beat. This means that the accuracy, *A*, of the keypress was 1 if the keypress began

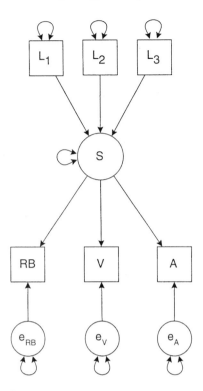

Figure 5.4
Path diagram of the entropy prediction model. Single-headed arrows are regression coefficients and double-headed arrows are variances. L_1, L_2 and L_3 are entropy of features of
length 1, 2, and 3 respectively. Again, S is the latent perceived structure of the rhythmic
pattern, RB is the response within the beat, A is the accuracy of the response and V is the
velocity of the response. e_{RB}, e_{RB} and e_{RB} are the residuals remaining after prediction. P_{run} and
P_{gap} are the regression coefficients by which the Run and Gap variables predict the perceived
structure S.

simultaneously with the onset of the stimulus beat, and the accuracy was
0 if the keypress occurred halfway between two stimulus beats.

5.5 Local Information Predictions

We constructed a similar latent variable model to test the fit of the local
information content predictions to the data from experiments 1 and 2 (see
figure 5.4). We coded the outcome variables in the same manner as the run-
gap model. We calculated the predictor variables in terms of redundancy
for features of a particular size.

   For each beat x in a rhythmic sequence, three local measures of information content were calculated according to equations 6 and 7: (1) the

local information for features of size 1, $L_1(x)$; (2) the local information for features of size 2, $L_2(x)$; and (3) the local information for features of size 3, $L_3(x)$. We used these three variables, each of which has a fixed value for each beat of each rhythmic sequence, to predict where the segmentation would occur.

5.6 Results

We first describe the results of the experiment using histograms to show distribution patterns, and then we summarize the results of model fitting.

Response Distributions for Selected Stimulus Patterns
In this section we present histograms of the response distributions for the stimuli that are pertinent to the theory and models under discussion.

In figure 5.5 we show the distributions of responses to two stimuli. For instance, in figure 5.5A we graph the distribution of responses to one stimulus: an eight-beat pattern in which four beats are sounded and four are silent. In the label for each histogram we give a binary representation of the stimulus pattern. Elapsed time increases from left to right and intervals between ticks on the abscissa represent 250 ms. We show the starting point of the rhythmic stimulus predicted by the run and gap principles on the far left side of the histogram, and this point is also the first binary digit in the label.

Note that although we numbered the abscissa of figure 5.5A from 0 to 8, there are only 8 beats in the measure [1 1 1 0 1 0 0 0]. It is the eight gaps between the sequence 0 to 8 that represent the durations of the eight beats within this measure. Thus responses that occurred just after the predicted starting point appear at the left edge of the histogram, and the responses which occurred at the end of the duration of the last beat appear at the right edge of the histogram. Since the stimulus is cyclic, responses that occur at the end of the last beat also occur just before the first beat. Therefore, figure 5.5A can be read as a distribution of responses with a mode just before the predicted starting point of the measure.

Figure 5.5 highlights the inconsistency of the run and gap principles. The responses in figure 5.5A to pattern [1 1 1 0 1 0 0 0] are predicted by the run-gap principles, whereas the pattern in figure 5.5B, [1 1 1 0 0 1 0 0], is almost identical and yet the responses are not predicted by the run and gap principles. Any theory of organization of rhythmic perception must take into account this type of shift. A number of these inconsistencies appear in our data.

Model Fitting Results
We fit the two models to the data from experiment 1 and experiment 2 using the structural Equation modeling procedure in SAS (PROC CALIS)

A. Distribution of Beats for [1 1 1 0 1 0 0 0]

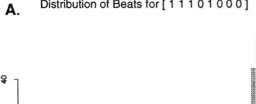

[11101000]

B. Distribution of Beats for [1 1 1 0 0 1 0 0]

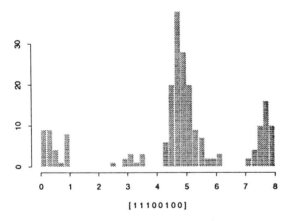

[11100100]

Figure 5.5
Response distributions for two stimulus patterns. (A) Histogram showing response distributions for one stimulus pattern which elicited responses predicted by the run and gap principles; (B) Histogram showing response distributions for a nearly identical stimulus pattern that elicited responses not predicted by the run-gap principles.

Table 5.1
Comparison of prediction model parameters and χ^2 for models fit to the data from experiment 1 and experiment 2

	Null	Run-Gap	Entropy
Experiment 1			
χ^2	923649	2623	79
DF	10	4	6
N	174781	174781	174781
Experiment 2			
χ^2	541596	388	59
DF	10	4	6
N	104512	104512	104512

and present the results of fitting the run-gap model and the local information model in table 5.1. The estimated parameters and χ^2 statistics are presented side by side for the two models.

The run-gap model has a χ^2 fit statistic of 2623 with 4 degrees of freedom (DF). Although this might seem large, the effective sample size is 174,781 separate stimulus response pairs which contribute to a null model χ^2 of 923,649 with 10 DF. The run-gap model fits much better than the null model, but the local information (entropy) model has a χ^2 of only 79 with 6 DF. Although these two models are not nested and so cannot be compared precisely in terms of χ^2 goodness of fit, the difference in χ^2 is so great that it overwhelms the possible loss of accuracy due to the nonnested nature of the comparison.

Table 5.1 also presents the results of the analysis of experiment 2. The run-gap model has a χ^2 fit statistic of 388 with 4 DF compared to a null model χ^2 of 541,596 with 10 DF. The local information (entropy) model has a χ^2 of 59 with 6 DF. As in experiment 1, the two models are not nested, but the difference in χ^2 between the two models is so large that we do not hesitate to prefer the local information model over the run-gap model.

5.7 Discussion

A local information structural equation model (entropy model) based on ideas advanced by Barlow (1961) fits our data much better than does the run-gap model. This entropy model suggests that perceptual segmentation is based on principles of "minimum redundancy," or alternately put, "maximum surprise." By segmenting an incoming signal with respect to maxima of local information, redundancy can be removed from the perceived signal.

Other systems concerned with the efficient transmission and storage of information have been shown to obey the laws of information theory and their physical cousins, the laws of thermodynamics. These laws provide a way of measuring relative organization and disorganization. Entropy not only provides a metric for the process by which the universe becomes more disorganized over time, it also provides a metric for the process by which the brain organizes input over time.

Perceptual systems other than auditory are likely to obey these laws of minimization of redundancy while they discover structure in the environment. There is no reason why higher cognitive areas of the brain would be immune to these laws for the communication of information and organization of structure. Thus one might speculate that abstract constructs such as the syntactic and grammatical structure of language should also behave according to general laws of organization.

The importance of an entropic Weltanschauung should not be underestimated. The systematic observation of human behavior inevitably involves measurement of the perception and expression of the organization of structure. Re-expressing psychometric measurement of perceptual tasks in terms of an information theoretic metric may provide a foundation upon which to build structural models of cognition.

Acknowledgments

We thank John Nesselroade for his friendship and thoughtful advice during the development of this project, Jay Friedenberg for helping to carry the experiments to a successful conclusion, and Jack McArdle for helping to achieve the stimulus-response simplicity of the structural models. We would also like to acknowledge Charles Collyer and an anonymous reviewer whose careful and helpful comments substantially improved this chapter. This research was supported by NIMH grant number 5-R01 MH47317 to the University of Virginia, Michael Kubovy, P.I., and also supported by the Institute for Developmental and Health Research Methodology at the University of Virginia.

References

Attneave, F. (1954). Some informational aspects of visual perception. *Psychological Review, 61,* 183–193.

Barlow, H. B. (1961). Possible principles underlying the transformation of sensory messages. In W. A. Rosenblith (ed.), *Sensory Communication* (pp. 217–234). Cambridge, MA: MIT Press.

Boker, S. M. (1994). The Perception of Structure in Simple Auditory Rhythmic Patterns. Master's thesis, University of Virginia, Charlottesville.

Boker, S. M., & Kubovy, M. (1998). Predicting the grouping of rhythmic sequences using local estimators of information content. In D. Rosenthal & H. G. Okuno (eds.), *Readings in Computational Auditory Scene Analysis*. Hillsdale, NJ: Lawrence Erlbaum Associates.

Bollen, K. A. (1989). *Structural Equations with Latent Variables*. New York: John Wiley & Sons.

Garner, W. R. (1974). *The Processing of Information and Structure*. Hillsdale, NJ: Lawrence Erlbaum Associates.

Garner, W. R., & Gottwald, R. L. (1968). The perception and learning of temporal patterns. *Quarterly Journal of Experimental Psychology, 20,* 97–109.

Garner, W. R., & Hake, H. W. (1951). The amount of information in absolute judgments. *Psychological Review, 58,* 446–459.

Redlich, N. A. (1993). Redundancy reduction as a strategy for unsupervised learning. *Neural Computation, 5,* 289–304.

Royer, F. L., & Garner, W. R. (1966). Response uncertainty and perceptual difficulty of auditory temporal patterns. *Perception & Psychophysics, 1,* 41–47.

Shannon, C. E., & Weaver, W. (1949). *The Mathematical Theory of Communication*. Urbana: University of Illinois Press.

Chapter 6

Musical Motion in Perception and Performance

Bruno H. Repp

Abstract

A series of experiments has demonstrated that the relative difficulty of detecting a small change in the duration of a single inter-onset interval (IOI) in an otherwise iso-chronously played musical excerpt is closely related to the relative lengthening of that IOI in a typical expressive performance of the music. These results suggest that musical structures have kinematic implications that not only compel performers to modulate their tempo in certain ways but also induce corresponding perceptual biases in (musically trained) listeners. The perceptual effects may be understood as a form of perceptual-motor interaction. Unlike expressive timing in performance, which is under cognitive control ("interpretation"), the perceptual biases elicited by a piece of music may reflect a precognitive, obligatory response to implied musical motion.

6.1 Introduction

Expressive Timing In Music Performance

The timing of interest in this chapter is not the hierarchically structured regularity of acoustic events that conveys rhythm and meter, that is represented in musical notation, and that has been the primary concern of music theorists and psychologists interested in the temporal structure of music (e.g., Cooper and Meyer, 1960; Povel and Essens, 1985; Jones and Boltz, 1989). Rather, the focus is on systematic *deviations* from this regularity, which are difficult to capture in symbolic notation but are an important aspect of expressiveness in music performance (see Seashore, 1938; Epstein, 1995). Without these deviations, a performance sounds mechanical and artless. At least this is so for music that is intended to be played with expressive timing, the prime example of which is European art music from the nineteenth century.

The variability that constitutes expressive timing is far from random. To be sure, a random component exists, reflecting the limited precision of musicians' motor control as well as, perhaps, uncontrolled variability in their expressive intentions. Typically, however, most of the timing variance among nominally equal inter-onset intervals (IOIs) is due to a musician's stable intentions, as is evident in the high replicability of timing patterns across repeated performances of the same music (Palmer, 1989; Repp, 1995b).[1] These intentions with regard to timing are rarely explicit and conscious, however; rather, they emerge from a musician's conception of the structure and character of a particular composition (Palmer, 1989; Shaffer, 1995) in combination with acquired (sometimes idiosyncratic) strategies for communicating this conception to listeners.

The precise timing of a performance can be measured—laboriously, and with some margin of error—from the digitized waveform of a sound recording (see, e.g., Gabrielsson, 1987; Repp, 1992b), or it can be obtained more quickly and accurately via MIDI (Musical Instrument Digital Interface) if the music was played on a computer-controlled instrument, typically a piano (see Palmer, 1989; Repp, 1995b). One way of representing the timing information is to plot normalized interonset intervals (IOIs) as a function of metrical (score) position.[2] The resulting graph constitutes the timing pattern or *timing profile* of a performance.

Different artists' performances of the same music have different timing profiles. For the purpose of the present research, it was desirable to obtain a representative or *typical* timing profile (TTP) of the music used in a particular experiment. This requires analysis of a number of performances by different artists. Their average timing profile provides a reasonable estimate of what is typical of these performances, especially if individual differences are not very large, as is often the case with groups of young artists (Repp, 1995b, 1997).

The shape of the TTP for a given piece of music is a complex function of the compositional structure, especially of rhythmic grouping (Lerdahl and Jackendoff, 1983) but also of melodic contour and harmonic progression. These structural factors generate implications—tension and relaxation, continuation and closure—that seem to propel the music forward in time with varying degrees of urgency, and therefore their total effect is often referred to as *musical motion* (see Epstein, 1995; Shove and Repp, 1995). Musicians realize musical motion through physical movement on instruments, and the TTP therefore represents instantiated musical motion—the actual timing of musical events. Several researchers, most notably Todd (1985, 1995), have attempted to devise algorithms that lead from musical structure to typical expressive timing. This will no doubt be an area of intensive investigation in the near future, eventually leading to the successful computer synthesis of expressive music performances.

An example of a TTP is shown in figure 6.1. The musical excerpt is the initial phrase of Chopin's *Etude in E-major*, op. 10, No. 3, terminated with a chord to provide closure. The TTP represents the average IOIs of performances by nine graduate student pianists, each of whom played the excerpt three times on a digital piano (Repp, 1997, in press, a). The initial

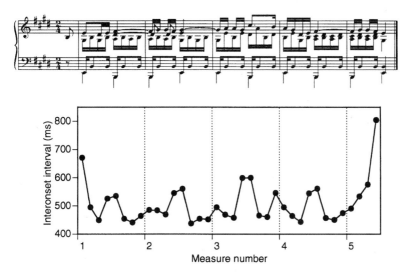

Figure 6.1
A typical expressive timing profile for the initial phrase of Chopin's Etude in E major, op. 10, No. 3.

eighth-note upbeat is not included in the graph. All other IOIs represent sixteenth-note intervals, measured (via MIDI) between the onsets of the highest notes in successive positions. There seems to be a "floor" at about 450 ms, corresponding to a basic tempo of about 133 events (or 33 quarter-note beats) per minute, and the longer IOIs constitute expressive lengthenings with respect to this baseline. The initial and final IOIs are lengthened dramatically, marking the boundaries of the phrase. A gradual slowing towards the end of the phrase can be seen in measure 5. Inside the phrase there are four double peaks and one single peak. Each double peak marks the end of a melodic segment: The pianists lengthened the final IOI as well as the IOI between the final long melody note (in the soprano voice) and the following accompanying note (in the alto voice). The single peak at the end of measure 3 emphasizes the anacrusis (upbeat) unique to the fourth melodic segment. This TTP will serve as a reference in the perceptual experiment to be described.

Detecting Deviations from Isochrony
At first blush, the task of detecting small perturbations in the timing of a regular stream of acoustic events seems to have little to do with music perception. It is a psychophysical paradigm for the determination of temporal discrimination thresholds and for the testing of theories about time-keeping mechanisms in the human brain (see, e.g., Schulze, 1978; Hibi,

1983; Hirsh et al., 1990; Monahan and Hirsh, 1990). However, some previous research and informal observations have suggested that the paradigm can be used to reveal more than just a listener's auditory acuity.

Several studies have shown that an increment in one inter-stimulus interval in a regular sequence of tones separated by silent intervals is more difficult to detect at a structural boundary than within a structural unit, both for adults (Fitzgibbons, Pollatsek, and Thomas, 1974) and for infants (Thorpe et al., 1988; Thorpe and Trehub, 1989). In these experiments, the boundary was defined by a change in pitch, so the results are consistent with the phenomenon of perceptual segregation as a function of pitch difference (Noorden, 1975; Bregman, 1990) and with the well-established psychophysical finding that the gap detection threshold increases with the spectral difference between the delimiting sounds (e.g., Perrott and Williams, 1971; Williams and Perrott, 1972; Collyer, 1974; Divenyi and Danner, 1977; Neff, Jesteadt, and Brown, 1982; Formby and Forrest, 1991). In other words, these findings may reflect an elementary principle of auditory organization: Time is more accurately perceived within than between auditory channels or streams.

Similar results have been obtained with more complex materials. Krumhansl and Jusczyk (1990) and Jusczyk and Krumhansl (1993) demonstrated that infants prefer to hear pauses between rather than within phrases of Mozart minuets (as adults undoubtedly would), and analogous findings have been reported for passages of speech containing prosodically marked phrase boundaries (Hirsh-Pasek et al., 1987; Jusczyk et al., 1992). Short pauses are also more difficult to detect at these points (Boomer and Dittman, 1962; Butcher, 1980). A slowing down of the event rate and a lowering of the pitch contour are common correlates of phrase boundaries in both speech and music. These findings, too, could be explained by principles of auditory grouping and segregation.

Not all boundaries are equal in speech and music. Butcher (1980) reported that the relative detectability of boundary pauses in speech was inversely related to the relative depth of the boundary in the hierarchical phrase structure. This observation parallels the finding of Gee and Grosjean (1983) that pause durations in controlled speaking tend to be proportional to boundary depth. In music, too, there is a tendency for larger *ritardandi* in expressive timing to be associated with deeper structural boundaries (Todd, 1985), so one might predict that there will be a corresponding perceptual phenomenon: Hesitations may be more difficult to detect at deep boundaries than at shallow boundaries, and more difficult at shallow boundaries than within melodic units. This prediction was confirmed by Repp (1992c) in the initial experiments of what turned out to be a long series. These experiments went further by probing not just the boundaries but the *entire time course* of a musical structure, to determine whether per-

ception—measured in terms of the relative detectability of hesitations—
is modulated as quasi-continuously as is the timing of an expressive performance. This research demonstrated that the *detection accuracy profile*
(DAP, percent correct as a function of score position) for IOI increments
is inversely related to the TTP. A small increment is the more difficult to
detect the longer the IOI tends to be in expressive performance.

This step from a focus on boundaries to the quasi-continuous probing
of a whole temporal shape shifted attention from acoustic and auditory
determinants of detectability to perception–performance relationships.[3]
Although lower detectability of hesitations at major boundaries may have
more or less obvious psychoacoustic causes, it is less clear whether the
acoustic surface structure of music or principles of auditory processing can
explain the whole DAP. At the time of writing, the author has completed
19 experiments of similar design that explore this perception-performance
parallelism and its possible causes. Here there is space to describe only
one of them. The tenth in the series, it occupies a central position and has
served as a baseline for all following experiments. (For details omitted
here, see Repp, in press, a Exp. 1.)

6.2 Experiment

Method

The music was the Chopin excerpt shown in figure 6.1. Apart from the
initial upbeat, which was included but never served as a detection target,
the music contains 36 sixteenth-note IOIs. It was synthesized on a Roland
RD-250s digital piano under computer control with a fixed baseline IOI
duration of 500 ms. All simultaneous tones had synchronous onsets, and
successive tones followed each other without any intervening silence,
resulting in *legato* articulation throughout. The pedal was not used. The
relative intensities (MIDI velocities) of the tones were copied from an
expressive performance on the Roland.

The task required the detection of deviations from isochrony. The
musical excerpt was presented repeatedly, and each presentation contained
between 0 and 4 IOIs (separated by at least four baseline IOIs) whose
duration had been changed. Increment and decrement detection were
tested in separate parts of the experiment. Each part consisted of 5 famil-
iarization trials and three test blocks of 18 trials each, in the course of
which each of the 36 IOIs served as a target once. The amount of duration change decreased across the three blocks, from 42 to 31 to 21 ms.
The change was made in the MIDI instructions to the digital piano by
lengthening or shortening the note(s) filling the target IOI and delaying or
advancing the onsets of all following notes. This amounted to a rhythmic

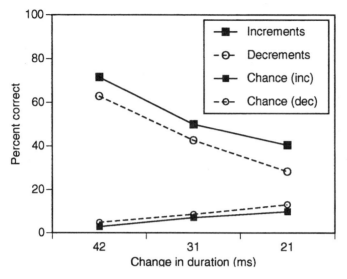

Figure 6.2
Percent correct detection ("hits") as a function of change in IOI duration.

phase shift, perceived as a momentary hesitation or acceleration, with *legato* articulation held constant.

The subjects were 14 musically trained college students. They marked their responses by circling notes in copies of the musical score on prepared answer sheets. Circling of a note adjacent to the correct one was considered a correct response, as such near misses were quite frequent. Other responses were considered false alarms.

Results

Figure 6.2 shows the average percent correct scores ("hits") as a function of the change in IOI duration. Chance level estimates derived from the false alarm rates are shown as well. It can be seen that detection scores declined across blocks but were still better than chance in the most difficult condition. This level of performance was optimal for avoiding floor and ceiling effects in the DAPs. Increment detection was significantly easier than decrement detection [$F(1, 13) = 12.57, p < .004$].

Figure 6.3a shows the DAPs for increment and decrement detection, respectively, averaged across subjects and blocks. It is evident that there was tremendous variation in detection scores as a function of position in the music. The two DAPs are negatively correlated ($r = -0.53, p < .01$). On the whole, decrements were easier to detect where increments were more difficult to detect. As predicted, the DAP for increments is inversely

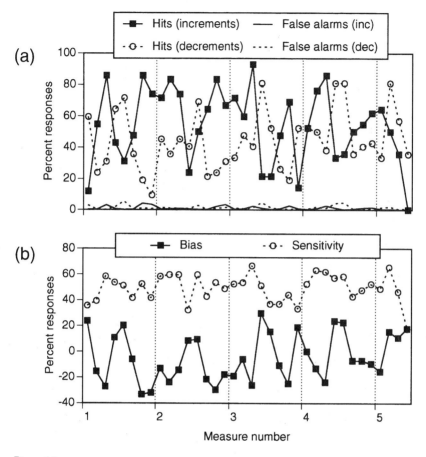

Figure 6.3
(a) The DAPs for increments and decrements; (b) the derived sensitivity and bias profiles.

related to the TTP shown in figure 6.1 ($r = -0.82, p < .001$), whereas the DAP for decrements shows a positive correlation with the TTP ($r = 0.70$, $p < .001$).[4] These findings indicate that it is more difficult to detect a duration increment, but easier to detect a duration decrement, in positions that typically exhibit expressive lengthening in performance. Conversely, increments are easier to detect and decrements harder to detect in positions where pianists tend to speed up.

The inclusion of both increment and decrement detection tasks made it possible to distinguish between two hypothetical factors affecting detection accuracy, namely *sensitivity* and *bias*. These concepts are familiar from signal detection theory (see, e.g., Macmillan and Creelman, 1991), but d' and beta indices could not be computed in the present paradigm because the task did not require a forced choice and because false-alarm responses were too sparsely distributed (see figure 6.3a) to yield reliable probability estimates. The following simple logic seemed applicable: Differences in sensitivity to temporal change across positions in the music should have a similar effect on increment and decrement detection; therefore, the average of the two DAPs yields an estimate of positional variations in sensitivity, a "sensitivity profile." Differences in bias, on the other hand, should affect increment and decrement detection in opposite ways; therefore, the difference between the two DAPs yields an estimate of positional variations in bias, a "bias profile."[5] Of these two profiles, it is the bias profile that should be correlated with the TTP, whereas the sensitivity profile should exhibit no such relationship. The two profiles are shown in figure 6.3b. The bias profile, computed by subtracting the increment DAP from the decrement DAP and dividing by two, indeed shows a remarkably close match with the TTP in figure 6.1 ($r = 0.85, p < .001$), whereas the sensitivity profile is unrelated to the TTP. These results provide strong evidence for a connection between perception and production of timing in music.

6.3 Discussion

Representativeness of the Data Shown
The overall accuracy results shown in figure 6.2 are typical for this type of task. Somewhat higher accuracy was obtained in unpublished experiments that used monophonic tunes, whereas accuracy was lower with music that contained some IOIs of longer duration (Repp, 1992c: Exp. 2). Elimination of variation in expressive dynamics makes duration differences somewhat easier to detect (Repp, 1992a; in press, a). Naturally, the task becomes much more difficult (but not impossible) when deviations from an expressively timed baseline are to be detected (Clarke, 1989; Repp, in press, b). Subjects without musical training often have difficulty perceiving small timing deviations (Repp, 1995a); therefore, musically trained subjects were used in most experiments. A reliable overall advantage of increment over decrement detection is not always observed, and there are also considerable individual differences in that regard. When the baseline contains variable IOIs, decrement detection is easier overall than increment detection (Repp, in press, b).

The early experiments in this series included only an increment detection task, whereas most later experiments tested both increment and decrement detection. A significant negative correlation between the DAP for increments and some estimate of the TTP has always been obtained:

with different original excerpts from the piano literature (Repp, 1992c), with simplified versions of the Chopin etude excerpt (Repp, in press, a), even with monophonic experimental tunes (Repp, 1992a; 1995a). The monophonic materials yielded DAPs and TTPs with little internal structure, however, so that the perception-performance relationship rested mainly on the final *ritardando* in performance and the corresponding decline in detection scores towards the end of the tune. In order to demonstrate a convincing perception-performance correlation, it is necessary to use music that elicits a finely differentiated timing profile from musicians. This requires a certain degree of rhythmic and harmonic complexity, as well as a tempo, character, and style that encourage expressive tempo modulations.

The inverse relation between the DAPs for increments and decrements and the positive correlation between the DAP for decrements and the TTP are *not* reliable findings. Most subsequent experiments failed to replicate these correlations (Repp, in press, a; in press, b). The bias profile calculated from the two DAPs, however, invariably did correlate with the TTP. There are two ways of interpreting these results. One is that the two hypothetical underlying factors, sensitivity and bias, reinforce each other in the DAP for increments but tend to cancel each other in the DAP for decrements. This is certainly true with respect to the final IOIs, where an increase in bias accompanies a decline in sensitivity (see figure 6.3b). From this perspective, the original DAPs are best ignored and only the derived sensitivity and bias profiles are to be considered. The other possibility is that the detection of decrements is indeed less related to music performance than is the detection of increments. This suggestion has some plausibility in view of the fact that expressive timing is not a symmetric process. Expressive lengthening prolongs tension and conveys emphasis, whereas relative shortening has no particular expressive function and may simply represent a return to some baseline tempo or compensate for lengthening in the vicinity. Listeners' expectations about expressive timing (i.e., their perceptual biases) thus may be formulated in terms of increments rather than decrements. This interpretation has found support in two recent experiments (Repp, in press, b): When the baseline is expressively modulated by the full or attenuated TTP, so that listeners' expectations are satisfied, as it were, the perceptual bias is neutralized in increment but not in decrement detection. Decrements are easy to detect in short IOIs and difficult to detect in long IOIs, even when the changes are proportional to IOI duration.

In theory, it would seem that false-alarm responses should be a direct reflection of perceptual bias, namely the tendency to perceive certain IOIs as longer or shorter than they really are. The frequency of these responses varies dramatically from subject to subject, however, and many subjects give only very few false-alarm responses. Moreover, as already pointed out, these responses are distributed over many positions, which makes the resulting false-alarm profile (FAP) somewhat haphazard and unreliable. In most experiments the FAP correlated positively with the corresponding DAP, but the correlation did not always reach significance. Similarly, the negative correlation between the FAP for increments and the TTP was significant only in some experiments. The FAP results thus are consistent with the DAP results, but they are far less robust.

Possible Psychoacoustic Factors

Music, even a simple monophonic tune played on the piano, is a rather complex stimulus from the perspective of research in psychoacoustics and auditory scene analysis (Bregman, 1990). It is possible, even likely, that the detectability of changes in IOI duration varies as a function of acoustic surface properties of the music. Even if the shapes of the DAPs (and/or of the sensitivity and bias profiles) could be explained entirely on the basis of auditory processing phenomena, however, the question would remain why there is a relationship between perception and expressive timing in performance. The answer would have to be that performers are subject to the same auditory effects as ordinary listeners, and that expressive timing is a sort of compensatory action to smooth out perceived rhythmic irregularities caused by these effects (Drake, 1993). This seems rather implausible, but let us see first whether the variation in detection scores can be rationalized on a psychoacoustic basis.

Psychoacoustic effects on sensitivity and on bias should be distinguished first. The former affect detectability regardless of the direction of the deviation, whereas the latter are directional; they can also be described as a constant error. Effects on sensitivity are not of particular interest here because they are irrelevant to the perception-performance relationship, which, as we have seen, rests on the variation in perceptual bias. Examples of sensitivity effects are the reduced detection scores in the initial and final positions of a musical excerpt.[6]

The crucial question is whether the positional variations in bias can be accounted for on psychoacoustic grounds. One relevant phenomenon is the "auditory kappa effect" (Shigeno, 1986; Crowder and Neath, 1995). When three successive tones are separated by unequal pitch distances but equal temporal intervals, the temporal interval between the two tones closer in pitch seems to be shorter than that between the two tones farther apart in pitch. In the present experiments, however, there was no evidence for a positive relation between bias and the absolute or directional pitch distance between successive tones. Thus, the auditory kappa effect did not seem to operate, either because of the greater complexity of the stimuli or perhaps because there were no silent intervals between tones. Instead, significant correlations were found between bias and the absolute pitch height of the highest tone occupying the target IOI (the target tone), and between bias and the directional intensity (MIDI velocity) difference between the two highest tones delimiting the IOI (Repp, in press, a).[7] In other words, an IOI tended to be heard as relatively *short* when the target tone was high in pitch or when the following tone was more intense than the target tone. These findings do not correspond to known auditory phenomena such as the kappa effect. They could have been due to the musical structure and its implications for performance timing, rather than to some independent auditory interactions between duration, pitch, and intensity.

Of course, it is difficult to separate the acoustic surface structure of music from the underlying structure described in music-theoretic terms, although a manipulation performed on the Chopin excerpt proved enlightening (Repp, in press, a: Exp. 2). In that study, the long melody notes (see figure 6.1) were broken up into repeated sixteenth notes of the same pitch and intensity. This enabled listeners (in theory) to detect deviations from isochrony by tracking the melody tones only, instead of jumping back and forth between melody and accompaniment. In fact, however, the manipulation had little effect on the results, which were quite similar to those shown in figure 6.3. Within the sixteenth notes of the melody, there was no correlation between bias and either pitch height or intensity difference. This finding suggests that the listeners tracked the whole musical structure, not just individual tones in one voice. Admittedly, there may be other incarnations of a bottom-up auditory processing hypothesis, for example one that takes the full spectral content and energy distribution of each chord into account and that models temporal integration (see, e.g., Todd, 1994). For the time being, however, an explanation in terms of structural and musically relevant concepts seems more promising.

Musical Motion and Structure
It seems only parsimonious to couch an explanation of the perceptual bias effects in the same terms as an explanation of expressive timing in music performance. Despite ubiquitous individual differences, expressive timing is governed by certain principles and constraints, and listeners evidently possess implicit knowledge of these principles, which leads them to expect lengthening of IOIs where performers typically linger and shortening of IOIs where performers typically rush. When music is played without any expressive timing, as in the present experiments, IOIs that are expected to be long sound too short (a positive bias, as bias is defined here), whereas IOIs that are expected to be short sound too long (a negative bias). These biases seem to be elicited automatically by the same structural properties that cause performers to modulate their timing.

What are these structural properties? The determinants of expressive timing are not fully understood at present, and a detailed discussion of this complex topic cannot be provided here. In the present Chopin Etude excerpt (figure 6.1), however, the major factor clearly is the segmentation of the melody: Each group of notes is associated with a final *ritardando*, and the final group has extra lengthening. In addition, there is initial lengthening in the first and fourth groups. This is consistent with an archetypal acceleration-deceleration shape within groups, as described in Todd's (1985) model of expressive timing. Todd (1995) has also argued that the precise shape of the timing curve at a coarser grain of analysis is subject to a constraint of linear tempo change, in analogy to forms of physical or biological motion. It would be difficult to apply this idea at the level of detail considered here. The precise timing of small IOIs seems to be modulated by factors in addition to group boundaries, such as melodic contour, harmonic dissonance, and metrical position. Thus, the fact that there is lengthening at the onset of the fourth group (position 3-8) but not at the onsets of the second and third groups, may be due to metrical position (immediately preceding a strong beat) and/or to the greater length of the fourth melodic gesture. The lengthened IOI in the fifth position of each measure may not represent group-final lengthening —after all, it *follows* the final note—but rather may serve to segregate the melody from the accompaniment, which otherwise might be heard as a continuation of the melody with lowered dynamics. At points of melodic re-entry, no lengthening is observed because the melody can hardly be mistaken for an accompaniment. The extent of mid-measure lengthening can be seen to increase from measure 1 to 2 to 3 and to decrease in measure 4; this trend follows the melodic pitch contour and the correlated changes in tension and dynamics.

It is not necessary to have a complete theory of expressive timing to appreciate the parallelism between perception and performance demonstrated in the present research, just as musicians and listeners need not have explicit knowledge of the principles that underly their behavior. The TTP represents the sum and interaction of all structural factors that generate musical motion, as filtered through a typical musician's mind and body. As an empirical measure of musical motion, it is superior to structural descriptions that may include many features that are not communicated (or not communicable) in the typical performer's movements.[8] It is only a small step from this argument to the claim that the (typical or average) perceptual bias profile, too, is a measure of communicatively relevant musical motion. The high correlation between the TTP and the bias profile suggests that whatever moves the typical musician also moves the typical listener.

Individual Differences

The perceptual bias profile is interesting because it is in some sense an even more direct measure of musical motion than the TTP. It is obtained in a detection task and thus presumably excludes any conscious decision making on the listener's part. In other words, it is an obligatory and automatic response to the music. Musicians, on the other hand, can modify, suppress, and even reverse their kinematic strategies in response to music in order to achieve variety and originality. A listener in the present type of experiment does not seem to have that choice.

In part, musicians' individual differences in expressive timing are not cognitive but organismic in origin; they represent their different body structures, personalities, technical training, and musical experience. The extent and nature of individual differences in perceptual bias profiles are not known. The present experiments never yielded enough responses from single individuals to determine reliable individual profiles that could be compared with each other. Effects of musical experience were examined correlationally in some early experiments (Repp, 1992c), without clear results. Repp (1995a) compared three groups of subjects with different degrees of musical training, but the shapes of their average DAPs for increments did not differ. Thus, there is no evidence yet for significant individual differences in perceptual profiles, but this is an issue that deserves further investigation. It would be particularly interesting to find a relationship between individual differences in perceptual bias and in performance timing among pianist subjects, but such an investigation is difficult, not only because of the large number of sessions required but also because young pianists tend to have rather similar timing profiles (Repp, 1995b, 1997).

If there is indeed less individual variation in the perceptual bias profile than in the timing profile, this has interesting implications for the aesthetics and evaluation of musical performance. The TTP, by virtue of its similarity to the bias profile, may then be understood as a precognitive, pre-interpretative measure of musical motion. This does not mean that a performance whose timing matches this profile is better than others. It may well be perceived as the most naturally timed performance, however, and it may be preferred under certain circumstances. The duality of typicality and individuality with respect to performance aesthetics is discussed in more detail, with preliminary data, in Repp (1997).

Mechanisms of Timing Perception

The detection of deviations from isochrony requires the tracking and prediction of regularly timed events by means of some internal time-keeping mechanism. This could be a mental clock or oscillator, as postulated by many theorists (e.g., Schulze, 1978; Povel and Essens, 1985; Jones and

Boltz, 1989; Desain, 1992; Large and Kolen, 1994), or it could be a memory for interval durations (Keele et al., 1989; Ivry and Hazeltine, 1995). One theoretical question of interest is whether the predictions of this internal time-keeper are directly modulated by the perceptual bias profile or whether the bias has its effect at some later decision stage.

Clearly, a listener could not simply expect events to occur at intervals that match the TTP. This would make it impossible to detect deviations from isochrony with any degree of accuracy. If the internal time-keeper is modulated by expectations, then these modulations must be much smaller than the deviations observed in the TTP. Even so, one would expect accuracy to be lower and false-alarm rates to be higher than they actually were. In fact, many listeners hardly gave any false-alarm responses, and accuracy was not much lower than in a psychophysical discrimination task. This suggests that the internal time-keeper was unmodulated, and that the bias had its effect at a subsequent stage that determined whether or not deviations from isochrony gained access to consciousness.

What kind of timing mechanism do the subjects employ to perform the task? One finding of the present experiments—not discussed so far— may provide a clue. It is the frequent occurrence of "late" responses in the increment detection task, that is, the circling of the note or chord following the correct position in the score. Typically, about one third of all correct responses were late in this sense, whereas "early" responses were far less frequent. Some of the late responses may have been due to subjects' failure to backtrack in the score; after all, they had to wait for the tone or chord ending an IOI in order to determine whether the IOI was longer or shorter than usual. If that had been the sole cause, however, late responses should have been equally frequent in increment and decrement detection tasks. It turned out, however, that they were much less common in decrement than in increment detection (Repp, in press, a). Thus, it seems that the majority of late responses in the increment detection task had a perceptual cause: The IOI following a lengthened IOI tended to be perceived as lengthened, at least if the actual lengthening was not detected.[9] Moreover, late responses tended to be relatively more frequent when the following IOI was one in which actual lengthening was easy to detect; thus they were subject to the same perceptual bias that shaped the DAP, which also argues for a perceptual origin of the phenomenon. Late responses in the decrement task not only were much less frequent but also did not show any systematic bias effects (Repp, in press, a).

These results seem more compatible with an oscillatory time-keeping mechanism than with an interval-based memory. An oscillator is perturbed by IOI duration increments or decrements, which amount to phase shifts in the isochronous rhythm. Adjustment to such phase shifts is probably not instantaneous but takes several cycles (Large and Kolen, 1994). When a target IOI is lengthened, the event that terminates it occurs immediately after a beat (tick, prediction) issued by the oscillator. As a result, the next beat will have to be delayed by lengthening the period of the oscillatory cycle, but unless this adjustment is complete, the next beat will again fall short of the event marking the end of the next IOI, hence the tendency to also perceive it as lengthened. By the same reasoning, one might predict that an IOI following a shortened target IOI should be perceived as shortened, but this did not happen. The reason may lie in the fact that the event marking the end of the target IOI occurs shortly *before* the oscillator issues its beat. This may have the effect of precipitating the beat, thereby leading to an immediate phase shift (assuming that the period of the oscillator remains constant). The difference in the frequency of late responses in increment and decrement detection thus can be explained by the directionality and irreversibility of time.

Unlike an oscillatory process, an interval-based memory need not adjust to a single mismatched IOI. The best strategy would be to hold on to the memory of the baseline interval. A modified target IOI may perturb that memory slightly, but there is no particular reason why the following IOI should be perceived differently (if anything, a contrast effect might be predicted), or why there should be a difference between increment and decrement detection. The present data thus favor an explanation in terms of an oscillatory time-keeping mechanism. It must be added, however, that individual differences in the percentage of late responses were very large. Some subjects gave hardly any late responses, while others gave more than 50%. Thus, individuals may differ in their strategies, as both timing processes seem to be available in principle (Keele et al., 1989).

Whichever mechanism is used in detecting deviations from isochrony, it seems to be subject to the performance-related biases. There is no indication so far that any listener is immune to this bias. It is tempting to speculate that it represents a form of perceptual-motor interaction (Viviani and Stucchi, 1992b).

Viviani and Stucchi (1992a)—and long before them, Derwort (1938)—have shown that a uniform movement of a light point along a path varying in curvature is perceived as nonuniform in velocity (too fast around the narrow curves, too slow along the straight portions), whereas a nonuniform movement varying lawfully with curvature is perceived as constant. Musical motion may be subject to similar laws that can be demonstrated by translating expressive timing into spatial movement (Truslit, 1938; Repp, 1993). The structural properties of music imply nonuniform timing, so that a compensatory effect is observed in perception when the actual timing is uniform. This mechanism may be analogous to that in vision, except that the compensation is not complete, only a tendency. Certainly, no careful listener would judge the TTP of the Chopin etude (figure 6.1) to be uniform, but a more subtle timing modulation may be perceived in that way (Repp, in press, b). Similarly, there is only weak evidence from false-alarm responses that an isochronous performance sounds nonuniform to listeners. If there is a perceptual-motor interaction here, it is less direct than in vision because it does not actually affect the time-keeping mechanism; the bias must be operating at a subsequent stage in processing.

Toward the Future
Three recent experiments (Repp, in press, c) have provided new information about the nature of the perceptual bias. One experiment showed that repeated exposure to an *atypically* timed performance leaves the bias profile quite unaffected. A second experiment showed that there is no systematic bias when the task is to detect deviations from isochrony in a sequence of clicks while *imagining* the Chopin excerpt and marking the responses in the score. The third experiment did obtain the typical bias profile when the clicks were superimposed on the music, even though the subjects had been instructed to ignore the music and pressed a button rather than marking responses in a musical score. These results show that the bias is contingent on the auditory processing of a musical structure and that it is resistant to modification.

An important question for future research is whether the bias reflects familiarity with classical music and/or expressive performance. To the extent that the perception-performance relationship demonstrated here rests on processes of auditory segmentation and grouping, it may well be independent of specific musical experience (Deliège and El Ahmadi, 1990). This would imply that the TTP, too, is largely the reflection of elementary grouping processes. In other words, there may be a close connection between grouping and timing, as some of the studies cited in the introduction have already suggested. This would be a rather straightforward conclusion, but it is probably not the whole story.

Acknowledgments

This research was supported by NIH grant MH-51230. Thanks are due to Charles Nichols, Linda Popovic, and Lisa Robinson for their assistance and to Steven Boker, Geoffrey Collier, Carol Krumhansl, and David Rosenbaum for helpful comments on the manuscript.

Notes

1. Some of this replicable timing variation may be due to technical difficulties (e.g., extra time required for rapid changes in hand position), although most investigations of expressive timing have focused on slow music in which such technical factors are minimized.

2. Other possibilities are percentage deviations from the average IOI (Gabrielsson, 1987; Palmer, 1989), local tempo estimates (i.e., reciprocal IOIs), or event onset times as a function of real time (see Todd, 1995).

3. A study by Clarke (1989) proved very stimulating. Although his main purpose was to determine the detection threshold for small timing deviations in a few positions of a musical excerpt, selected without particular reference to musical structure, his discussion made extensive reference to expressive performance and inspired the author to undertake his initial experiments (Repp, 1992c).

4. The final IOI was omitted in these correlations because of its extreme length in the TTP and the corresponding floor effect in the DAP for increments.

5. The bias of interest here is a *perceptual* bias (i.e., a constant error), not a response bias. It refers to listeners' tendency to perceive some IOIs a priori as shorter (longer) than others. It is defined as the extent to which an increment is more difficult to detect than a decrement in a given position.

6. The initial IOI is either the first IOI encountered or is shorter than the preceding IOI, so that its deviation from isochrony can be judged only retrospectively, with reference to a fraction of the preceding IOI, or with the aid of memory for a previous presentation of the musical excerpt. Similarly, the final IOI is followed by a longer tone or chord of vague duration (since no event onset follows it) and thus can be judged only relative to preceding IOIs (see also Monahan and Hirsh, 1990). Another factor that may affect sensitivity to changes in IOI duration is the pitch distance between two successive tones, which is known to affect the psychoacoustic gap detection threshold and duration discrimination at auditory group boundaries, as mentioned earlier in this chapter. No evidence for such an effect was obtained (Repp, in press, a), however, probably because of the relatively long duration of the IOIs and because they were filled with decaying sound rather than with silence. One factor that was found to have an effect on sensitivity was the relative intensity of the tones delimiting the IOI. Higher intensity led to higher detection scores (Repp, in press, a).

7. Whenever several tones occurred simultaneously as a chord, it was assumed that the highest tone was perceptually most salient because of its melodic function and higher intensity.

8. It should be kept in mind, however, that timing is only one aspect of expressive performance. Important additional information is conveyed by dynamics and articulation.

9. Circling of two adjacent positions in the music was extremely rare; however, the subjects knew that two modified IOIs could not be adjacent to each other.

References

Boomer, D. S., & Dittman, A. T. (1962). Hesitation pauses and juncture pauses in speech. *Language and Speech, 5*, 215–220.

Bregman, A. S. (1990). *Auditory scene analysis.* Cambridge, MA: MIT Press.

Butcher, A. (1980). Pause and syntactic structure. In H. W. Dechert & M. Raupach (eds.), *Temporal variables in speech: Studies in honour of Frieda Goldman-Eisler* (pp. 85–90). The Hague: Mouton.

Clarke, E. F. (1989). The perception of expressive timing in music. *Psychological Research, 51*, 2–9.

Collyer, C. E. (1974). The detection of a temporal gap between two disparate stimuli. *Perception & Psychophysics, 16*, 96–100.

Cooper, G., & Meyer, L. B. (1960). *The rhythmic structure of music.* Chicago: University of Chicago Press.

Crowder, R. G., & Neath, I. (1995). The influence of pitch on time perception in short melodies. *Music Perception, 12*, 379–386.

Deliège, I., & El Ahmadi, A. (1990). Mechanisms of cue extraction in musical groupings: A study of perception on *Sequenza VI* for viola solo by Luciano Berio. *Psychology of Music, 18*, 18–44.

Derwort, A. (1938). Untersuchungen über den Zeitablauf figurierter Bewegungen beim Menschen. *Pflügers Archiv für die gesamte Physiologie des Menschen und der Tiere, 240*, 661–675.

Desain, P. (1992). A (de)composable theory of rhythm perception. *Music Perception, 9*, 439–454.

Divenyi, P. L., & Danner, W. F. (1977). Discrimination of time intervals marked by brief acoustic pulses of various intensities and spectra. *Perception & Psychophysics, 21*, 125–142.

Drake, C. (1993). Perceptual and performed accents in musical sequences. *Bulletin of the Psychonomic Society, 31*, 107–110.

Epstein, D. (1995). *Shaping time: Music, the brain, and performance.* New York: Schirmer Books.

Fitzgibbons, P. J., Pollatsek, A., & Thomas, I. B. (1974). Detection of temporal gaps within and between perceptual tonal groups. *Perception & Psychophysics, 16*, 522–528.

Formby, C., & Forrest, T. G. (1991). Detection of silent temporal gaps in sinusoidal maskers. *Journal of the Acoustical Society of America, 89*, 830–837.

Gabrielsson, A. (1987). Once again: The theme from Mozart's Piano Sonata in A major (K.331). In A. Gabrielsson (ed.), *Action and perception in rhythm and music* (pp. 81–103). Stockholm: Royal Swedish Academy of Music Publication No. 55.

Gee, J. P., & Grosjean, F. (1983). Performance structures: A psycholinguistic and linguistic appraisal. *Cognitive Psychology, 15*, 411–458.

Hibi, S. (1983). Rhythm perception in repetitive sound sequence. *Journal of the Acoustical Society of Japan (E), 4*, 83–95.

Hirsh, I. J., Monahan, C. B., Grant, K. W., & Singh, P. G. (1990). Studies in auditory timing: 1. Simple patterns. *Perception & Psychophysics, 47*, 215–226.

Hirsh-Pasek, K., Kemler Nelson, D. G., Jusczyk, P. W., Wright Cassidy, K., Druss, B., & Kennedy, L. (1987). Clauses are perceptual units for young infants. *Cognition, 26*, 269–286.

Ivry, R. B., & Hazeltine, R. E. (1995). Perception and production of temporal intervals across a range of durations: Evidence for a common timing mechanism. *Journal of Experimental Psychology: Human Perception and Performance, 21*, 3–18.

Jones, M. R., & Boltz, M. (1989). Dynamic attending and responses to time. *Psychological Review, 96*, 459–491.

Jusczyk, P. W., Hirsh-Pasek, K., Kemler Nelson, D. G., Kennedy, L., Woodward, A., & Piwoz, J. (1992). Perception of acoustic correlates of major phrasal units by young infants. *Cognitive Psychology, 24*, 252–293.

Jusczyk, P. W., & Krumhansl, C. L. (1993). Pitch and rhythmic patterns affecting infants' sensitivity to musical phrase structure. *Journal of Experimental Psychology: Human Perception and Performance, 19*, 627–640.

Keele, S. W., Nicoletti, R., Ivry, R. I., & Pokorny, R. A. (1989). Mechanisms of perceptual timing: Beat-based or interval-based judgments? *Psychological Research, 50*, 251–256.

Krumhansl, C. L., & Jusczyk, P. W. (1990). Infants' perception of phrase structure in music. *Psychological Science, 1*, 70–73.

Large, E. W., & Kolen, J. K. (1994). Resonance and the perception of musical meter. *Connection Science, 6*, 177–208.

Lerdahl, F., & Jackendoff, R. (1983). *A generative theory of tonal music.* Cambridge, MA: MIT Press.

Macmillan, N. A., & Creelman, C. D. (1991). *Detection theory: A user's guide.* New York: Cambridge University Press.

Monahan, C. B., & Hirsh, I. J. (1990). Studies in auditory timing: 2. Rhythm patterns. *Perception & Psychophysics*, 47, 227–242.

Neff, D. L., Jesteadt, W., & Brown, E. L. (1982). The relation between gap discrimination and auditory stream segregation. *Perception & Psychophysics*, 31, 493–501.

Noorden, L. P. A. S. van (1975). *Temporal coherence in the perception of tone sequences*. Unpublished doctoral dissertation, Eindhoven University of Technology, The Netherlands.

Palmer, C. (1989). Mapping musical thought to musical performance. *Journal of Experimental Psychology: Human Perception and Performance*, 15, 331–346.

Perrott, D. R., & Williams, K. N. (1971). Auditory temporal resolution: Gap detection as a function of interpulse frequency disparity. *Psychonomic Science*, 25, 73–74.

Povel, D. -J., & Essens, P. (1985). Perception of temporal patterns. *Music Perception*, 2, 411–440.

Repp, B. H. (1992a). Detectability of rhythmic perturbations in musical contexts: Bottom-up versus top-down factors. In C. Auxiette, C. Drake, & C. Gérard (eds.), *Proceedings of the Fourth Rhythm Workshop: Rhythm perception and production* (pp. 111–116). Bourges, France: Imprimérie Municipale.

Repp, B. H. (1992b). Diversity and commonality in music performance: An analysis of timing microstructure in Schumann's "Träumerei". *Journal of the Acoustical Society of America*, 92, 2546–2568.

Repp, B. H. (1992c). Probing the cognitive representation of musical time: Structural constraints on the perception of timing perturbations. *Cognition*, 44, 241–281.

Repp, B. H. (1993). Music as motion: A synopsis of Alexander Truslit's "Gestaltung und Bewegung in der Musik." *Psychology of Music*, 21, 48–72.

Repp, B. H. (1995a). Detectability of duration and intensity increments in melody tones: A partial connection between music perception and performance. *Perception & Psychophysics*, 57, 1217–1232.

Repp, B. H. (1995b). Expressive timing in Schumann's "Träumerei": An analysis of performances by graduate student pianists. *Journal of the Acoustical Society of America*, 98, 2413–2427.

Repp, B. H. (1997). The aesthetic quality of a quantitatively average music performance: Two preliminary experiments. *Music Perception*, 14, 419–444.

Repp, B. H. (in press, a). Variations on a theme by Chopin: Relations between perception and production of timing in music. *Journal of Experimental Psychology: Human Perception and Performance*.

Repp, B. H. (in press, b). The detectability of local deviations from a typical expressive timing pattern. *Music Perception*.

Repp, B. H. (in press, c). Obligatory "expectations" of expressive timing induced by perception of musical structure. *Psychological Research*.

Schulze, H.-H. (1978). The detectability of local and global displacements in regular rhythmic patterns. *Psychological Research*, 40, 173–181.

Seashore, C. E. (1938). *Psychology of music*. New York: McGraw-Hill (Reprinted by Dover Publications, 1967).

Shaffer, L. H. (1995). Musical performance as interpretation. *Psychology as Music*, 23, 17–38.

Shigeno, S. (1986). The auditory tau and kappa effects for speech and nonspeech stimuli. *Perception & Psychophysics*, 40, 9–19.

Shove, P., & Repp, B. H. (1995). Musical motion and performance: Theoretical and empirical perspectives. In J. Rink (ed.), *The practice of performance: Studies in musical interpretation* (pp. 55–83). Cambridge, UK: Cambridge University Press.

Thorpe, L. A., & Trehub, S. E. (1989). Duration illusion and auditory grouping in infancy. *Developmental Psychology*, 25, 122–127.

Thorpe, L. A., Trehub, S. E., Morrongiello, B. A., & Bull, D. (1988). Perceptual grouping by infants and preschool children. *Developmental Psychology, 24,* 484–491.

Todd, N. [P. McA.] (1985). A model of expressive timing in tonal music. *Music Perception, 3,* 33–58.

Todd, N. P. McA. (1994). The auditory "primal sketch": A multiscale model of rhythmic grouping. *Journal of New Music Research, 23,* 25–70.

Todd, N. P. McA. (1995). The kinematics of musical expression. *Journal of the Acoustical Society of America, 97,* 1940–1949.

Truslit, A. (1938). *Gestaltung und Bewegung in der Musik.* Berlin-Lichterfelde: Chr. Friedr. Vieweg.

Viviani, P., & Stucchi, N. (1992a). Biological movements look uniform: Evidence of motor-perceptual interactions. *Journal of Experimental Psychology: Human Perception and Performance, 18,* 603–623.

Viviani, P., & Stucchi, N. (1992b). Motor-perceptual interactions. In G. E. Stelmach & J. Requin (eds.), *Tutorials in motor behavior II* (pp. 229–248). Amsterdam: Elsevier.

Williams, K. N., & Perrott, D. R. (1972). Temporal resolution of tonal pulses. *Journal of the Acoustical Society of America, 51,* 644–647.

Chapter 7

Concurrent Processing during Sequenced Finger Tapping

Heather Jane Barnes

Abstract

This chapter investigates the process that prepares the timing of sequenced finger tapping. If a subject is required to tap at a specified rate and then switch to a different rate of tapping and if the subject knows when and how the timing demands are to change, when does the subject specify the timing of the later portion of the task? The experiment to be discussed demonstrates that examination of one dependent variable, mean interresponse interval, leads to the conclusion that subjects do not take advantage of advance information to prepare for timing changes during execution of a rhythmic sequence. That is, subjects do not take advantage of concurrent processing. However, examination of another dependent variable, peak finger displacement, indicates performance changes related to changes in timing demands. This measure, in other words, indicates that subjects do take advantage of concurrent processing. The results extend previous conclusions concerning factors influencing the preparation of forthcoming timing changes.

7.1 Introduction

The process by which individuals retrieve, process, and store information in order to plan and carry out decisions and actions lies at the heart of the information processing approach. This processing approach posits various stages such as stimulus identification, response selection, response preparation, and execution. Through these stages, information is gathered and manipulated, decisions are made, and actions are carried out. Working within the information processing approach, Keele (1968) proposed the motor program as a construct that serves in identifying and preparing a motor skill for execution. In order for a motor skill to be performed, the parameters of the motor program must be specified. These parameters define a particular movement and include factors such as effector, direction, force, and timing of the movement. Based on the motor program framework, once the movement parameters are specified, the motor program is executed, resulting in performance of the motor skill. This process of preparing and executing a motor program is integrated within the general stages of information processing. That is, the response selection stage includes the selection of a motor program, the response preparation stage includes specifying the parameters of the motor program, and the execution stage includes execution of the motor program.

Although it has been widely assumed that information processing stages occur sequentially, evidence indicates that some processing stages can occur concurrently with the execution of a motor skill. Thus, while an individual is performing a motor skill, he or she might be performing one of the earlier information processing stages while executing an action. Two examples that illustrate this capability include musical performance and automobile driving. Beginning musicians identify one note to be played and then perform that note, next identify the subsequent note and then perform the next note. As musical skill improves, musicians string together notes and then execute the phrases of notes. Finally, the skilled musician is able to identify upcoming notes and rhythms in the musical score while performing the present rhythm with virtually no noticeable affect on the musical rhythms being performed. Hence, the musician seems to progress from a mode of purely sequential processing to a mode of concurrent or cascade processing (Pew, 1974; Rosenbaum, Hindorff, and Munroe, 1987). Late in the learning process when skilled performance has developed, several motor elements are apparently prepared together as a unit while earlier units are being executed. Such concurrent processing has been seen in writing (Portier, Van Galen, and Meulenbrook, 1990), musical performance (Shaffer, 1976), and key pressing (Rosenbaum, Hindorff, and Munroe, 1987; Semjen, 1992; Verway, 1994, 1995).

One way to investigate concurrent preparation and execution is to ask under what circumstances concurrent preparatory processes and execution occur without interfering effects. Several factors have been identified in relation to this issue. Two of them are practice and sequence length.

Key pressing tasks have been used to investigate the effects of practice and sequence length on concurrent processing. In general, key pressing tasks consist of the subject pressing a sequence of keys in which the lengths of the sequences might vary (one, three, or five key presses). Each sequence consists of a fixed portion and a portion that is stimulus dependent. Thus, in a three key press condition, the subject starts the trial by depressing the [5] key on a standard number pad. A warning signal is given in the center of the computer screen. After a delay, the imperative signal appears either to the left or to the right of where the warning signal had previously been located. If the imperative signal appears to the left of the warning signal, the sequence to be performed is to key [8 5 4] on a standard number pad. If the imperative signal appears to the right of the warning signal, the sequence to be performed is to key [8 5 6]. In this three key press example, the fixed portion of the sequence consists of [8 5] and the stimulus dependent key press is the last key press of the sequence.

The question underlying this task is when the stimulus dependent portion of the sequence is prepared in relation to the fixed portion. Preparation for the stimulus dependent key could occur after the imperative signal and before any key presses occur. This would result in increased reaction times compared to conditions where the entire three key press sequence is known before the imperative signal. Alternatively, preparation for the stimulus dependent key could occur during execution of the fixed portion of the sequence. This concurrent processing might result in interresponse delays or in increased variability of the responses during the fixed portion of the sequence. Preparation for the stimulus dependent key could also occur upon completion of the fixed portion of the task. This would result in an interresponse delay between the last response in the fixed portion of the sequence and the stimulus dependent key.

Garcia-Colera and Semjen (1987) and Verway (1995) used a key pressing task with assumptions similar to those described and demonstrated that practiced subjects could prepare forthcoming key presses while earlier key presses were being executed. That is, with practice interference free concurrent processing occurred. Portier, Van Galen, and Meulenbrook (1990) used a handwriting task and concluded that with practice the amount of concurrent processing increases.

Using a key pressing task similar to the one just described, Verway (1995) concluded that with practiced subjects the interfering effects of concurrent processing on sequence execution were reduced as the sequence length increased. Verway and Dronkert (1996) found that longer sequences provided more opportunity for subjects to take advantage of concurrent processing. Garcia-Colera and Semjen (1988) also used a key pressing task with a similar assumption. Their task consisted of a fixed sequence of eight finger taps. The location of a stimulus dependent accentuated tap and the hand to use in execution was varied. The effects associated with the accentuated tap on sequence production disappeared when the accentuated tap occurred late in the sequence. Thus, both practice and sequence length influenced concurrent processing.

The effects discussed previously can by classified in terms of the preparatory processes that occurred during execution. Some of the studies examined the response selection stage of processing during execution Verway (1995) and Rosenbaum, Hindorff, and Munroe (1987) used tasks in which various key presses in the sequence were left to be identified based on the imperative signal. Thus, during concurrent processing the response selection stage could have co-occurred with the execution stage. Garcia-Colera and Semjen (1988) used a task in which the key presses in the sequence were the fixed portion of the sequence and thus the response selection stage could be completed in advance of the imperative signal. Certain aspects of the sequence, accentuated key press (force) and hand (effector), were stimulus dependent. Thus, these movement parameters could not be prepared until after the imperative signal appeared.

Another movement parameter that has received attention in the literature is the timing of the movement. Several models of timing are currently popular. The Wing and Kristofferson (1973) model has been integrated with the information processing approach and the motor programming framework (Keele and Ivry, 1987). According to this model, the timing of a movement is the result of two independent processes, the clock process and the implementation process. The clock process involves a central time keeper metering out the required temporal delay for a specific movement. The implementation process involves sending the appropriate muscle commands to execute the movement. The success of the model is seen in various studies aimed at testing specific predictions of the model (Keele et al., 1985; Ivry and Keele, 1989). A possible application of the Wing and Kristofferson model is to imagine that in order for the clock process to begin, the timing parameter of the motor program must be specified as part of the response preparation stage of information processing. Once the timing parameter is specified, the clock process can begin with the resultant implementation process occurring as part of the execution stage of information processing.

If a subject is required to tap at a specified rate and then switch to a different rate of tapping and if the subject knows when and how the timing demands are to change, there are several possibilities for specifying the timing of the later portion of the task. One possibility is that, because the subject has information about the second tapping rate before the task begins, he or she can use this information to prepare for the second rate before any tapping takes place. A second possibility is that the subject holds the temporal information in memory and prepares the timing of the later portion of the task during tapping at the first rate. A third possibility is that the subject holds the temporal information in memory and prepares the timing of the later portion of the task once tapping at the first rate is completed.

Inhoff et al. (1984), Rosenbaum, Inhoff, and Gordon (1984), and Sternberg et al. (1978) found support for the adoption of the first strategy—preparing the second tapping rate before the task begins. During key pressing tasks, sequences were completely prepared (response selection) before execution of the sequences began. This result was evidenced through the finding that reaction times to begin the sequences increased as a function of the amount of response preparation (number of key presses to be prepared) based on the imperative signal.

Adoption of the second strategy, holding temporal information in memory and preparing the timing of the later portion of the task during tapping at the first rate requires concurrent processing. Semjen (1992) and

Verway (1994) reported that subjects prepared (response selection) for a later key press or a series of key presses during execution of the first portion of the sequence. Concurrent processing during execution was evidenced by increased interresponse intervals (IRIs) in anticipation of later key presses.

Adoption of the third strategy, holding the temporal information in memory and preparing the timing of the later portion of the task once tapping at the first rate is completed has also been demonstrated in key pressing tasks (Semjen, 1992; Verway, 1994). In a key pressing task subjects were given information concerning the choice of a key press in the sequence. Subjects did not take advantage of the advance information, but instead waited until just before the choice key press to prepare (select responses) for the remaining key presses in the sequence. A lengthening in the interresponse interval immediately before the choice key press suggested that selection of the key press did not occur until just prior to its execution.

In trying to understand a mechanism that accommodates concurrent processing, a plausible model is provided by Peters (1985a, 1985b) and Peters and Schwartz (1989). Peters and his colleagues proposed a model of attention for bimanual timing. It seems appropriate that the model be adapted to concurrent preparatory processing and execution. According to the original model, during bimanual timing, one hand is under the guidance of direct attention and the other is under the guidance of indirect attention. According to Peters and his colleagues, direct attention is allocated by a central mechanism capable of redirecting attention to different task components. Although Peters and his colleagues did not directly examine the costs associated with redirecting attention, they proposed a cost associated with the reallocation of attention. In the adapted version of the model, execution of the first portion of a timing task is under the guidance of direct attention. Again, attention is allocated by a central mechanism capable of redirecting attention to different task components. One component to which indirect attention might be allocated is toward preparatory processes. Under certain conditions, indirect attention might be reallocated to preparatory processes during execution of the task at hand. This would result in concurrent processing. The cost associated with redirecting indirect attention might result in the changes in performance. One question that arises is, What are the conditions under which indirect attention can be reallocated? Possible alternatives include the conditions currently investigated in relation to concurrent processing, namely, practice and sequence length.

The primary question in the present work is, when do subjects prepare for a known timing change in a rhythmic sequence? This question extends previous investigations of concurrent processing. Much of the previous work investigated concurrent response selection during execution. One exception is Garcia-Colera and Semjen (1988), who concluded that preparatory parameter setting (force and effector) can co-occur with execution of finger tapping. Setting the timing parameter during execution raises an interesting question. Peters (1977, 1990) concluded that timing is the limiting factor in dual task performance. That is, if the timing of two activities cannot be integrated into one rhythmic structure, the differing timing demands cannot be met simultaneously. Thus, the question arises: Can subjects set the timing parameter of the motor program during the execution of a task requiring strict temporal control?

A secondary question in the present work is whether there are measures that are more sensitive to concurrent processing effects than others. Van Donkelaar and Franks (1991) raised a similar question when investigating preprogramming versus on-line control of arm movements. Van Donkelaar and Franks pointed out that although interresponse intervals within arm movement sequences had been used to investigate this issue, other measures that might be sensitive to differences between preprogramming and on-line control were not frequently used. In their experiment using human arm movements, Van Donkelaar and Franks found that reaction times to begin arm movements did not increase with the complexity of the arm movements, but evidence for increased movement complexity was seen in acceleration traces. Extrapolating from this finding to the present task, it might be that when investigating the preparation for a known timing change in a rhythmic sequence, interresponse times might be sensitive to some aspects of preparation while another measure like finger displacement might be sensitive to other aspects.

7.2 Method

Participants
Five students from the University of Massachusetts, Amherst, community participated in the study. One male undergraduate, three male graduate, and two female graduate students participated in the experiment. Each subject was paid for his or her participation.

Apparatus
The subject sat facing a Macintosh Computer and wore a "tapping glove" —a right-handed leather archer's glove with wire interwoven on the underside of the index finger cup. Tapping responses were made by tapping the right index finger on a metal plate. Upon contact with the metal, the wires completed a circuit so that tap time could be recorded. The experiment was controlled by a Lightspeed Pascal computer program and a Logical Solu-

tions I/O interface. In addition, an infrared emitting diode was attached to the "tapping glove" above the subject's right index fingernail. The diode sent a signal to a Northern Digital Optotrack System used for measurement of finger kinematics.

Procedure

The task involved performing manual responses (right index finger tapping) at different rates. In a trial, the subject was required to tap at one of the goal rates and then to tap at the same or another goal rate. The goal tapping intervals used were: 200, 400, and 600 ms. The conditions were formed by crossing first and second goal rates in all possible ways. The numerical values of the first and second goal tapping rates were not revealed to the subject. Instead, the values were referred to as "fast," "medium," and "slow," respectively.

The goal tapping rates were presented to the subject as computer generated tones. On a given trial, nine tones were presented. The first four tones represented the first goal tapping rate, and the second five tones, which immediately followed, represented the second goal tapping rate. This created four IRIs at the first tapping rate and four IRIs at the second. The first tone marked the beginning of the first interval at the first rate. The fifth tone marked the end of the first rate and simultaneously marked the beginning of the second rate.

Once the tones ended, the subject began tapping when he or she was ready. There was no reaction time pressure. The subject was supposed to tap four times at the first rate (preswitch taps) and then to tap five times at the second rate (postswitch taps). The subject was instructed to count silently as the tones were being generated and aloud as he or she tapped to reproduce the sequence. The count was "1, 2, 3, 4, 1, 2, 3, 4, stop." Finger tapping was monitored through the Northern Digital Optotrack System. For each trial, index finger tapping was sampled at a rate of 100 Hz.

As the subject tapped, the interval between each tap was measured to the nearest millisecond, and immediately following the last tap of the trial, feedback was presented on the computer screen. An example of the feedback is presented in figure 7.1. The horizontal line indicates the goal tapping time, and the asterisks represent the intervals produced by the subject. The height of the asterisk above or below the horizontal line represents the proportional error in the produced interval above or below the target interval. Asterisk positions from left to right correspond to interval numbers (first to last).

Each subject participated in 20 repetitions of each first x second goal tapping rate condition. On each of two sessions, subjects completed 10 blocks of trials. A block consisted of nine trials. Within a block of trials, the first goal tapping rate was constant and the second rate was randomized

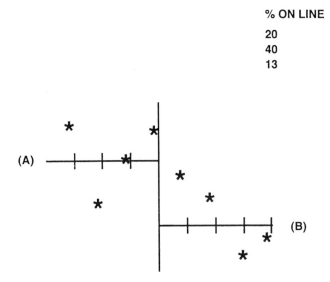

% ON LINE
20
40
13

Figure 7.1
Example of presentation of first and second goal tapping times in experiment 1: (A) first goal tapping time, (B) second goal tapping time. As the subject taps, interresponse intervals were measured and the corresponding interresponse times were graphed (*) on the screen at a distance from the line proportional to the goal tapping time. Sample number is represented on the abscissa. The subject also received feedback in the form of the percentage of taps in which the "*" fell on the goal tapping lines. See text for an explanation.

such that each condition was presented once in a block. Each session consisted of a guided introduction to the procedure and 10 blocks of experimental trials. Each session lasted 1 hour and was performed on consecutive days.

7.3 Results

Mean Interresponse Time
To use the data from subjects when they were most practiced, only data from day two were analyzed for this report. An ANOVA was conducted that evaluated the effects of first goal tapping rate (200, 400, 600 ms) × second goal tapping rate (200, 400, 600 ms) × location (preswitch, postswitch) × distance (1, 2, 3, 4). Several effects and interactions were significant.

Figure 7.2 shows the mean IRI before and after the switch for each of the nine conditions. The four-way interaction (first goal tapping rate × second goal tapping rate × location × distance) was significant, $F(12, 48) =$

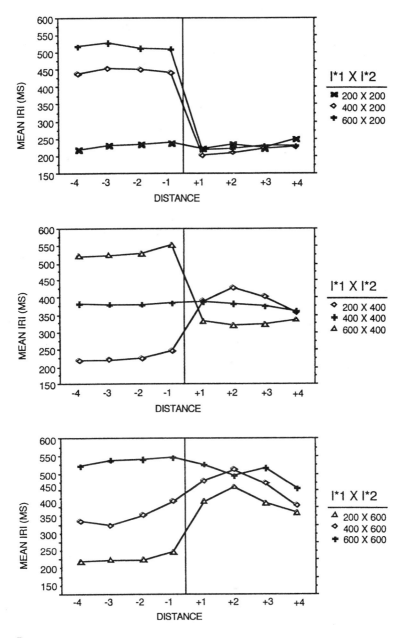

Figure 7.2
Mean IRI as a function of first goal tapping rate, second goal tapping rate, location, and distance from the switch.

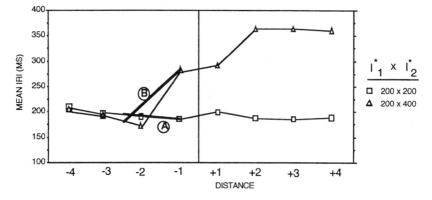

Figure 7.3
Illustration of differences being subjected to contrast tests. The line labeled "A" represents the control difference. The line labeled "B" represents the comparison difference. See text for explanation.

1.97, $p < .04$. The result to note in this four-way interaction is that mean IRIs approximated the goal tapping rates with the exception of some context effects. For example, when 400 ms was followed by 400 ms, subjects underestimated the initial goal tapping rate by approximately 25 ms, but when the 400 ms was followed by 200 ms, subjects overestimated the initial goal tapping rate by approximately 25 ms. Thus, in some conditions, production of the goal tapping rate was influenced by the context in which it was performed.

Contrast tests were conducted on the mean IRIs for the four-way interaction shown in figure 7.2. The first question addressed was whether there were changes in tapping performance during the first rate associated with later timing demands. The specific contrast compared two differences. Figure 7.3 provides an example. The first difference in question served as the control. It is labeled "A" in figure 7.3. This was the difference between the last IRI at the first rate and the mean of the nonboundary intervals at the first rate when the first and second rates were equal. Nonboundary intervals are those intervals that do not surround the required switch, begin the sequence, or end the sequence. In this experiment the non-boundary intervals include distance 2 and 3. Theoretically, there should be no differences in the control difference since there are no changes in the timing demands of the task. The second difference in question served as the comparison. It is labeled "B" in figure 7.3. This was the difference between the last IRI at the first rate and the mean of the nonboundary intervals at the first rate when the first and second rates differed. Theoretically, if subjects prepare for changes in anticipation of the changing timing demands, changes in tapping performance should reflect this added process. Thus, one might expect that the interval just prior to the required switch would be elevated compared to the other intervals. To ensure that any changes in performance reflect processes associated with changes in the timing demands of the task, the two differences just described, the control and comparison differences, were subjected to contrast tests. If the control difference and the comparison difference are equal (e.g., the slope of A equals the slope of B), one can conclude that there were no changes in performance related to timing preparation. If the control difference and the comparison difference yield different patterns (e.g., the slope of B is greater than the slope of A), then one can conclude that the differences reflect preparation for the timing change.

Contrasts were conducted for each first goal tapping rate. For example, for conditions in which the first rate equaled 200 ms, the first contrast tested the 200 × 200 ms condition versus the 200 × 400 ms condition. The second contrast tested the 200 × 200 ms condition versus the 200 × 600 ms condition. This procedure was repeated for the data in each left panel in figure 7.2. No significant results were found.

A similar contrast was conducted for the first interval after the required switch related to the changes in the timing demands. The question of interest was whether there were changes in tapping performance at the first interval after the required switch that reflected changes in the timing demands. Again, the specific contrast compared two differences, the control and comparison. The control difference was the difference between the IRI at the first interval at the second tapping rate and the mean of the nonboundary intervals at the second rate when the first and second rates were equal. The comparison difference was the difference between the IRI at the first interval at the second tapping rate and the mean of the nonboundary intervals at the second tapping rate when the first and second rates differed. As with the preswitch intervals, contrast tests were conducted twice for each second goal tapping rate (200, 400, and 600 ms). No significant differences were found. Thus, there was no evidence in the mean IRI data for concurrent timing preparation during execution, and there was no evidence in the mean IRI data for subjects preparing for the timing change at the first interval after the required switch (at the "last possible moment").

Log Standard Deviation
An ANOVA was conducted to evaluate the effects of the first goal tapping rate (200, 400, 600 ms) × the second goal tapping rate (200, 400, 600 ms) × location (preswitch, postswitch) × distance (1, 2, 3, 4) on log(sd) (Myers and Well, 1991). Several main effects and interactions were significant.

Figure 7.4 shows the mean log(sd) before and after the switch for each of the nine note sequences. The three-way interaction (first goal tapping rate × the second goal tapping rate × distance) was significant; $F(12, 48) = 2.25$, $p < .01$. In each of the three graphs, the second goal tapping rate is constant. The result to note is that in the three conditions where subjects started at a relatively slow rate and switched to a faster rate (e.g., 600×200, 400×200, 600×400), log(sd)s were higher than in the other conditions.

Contrast tests were conducted on mean log(sd) for the three-way interaction shown in figure 7.4. The specific question was whether there were changes in tapping performance during the first rate associated with later timing demands. The contrast tests were similar to those used in the mean IRI data (see figure 7.3). Two significant differences were found. The slopes of the comparison differences were greater than the slopes of the control differences when comparing the 200×200 versus 400×200 and when comparing the 600×600 versus 200×600 ms conditions. Thus, there was evidence in the log(sd) data for concurrent timing preparation during execution.

Finger Displacement
An ANOVA was conducted that evaluated the effects of the first goal tapping rate (200, 400, 600 ms) × the second goal tapping rate (200, 400, 600 ms) × location (preswitch, postswitch) × distance (1, 2, 3, 4) on finger displacement. Several main effects and interactions were significant.

Figure 7.5 shows the mean finger displacement for the intervals before and after the switch for each of the nine note sequences. The four-way interaction (first goal tapping rate × second goal tapping rate × location × distance) was significant, $F(12, 48) = 2.34$, $p < .05$. In each of the three graphs the second goal tapping rate is constant. The first result to note is the systematic increases in the peak vertical finger displacements as the required switch approached and as the end of the sequence approached. A second result to note is that the peak finger displacement at the last interval before the required switch is larger for some conditions requiring a timing change than for corresponding control conditions. This result was confirmed with *t*-tests for 200×200 compared to 600×200, for 200×200 compared to 400×200, and for 600×600 compared to 200×600 ms.

Contrasts were conducted for each first goal tapping rate (200, 400, 600 ms) condition as described previously (see figure 7.3). Two significant differences were found. The slopes of the comparison differences were greater than the slopes of the control differences when comparing 200×200 and 400×200 and when comparing 200×200 and the 600×200.

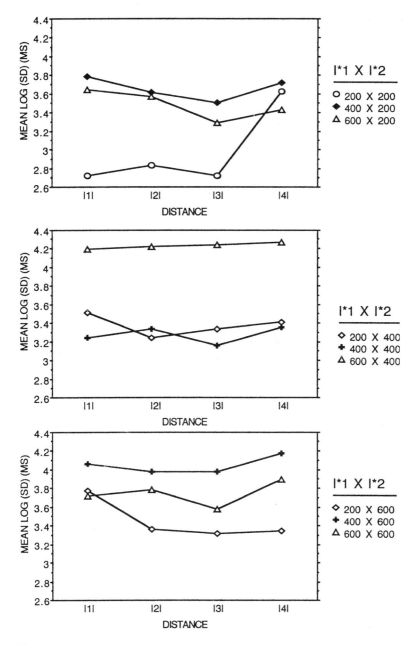

Figure 7.4
Mean log(sd) as a function of first goal tapping rate, second goal tapping rate, and absolute distance from switch.

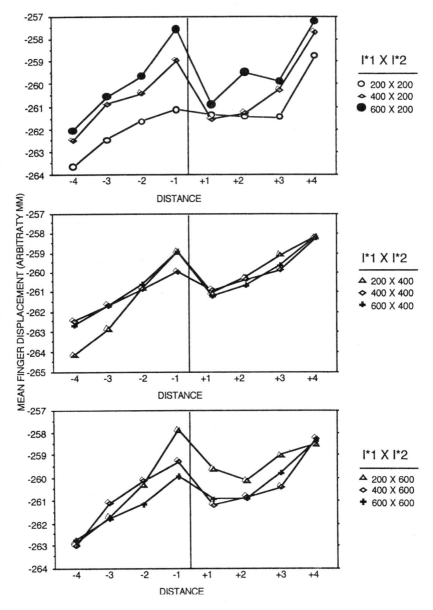

Figure 7.5
Mean peak vertical finger displacement as a function of first goal tapping rate, second goal tapping rate, location, and distance from switch.

Thus, there is evidence in the mean vertical displacement data for concurrent timing preparation during execution.

A similar question was asked for the tapping performance at the first interval after the required switch. One significant difference was found. The slope of the comparison difference was greater than the slope of the control difference when comparing 200 × 200 and 400 × 200. Thus, there was also evidence in the mean vertical finger displacement data for timing preparation taking place at the "last possible moment."

7.4 Discussion

If a subject is required to tap at a specified rate and then to switch to a different rate of tapping and if the subject knows when and how the timing demands are to change, when does the subject specify the timing of the later portion of the task? The present results suggest that the choice of dependent variable affects the conclusion drawn. Using mean IRI data, there is no evidence of concurrent timing preparation during execution of the first portion of the task. But using log(sd) and peak finger displacement data, there is evidence that subjects prepared for the upcoming timing change during the first portion of the task.

The log(sd) data provide weak evidence of changes in performance related to timing changes. In several conditions requiring a timing change, the log(sd)s of IRIs were higher than the corresponding control conditions. The conditions with increased log(sd)s were conditions in which subjects started tapping at a relatively slower rate and then switched to a relatively faster rate (e.g., 600 × 400, 600 × 200, and 400 × 200). Finger position data also provide some evidence for preparation of late rates during execution of earlier rates. Peak vertical finger displacements increased systematically as the required switch approached. Also, peak vertical finger displacement for the last interval before the required switch for some conditions requiring a timing change were larger than corresponding control conditions.

The data, however, do not provide clear evidence that the log(sd) and peak finger displacement results are due to concurrent preparation. Another possibility is that the sequences did not contain enough intervals to allow subjects to settle into a steady rate of tapping. This possibility is supported by the finding that in some conditions the log(sd) of IRIs during control conditions equaled the log(sd)s of conditions requiring a timing change. Also, systematic increases in peak vertical finger displacement as the "required switch" approached in control conditions (with no actual timing change) suggest that subjects might not have reached a steady state in tapping. One might assume that if a steady state of tapping was reached, then log(sd)s and finger displacements should plateau.

What is the criterion or appropriate measure for steady state tapping? The presence of steady state tapping depends on the dependent measure. Mean IRIs plateau at or near the goal tapping rates suggesting steady state tapping, but peak finger displacements from the same subjects do not plateau and thus suggest the absence of steady state tapping.

Barnes (1996) addressed the question of steady state tapping in a follow-up study. The task was identical to the one used in this report except that the subjects produced longer sequences. The sequences had eight intervals at the first goal tapping rate immediately followed by eight intervals at the second goal tapping rate. The answer to the question of whether subjects reach a steady state of tapping with longer sequences depends on the dependent variable. As in the experiment presented in this report, the mean IRI data indicate steady tapping through plateaus at or near the goal tapping rates. However, systematic changes in log(sd) and peak finger displacement do not support the presence of steady state tapping because there were increases in log(sd)s and peak finger displacements as the required switch approached and as the required end of the sequence approached. Assuming the increased sequence length allowed subjects to reach a steady state of tapping, we are still left with the alternative that the log(sd) and finger displacement results reflect concurrent processing. In support of this conclusion it is useful to recall that Garcia-Colera and Semjen (1988) used sequences of eight key presses and subjects prepared for accentuated key presses during execution of the sequence. These researchers found that when the accentuated key press occur late in the sequence, subjects were more likely to use concurrent processing. The longer sequences used in the follow-up study (Barnes, 1996) were similar in length to those used by Garcia-Colera and Semjen. Given the similarity of the log(sd) and finger displacement results with shorter and longer sequences, the patterns of results can be taken as evidence for concurrent processing during rhythmic finger tapping in the short as well as the long sequences.

One question that remains is why control conditions and conditions requiring a timing change have increases in finger displacements as a function of distance from the switch. A way to answer this question is to consider a study by MacKenzie and Van Eerd (1990) who reported systematic changes in mean internote intervals (INIs) during piano scale playing. The pattern of INIs as a function of note position in the sequences was scalloped. That is, as a scale was played there was an organization in terms of the finger used to press the key. In these scales fingerings were $T, I, M, T, I, M, R, T, I, M, R, P$, where T is thumb, I is index, M is middle, R is ring, and P is pinkie. The INIs increased each time the thumb was used and then immediately decreased with the index finger key press.

This scallop pattern repeated with the beginning of each new hierarchical subsection in the sequence. These results are similar to the peak finger displacement data reported here. Consequently, the pattern of increasing peak finger displacements to the required switch and to the end of the sequence might indicate the underlying structure of the sequence. The pattern might also be evidence of performance changes related to the timing change. A more controlled investigation is needed to separate the effects of sequence structure and effects due to concurrent processing.

Based on the log(sd) and peak finger displacement data, it appears that subjects took advantage of advance timing information, held that information in memory, and then prepared for the timing change during execution of the first portion of the sequence. In addition to preparing for the required timing change during execution of the first portion of the task, it appears that subjects also prepared for the required end of the sequence during execution of the second portion of the task. The clearest evidence is provided by the peak finger displacement data. Not only did peak finger displacement systematically increase as the required switch approached, but it also systematically increased as the required end of the sequence approached. The basis for arguing that subjects prepared for the end of the sequence stems from the fact that subjects had to prepare to stop tapping. Early in the experiment some subjects continued tapping beyond the length of the sequence. When this occurred the subject was instructed that the counting strategy should be used to guide tapping so that when the "stop" count occurred, tapping should stop. Garcia-Colera and Semjen (1988) relied on IRI data as evidence for subjects preparing to stop during finger tapping.

In trying to adapt the Peters (1985a, 1985b) and Peters and Schwartz (1989) model of attention for bimanual timing to concurrent processing, one question that arises is, what are the conditions under which indirect attention can be reallocated to preparatory processes? Possible alternatives include the conditions currently investigated in relation to concurrent processing, namely, sequence length and practice.

In terms of sequence length the adapted version of the model suggested that as the length of a sequence increased subjects had more opportunity to use concurrent processing. When comparing the patterns of peak finger displacements in the shorter sequences reported here and the longer sequences used in the follow-up study (Barnes, 1996), the main finding was that the pattern of results was the same for longer and shorter sequence lengths. Peak finger displacement increased as the required switch approached and as the end of the sequences approached. The slopes of the increases were steeper in the shorter sequences. This difference in slopes might be capturing the fact that with longer sequences the demands of concurrent processing are less severe.

In terms of practice the model predicted that with more experience subjects should be able to take greater advantage of concurrent processing. As a task is practiced it becomes more automatic and the cost of redirecting indirect attention should not be as great. In support of this prediction, Garcia-Colera and Semjen (1987) and Verway (1995) demonstrated that with practice interference free concurrent processing occurs. The present report only utilized the Day 2 data. How these data corresponded to Day 1 data not yet been addressed.

The use of alternative measures to capture concurrent processing was a secondary question in the present research project. It appears that mean IRIs capture some aspects of performance and not others, just as it appears peak finger displacements capture some aspects of performance and not others. For example, based on mean IRI data in the present experiment and the follow-up experiment (Barnes, 1996), it appears that subjects did not prepare for the required timing change. As previously discussed, however, the finger displacement data indicate that subjects not only prepared for the required timing change during execution of the first portion of the task but also prepared for the required end of the sequence during the second portion of the task. One explanation as to why IRI data might not be sensitive to these effects though the finger displacement data are is related to the window of time in which the effect occurs. That is, if the effects of concurrent processing are present for some amount of time and the interval of measurement is shorter than that amount of time, the effects will go unnoticed. If, however, the interval of measurement is longer than the amount of time that the effect is present, then the effect will be captured. According to this analysis, the finger displacements, which occurred over a shorter time span than the mean intervals, may have been more diagnostic. The more general lesson, then, is that using multiple dependent variables to investigate concurrent processing allows for a more accurate description of the underlying processes.

In conclusion, the results of the present project suggest that concurrent timing preparation can co-occur with execution of the rhythmic sequence being performed. Most important, while several factors including practice (Semjen, 1992; Verway, 1995), sequence organization (Barnes, 1995), appropriate counting strategies (Barnes, 1995), and sequence length (Semjen, 1992; Verway, 1995) affect concurrent processing, the conclusions drawn about such factors are influenced by the choice of dependent variable.

Acknowledgments

The author thanks Rachel Clifton and Neil Berthier for the use of their lab and equipment at the University of Massachusetts, Amherst.

References

Barnes, H. J. (1996). Concurrent processing during rhythmic finger tapping. Paper presented at the annual meeting of New England Sequencing and Timing, March, Providence, RI.

Barnes, H. J. (1995). Advance preparation in rhythmic finger tapping. Paper presented at the annual meeting of New England Sequencing and Timing, March, Providence, RI.

Garcia-Colera, A., & Semjen, A. (1987). The organization of rapid finger movement sequences as a function of sequence length. *Acta Psychologica, 66,* 237–250.

Garcia-Colera, A., & Semjen, A. (1988). Distributed planning of movement sequences. *Journal of Motor Behavior, 20,* 341–367.

Inhoff, A. W., Rosenbaum, D. A., Gordon, A. M., & Campbell, J. A. (1984). Stimulus-response compatibility and motor programming of manual response sequences. *Journal of Experimental Psychology: Human Perception and Performance, 10,* 724–733.

Ivry, R., & Keele, S. (1989). Timing functions of the cerebellum. *Journal of Cognitive Neuroscience, 1,* 136–152.

Keele, S. (1968). Movement control in skilled motor performance. *Psychological Bulletin, 70,* 387–403.

Keele, S., & Ivry, R. (1987). Modular analysis of timing in motor skill. In G. Bower (ed.) *The psychology of learning and motivation: advances in research and theory* (pp. 183–228). New York: Academic Press.

Keele, S., Pokorny, R., Corcos, D., & Ivry, R. (1985). Do perception and motor production share common timing mechanisms: A correlational analysis. *Acta Psychologica, 60,* 173–191.

MacKenzie, C. L., & Van Eerd, D. L. (1990). Rhythmic precision in the performance of piano scale: Motor psychophysics and motor programming. In M. Jeannerod (ed.), *Attention and performance* XIII (pp. 375–408). Hillsdale, NJ: Erlbaum.

Myers, J. L., & Well, A. (1991). *Research design & statistical analysis.* New York: Harper Collins.

Peters, M. (1977). Simultaneous performance of two motor activities: the factor of timing, *Neuropsychologia, 15,* 461–465.

Peters, M. (1985a). Attentional asymmetries during concurrent bimanual performance. *Quarterly Journal of Experimental Psychology, 33A,* 95–103.

Peters, M. (1985b). Constraints in the performance of bimanual tasks and their expression in unskilled and skilled subjects. *Quarterly Journal of Experimental Psychology, 37A,* 171–196.

Peters, M. (1990). Interaction of vocal and manual movements. In G. Hammond (ed.). *Advances in psychology: Cerebral control of speech and limb movement* (pp. 535–574). Amsterdam: North Holland.

Peters, M., & Schwartz, S. (1989). Coordination of the two hands and effects of attentional manipulation in the production of bimanual 2:3 polyrhythm. *Australian Journal of Psychology, 41,* 215–224.

Pew, R. W. (1974). Human perceptual-motor performance. In B. H. Kantowitz (ed.), *Human information processing: Tutorials in performance and cognition* (pp. 1–39). New York: Wiley.

Portier, S. J., Van Galen, G. P., & Meulenbroek, R. G. J. (1990). *Journal of Motor Behavior, 22,* 474–492.

Rosenbaum, D. A., Hindorff, V., & Munro, E. M. (1987). Scheduling and programming of rapid finger sequences: Tests and elaborations of the hierarchical editor model. *Journal of Experimental Psychology: Human Perception and Performance, 13,* 193–203.

Rosenbaum, D. A., Inhoff, A. W., & Gordon, A. M., (1984). Choosing between movement sequences: A hierarchical editor model. *Journal of Experimental Psychology: General, 113,* 372–393.

Semjen, A. (1992). Plan decoding and response timing during execution of movement sequences. *Acta Psychologica, 79,* 255–273.

Shaffer, L. H. (1976). Intention and Performance. *Psychological Review, 83,* 375–393.

Sternberg, S., Monsell, S., Knoll, R. L., & Wright, C. E. (1978). The latency and duration of rapid movement sequences: Comparisons of speech and typewriting. In G. E. Stelmach (ed.), *Information processing in motor control and learning* (pp. 117–152). New York: Academic Press.

Van Donkelaar, P., & Franks, I. M. (1991). Preprogramming vs. on-line control in simple movement sequences. *Acta Psychologica, 77,* 1–19.

Verway, W. B. (1994). Evidence for the development of concurrent processing in a sequential key pressing task. *Acta Psychologica, 85,* 245–262.

Verway, W. B. (1995). A forthcoming key press can be selected wile earlier ones are executed. *Journal of Motor Behavior, 27,* 275–284.

Verway, W. B., & Dronkert, Y. (1996). Practicing a structured continuous key pressing task: motor chunking or rhythmic consolidation. *Journal of Motor Behavior, 28,* 71–79.

Wing A., & Kristofferson, A. (1973). Response delays and the timing of discrete motor responses. *Perception and Psychophysics, 14,* 5–12.

Chapter 8

Memory Mixing in Duration Bisection

Trevor B. Penney, Lorraine G. Allan, Warren H. Meck, and John Gibbon

Abstract

We studied the effects of stimulus modality and stimulus spacing on duration classi-fication in the human temporal bisection task. When auditory and visual signals were presented in the same test session, visual signals were judged shorter than auditory signals that had equivalent durations, but, when subjects were exposed to a single modality within a session there was no difference between auditory and visual signal classifications. We posit a model in which visual and auditory signals evoke different, variable memory representations for the same objective-time duration signal. This dif-ference is revealed only when subjects experience both modalities in the same session and the memory for the target duration is a mixture of representations generated on both auditory and visual trials. We also apply this memory mixing notion to the stimulus spacing literature as one possible mechanism that can account for the differ-ence in psychometric functions when stimuli are either logarithmically or linearly spaced.

8.1 Introduction

The study of modality effects on perceived duration has had a checkered history. In a series of studies, Goldstone and Goldfarb (1964; see Allan, 1979) reported that a filled auditory interval was judged longer than a filled visual interval of the same duration. Some researchers have found similar modality differences (e.g., Behar and Bevan, 1961; Stevens and Greenbaum, 1966), but others have not (e.g., Hawkes, Bailey, and Warm, 1961; Bobko, Thompson, and Schiffman, 1977; Brown and Hitchcock, 1965). These conflicting results are difficult to reconcile because a variety of different experimental procedures were used in the studies. Also, most of the research concerned with modality effects on temporal judgments was conducted many years ago, and there has been, in recent years, sub-stantial progress in methodology and quantitative analyses.

Recently, we began to examine the influence of signal modality on duration classification by human subjects using the temporal bisection task. Our studies use an analogue of the procedure employed by Church and Deluty (1977) to study temporal bisection by rats. In the Church and Deluty (1977) procedure, the rat is trained to perform one response following one signal duration and a different response following another signal duration. The animal receives reinforcement for making a "short" response, R_S (e.g., left lever press) when the signal duration is short (S), and for making a "long" response R_L (e.g., right lever press) when the signal duration is long (L). After this discrimination has been established, probe signals of intermediate duration T, $S < T < L$, are presented, for which no response is reinforced, along with S and L.

On each trial of a human temporal bisection task, the subject is presented with a temporal interval, T, $S \leq T \leq L$, and is required to categorize the presented interval as R_S or R_L. In some studies, the "similarity" procedure has been used: S and L are explicitly identified as standards, by providing feedback periodically on S and L trials (e.g., Allan and Gibbon, 1991) or by presenting the S and L intervals at the beginning of a block of trials (e.g., Wearden, 1991; Wearden and Ferrara, 1995,1996). In other studies, the "partition" procedure has been used: No members of the set are explicitly identified as standards (e.g., Wearden and Ferrara, 1995, 1996).

The temporal bisection procedure generates psychometric functions relating the proportion of "long" responses, $P(R_L)$, to signal duration T. The bisection point ($T_{1/2}$) or point of subjective equality (PSE), is the value of T at which R_S and R_L occur with equal frequency, $P(R_L) = .5$. Many animal studies (e.g., Church and Deluty, 1977; Meck, 1983, 1986) have shown that the bisection psychometric function is ogival with $T_{1/2}$ at about the geometric mean (GM) of the two training stimuli, S and L; $GM = (S * L)^{1/2}$.

Bisection at the GM of the S and L signal durations has also been reported for human bisection data (Allan and Gibbon, 1991). Wearden (1991), in contrast, reported human data with the bisection point not at the GM, but located just below the arithmetic mean (AM) of S and L; $AM = 1/2(S + L)$.

In previous studies of human bisection, the temporal intervals were auditory signals only, either filled (Allan and Gibbon, 1991; Wearden and Ferrara, 1995, 1996) or empty (Wearden, 1991). Here we present new data from experiments that examined bisection of filled visual and auditory intervals. In some conditions durations were marked in a single modality (auditory or visual), whereas in other conditions subjects were required to time auditory and visual intervals in the same session. We also discuss data, some previously published, that address the effect of stimulus spacing on the placement of the bisection function.

In the remainder of the chapter we describe scalar timing and its application to our experiments. We then develop the ideas used to explain the modality effect in the domain of stimulus spacing.

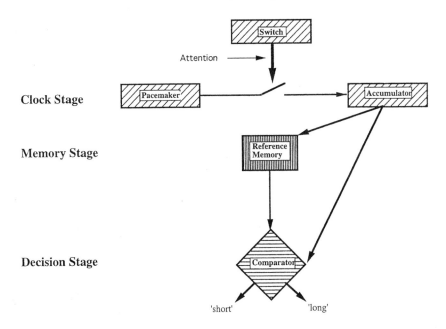

Figure 8.1
Information-processing model of interval timing with clock, memory, and decision stages.

8.2 Scalar Timing Model

The information processing components of scalar timing are shown in figure 8.1. The clock stage consists of a pacemaker, a mode switch, and an accumulator (temporal integration mechanism). The pacemaker emits pulses at some (high) rate, and these are gated into an integrating component, the accumulator, through the switch that closes when a timing signal is present. The record in the accumulator is compared to the representation of S and of L in reference memory. The decision to respond R_S or R_L is made by a ratio comparison of the similarity of the value of T in the accumulator to the remembered values of S and L in reference memory. In effect, the subject asks, whether T is more similar to L or to S. The values of these comparisons, which represent the similarity of the sample to the two referents, are themselves composed of a ratio. The decision to respond R_L occurs when the similarity of S to T is less than the similarity of T to L. A response, possibly biased in favor of R_L, is made when

$$\mathrm{SIM}(x_S, x_T)/\mathrm{SIM}(x_T, x_L) < \beta, \tag{8.1}$$

where x_T is a variable representing the accumulation of current time T on a given trial, x_S and x_L are samples from memory for S and L, β is a

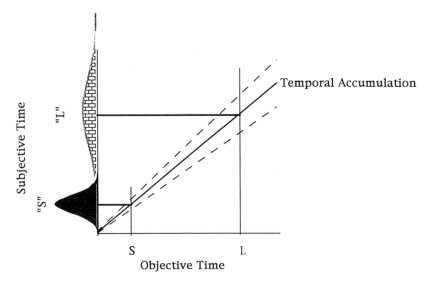

Figure 8.2
Variability in memory encoding across trials, represented by the dashed diagonal lines, results in distributions in memory rather than single points.

bias parameter, and the similarity metric for two values is their ratio, $\mathrm{SIM}(x, y) = \min(x, y)/\max(x, y)$.

S and L have memory distributions associated with them rather than single point values because of noise in the timing system. One way variability in memory may result is illustrated in figure 8.2. Objective time is on the abscissa and the short and long anchor values are demarcated by S and L respectively. Subjective time is on the ordinate. The solid diagonal represents temporal accumulation on the current trial. In the model developed later, we assume minimal variability in temporal accumulation (clock-rate variability) but relatively high variability in the memory encoding process. The two dashed diagonal lines show the effect of this encoding variability. Note that what is stored in memory is some variable multiplicative translation of the accumulation. As a consequence, the S and L values are distributions in memory rather than single points.

Scalar timing allows for constant (switch variability) and Poisson (pacemaker variability) sources of variation, as well as scalar sources of variability. Gibbon (1981) has shown that for temporal accumulations that are large relative to the interpulse interval of the pacemaker, the scalar sources dominate. In the version of the model used by Allan and Gibbon (1991), "Sample Known Exactly" (SKE), variance in the representation of the current time in the accumulator is negligible and the scalar sources of variance in memory are assumed to be the major contributors to the scalar property in performance. For this case there are only two parameters. The sensitivity parameter, γ, is the coefficient of variation of remembered time. It reflects the degree of noise in the memory representation of the short and long signal durations and is comparable to, but not identical to, the empirically-based Weber ratio. The location parameter, β, may be thought of as a bias parameter for the report of R_L. For the SKE model, it is assumed that there is no variability in β, or in x_T, the percept of current time.

Mean subjective time is assumed to be linear with objective time, and the standard deviation of subjective time is linear with the mean, the scalar property. It is this feature that implies a constant coefficient of variation, γ, in the memory distributions. The scalar property of the standard deviation implies Weber's law, and can be thought of as a linear relationship between variability in subjective time, as indexed by standard deviation, and mean subjective time. Scalar timing imposes a stronger requirement than Weber's law however, namely that psychometric functions plotted against $T/T_{1/2}$ superpose for all $S:L$ ratios.

The decision rule to respond long is equivalent to

$$[\mu(T)]^2 > (x_S x_L)/\beta, \tag{8.2}$$

where $\mu(T)$ represents mean subjective time, which for the present approximation may be taken as proportional to objective time, and x_S and x_L are samples from Gaussian memory distributions for the S and L intervals respectively. The product variate on the right of equation 8.2 is non-normal, but for reasonable values of the sensitivity parameter γ, the positive skew is small and can be ignored (c.f. discussion in Gibbon, 1981). Equation 8.2, then, implies a cumulative normal psychometric function where the mean bisection point ($R_L = .5$) is

$$E[\mu(T_{1/2})^2] = E(x_S x_L)/\beta,$$

which implies

$$T_{1/2} = GM/(\beta)^{1/2} \tag{8.3}$$

for $GM = (S * L)^{1/2}$. Bisection is at the GM corrected by the bias parameter β; that is, bisection = GM when $\beta = 1$.

8.3 Signal Modality Experiments

Experiment 1: One Modality
To study the effects of signal modality on bisection performance, we trained two groups of 12 subjects each (all Columbia University under-

graduates) on a duration bisection task in which they were exposed to one signal modality, either auditory or visual. The auditory-alone group experienced only auditory signals and the visual-alone group experienced only visual signals. A Macintosh computer was used to present all experimental stimuli and to record responses. The auditory signals were 440 Hz tones produced by the computer tone generator and played over headphones. The visual signals were black squares measuring approximately 5 cm by 5 cm on the computer monitor. Both signals were well above detection threshold. Each subject had one test session at each of two anchor duration pairs (3s vs 6s and 4s vs 12s). In the 3s versus 6s test the stimulus durations occupied the 3–6 sec range as follows: 3.00, 3.67, 3.78, 4.24, 4.76, 5.34, and 6.00 seconds. In the 4s versus 12s test the stimulus durations occupied the 4–12 second range as follows: 4.00, 4.80, 5.77, 6.93, 8.32, 9.99, and 12.00 seconds. The order of session presentation was counterbalanced across subjects. Each session consisted of 10 training trials, of which 50% were the short anchor and 50% the long anchor. The testing phase consisted of 100 trials of which 30% were the anchor durations and the remaining 70% were divided equally among the five intermediate durations. Subjects received feedback indicating whether or not a signal had been classified correctly on all training trials and on those test trials where the signal was the same duration (short or long) as an anchor duration learned in training. Feedback was not given for any of the intermediate duration signals.

Group mean data for both the auditory-alone and visual-alone conditions for each pair of anchor durations (3s vs 6s and 4s vs 12s) are shown in figure 8.3. Duration is on the abscissa and the probability with which a duration is called long, $P(R_L)$, is on the ordinate. The 4s versus 12s functions nearly superimpose, and while the 3s versus 6s auditory and visual functions are somewhat less similar, the PSEs and DLs of both pairs of functions are not statistically different.

As noted previously, scalar timing theory requires that psychometric functions from different anchor pairs superpose when plotted against $T_{1/2}$. $T_{1/2}$ was calculated for the group average response functions and the functions were normalized. The top panel of figure 8.4 shows that for the visual functions there is reasonable superposition. In the bottom panel, however, it is clear that superposition fails for the auditory functions. The 3s vs 6s function is steeper in relative time (better discrimination) than the 4s vs 12s function. The absence of superposition for the auditory functions may reflect a range effect for difficulty level, a point to which we will return.

Experiment 2: Two Modalities
In experiment 2, our interest centered on performance when both modalities are present. Twenty additional subjects participated in the second

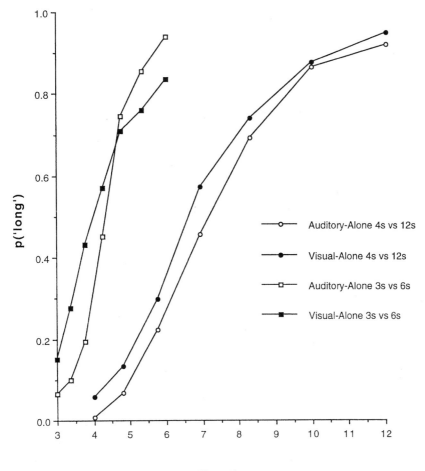

Figure 8.3
Proportion of "long" responses as a function of duration for the Auditory Alone and Visual Alone conditions. Anchor durations were either 3s vs 6s or 4s vs 12s.

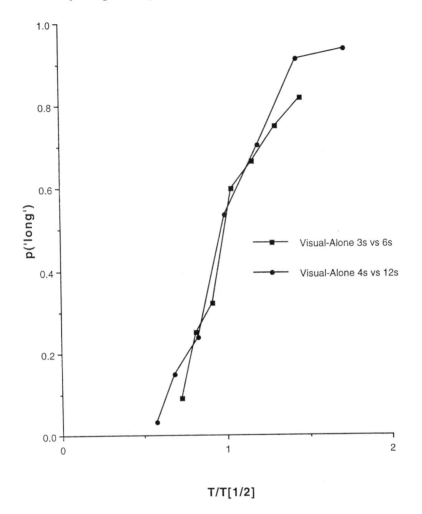

Figure 8.4
Proportion of "long" responses as a function of relative duration ($T/T_{1/2}$) for the both-same conditions. Anchor durations were either 3s vs 6s or 4s vs 12s. Visual functions are displayed in the top panel and auditory functions are displayed in the bottom panel.

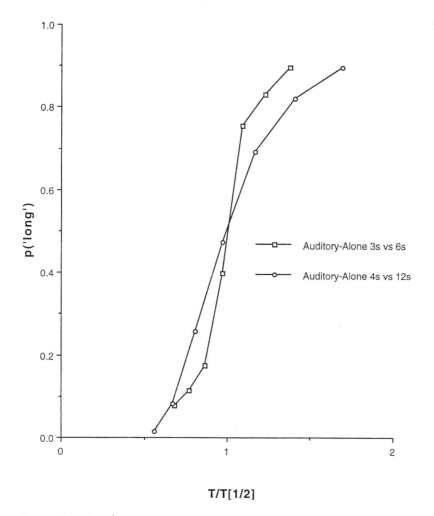

Figure 8.4 (continued)

experiment. The key difference between experiment 2 and experiment 1 was that, whereas only a single modality was tested within a session in experiment 1, both modalities (visual and auditory) were tested in a session in experiment 2. Signals were presented singly and the order of signal presentation with respect to modality and duration was randomized. For 10 subjects, 3s and 6s were the anchor durations for both modality signals (group both-same 3s vs 6s), whereas for another 10 subjects, 4s and 12s were the anchor durations for both modality signals (group both-same 4s vs. 12s). The intermediate probe durations and feedback were the same as those used in experiment 1. Training sessions consisted of 20 trials divided evenly among short/long anchors and single auditory and single visual trials. Subjects were instructed that both signal modalities had the same objective-time anchor durations. The test phase consisted of 200 trials divided evenly among the auditory and visual modalities. Thirty percent of the trials were the anchor durations and the remaining 70% were divided equally among the five intermediate durations.

Figure 8.5 indicates that the visual function lay to the right of the auditory function for both anchor duration pairs. The PSEs for the visual bisection function were significantly larger than for the auditory function for both pairs of anchor durations [$F(1, 9) = 11.503$, $p. < 0.05$ for 3s vs. 6s and $F(1, 9) = 10.557$, $p < 0.05$ for 4s vs. 12s].

Figure 8.6 shows that the auditory and visual functions superpose within a particular pair of anchor durations when plotted as $T/T_{1/2}$. Superposition fails, however, across anchor duration pairs, as was the case for the alone conditions in experiment 1.

8.4 Modifications Of The Scalar Timing Model

Within the framework of the scalar timing model, an explanation of the modality effect requires that we build on previous work in our laboratories, using animals as subjects, which has examined two possible mechanisms for differential subjective-time accumulation (Penney, Holder, and Meck, 1996; Meck and Church, 1987; Meck, 1983, 1986): onset-latency to close the switch, and clock-rate differences. We describe these mechanisms and expand upon them next.

Onset Latency

Posner (1978) suggested that auditory signals are processed automatically whereas visual signals require attention. If perception of the onset of the visual signal lags behind that for the auditory signal, one might expect switch closure to take longer, on average, for visual than for auditory signals. As a consequence, a visual signal would be perceived as shorter than an auditory signal with the same duration. If a single memory distribution is used for both signal modalities, the PSE for visual signals would lie to the right of that for auditory signals. If memories for the anchors are modality specific, however, the difference in switch closure time would not be revealed by differences in PSE, as illustrated in figure 8.7. Here it is seen that there are four memory distributions on the ordinate, one for each of the short and long duration signals of both modalities. Objective time is on the abscissa. The solid diagonal and dashed diagonal lines represent the subjective accumulations of time for the auditory and visual signals, respectively. The visual accumulation begins incrementing later than the auditory accumulation because onset latency to begin timing is

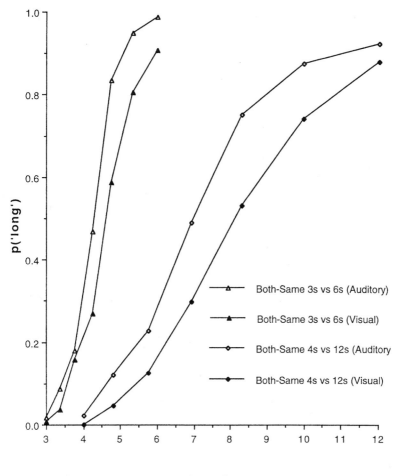

Figure 8.5
Proportion of "long" responses as a function of duration for the Both-Same conditions. Anchor durations were either 3s versus 6s or 4s versus 12s.

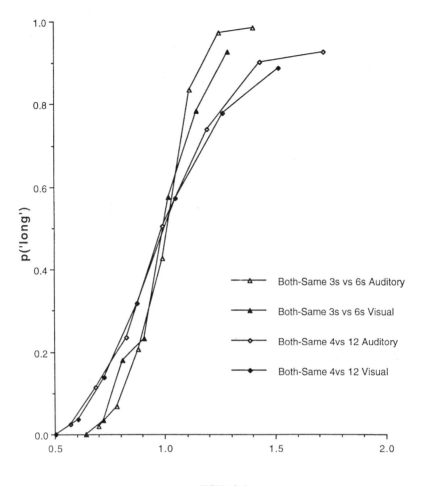

Figure 8.6
Proportion of "long" responses as a function of relative duration $(T/T_{1/2})$ for the both-same conditions. Anchor durations were either 3s versus 6s or 4s versus 12s.

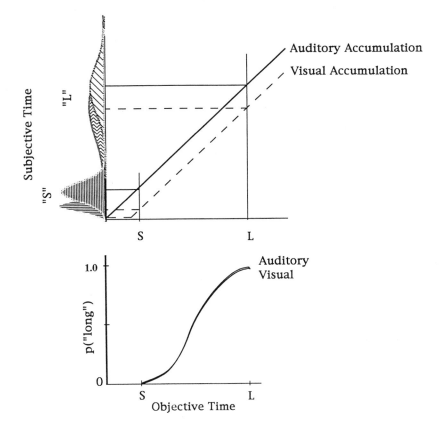

Figure 8.7
Information processing model of modality differences in interval timing: An onset-latency model with independent memories for auditory and visual signals is illustrated in the top panel. Timing onset is delayed for the visual signal. The predicted proportion "long" responses for each modality signal is shown in the bottom panel.

longer for visual signals. This onset latency difference is represented by the rightward displacement of the dashed diagonal line. As a result, there is a smaller subjective time accumulation for a visual signal than for an auditory signal of equivalent duration. But because the memories for the two modalities are distinct, the subject should classify equivalent duration signals for each modality the same way, even though the subjective accumulation is different, as long as the subject compares a given modality accumulation on the current trial with the appropriate modality "short" and "long" memories. The bottom panel of figure 8.7 shows that the behavioral outcome of such a comparison process is that the two functions are nearly identical.

Clock Speed
It is also possible that signal modalities drive the internal clock at different rates. Clock speed is determined by the rate of pulse generation, which may occur at a higher frequency when the signal driving the clock is auditory than when it is visual. Alternatively, the accumulation rate or clock speed may be higher for auditory than for visual signals because the mode switch closes more efficiently for auditory than for visual signals. The mode switch may be thought of as oscillating or flickering between an open and a closed state. When the switch is closed, pacemaker pulses are accumulated, but when it is open they are not. If the signal duration must be attended to continuously for the switch to close and remain closed, and if auditory signals capture attention more easily than visual signals, they may also cause the mode switch to flicker less, resulting in larger pulse accumulations for the auditory signals.

The flickering-mode-switch account is similar to the onset latency account described above in that it has an attentional component, yet it suggests a *multiplicative* rather than an *additive* difference. With the onset latency model, one expects a visual signal to be subjectively shortened by a constant absolute amount no matter what the duration of the signal. With a flickering mode switch, however, the amount of "lost" time will be a constant proportion of the signal duration.

We prefer the flickering mode switch account because it incorporates an attentional explanation of the effect and also because it receives support from the superposition data described earlier. We obtained "across modality" superposition in experiment 2 in the both-same condition for the 3s versus 6s and the 4s versus 12s anchor durations. Functions superpose following normalization by the PSE when the difference between the functions is a multiplicative transform, not when it is an additive difference. This evidence, although not conclusive, favors a clock rate rather than an onset latency explanation. It is important to note, however, that neither of the explanations offered above can account for our observed modality effects if the subject maintains separate memory distributions for both signal modalities.

Mixed Memories
The models described previously cannot adequately account for our duration bisection results because modality-specific memories in the both-same conditions in experiment 2 would have rendered the same response functions as those obtained in experiment 1 in the alone conditions where memories were independent. Models in which the subject uses a single, mixed memory representation of "short" and "long" for both signal modalities can account for the data.

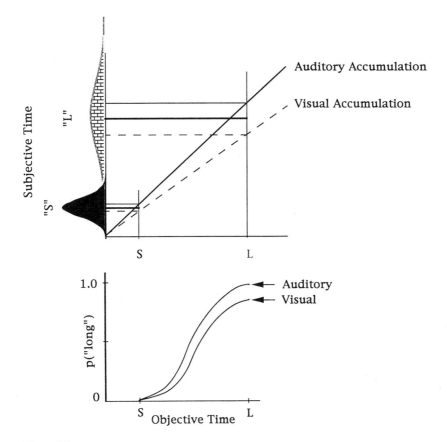

Figure 8.8
Information processing model of modality differences in interval timing: A clock rate model with mixed memories for auditory and visual signals is illustrated in the top panel. Clock rate is slower for visual signals. The memories are a mixture of the accumulations for the auditory and visual signals. The predicted proportion "long" responses for each modality signal is shown in the bottom panel.

A mixed-memory model results in a classification difference between the two signal modalities, as illustrated in figure 8.8. There are two memory distributions on the ordinate, one for the short and one for the long duration signals. Objective time is on the abscissa. The solid diagonal and dashed diagonal lines represent the subjective accumulations of time for the auditory and visual signals respectively. We posit a slower clock rate for visual signals resulting in a smaller subjective time accumulation for visual signals. The memory distributions are slightly skewed because the memories are a mixture of the accumulations for the auditory and visual signals. Because of the different clock rates for the two modalities the mean of the memory distribution for each anchor will be slightly larger than the mean visual accumulation and slightly smaller than the mean auditory accumulation. Therefore, a given duration visual signal will seem shorter than an equivalent-duration auditory signal when compared to the combined short and combined long memory values. The bottom panel of figure 8.8 illustrates the behavioral predictions of this model. The visual response function lies to the right of the auditory response function, matching the empirical data shown earlier in figure 8.5.

The absence of a PSE difference between the auditory-alone and visual-alone conditions in experiment 1, in combination with the difference shown by the both-same groups in Experiment 2, indicates that both auditory and visual signals must be present in the same session to obtain the modality effect. Earlier we claimed that the presence of independent memories for each modality would preclude any classification difference even if the rate of pulse accumulation for visual signals were slower than that for auditory signals. Clearly, comparing a group of subjects who experienced only auditory signals to a group of subjects who experienced only visual signals is a comparison of independent memories of the anchor durations. When both signal modalities are present in the same session and the anchor durations are the same for both modalities, however, it appears that differential subjective time accumulation combined with memory mixing results in classification differences.

Experiment 3: Different Anchor Durations
To further investigate our memory-mixing model we tested a group of 10 subjects who experienced both signal modalities in the same session but had 3s versus 6s as the auditory anchor points and 4s versus 12s as the visual anchor points (both-different condition). The intermediate probe durations and feedback were the same as in experiment 1. Training sessions consisted of 20 trials divided evenly among short/long anchors and auditory-alone and visual-alone trials. Subjects were instructed that the two signal modalities had *different* objective-time anchor durations and that during the test signals were to be classified relative to the short and long anchors of the same modality. The test phase consisted of 200 trials divided evenly among the auditory and visual modalities. Thirty percent of trials were the anchor durations and the remaining 70% were divided equally among the five intermediate durations. The order of signal presentation with regard to both modality and duration was random.

If the modality effect was simply due to the presence of both modalities in the same test session and did not depend on memory mixing, one would expect the 4s versus 12s function for the both-different condition to look the same as the 4s versus 12s function for the both-same condition in experiment 2. If the modality effect requires the objective time anchor durations to be equivalent for both signal modalities, then the both-different (visual) 4s versus 12s function in experiment 3 should be indistinguishable from the visual-alone 4s versus 12s function in experiment 1.

The group response functions for the visual signals of the 4s vs 12s anchors for subjects in the visual-alone condition in experiment 1, in the both-same condition in experiment 2, and in the both-different condition in experiment 3 are shown in figure 8.9. The visual-alone and both-different functions are similar, whereas the both-same function lies to the right. A one-way between subjects ANOVA confirmed a reliable effect of condition on PSE $[F(2, 29) = 7.797, p < 0.05]$. Post-hoc comparisons (Fisher's Protected LSD) indicated that the both-same condition was different from the visual-alone and the both-different conditions, which did not differ from each other. The absence of a difference between the visual-alone and the both-different conditions implies that the objective-time anchor durations used for the two signal modalities were important in determining whether or not the modality effect occur. Evidently, memory mixing did not occur in the both-different condition because six seconds of an auditory signal was quite distinct from 12 seconds of a visual signal even if the temporal accumulation was smaller for the visual signals. That is, the visual signals were (appropriately) compared to the memories for the visual anchors alone.

The group response functions for the auditory signals of the 3s versus 6s anchors for subjects in the auditory-alone condition in experiment 1, in the both-same condition in experiment 2, and in the both-different condition in experiment 3 are shown in figure 8.10. Although there appears to be some separation of the three functions at longer durations, the PSEs and DLs were not reliably different. This outcome suggests that the memory representations of short and long were similar in the three conditions.

Auditory-Dominant Mixed-Memory Model
The simple clock-rate mixed-memory model described earlier makes some quantitative predictions for auditory and visual signals in the both-same condition that were not confirmed. Within this model, an auditory duration is compared to a mixed memory that was generated by combining pacemaker accumulations for the anchors on both auditory and visual trials. Because pulse generation is faster for auditory than for visual signals, a given duration auditory signal will seem longer when it is compared to a mixed memory distribution that is a combination of visual and auditory subjective times than would an equivalent-duration auditory signal that is compared to a pure auditory memory distribution. Therefore, the clock-speed mixed-memory model predicts that the auditory functions for the both-same condition should lie to the left of the function for the auditory-alone condition. As described earlier, although there is some separation

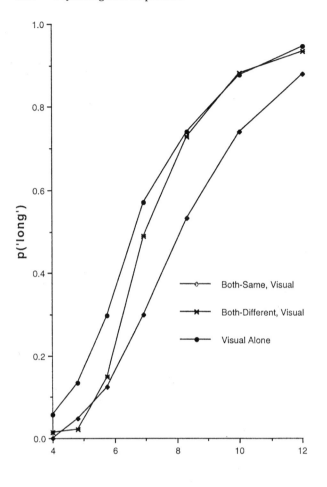

Duration

Figure 8.9
Proportion of "long" responses as a function of duration for the visual signals for subjects in the visual-alone condition of Experiment 1, in the both-same anchors condition of Experiment 2, and in the both-different anchors condition of Experiment 3. Anchor durations were 4s vs 12s.

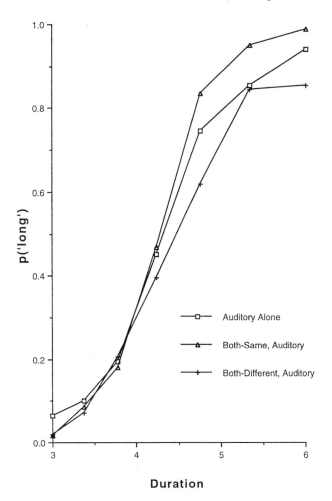

Figure 8.10
Proportion of "long" responses as a function of duration for the visual signals for subjects in the auditory-alone condition of Experiment 1, in the both-same anchors condition of Experiment 2, and in the both-different anchors condition of Experiment 3. Anchor durations were 3s vs 12s.

of the response functions (see figure 8.10), the PSE differences were not reliable.

A slightly modified version of the mixed-memory model predicts a minimal difference, if any, between the auditory functions for the different auditory conditions. If the memory-mixture is dominated by the auditory modality, one would expect minimal differences among the auditory functions for the different conditions, but this account would still anticipate the auditory-visual modality effect. This is the case because when auditory time accumulations dominate in memory, the mixed memory distribution is very similar to the memory distribution created when only auditory signals are presented. As a consequence, there should be minimal differences between the functions from the auditory-alone condition and the mixed conditions, both-same and both-different. The visual difference should still be present, of course, because a visual signal of given duration will seem shorter when compared to a memory that was dominated by an auditory accumulation with a faster clock than it would if compared to a pure visual memory where the clock rate on both the current trial and the remembered trial was the same.

This auditory-dominant mixed-memory model is presented in figure 8.11. Once again there are two memory distributions on the ordinate, one for the short and one for the long duration signal. The solid diagonal and dashed diagonal lines represent the subjective accumulations of time for the auditory and visual signals respectively. Again we posit a slower clock speed for visual signals than for auditory signals, resulting in a smaller subjective time accumulation for visual short and long anchors. This time, however, the subject compares temporal accumulation on the current trial with memory representations that are generated by the auditory accumulations only. Because the visual signal supports a slower clock speed, a given duration visual signal seems shorter than an equivalent duration auditory signal when compared to the auditory memory values, but auditory signals will be classified in the same way whether they occur alone in a session or in a session that also has visual trials.

Mixed-Memory SKE Model
We have modified the standard SKE model described previously to include two new parameters, RR and Pa. RR is the ratio of the visual clock speed to the auditory clock speed, and Pa is the proportion of the memory mixture contributed by the auditory modality signal. RR equals one when the auditory and visual clock speeds are equivalent and is less than one when the auditory clock speed is faster. Pa, which equals 1-Pv, can range from zero, meaning no auditory contribution to the memory, to one, meaning complete auditory dominance of the memory.

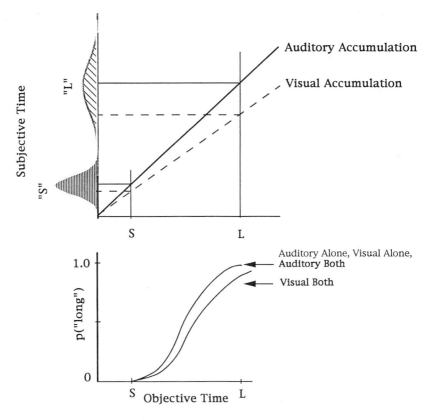

Figure 8.11
Information processing model of modality differences in interval timing: A clock rate model with mixed memories for auditory and visual signals in which the auditory modality dominates the memory mixture is illustrated in the top panel. Clock rate is slower for visual signals. The memories are an unequal mixture of the accumulations for the auditory and visual signals. The predicted proportion "long" responses for each modality signal are shown in the bottom panel.

According to the SKE model developed by Gibbon (1981) the bisection function is approximately

$$P(T; S, L) = \phi[C(T; S, L)], \tag{8.4}$$

where $P(T; S, L)$ is the probability of a "short" response after Ts, given training on S and L anchors. ϕ is the cumulative normal distribution function and C is the bisection criterion

$$C(T; S, L) = (1 - \beta(T/\sqrt{S^*L})^{2p})/(\gamma\sqrt{\gamma^2 + 2}). \tag{8.5}$$

As described earlier, β is a location parameter that may be thought of as a bias for the report of "long," and γ is the coefficient of variation of remembered time. The sources of variability represented by γ include encoding and decoding variability in the representation of the anchor durations as well as variability in the representation of current accumulated time. We assume that subjective time is linear with objective time so p equals 1.0.

To allow for modality dependent clock speeds and memory mixing, however, we require separate bisection function criteria for auditory (C_A) and visual (C_V) signals:

$$C_A = \frac{1 - \beta\{(T/\sqrt{S^*L})(1/Pa + Pv\,RR)\}^{2p}}{(\gamma\sqrt{\gamma^2 + 2})}. \tag{8.6}$$

$$C_V = \frac{1\beta\{(T/\sqrt{S^*L})(RR/Pa + 2Pv\,RR)\}^{2p}}{(\gamma\sqrt{\gamma^2 + 2})}. \tag{8.7}$$

The best fit this model provides for the both-same 3s versus 6s group mean response function is shown in figure 8.12. The fit was obtained via an exhaustive search of the parameter space for β, γ, RR, and Pa under the constraint that β, RR, and Pa are the same for both modalities; γ was permitted to differ across modalities. The obtained β was 0.94, indicating minimal response bias, γ was 0.179 for the auditory condition and 0.227 for the visual condition. The auditory signal dominated memory ($Pa = 0.76$) and the auditory clock speed was about 10% faster than the visual ($RR = 0.92$). The model accounted for 99.8% of the variance in the auditory data and 98.8% of the variance in the visual data.

8.5 Stimulus Spacing

There are conflicting results in the animal and human interval timing literature on the effects of stimulus spacing. We believe that memory mixing may determine whether or not such context effects are revealed in the bisection task.

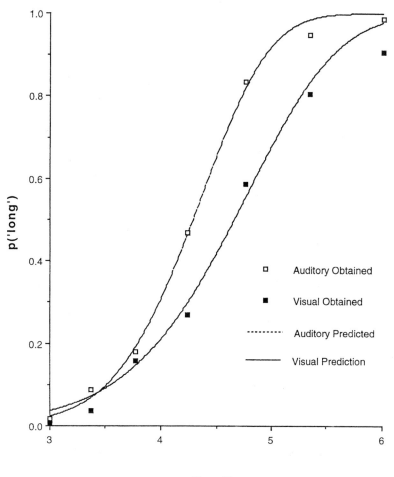

Figure 8.12
The solid lines are the response functions predicted by the auditory dominant model for the
auditory and visual signals of the both-same anchors 3s versus 6s condition.

When rats served as subjects and an $L:S$ ratio of 4:1 for several different anchor pairs was used, no differences in the location of the PSE were observed when different probe duration spacings were evaluated (Church and Deluty, 1977). Raslear (1983, 1985) found that the PSE for linearly spaced probe signal durations was significantly larger than that for logarithmically spaced signals when an $L:S$ pair of 10s:0.1s (100:1) was used. No spacing effect was observed with smaller $L:S$ ratios.

When humans served as subjects and difficult discrimination ratios with probe durations in the seconds range were used, no effect of linear versus logarithmic stimulus spacing on the location of the PSE was found (Allan and Gibbon , 1991). However, Wearden and Ferrara (1995, 1996) showed a significant effect of stimulus spacing on PSE using logarithmic versus linear spacing when the $L:S$ ratio was 9:1 but not when it was 4:1. We have also obtained a significant effect of linear versus logarithmic spacing in our lab using short and long anchor points of 100 and 200 msec.

The data for humans, data from Allan and Gibbon (1991), from Wearden and Ferrara (1995), and our previously unpublished stimulus spacing data, are presented in figure 8.13. The ordinate plots the difference between the PSE obtained with linear spacing and with logarithmic spacing divided by the geometric mean of the anchor durations. Normalizing by the geometric mean of the anchor durations corrects for the very different training ranges used. The abscissa is the $L:S$ ratio. The 4:1 and 9:1 ratio values are the means of the similarity and partition values from Wearden and Ferrara (1995). It is clear that the size of the difference between linear and logarithmic spacing increases with the $L:S$ ratio.

Wearden and Ferrara (1995) explain the stimulus spacing effect by proposing that subjects calculate the midpoint of the distribution of probe durations, and base their classification upon the duration of the current test probe relative to the calculated midpoint duration. Although their explanation works well for some data, it does not account for the influence of the $L:S$ ratio on whether or not spacing effects are found.

Our approach to modeling the bisection procedure is different from that of Wearden and Ferrara (1995). As described earlier, we argue that subjects generate a representation of both the short and long anchor durations during training. When a discrimination is difficult (i.e., when there is a small $L:S$ ratio such as 2:1) they must maintain an accurate representation of the short and the long anchor points to ensure that these signal durations will be classified correctly. In contrast, when the discrimination ratio is large (e.g., 9:1) the subject is able to maintain a high level of performance on the anchor points with a less accurate representation of short and long.

We propose that the representation becomes less accurate because the subject uses more than the shortest and longest probe durations to gen-

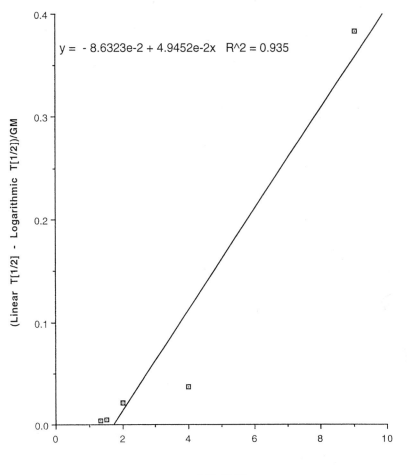

$$y = -8.6323e\text{-}2 + 4.9452e\text{-}2x \quad R^{\wedge}2 = 0.935$$

Figure 8.13
Temporal bisection data from Allan and Gibbon (1991), Wearden and Ferrara (1995), and our previously unpublished stimulus spacing data. The ordinate plots the difference between the PSE obtained with linear spacing and with logarithmic spacing divided by the geometric mean of the anchor durations. The 4:1 and 9:1 ratio values are the means of the similarity and partition values from Wearden and Ferrara (1995).

erate the memory representation for short and long. Probe values that are close to the very shortest and very longest durations may also enter into the memory representation for short and long. This is likely to occur when relatively easy discrimination ratios are used because it is not necessary for the subject to pay full attention to the task in order to maintain near perfect discrimination at the extremes.

The consequence of allowing values that are close to the anchor durations to contribute to the anchor duration memories is that the subjective short becomes slightly longer than the true short and the subjective long becomes slightly shorter than the true long. If the values that are close to the anchor durations are mixed together to form the representations of short and long, one might expect different function placement depending upon the stimulus spacing used. With logarithmic spacing, the values around the short anchor point are closer together than are these values for linear spacing; but the values at the long end are farther apart with logarithmic than with linear spacing. As a consequence, the memory representations for the short and the long anchor durations for the linear spacing condition lie to the right of those for the log spacing condition, resulting in equivalent durations being judged longer in the logarithmic condition than the linear condition.

This is illustrated in figure 8.14. The solid diagonal line represents temporal accumulation. The objective S and L durations (100 and 900 msec) are demarcated on the abscissa by a thick solid line and a thick dashed vertical line respectively. Two adjacent durations for the linear spacing condition (200 and 800 msec) and two adjacent durations for the logarithmic spacing condition (132 and 684 msec) are indicated on separate abscissas. These adjacent durations are mixed with the true S and L when an easy discrimination ratio is used. The subjective temporal representations for the linear and logarithmic spacing conditions are shown on the left and right ordinates respectively. For each spacing condition, the inner ordinate shows temporal representations for the anchor durations and the immediately adjacent probe duration. The outer ordinates show the mixed memories that result from the combination of an anchor duration and an adjacent duration. Because the adjacent durations have different values for linear and logarithmic spacing, the mean of the mixed memory is longer in the linear spacing condition than in the logarithmic spacing condition for the short and long signal durations. Note that the difference between representations of the long signal duration for the linear and logarithmic spacing conditions is much greater than the difference between representations of the short signal duration. This means that when a subject is classifying a given probe duration, (i.e., making a ratio judgement that utilizes current accumulated time as well as the memory representations of the short and long durations), the duration

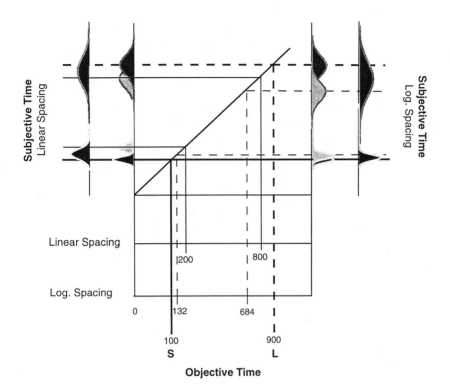

Figure 8.14
Memory mixing model of spacing effects in interval timing.

will seem longer when the intermediate stimuli are logarithmically spaced than when they are linearly spaced.

Of course, the difficulty of the discrimination in terms of the ratio of short to long anchors may not be the only factor that determines whether or not mixing occurs. It seems likely that the absolute difference between the anchor durations and the adjacent probe durations may determine which non-anchor values, if any, contribute to the short and long memory representations.

8.6 Summary

We obtained an effect of signal modality (auditory or visual) on duration classification in some experimental conditions but not in others. When subjects classified auditory and visual signals in the same test session, the visual signals appeared shorter than equivalent duration auditory signals, but when the response functions of subjects who experienced only auditory signals were compared to those of subjects who experienced only visual signals, there were no significant differences. Also, classification of signals was not distorted when both signal modalities were experienced in the same test session, but the anchor durations used for each modality were different.

We proposed that the modality effect we obtained is due to clock speed differences in combination with memory mixing across modalities for the short and long anchors. A subject's reference memory for the short and long signals is a mixture of accumulations obtained for auditory and visual signals experienced in training rather than a separate memory for each modality. Because temporal accumulation is faster for auditory than visual signals a given visual signal will appear shorter than an auditory signal of equivalent duration when it is compared to the mixed memory.

Memory mixing in combination with differential clock speed may account for previous findings concerning modality effects on duration perception. It is of interest that two of the studies cited in the introduction that failed to find modality effects used a between subjects designs, which, according to our model, would not reveal a modality difference (Bobko, Thompson and Schiffman, 1977; Brown and Hitchcock, 1965). Hawkes, Bailey, and Warm (1961) used a within subjects design but varied modality between sessions and also failed to find a modality difference. Of the three studies cited in support of modality effects, two used within subjects designs (Behar and Bevan, 1961; Stevens and Greenbaum, 1966) and the third used within and between subjects designs (Goldstone and Goldfarb, 1964).

Our failure to obtain superposition across anchor duration pairs suggests a range effect. Easy discrimination ratios allow the subject to perform accurately on the endpoints even if the timing process is not very precise or if attention wanders. The result is that subjects are less consistent in classifying the intermediate durations while still maintaining accurate anchor discrimination. The response function generated from an easy discrimination, normalized by the PSE, will not superpose with a PSE normalized function generated from a difficult discrimination ratio on which the subject performed as precisely as possible in order to maintain accurate anchor discrimination. It is as though subjects must "do their best" to maintain accuracy on difficult discriminations. The result in the theory is the lowest possible coefficient of variation (γ).

A combination of memory mixing and range effects may allow us to explain the presence of stimulus spacing effects in some experimental conditions but not others. When exposed to an easy discrimination ratio, subjects may be inclined to form less accurate representations of the shortest and longest signal durations. If this representation included the durations adjacent to the anchors, the ratio of the short to the long memory representation would be different for the linear and logarithmic spacing conditions. The response function for the logarithmic spacing condition would fall to the left of that for the linear spacing condition.

References

Allan, L. G. (1979). The perception of time. *Perception and Psychophysics, 26,* 340–354.

Allan, L. G., & Gibbon, J. (1991). Human bisection at the geometric mean. *Learning and Motivation, 22,* 39–58.

Behar, I., & Bevan, W. (1961). The perceived duration of auditory and visual intervals: Cross modal comparison and interaction. *American Journal of Psychology, 74,* 17–26.

Bobko, D. J., Thompson, J. G., & Schiffman, H. R. (1977). The perception of brief temporal intervals: Power functions for auditory and visual stimulus intervals. *Perception, 6,* 703–709.

Brown, D. R., & Hitchcock, L. (1965). Time estimation: Dependence and independence of modality specific effects. *Perceptual and Motor Skills, 21,* 727–734.

Church, R. M., & Deluty, M. Z. (1977). The bisection of temporal intervals. *Journal of Experimental Psychology: Animal Behavior Processes, 7,* 242–268.

Gibbon, J. (1981). On the form and location of the bisection function for time. *Journal of Mathematical Psychology, 24,* 58–87.

Goldstone, S., & Goldfarb, J. L. (1964). Auditory and visual time judgment. *Journal of General Psychology, 70,* 369–387.

Hawkes, G. R., Bailey, R. W., & Warm, J. S. (1961). Method and modality in judgments of brief stimulus duration. *Journal of Auditory Research, 1,* 133–144.

Meck, W. H. (1983). Selective adjustment of the speed of internal clock and memory storage processes. *Journal of Experimental Psychology: Animal Behavior Processes, 9,* 171–201.

Meck, W. H. (1986). Affinity for the dopamine D_2 receptor predicts neuroleptic potency in decreasing the speed of an internal clock. *Pharmacology Biochemistry & Behavior, 25* 1185–1189.

Meck, W. H., & Church, R. M. (1987). Nutrients that modify the speed of internal clock and memory storage processes. *Behavioral Neuroscience, 101,* 465–475.

Penney, T. B., Holder, M. D., & Meck, W. H. (1996). Clonidine-induced antagonism of norepinephrine modulates the attentional processes involved in peak-interval timing. *Experimental and Clinical Psychopharmacology, 4,* 1–11.

Posner, M. I. (1978). *Chronometric exploration of mind.* Hillsdale, NJ: Erlbaum.

Raslear, T. G. (1983). A test of the Pfanzagl bisection model in rats. *Journal of Experimental Psychology: Animal Behavior Processes, 9,* 49–62.

Raslear, T. G. (1985). Perceptual bias and response bias in temporal bisection. *Perception and Psychophysics, 38,* 261–268.

Stevens, S. S., & Greenbaum, H. B. (1966). Regression effect in psychophysical judgment. *Perception and Psychophysics, 1,* 439–466.

Wearden, J. H. (1991). Human performance on an analogue of an interval bisection task. *Quarterly Journal of Experimental Psychology, 43B,* 59–81.

Wearden, J. H., & Ferrara, A. (1995). Stimulus spacing effects in temporal bisection by humans. *Quarterly Journal of Experimental Psychology, 48B,* 289–310.

Wearden, J. H., & Ferrara, A. (1996). Stimulus range effects in temporal bisection by humans. *Quarterly Journal of Experimental Psychology, 49B,* 24–44.

Chapter 9

The Regulation of Contact in Rhythmic Tapping

Jonathan Vaughan, Tiffany R. Mattson, and David A. Rosenbaum

Abstract

The study of the planning of movement has demonstrated how the performance of repetitive tasks (such as tapping to a metronome beat) depends on the similarity between the task definition (speed and force of tapping) and the optimal biomechanical properties of each limb segment. The pattern of tapping may not be completely determined by the task requirements. To explore the effect of immediately prior experience on how people elect to tap, 15 subjects were instructed to tap the forefinger on a strain-gauge mounted bumper in time with an adjustable metronome beat. Tapping at a moderate rate (1.75 taps/sec) was examined under two conditions: when it followed fast tapping (3 taps/sec) and when it followed slow tapping (0.5 taps/sec). The duration of contact with the bumper during each tap demonstrated a hysteresis effect. Contact duration at the intermediate rate of tapping depended on whether it immediately followed fast or slow tapping. Hysteresis may be taken as evidence of the conservation of a motor program, in the service of the efficiency of planning and performance.

9.1 Introduction

When people perform an action, it is necessary for them to choose from among a highly redundant set of possible movements or postures that will accomplish the goals of the task at hand. Ordinarily, specifying the goal does not completely determine all the details of the action. For example, recently, when one of the authors was leaving the departmental shop with both hands encumbered, he decided to turn off the light by gently tapping the switch with the end of one of the sticks of wood that he was carrying. He could have done so with the hand, as is conventional, or the elbow instead. Ignoring, for the moment, whether the action was potentially detrimental to the light switch, this example illustrates how action selection is adaptable to encumbrance and tool use.

The vignette illustrates what the Russian physiologist Nikolai Bernstein (1967) identified as the *degrees of freedom* problem. For most tasks, our skeletal system affords more degrees of freedom in the motion of our joints than are required for accomplishing a goal. A surplus of degrees of freedom is fortunate because it allows us to adapt to impediments such as obstacles that may be in the most direct path of movement or to disease that might restrict habitual movements. To take a realistic example, suppose one enjoyed both skateboarding and playing the cello. Imagine that a spectacular skateboarding accident resulted in a marked reduction in the range of pronation and supination of the right wrist. In order that the fluidity of cello bowing would not be noticeably affected, whenever a large degree of supination would ordinarily have been used, other axes of articulation of the wrist, elbow, and shoulder would have to be recruited to compensate for the attenuated degree of freedom in wrist motion.

Fortunately, in both free movement and in compensation for injury or disease, actors may exploit their surplus degrees of freedom. What implicit knowledge do people have about the biomechanics of the different limb segments, and how effectively is this knowledge exploited in planning? A complete answer to this question would require us to know the full dynamics of movement, but we can learn a great deal by simply observing how performance varies in simple tasks.

Control of Tapping
The work that we will describe addresses the flexibility of action selection in a specific domain of performance, rhythmic tapping to a metronome beat, which we used as an example of the general problem of action selection. The present paper has three goals. First, we briefly describe a recently developed model of tapping, consider where it has been successful, and then explore how it may be further tested. Second, we examine how a surplus of degrees of freedom of action might not only afford flexibility in action, but also afford consistency by allowing similar patterns of action to be used in more than one setting. Finally, we report the results of an experiment that evaluated the flexibility of tapping.

Although the task of tapping at an assigned rate is intuitively familiar to subjects, it can encompass a number of different variations in performance. For example, tapping against a bumper may vary not only in rate, but in a number of other, possibly redundant, parameters: impulse of collision (intensity of the initial contact); dwell time (duration of contact with the bumper); sustained force of contact with the bumper; amplitude of movement (distance of the fingertip away from the bumper during the backswing phase); and temporal accuracy (extent to which tapping leads or lags the metronome cue). Therefore, tapping may serve as a model system for exploring how performance is controlled.

Control of Limb Segments: Toward a Model of Tapping Control
Even when the defining attributes of the task (such as the rate and impulse of collision of tapping) are controlled, different segments of the arm may contribute to fingertip movement. The displacement of the fingertip

through a particular amplitude may be accomplished either by flexion of the finger about the knuckle joint, the hand about the wrist joint, or the forearm about the elbow joint, as well as any of an infinite number of combinations of movements of these three joints, among others. The variability inherent in the varieties of tapping movement means that not all tapping may be equivalent. There are individual differences in the variability of forces produced in tapping that tend to covary with the temporal accuracy of tapping (Keele, Ivry, and Pokorny, 1987). Similarly, the mode of tapping may affect accuracy. For instance, Wing (1977) compared the accuracy of tapping that was accomplished by finger flexion, wrist flexion, forearm elevation, or forearm pronation. He observed greater variance in the inter-tap times when the finger, rather than the hand or forearm, was used to tap. In the face of such results, we might hypothesize that one segment or another might be best suited to a particular tapping task. Segments have different masses, and the stiffness of their proximal joints may vary. Furthermore, as Wing (1977) suggests, some sets of muscles might require more complex motor programming, leading to greater variability in movement. Similarly, the joints' ranges of motion differ. All of these parameters may contribute to the efficiency with which each segment might oscillate at a particular frequency or amplitude.

Recent work (Rosenbaum, et al., 1991; Vaughan et al., 1996) has demonstrated that, when different rates of waving (or different rates and intensities of tapping) are required, correspondingly different patterns of contribution to the movement are observed in the finger, hand, and arm. Under different rate and amplitude requirements, oscillation of the fingertip was produced primarily by the segment (finger, hand, or forearm) whose "most comfortable" frequency and amplitude of oscillation most closely matched the required task (Rosenbaum et al., 1991). We also observed that when the tapping rate and intensity were particularly well matched to one of the limb segments, that segment tended to contribute relatively more to the oscillation of the fingertip (Vaughan et al., 1996). Tapping that was fast and soft elicited more finger movement, whereas slow, hard tapping was accomplished by more arm movement.

The fact that tapping exploits different limb segments to different degrees suggests that people have implicit or procedural knowledge about what kinds of movements are most efficiently performed by their limb segments. The reader is invited to freely oscillate the wrist at a rate of 2 Hz through a distance of about 10 to 15 cm (measured at the tip of the extended index finger). Such a movement is judged to be relatively comfortable by subjects. Increasing the rate of oscillation about the wrist to 4 Hz is possible, but the faster rate is accompanied by a decrease in oscillation amplitude because the wrist joint must be stiffened. The reciprocal relationship between the amplitude and the frequency of most efficient oscillation is characteristic of harmonic oscillators. Increasing the stiffness of a harmonic oscillator increases its resonant frequency while decreasing the amplitude produced by a constant driving force (Feynman, Leighton, and Sands, 1963). The modulation of stiffness is an appropriate mechanism for the modulation of the rate of oscillation of limb segments. A predictable consequence of using such a mechanism would be an inverse relationship between the amplitude and the frequency of oscillation. When subjects are required to oscillate at different frequencies, this inverse relationship is observed (Kay et al., 1987; Rosenbaum et al., 1991; Vaughan et al., 1996). Furthermore, the preferred rate of rhythmic movement corresponds to the resonant frequency of the oscillated system (Hatsopoulos and Warren, 1996).

Harmonic oscillation has inspired a model of tapping based on the concept of a virtual amplitude of tapping (Diedrich, 1990; Vaughan et al., 1996). In this "virtual amplitude" model, tapping is considered to be an interrupted sinusoidal motion aimed at a point beyond the striking surface. Control of tapping rate is achieved by modulating joint stiffness; control of tapping impulse is achieved by modulating the virtual amplitude of oscillation. To test this model, the required intensity and rate of tapping were varied (Vaughan et al., 1996). Both the amplitude of the backswing and the dwell time (duration of contact with the bumper) varied, at least qualitatively, as predicted by the model. In one of the experiments we were able to record the full trajectory of the fingertip from tap to tap. A sample of these trajectories is shown in figure 9.1, in which the position of the fingertip, relative to the bumper, was measured while the subject tapped at each of three intensities: 1, 3, and 5 Hz. At many combinations of frequency and required force of tapping (particularly at higher frequencies and softer tapping), the trajectory of the fingertip was very similar to an interrupted sinusoid, which is the pattern that would be produced by a harmonic oscillator mechanism of reciprocal movement. At the same time, the relatively asymmetrical trajectory at other task combinations (low frequency and hard tapping) suggests that the model may not apply equally well in its unmodified form to all domains of performance.

Repetitive movement at high rates is central to locomotion as well as tapping. One of the important features of bipedal and quadrupedal locomotion is that the alternate storage and release of elastic energy between periodic impacts with a surface contribute to the efficiency of limb movements in running (Alexander, 1984; see also Chapter 12). Similarly, the storage of energy during the contact phase of tapping is an essential component of the virtual amplitude model. Stored energy can be exploited for initiating the backswing phase of tapping, just as it is exploited

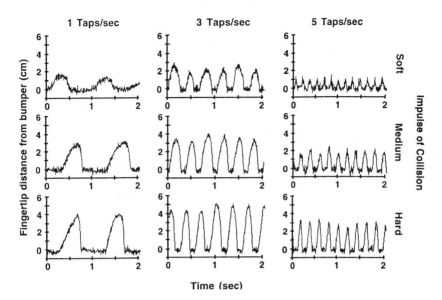

Figure 9.1
Displacement of the fingertip from the bumper at three different tapping rates and three different tapping intensities. (Reprinted, with permission, from Diedrich, 1990; see Vaughan et al., 1996, Experiment II, for details. The distance of the fingertip from the bumper was measured at 200 samples/sec, using an infrared emitting diode and the Wat-Smart recording system.)

in the contact phase of mammalian locomotion. For an ideally elastic collision, the force exerted on the bumper would increase during deceleration of the fingertip after it contacts the bumper, and decrease at the beginning of the opposite phase of movement. The sinusoidal motion could be maintained by a virtual trajectory of force that is complementary to the trajectory that the fingertip follows when it is not in contact with the bumper. Our earlier studies could not directly test this hypothesis, because they did not continuously monitor the bumper force. Therefore, one goal of the present work was to examine the time course of forces on the bumper during the contact phase of the tapping oscillation.

Hysteresis
A second goal of the present work was to examine the degree to which the adoption of a particular pattern of action persists in time. Flexibility of movement selection is inherent in Bernstein's degrees of freedom problem. Because there is typically a surplus of degrees of freedom, there are many ways to accomplish each task. We might predict that if conditions change, the most efficient method for performing the task would also

change. However, just as redundant degrees of freedom may allow an actor to perform the same task in different ways, having redundant degrees of freedom may also allow the actor to perform different tasks in the same way. In other words, surplus degrees of freedom may permit the conservation of qualitative aspects of performance from one task to another.

How resistant, then, is the motor system to change? Does it tend to persist in previous ways of moving, so that performance at a particular condition can exploit the planning of the immediately previous conditions? The answer is yes: A cogent demonstration of the cost of having to change a motor plan is the parameter remapping effect (Rosenbaum et al., 1986; Rosenbaum, 1991), in which people recite several letters more slowly if the stress that must be imposed on a particular letter is inconsistent each time it is recited.

More global hysteresis effects have been observed in the selection of arm movements in several tasks. In a grasping task, Rosenbaum and Jorgensen (1992) asked subjects to pick up a bar (a section of broomstick handle) and place its marked end on one of 14 different targets whose heights varied in 5-cm increments. For lower targets, it was more comfortable to have grasped the rod with the marked end near the thumb, whereas for higher targets the grip with the thumb away from the marked end was more comfortable. To evaluate hysteresis, the 14 targets were tested sequentially in either ascending or descending order. As predicted, in the middle of the sequence, placement was accomplished more frequently with the grip that had been used for the immediately prior target.

In a drawing task, Meulenbroek and colleagues (1993) required participants to draw a series of lines using a pen that could be displaced by a combination of upper arm, forearm, hand, and finger movements. Over the course of several seconds of continuous oscillation, subjects were required either to consistently increase or consistently decrease line length. As expected, the larger limb segments made relatively greater contributions to longer lines. Furthermore, the contribution of the segments varied depending on recent experience: The contribution of the upper arm was greater in descending trials (progressing from long to short lines), whereas the contribution of the hand was greater in ascending trials.

Finally, in a tapping task, Boak (1989) explored the existence of hysteresis effects. He observed large differences in the contribution of the arm during tapping at 2 taps/sec, depending on whether the subject was just beginning to tap or had recently been tapping at a higher (6 taps/sec) rate. During initial tapping at 2 taps/sec, 60% of the fingertip movement was attributed to forearm flexion about the elbow joint; however, in identical (2 taps/sec) tapping that immediately followed 6 taps/sec, only 30% of the fingertip movement was produced by forearm flexion. Complementary changes were observed for the contribution of the wrist joint to the tapping movement.

To extend Boak's observations and explore hysteresis effects in a more systematic manner, the present experiment was designed to observe how tapping at an intermediate rate varied depending on the immediately preceding performance (fast or slow). On each trial, the subject was required to tap for 20 seconds. For the first 10 seconds, one rate of tapping (0.5 or 3 taps/sec) was required. For the remainder of each trial, a tapping rate of 1.75 taps/sec was required.

9.2 Method

Subjects

Fifteen right-handed college students gave written consent and were paid to participate in the 45-minute experimental session. The data were collected at Hamilton College after approval of the experimental protocol by the Hamilton College Institutional Review Board for the use of human subjects.

Apparatus and Procedure

A vertically oriented bumper (15 × 36 mm), with 4 mm of hard rubber glued to the face, was mounted on a Grass model FT 10D force displacement transducer, equipped with 2 Kgm range springs (Grass Instrument Company, 1984). The center of the bumper was mounted 20.1 cm above a tabletop, approximately 41 cm from the front of the table, and 7 cm from the left side of the table. Subjects sat on a chair 45 cm high at a table 74 cm high and were instructed to align the inside of their left leg with the outer side of the table while placing their right leg comfortably beneath the table. The table was secured to the wall to prevent its vibration due to tapping.

All subjects held the right hand so the middle, ring, and little fingers were flexed, the thumb rested on the flexed middle finger, and the index finger was extended; the forearm was held perpendicular to the bumper. During tapping, the subject was told to keep the eyes fixated on the bumper and shoulders parallel to the front edge of the table. In this position, the subject was able to comfortably strike the center of the bumper with the soft, fleshy area of the fingertip. Seven subjects placed an arm rest (16 cm high, consisting of 12.5 cm hard plastic for stability and 3.5 cm of foam on top for comfort) to restrain the upper part of the right arm; the other eight subjects adopted a slightly different posture that permitted free elbow movement, without noticeable upper arm movement. Because the data acquired using the two postures did not differ, observations using both postures were combined in subsequent analyses.

Each trial began with the finger resting against the bumper during two beeps (6000 Hz, 67 msec tones), which indicated the beginning of the trial. Then, a computer-controlled metronome provided a (3000 Hz, 100 msec tones) model for tapping rate. In the first nine trials, each subject tapped for three 20 second trials at each of the tapping rates (0.5, 1.75, or 3 taps/sec). These nine trials served to acquaint the subject with the tapping task, and will not be discussed further. During the next eight trials, the rate of the metronome tones changed halfway through the trial. In the ascending sequence condition, the metronome began at a rate of 0.5 beats/sec and continued for 10 seconds, then it changed to 1.75 beats/sec for another 10 seconds. In the descending sequence condition, the metronome ran at a rate of 3 beats/sec for 10 seconds, then changed to 1.75 beats/sec for another 10 seconds. Four blocks of each sequence (ascending or descending rate change) were conducted. Throughout the 20 seconds, the force on the bumper was sampled 240 times/sec by digitizing the voltage derived from the force displacement transducer using a bridge circuit.

9.3 Results

Examples of the recorded profile of tapping forces during two representative trials of one subject's performance are shown in figures 9.2 and 9.3. Figure 9.2 shows a single ascending sequence trial. The metronome began at 0.5 beats/sec for 10 seconds, followed by 1.75 beats/sec for 10 seconds. Figure 9.3 shows a descending sequence trial in which 3 beats/sec was followed by 1.75 beats/sec. In each of the figures each of the six rows represents 3.33 seconds. The ordinal number of each tap is indicated by the numbers in Roman type, and the ordinal number of each beat by the numbers in italic type. The interrupted horizontal line in each row denotes contact with the bumper. The continuous line represents the force exerted on the bumper during that contact (downward deflections indicate more force), and the filled circles represent the instant of the metronome beat, counting from the beginning of the trial. Each trial began with the finger in contact with the bumper (labelled tap zero). In the ascending sequence (figure 9.2) the metronome began at 0.5 beats/sec. In this trial, taps 2 through 5 were generated nearly in synchrony with the metronome. Then the subject apparently anticipated the rate change, because the onset of tap 6 relative to the corresponding metronome beat is earlier than the preceding taps, and the subject extended tap 6 through beat 7 (the first beat at the faster rate). As a consequence, tap 7 coincided with metronome beat 8, from which point synchrony between the taps and metronome beats was established at 1.75 beats/sec.

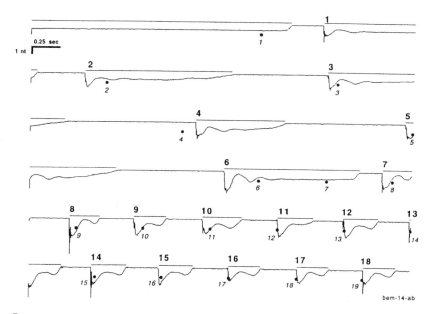

Figure 9.2
Tapping forces produced on the strain-gauge bumper by one subject for 10 seconds of tap-ping at 0.5 taps/sec, followed by 10 seconds of tapping at 1.75 taps/sec. (The continuous line represents the force exerted on the strain gauge during the 20 seconds of tapping. Down-ward movement represents greater force, and the scale indicates 1 newton and 0.25 seconds. The filled circles represent metronome beats. The interrupted line above the strain-gauge record denotes the duration of contact with the strain-gauge bumper, as determined from the force record. Ordinal position is indicated above each tap; numbers in italics indicate the ordinal position of each metronome beat.)

In the descending sequence (figure 9.3), the subject began tapping to 3 beats/sec, achieving synchrony on tap 5 (beat 6). When the metronome slowed after beat 31, tap 31 was made at the time the next beat was ex-pected at the fast rate; two beats were then skipped, and synchrony was established at 1.75 taps/sec on beat 34.

The information of greatest interest in these two trials is the tapping force waveform in the second interval of each trial, when the prescribed tapping rate in both trials was 1.75 taps/sec. Qualitatively, the force pro-file of taps 7 through 18 in the ascending sequence (figure 9.2) is notice-ably different from the force profile of the corresponding taps after the change (33 through 46) in the descending sequence (figure 9.3). Each tap's contact duration was longer in the ascending sequence, and there were two or more peaks of force in each tap. In the descending sequence, by contrast, there was a briefer and monotonic change in tap force dur-ing each contact. We now turn to the statistical tests of these apparent

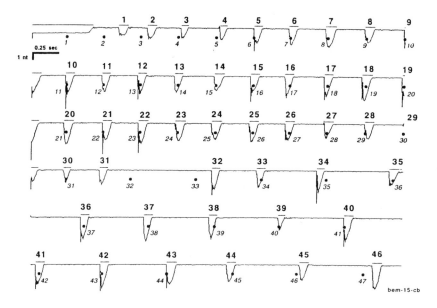

Figure 9.3
Tapping forces produced on the strain-gauge bumper by the same subject as figure 9.2, for 10 seconds of tapping at 3.0 taps/sec, followed by 10 seconds of tapping at 1.75 taps/sec. (Symbols as in figure 9.2.)

differences. First, we analyze tapping before and after the rate change; then, we concentrate on analyses that explicitly compare tapping at the same intermediate metronome rate after slow and fast tapping, in the second half of each trial.

Overall Analyses
In order to focus the analyses on the changes in the tap requirements, statistical analyses were directed at the five consecutive taps, through the last accurate tap, immediately preceding the change in metronome rate (0.5 or 3 beats/sec) and five consecutive taps after the change, beginning with the first tap synchronized with the new metronome beat (1.75 beats/sec).

Considering only these taps, the mean inter-tap intervals are shown in figure 9.4. Tapping intervals were accurate just before the rate change, and after tapping had become synchronized at the new rate.

The sequence of rates in each trial was categorized as either ascending (0.5 taps/sec to 1.75 taps/sec) or descending (3 taps/sec to 1.75 taps/sec). Taps were further categorized as coming from the first (pre-change) or the second (post-change) interval, and by tap number within each of these sequences. Finally, the amount of practice the subject had was repre-

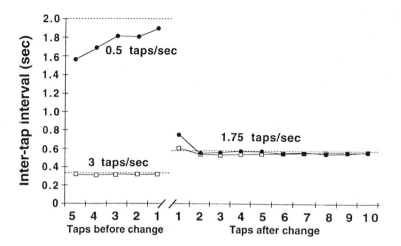

Figure 9.4
Inter-tap intervals for five taps prior to the rate change and 10 taps beginning with the first synchronized tap after the rate change. (Open squares represent tapping in the descending sequence trials, at 3 taps/sec during the first 10 seconds and 1.75 taps/sec during the second 10 seconds. Filled circles represent tapping in the ascending sequence trials, at 0.5 taps/sec during the first 10 seconds and 1.75 taps/sec during the second 10 seconds.)

sented by treating the four blocks separately. The tapping rate data were submitted to a four-way ANOVA in which the factors were sequence (ascending or descending), Interval (pre- or post-change), tap number (one through five), and block (first through fourth).

As expected, tapping rates (measured by the interval separating the beginning of contact on successive taps) differed across metronome beat conditions, as shown by the significant effects of interval, $F(1, 14) = 595.28$, $p = .0001$, sequence, $F(1, 14) = 2096.50$, $p = .0001$, and the interval × sequence interaction, $F(1, 14) = 1424.36$, $p = .0001$. Two interactions involving the tap number were significant, interval × tap number, $F(4, 56) = 13.08$, $p < .005$, and sequence × interval × tap number, $F(4, 56) = 8.63$, $p < .025$ (by conservative F tests; see Myers and Well, 1991). Inspection of figure 9.4 suggests that these interactions may have come about because of different accuracies of the tapping rate in different parts of the trial. During the pre-change interval of the ascending trials, tapping rate was not initially as accurate as during the pre-change interval of the descending trials, presumably because prior to the rate change on each trial there had been fewer taps in the ascending sequence. Nevertheless, by the final pre-change tap subjects had completed matching the metronome beat. In the post-change interval, regardless of sequence, the inter-tap interval was too long prior to the first synchronized tap, but

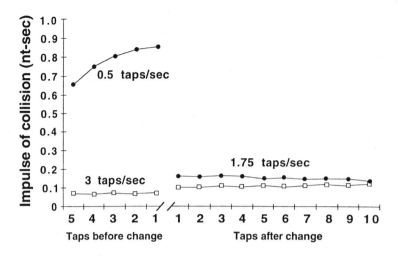

Figure 9.5
Impulse of collision for five taps prior to the rate change and 10 taps beginning with the first synchronized tap after the rate change. (Symbols as in figure 9.4.)

accurate thereafter. None of the other main effects or interactions were significant (by a conservative F test, where appropriate).

We selected two qualitative characteristics of tapping to analyze in detail: the impulse of collision (the integral of the force on the bumper over the duration of contact) and dwell time (the duration of contact with the bumper on each tap). Both of these characteristics could, in principle, vary even though tapping was performed at a particular rate, and even though the subjects' instructions imposed no constraints on them. Overall, the impulse of collision (figure 9.5) was larger in the pre-change interval than in the post-change interval, $F(1, 14) = 10.24$, $p = .0064$, and larger in the ascending sequence than in the descending sequence, $F(1, 14) = 12.43$, $p = .0034$; and there was an interval × sequence interaction, $F(1, 14) = 11.88$, $p = .0039$. No other main effects or interactions were significant.

Changes in dwell time were evaluated by an analysis of variance of dwell time as a function of tap condition. Dwell time (figure 9.6) was, overall, longer in the pre-change Interval, $F(1, 14) = 17.04, p = .001$, and for the ascending sequence, $F(1, 14) = 21.36, p = .0004$, and there was an Interval × Sequence interaction, $F(1, 14) = 19.81$, $p = .0005$. Again, there were no other significant main effects or interactions in the overall analysis of dwell time.

Analysis of Tapping after the Rate Change
The most important comparison of the experiment for the evaluation of hysteresis effects is the characteristics of tapping at the intermediate rate

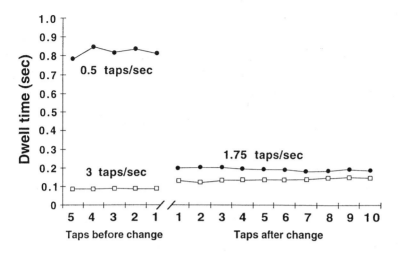

Figure 9.6
Duration of contact with the bumper on each tap, for five taps prior to the rate change and 10 taps beginning with the first synchronized tap after the rate change. (Symbols as in figure 9.4.)

in the post-change interval, depending on whether it had been preceded by fast or slow tapping. To explore these effects, a second set of analyses was conducted on the first 10 taps after the rate change. First, tapping rate after the rate change showed only a marginally significant effect of sequence, $F(1, 14) = 4.57, p = .0507$; however, there was a significant effect of tap number, $F(9, 126) = 5.47, p < .05$ (by a conservative F test). This interaction probably represents the elevated interval prior to the first synchronized tap after the rate change in both sequences (see figure 9.4); however, even if the first synchronized tap after the rate change was excluded from the comparison, tapping at the intermediate rate still differed between ascending and descending sequences, $F(1, 14) = 5.32, p = .0368$. Figure 9.4 shows this difference to be small in absolute terms.

Impulse amplitude after the rate change differed marginally between ascending and descending sequences, $F(1, 14) = 4.59, p = .0502$. Other main effects and interactions did not approach significance.

Finally, in contrast to tapping rate and impulse amplitude, dwell time after the rate change (figure 9.6) was affected by the prior tapping rate. Dwell time at 1.75 taps/sec was longer after 0.5 taps/sec than after 3 taps/ sec, $F(1, 14) = 9.27, p = .0087$, even though the objective definition of the task (tap at 1.75 taps/sec) was identical in both ascending and descending sequences. This difference persisted unchanged throughout the ten post-change taps; in contrast to the result for tapping rate, there was no tap number × sequence interaction, $F(1, 14) = 3.42, .05 < p < .10$.

9.4 Discussion

We observed large and consistent differences in the impulse amplitude and dwell time at different tapping rates, even though the subjects were not instructed to tap in any particular manner. These differences are closely related to differences in the apparent strategy that the subjects used to control tapping. Consistent with the virtual amplitude model, at the fast tapping rate (3 beats/sec) the virtual trajectory of the force of tapping was roughly symmetrical, like a truncated sinusoid, in a manner that is complementary to the observed trajectory of the fingertip in space (compare figure 9.3 with figure 9.1). Deviations from symmetry at the slow tapping rate may be attributed to differences in the reliance on elasticity during tapping at different rates. At 3 taps/sec, the force trajectory was unimodal, monotonic, and symmetrical, which is characteristic of what would be expected in a relatively elastic collision; whereas at 0.5 taps/sec the force trajectory both extended in time and had multiple force peaks, which are clearly inconsistent with an elastic collision. (For convenience, we will refer to the tapping that produces the first pattern of force changes as "elastic" tapping, recognizing that the collision of the fingertip may be only relatively, not perfectly, elastic. We will refer to the second pattern as "intermittent" tapping, to emphasize the biphasic control strategy that it requires).

The pattern of tapping that subjects adopted in the first half of each trial affected the later pattern. In the post-change interval, there were strong hysteresis effects. Dwell times for taps at 1.75 taps/sec were longer when the subject had been tapping at 0.5 taps/sec than at 3 taps/sec. Furthermore, this difference persisted over ten taps, and appears to have become more robust as subjects acquired greater experience with the task.

How are we to explain these hysteresis effects? A persisting theme of recent models of movement planning (for example, Rosenbaum et al., 1995) is the efficiency of movement, which implicitly refers to metabolic efficiency. But the metabolic cost of moving the limbs may not be the only cost that movement planning takes into account. Planning itself is presumably costly, a cost that may be minimized by maintaining similar movement patterns when it is possible to do so without compromising the efficient achievement of the task. Continuing to use the same movement pattern for different tasks has the advantage that less new planning is needed.

The data suggest that it may be possible to induce qualitatively different modes of tapping at intermediate tapping rates: intermittent tapping or elastic tapping. It is possible, therefore, that subjects vary the probability with which they use one method or the other depending on which method prevailed beforehand. The duration and waveform of the force exerted against the strain gauge may serve as a discriminator of the two kinds of tapping motion.

Intermittent tapping, as we have defined it, presumably depends on independent timekeeping of the contact and release phases of motion, whereas elastic tapping has the potential of exploiting the biomechanics of the oscillating segments to help maintain the consistency of the pace of tapping (Hatosopoulos and Warren, 1996). It is not yet clear, however, which tapping strategy is more accurate, or if subjects adopt different modes of tapping depending on their timing accuracy goals. The differences in impulse and dwell time at different tapping rates suggest an intimate connection between rhythm and the dynamics (intensity, in the musical sense) of performance. As Keele, Ivry, and Pokorny (1987) observed, varying the force of tapping may shift or otherwise distort the synchrony of timing.

Elastic tapping requires that people choose to either tap using joints whose resonant frequency matches the task or modulate the stiffness of the joints so the resonant frequency is adjusted to match the task. How might people modulate the stiffness of their joints? A general explanation may be made in terms of the co-contraction of antagonist muscle pairs, in which the stiffness of the joint is increased by greater degrees of co-contraction. While there are several models that describe the effects of different agonist/antagonist patterns of activation, we will discuss these in terms of one specific model, the λ-model of Feldman and Latash (Latash, 1993). The λ-model proposes that changing the central command to a muscle leads to a shift of the force-length characteristic of that muscle. The independently controlled variable of an intact muscle is the threshold for the tonic stretch reflex, referred to as λ.

The λ parameter specifies a threshold length of the muscle at and beyond which contraction of the muscle will be activated. At muscle lengths less than this threshold length, the muscle exerts little or no force, whereas the imposition of a supra-theshold length generates resisting forces in the muscle. Whether or not a muscle is activated depends, then, on both its λ setting and on the length imposed on it. Consider, now, an antagonistic pair of muscles, whose activations maintain a joint in an equilibrium position. What happens when this joint is to move in oscillation? If the λ thresholds are close together, both muscles will be at lengths that result in contraction. Oscillation in one direction will tend to produce a restoring force, which (coupled with energy storage in the muscle and tendon system) will be similar to the restoring force of a simple harmonic oscillator. By contrast, if the λ thresholds of the antagonist pair are more separated, then oscillation in one direction will not immediately elicit restoring contraction in the antagonist. Oscillation in the second case will require explicit alternating changes in the location of the λ threshold in each muscle to accomplish the same extent of joint movement.

Latash distinguishes two different kinds of activation of the antagonistic pairs: a reciprocal command changes equilibrium by moving the λ threshold of agonist and antagonist in opposite directions (one muscle longer, the other shorter). A reciprocal command has the effect of changing the equilibrium position of the joint so that, other things being equal, it assumes a different degree of flexion. A coactivation command, by contrast, changes the compliance characteristic of the joint without changing its equilibrium position. A coactivation command changes compliance by moving the λ threshold of agonist and antagonist in the same direction, both to longer or shorter lengths.

What would be the effects of adopting different degrees of coactivation on waving or tapping performance? Setting the activation threshold (λ) of both agonist and antagonist to shorter lengths (by means of a coactivation command) would increase the effective stiffness of the joint. In the context of the tasks investigated here, this would increase the resonant frequency of the joint and allow the actor to exploit the compliance characteristics of the joint to oscillate more efficiently at a higher frequency.

Setting the activation threshold of both agonist and antagonist to longer lengths, on the other hand, would have the effect of decreasing the effective stiffness of the joint, producing a much shallower length-stiffness function. In intermittent oscillation, movement of the joint would have to be more specifically programmed in each direction using alternating reciprocal commands, without reliance on the automatically elicited restoring force of the antagonist muscle to reverse direction. Therefore, the movements would lack the symmetry observed during harmonic oscillation.

In summary, the present study demonstrates that tapping performance may vary qualitatively, depending not only on the central task requirement (rate) but also on the immediate history of performance. This observation suggests that it will be fruitful to look more closely at the preservation of motor plans and the adaptation of performance in tapping and related tasks. Although the importance of biomechanical efficiency in performance is easily recognized, cognitive efficiency may also play a role in how performance is determined.

Acknowledgments

Preliminary versions of this paper were presented at the fifth New England Sequencing and Timing (NEST) meeting, Providence, March 8, 1996, and at the Psychonomic Society meeting, Chicago, November 3, 1996. We thank Leslie Allen, Kimberly Hurme, Öykü Kalaycioglu, and

Amira Rosberg for assistance with data analysis. Supported in part by the Hamilton College Faculty Research Fund (J.V.), the Howard Hughes Medical Foundation (T.R.M.), NSF grant SBR-94-96290 (J.V. and D.A.R.), and a NIMH Research Scientist Development Award (D.A.R.).

References

Alexander, R. M. (1984). Elastic energy stores in running vertebrates. *American Zoologist, 24,* 85–94.

Bernstein, N. (1967). *The coordination and regulation of movements.* London: Pergamon.

Boak, J. (1989). *Learning strategies within a constraint model of finger, hand, and arm movement.* Honors thesis, Psychology Department, Hamilton College, New York.

Diedrich, F. J. (1990). *Planning of simple tapping movements: The virtual target hypothesis.* Senior fellowship thesis, Psychology Department, Hamilton College, New York.

Feynman, R. P., Leighton, R. B., & Sands, M. (1963). *The Feynman lectures on physics.* Volume 1. Reading, MA: Addison-Wesley.

Grass Instrument Company. (1984). *Force Displacement Transducers, Models FT 03 and FT 10. Instruction Manual.* Quincy, MA: Grass Instrument Company.

Hatsopoulos, N. G., & Warren, W. H. (1996). Resonance tuning in rhythmic arm movements. *Journal of Motor Behavior, 28,* 3–14.

Kay, B. A., Kelso, J. A. S., Saltzman, E. L., & Schöner, G. (1987). Space-time behavior of single and bimanual rhythmical movements: Data and limit cycle model. *Journal of Experimental Psychology: Human Perception and Performance, 13,* 178–192.

Keele, S. W., Ivry, R. I., & Pokorny, R. A. (1987). Force control and its relation to timing. *Jourenal of Motor Behavior, 19,* 96–114.

Latash, M. L. (1993). *Control of Human Movement.* Champaign, IL: Human Kinetics.

Meulenbroek, R. G. J., Rosenbaum, D. A., Thomassen, A. J. W. M, and Schomaker, L. R. B. (1993). Limb-segment selection in drawing behavior. *The Quarterly Journal of Experimental Psychology, 46A,* 273–299.

Myers, J. L., & Well, A. D. (1991). *Research design and statistical analysis.* New York: Harper Collins.

Rosenbaum, D. A. (1991). *Human Motor Control.* San Diego: Academic Press.

Rosenbaum, D. A., & Jorgensen, M. J. (1992). Planning macroscopic aspects of manual control. *Human Movement Science, 11,* 61–69.

Rosenbaum, D. A., Loukopoulos, L. D., Meulenbroek, R., Vaughan, J., & Engelbrecht, S. E. (1995). Planning reaches by evaluating stored postures. *Psychological Review, 102,* 28–67.

Rosenbaum, D. A., Slotta, J., Vaughan, J., & Plamondon, R. (1991). Optimal movement selection. *Psychological Science, 2,* 86–91.

Rosenbaum, D. A., Weber, R. J., Hazelett, W. M., & Hindorff, V. (1986). The parameter remapping effect in human performance: Evidence from tongue twisters and finger fumblers. *Journal of Memory and Language, 25,* 710–725.

Vaughan, J., Rosenbaum, D. A., Diedrich, F. J., & Moore, C. M. (1996). Cooperative selection of movements: The optimal selection model. *Psychological Research, 58,* 254–273.

Wing, A. M. (1977). Effects of type of movement on the temporal precision of response sequences. *British Journal of Mathematical and Statistical Psychology, 30,* 60–72.

Part III

Computational Perspectives

Chapter 10
Broadcast Theory of Timing

David A. Rosenbaum

Abstract

Controlling the timing of behavior is one of the most remarkable achievements of the nervous system. Yet it has proven difficult to explain distinct aspects of timing data with a single control mechanism. Such a mechanism is proposed here. Its key property is reliance on the time needed for signals to travel different distances. With minimal assumptions, the model predicts a wide range of observed timing effects, including changes of interval standard deviation with interval mean, changes of interval standard deviation with change of relative phase (in two-hand coordination tasks), and the existence of special attractor intervals. The theory also provides a basis for common mechanisms underlying perception and production of timed intervals, and a possible answer to the question: How can information about temporally extended events be stored all at once?

10.1 Introduction

No less remarkable than the fact that we can control the timing of our behaviors is the fact that we can store in memory information that makes such timing possible. How do we store timing information? How do we keep in mind, without thinking of it consciously, the information that lets us lace our shoes, dribble basketballs, sing familiar songs, or ride bicycles? The difficulty of the problem is compounded by the fact that the information that makes such temporally extended behaviors possible is stored at any one moment. Thus, information is held simultaneously about behaviors that take seconds, minutes, hours or even days to unfold. How do we store simultaneously what takes time to transpire?

One possibility is that symbols for different temporal relations (e.g., "next" or "wait 150 ms") become associated with different behavioral elements. Thus, the way one remembers how to sing "Happy Birthday" is that the element for /ha/ is linked to the element for /pi/ via a "next" or "wait x time units" node in memory, and so on for other elements. This proposed solution is no solution at all, of course. It merely symbolizes what we wish to explain.

Representing timing with diagrams is another possibility (see figure 10.1). One can depict a delay from one element to another with an arrow,

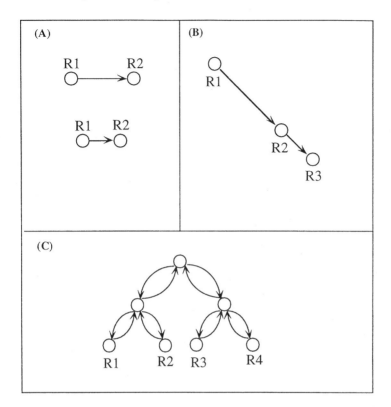

Figure 10.1
Representing timing with arrows. (A) Long or short intervals between response 1 (R1) and response 2 (R2). (B) A series of responses. (C) Hierarchical control of responses where control passes from the top node, down to the next lower left node, then down to the left terminal node (R1), then to the right terminal node (R2), and so forth. The process shown in (C) is called a tree-traversal process.

with the arrowhead being closer to the element that is supposed to come after the delay than the element that is supposed to come before the delay. Such a diagram can be elaborated in various ways. The length of the line can correspond to the length of the delay (figure 10.1A), a series of arrows can be connected to shows series of events (figure 10.1B), or the arrows can be embedded in a hierarchy (figure 10.1C) to account for the nesting relations suggested by the timing and accuracy of performance (MacKay, 1987; Restle, 1970; Rosenbaum, Kenny, and Derr, 1983; Simon, 1972). Again, however, drawing arrows merely makes visible one's conception of control, but begs the question of mechanism.

Relying on oscillators would seem to be another possible solution. Neural activity is rhythmic (Cohen, Rossignol, and Grillner, 1988), and the rhythmic properties of nervous activity influence behavior. That oscillations of one arm are influenced by oscillations of the other arm in ways that are not merely mechanical (von Holst, 1939; Swinnen, Heuer, and Casaer, 1994), attests to the functional importance of such effects. Still, the question remains: If the hand first goes to position *A* and then to position *B*, what information, short of instructions by a homunculus, directs the hand to move initially to *A* rather than *B*? The question remains of how timing is memorially represented.

In this chapter, I will present a theory that provides a solution to this problem. I will describe the theory informally at first and then more formally afterwards. Then I will explain why I believe the theory may help address some long-standing issues in the study of timing, most notably the existence of phenomena that have seemed explainable only in mutually exclusive theoretical frameworks. The final section concerns issues for future research.

10.2 Broadcast Theory

Overview of the Theory

The core of the theory is that the representation of timing takes advantage of neural processes, which themselves take time. The basis for the idea is simple. It takes time for signals to traverse neural fibers. Suppose then, that there is a connection between one neural element *A* and another neural element *B* such that the neuron that joins *A* to *B* sends signals from *A* to *B* but not the reverse. Thus, if *A* fires, *B* fires afterward, but if *B* fires, *A* does not fire afterward. The delay between the firing of *A* and the firing of *B* depends on the time for the signal to travel from *A* to *B*. The length of the delay between *A* and *B* can be controlled by forming a connection between *A* and *B* via a fiber that has the desired delay. Simple trial-and-error learning can lead to the appropriate connections being formed.

There is precedent for this idea. Helmholtz (1850/1948) measured the speed of nerve conduction and showed that, contrary to earlier belief, nerve conduction is sufficiently slow for longer neural distances to lead to longer signal delays. Pavlov (1928), in his studies of classical conditioning, argued that as neural excitation travels, it provides a time-varying gradient of excitation. Similar ideas have been considered in modern studies of spreading activation in cognitive networks (e.g., Collins and Loftus, 1975). Neurophysiological research on the cerebellum has also suggested that delays may be controlled by adjusting the number of synapses crossed by nerve signals as the signals travel along parallel fibers in the cerebellar cortex (Braitenberg and Atwood, 1958).

The theory proposed here is more explicitly concerned with timing than previous spreading-activation models (including Pavlov's), and is meant to provide a style of timing control that is richer, and that allows for longer delays, than the simple delay-line approach from cerebellar modeling (where controlled delays can typically last no more than a few milliseconds). The theory relies on geometry to impose constraints on the way timing and sequencing are controlled. These constraints force one to find solutions to timing and sequencing problems that seem to correspond to the kinds of solutions people (and animals) use. Curiously, these solutions seem to account for results which so far have appeared explainable only with mutually exclusive theories.

A major goal of the theory is to address the issue with which we started: How can information be held in memory about many temporally extended behaviors? The problem is solved by using space to represent temporal relations.

Assumptions of the Theory
The theory has six assumptions.

1. Units in an n-dimensional space receive and emit signals. The space I consider in this paper is 2-dimensional. The units being modeled need not be neurons but are meant to be neurologically plausible.

2. A unit can only receive a signal to which it is tuned, and when a unit receives such a signal, it transmits a signal. If unit B is tuned to unit A, then when unit B receives a signal from unit A, it transmits a signal. Tuning is all-or-none. It can be conceptualized as the closing of a switch (at which time receipt of the incoming signal is possible) or opening of a switch (at which time receipt of the incoming signal is impossible). If the switch is closed for the line allowing transmission of signals from A to B, then when A transmits a signal, B receives it and then transmits a signal on its own. Signal lines are assumed to allow for transmission of signals in just one direction (as is true of axons). Thus, the line from A to B allows for the transmission of signals from A to B but not the reverse.

3. A signal that is transmitted by a unit is a single pulse that travels away from the unit in all possible directions (i.e., along all the lines emanating from it) at one speed in a given transmission. Because the transmission is nonspecific, extending along all the lines emanating from the source unit, the transmission of a signal is like the sending of a signal from a broadcast source—hence the name *broadcast* theory.

4. When signals are transmitted from a unit on different occasions, the speed of the signals varies. The exact form of the variation need not be specified at this point in the theory's development.

5. Each unit involved in transmitting a signal adds a delay with a nonzero mean and variance to the signal's total travel time.

6. Because transmission times are affected by the lengths of the lines over which they travel, and because the maximum length of any line is relatively small given anatomical constraints, there is a maximum delay that is possible between the transmission of a signal from one unit and the receipt of that signal by another unit to which the sending unit is connected. For this reason, other units may have to be included to generate longer delays.

10.3 Clock Models Versus Coupled-Oscillator Models

I now discuss the predictions that arise from these assumptions. In this section, I focus on a debate in the timing literature: Is timing controlled with clocks or with coupled oscillators? An oscillator is a mechanism that displays periodicity or quasi-periodicity. Coupled oscillators are systems for which certain frequency combinations are special (e.g., more stable than others). A clock is an oscillator that also has a counter. In clock models, special events (e.g., initiations of responses) are triggered when a critical count has been reached.

As seen in the following, several phenomena have been obtained in similar behavioral contexts but have been explained exclusively in terms of one view or the other. This state of affairs is troubling, for it seems unlikely that results from experiments that vary only slightly in what the subject must do (e.g., tap with one finger or two) could be attributable to wholly different mechanisms. Broadcast theory provides a unified account of these phenomena.

Clock Models

Consider the production of a response at different rates. This task was popularized by Wing and Kristofferson (1973), who developed a two-process model to account for the associated results (see figure 10.2A). One process is waiting to trigger responses, under the control of a central timekeeper or clock. The other process is executing responses after they have been triggered, subject to a motor delay. Wing and Kristofferson assumed that the clock process and motor-delay process are stochastically independent. They derived separate estimates of the variance of the clock process and the variance of the motor-delay process. Representative data from Wing and Kristofferson are shown in figure 10.2B. As the mean interresponse interval increased, the estimated clock variance increased, but the estimated motor-delay variance remained roughly constant.

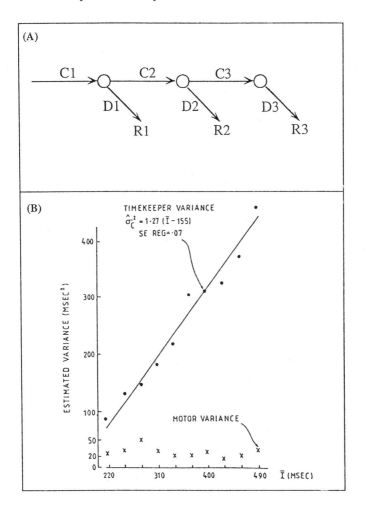

Figure 10.2
Two-process timing model and representative data of Wing and Kristofferson (1973). (A)
The two-process model, where responses, R1, R2, R3, ... are centrally triggered after clock
delays, C1, C2, C3, ..., respectively, and motor delays, D1, D2, D3, ..., respectively. (B)
Data from a finger-tapping experiment, reprinted from Wing (1980).

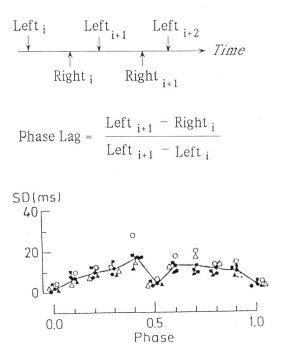

Figure 10.3
Task and results of the phase-lag study of Yaminishi, Kawato, and Suzuki (1980). Top panel: Task, and definition of phase lag. Bottom panel: standard deviation of inter-response interval as a function of phase lag, reprinted from Yaminishi, Kawato, and Suzuki (1980).

Coupled Oscillators

Next consider data that have been taken to support a coupled oscillator model rather than a clock model. The data to be discussed were reported by Yaminishi, Kawato, and Suzuki (1980). Their paradigm is shown in the top panel of figure 10.3. Subjects repeatedly made responses with the left hand followed, about 1 second later, by the right hand. The main independent variable was the phase lag of the left and right hands. Phase lag was defined as the time between the right-hand response and the following left-hand response, divided by the time between the two left-hand responses bounding the right-hand response. When the left hand and right hand responded in a regularly alternating fashion, the phase lag was .5. When the left hand and right hand responded simultaneously, the phase lag was 0 or, equivalently, 1; whether a phase lag is 0 or 1 simply depends on the cycle to which the right-hand response is nominally assigned. Intermediate delays had intermediate phase lags.

The results of the work of Yaminishi, Kawato, and Suzuki (1980) are shown in the bottom panel of figure 10.3. The standard deviation of the interresponse intervals was minimal at phase lags of 0, .5, and 1, and reached maxima at phase lags between these values.

Yaminishi et al. explained their data by assuming that the two hands are controlled with two oscillators, one for the left hand and one for the right hand. The oscillators are coupled so that certain phase lags (0, .5, and 1) are stable, whereas other phase lags are unstable.

The Apparent Incommensurability of the Two Models

Can both sets of results be accounted for with a single model? First, consider the possibility that the results of Yaminishi, Kawato, and Suzuki can be explained with a clock model like the one put forth by Wing and Kristofferson (1973). One can try to explain the results of Yaminishi and colleagues with such a model by assuming that *one* clock delay is required for phase lags of 0, .5, and 1 because these phase lags entail only one interval between (nonsimultaneous) responses, whereas *two* clock delays are required for phase lags other than 0, .5, and 1 because these phase lags entail more than one interval between (nonsimultaneous) responses. The lower variability of the 0, .5, and 1 phase lags can then be attributed to the reduced complexity of using one clock delay instead of two. A difficulty with this approach, however, is that for phase lags of 0 or 1 the standard deviation should be greater than for the phase lag of .5, because the clock delay is twice as long when the phase lag is 0 or 1 than when the phase lag is .5. Yet the standard deviations were about the same when the phase lags were 0, 1, or .5 in the study of Yaminishi, Kawato, and Suzuki. Thus, the extension of Wing and Kristofferson's model will not work.

A second difficulty for Wing and Kristofferson's model as applied to the results of Yaminishi, Kawato, and Suzuki is that the standard deviations for phase lags other than 0, .5, and 1 are not uniform. Instead, they reach a maximum just below and just above and .5. This is problematic for the application of Wing and Kristofferson's model because the sum of the two clock delays required for phase lags other than 0, .5, and 1 should be constant. In other words, because Wing and Kristofferson assumed that variance is linear with clock delay, variance (or standard deviation) should be the same for all intervals corresponding to phase lags whose total clock delays are equal. They are not, however, which poses a problem for the extension of Wing and Kristofferson's model to the results of Yaminishi, Kawato, and Suzuki (For another attempt to explain the results of Yaminishi, Kawato, and Suzuki with a variant of Wing and Kristofferson's model, see Wing, Church, and Gentner, 1989. This variant of the basic two-process also had problems with the Yaminishi, Kawato, and Suzuki data.)

Next, consider the possibility of extending the coupled oscillator model of Yaminishi, Kawato, and Suzuki to Wing and Kristofferson's data. To pursue this possibility, one would have to allow that one or more oscillators could control the delays to be produced and that none of the oscillators could have a counter. (Recall, that a clock is an oscillator with a counter.) The only way to achieve this form of control would be to vary the rate of oscillation of a single oscillator, so each response occurred at the completion of one cycle, and the period of that cycle varied with the delay to be produced. The problem with this idea is that variation in the period would have to be as large as the greatest delay that could be produced between two responses. Because this delay is effectively infinite, the period of a biological oscillator would also have to be effectively infinite as well, which is doubtful. It is also difficult to accept the idea that the variance (or standard deviation) of interresponse intervals could increase with the mean of the interval if some sort of counter or accumulator were not introduced (but see Church and Broadbent, 1990). Classically, the increasing-variance result has been ascribed to variability in the rate at which a counter accumulates endogenous "pulses" generated through a random process (e.g., a Poisson source). Without such pulses, it is doubtful that the increasing-variance effect could be obtained.

To summarize the preceding arguments, the status quo is that there are two sets of data, one for tasks in which subjects produce delays of varying magnitude, and one for tasks in which subjects produce polyrhythms. The model developed for each data set appears unable to account for the other.

Application of Broadcast Theory to "Clock Model Results"

Now consider how the broadcast system controls response rates. Focus on the tapping task of Wing and Kristofferson (1973) (figure 10.4). Suppose a unit transmits signals that give rise to an overt response. Call this an *output* unit (labeled O in figure 10.4). Units that do not directly give rise to overt responses are called *trigger* units. In the left panel of figure 10.4, A is a trigger unit for O because O is tuned to A. It also happens that A is tuned to O. Because of the mutual tuning relation, when A transmits a signal, after the signal has traveled to O, O transmits a signal that returns to A, A in turn transmits a signal that is picked up by O, and so on. The mean time for the signal to travel between A and O is just the distance between the units divided by the mean signal speed. When O transmits a signal, the signal is also picked up by the appropriate muscles (that is, the muscles tuned to O), which permits an overt response following a motor delay. The mean delay between successive productions of the overt response is simply the mean time for the signal to travel from O to A and back to O again, plus any difference between the mean motor delays for the two responses.

To increase the delay between successive responses, all that is needed is to tune O to a trigger unit that is farther away (see figure 10.4, right

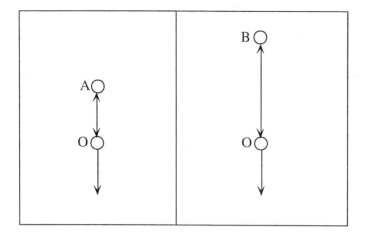

Figure 10.4
Control of interresponse intervals according to broadcast theory. Left panel: Short intervals produced with a unit, *A*, close to an output unit, *O*. Right panel: Longer intervals produced with a unit, *B*, farther from *O*.

panel). Here *O* is tuned to a trigger unit, *B*, that is farther from *O* than *A*. The mean delay between successive productions of the response is longer than before because the signal has a longer distance to travel between the output unit and the trigger unit.

How does this account for the variance of interresponse intervals? First, it should be clear that the variance of the motor delay remains constant as the response rate changes. This is because the motor delay does not change with response rate.

The variance of the delay between successive activations of the output unit, which corresponds to the clock delay in Wing and Kristofferson's model, should increase with the time for the signal to travel from the output unit to the trigger unit and back again. It happens that the variance should increase with the *square* of the mean travel time. This follows from the fact that as the mean travel time increases, the signal covers a longer distance. The variance of the time to cover the distance can be arrived at by multiplying the variance of the signal speed by a constant corresponding to the distance. The variance of a random variable multiplied by a constant equals the constant *squared* times the variance (Hays, 1988, p. 870). Hence, the theory predicts that the variance of the waiting process should increase with the square of the wait, not directly with the wait, contrary to Wing and Kristofferson's model (see Church and Gibbon 1982 for a similar argument). In fact, the preponderance of evidence in the timing literature now indicates that time-interval variance increases with the square of the timed interval. Ivry and Hazeltine (1995) reviewed this literature and provided new supportive data for the interval-squared relationship in three finger-tapping experiments. They also indicated that Wing and Kristofferson's (1973) own graphs relating interval variance to interval mean could be replotted to yield more sensible fits when interval-variance is plotted against the square of the interval mean than when interval-variance is plotted against the interval mean itself. In the former case, the best-fitting straight line has a positive intercept, whereas in the latter case, the best-fitting straight line has a negative intercept. Only a positive intercept can be sensibly interpreted as a baseline noise level. A negative intercept is meaningless.

Application of Broadcast Theory to "Coupled-Oscillator Results"
Consider next how broadcast theory can account for the results of Yamanishi, Kawato, and Suzuki (1980) (figure 10.5). First consider the production of left-and right-hand responses in regular alternation, with a phase lag of .5 (upper left panel). Regular alternation between two responses can be achieved with mutual tuning between their output units. The output unit for the right hand, R, is tuned to the output unit for the left hand, L, and vice versa. If L is activated by a trigger unit, A, it transmits a signal that is picked up by R, R in turn transmits a signal that is picked up by L, and this back-and-forth signaling process continues until the tuning relation is broken. The variance of the delay between the left- and right-hand responses depends on the variance of the delay between the activations of the output units.

Now consider the top right panel of figure 10.5. This panel shows how the broadcast system achieves production of simultaneous rather than regularly alternating responses. Here the phase lag is 0 or, equivalently, 1. To produce simultaneous responses, both output units are tuned to the trigger unit, A. When A is activated, it transmits a signal that is picked up at the same time, on the average, by the two output units. Each output unit transmits a signal that is picked up by the other output unit, so the signals from the two output units pass back and forth, without the continued involvement of A, as was the case when the phase lag was .5. The variance of the delay between the activations of L and R is exactly what it was when the responses were produced in an alternating rather than simultaneous fashion.

Finally, consider phase lags other than 0, .5, or 1 (middle panel of figure 10.5). A simple way to produce other phase lags is to have mutual tuning between the output unit for the left-hand response, L, and a trigger unit, A, that is located anywhere on a circle around L, such that the radius of the circle corresponds to half the cycle time for the sequence. When A transmits a signal, the signal passes to L, L transmits a signal that reactivates

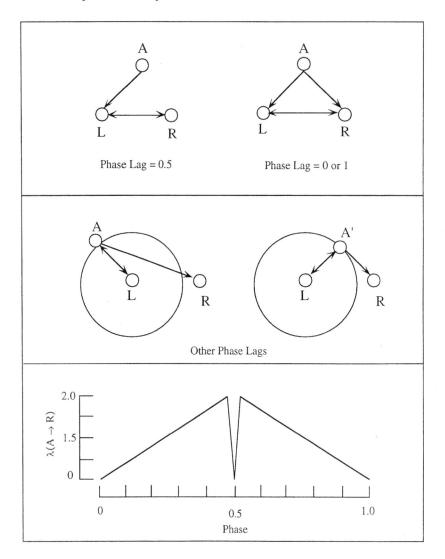

Figure 10.5
Broadcast theory's account of phase lag effects. Top and middle panels: Production of different phase lags depending on the location of a trigger unit A or A' in relation the output units
L and R for the left and right hand, respectively. The double arrow between L and R ensures
continued transmission between these units. Bottom panel: Length, λ, of the line between A
and R as a function of phase lag.

A, A then transmits a signal that returns to L, and so forth. The time for the signal to travel from L to A and back to L is the cycle time for the left-hand response. If A can also activate the output unit for the right-hand, R, then when A transmits a signal, it activates R as well as L. Varying the location of A on the circle around L affects the delay between the activations of L and R, which in turn alters the phase lag of the two output units.

The effect of shifting the location of A on the variability of timing can be understood by considering the formula for the length, $\lambda(A \rightarrow R)$ of the line connecting A to R:

$$\lambda(A \rightarrow R) = [(\lambda(A \rightarrow L) \cos \theta)^2 + (\lambda(A \rightarrow L) \sin \theta)^2]^{1/2}, \tag{10.1}$$

where θ is the angle of the line AL with respect to the horizontal. The bottom panel of figure 10.5 shows $\lambda(A \rightarrow R)$ as a function of phase lag. The length of the line from A to L is constant, so the sum of the two line lengths looks like this function. Because the variance of the time for a signal to travel along a line increases with the square of the line's length, the standard deviation of the travel time increases directly with the line's length. Therefore, the standard deviation function looks just like the function shown in the bottom panel of figure 10.5. This plot looks very much like the standard deviation data of Yaminishi, Kawato, and Suzuki (1980). For the present theoretical curve, there is a drop at the phase lag of 0.5 because no trigger unit is required during ongoing production of the response sequence, so the length of the line connecting A to R effectively goes to zero, and so does the standard deviation of the travel time between A and R.

These simulations, applied to the results of Yaminishi, Kawato, and Suzuki (1980) and the results of Wing and Kristofferson (1973), lead to the conclusion that a single model can account for results that previously were explained only with a clock model or only with a coupled-oscillator model.

10.4 Special Intervals

Recall that according to broadcast theory, the variance of delays between units should grow linearly with the square of the distance, d, between the units. Suppose this relation is written $\text{Var}(d) = kd^2$, where k is a positive constant. Recall as well that when a unit is interposed between two output units, it adds its own delay and variance. Call this delay u and call the associated variance $\text{var}(u)$. For convenience, assume $\text{var}(u) = ku^2$. If the actor's job is to minimize the variance of produced time intervals, it may be advantageous to subdivide the intervals, using an intermediate unit. That is, for $d = d_1 + d_2 + u$, it may be the case that

$$kd^2 > k(d_1)^2 + k(d_2)^2 + ku^2. \tag{10.2}$$

Would this strategy have any observed effect on timing behavior? A strong hint that it would comes from the observation that the square of a number is always larger than the sum of the squares of its additive components, provided none of the additive components is 0 (e.g., $4^2 = 16$, but $2^2 + 2^2 = 8$). From this observation, it follows that it is advisable to subdivide any interval greater than u.

Consider an interval d that is either shorter than u, equal to u, or larger than u. As seen in figure 10.6, when d is less than u, $\text{var}(d) = kd^2$. When $d = u$, it is possible to subdivide d such that $d = d_1 + d_2 + u$, in which case $\text{var}(d)$ drops from kd^2 to $k(d_1{}^2 + d_2{}^2 + u^2)$, assuming that the delays, d_1, d_2, and u, are independent of one another; the drop amounts to $k(-d_1{}^2 - u^2)$. If d must get still larger, there will come a point when its constituent delays can be subdivided further. The resulting variance function will be scalloped, as shown in figure 10.6A.

Discerning scallops in obtained interval variance data could be difficult in practice. Unless the decrease in variance associated with subdivision were large, a scallop function would be hard to distinguish statistically from a linear or other monotonic function. However, there is a consequence of the scallops which might be easier to detect than the scallops themselves. The existence of the scallops implies that there should be special intervals along the required-interval axis whose variances will be lower than the variance of *shorter* intervals. If these special intervals exist, and if subjects try to minimize interval variances while also producing intervals that are approximately correct, there should be "attractor intervals" that have especially low variance. If one plotted the subjects' produced intervals against the required intervals, the data would like roughly like the hypothetical data shown in figure 10.6B. Moreover, if one fitted a straight line to the produced intervals and then plotted the deviations of the observed points from the best-fitting straight line, the resulting residual function would be a zigzag like the one shown in figure 10.6C.

Data like these have been reported by Collyer, Broadbent, and Church (1992, 1994), as shown in figure 10.7; also see chapter 3). Collyer and colleagues suggested that these results reflect an underlying oscillator; in fact, they referred to their obtained functions as an oscillator signature. The analysis presented here suggests a possible source for the oscillator signature.

10.5 Perception of Time Intervals

So far, I have only discussed production of time intervals, but production cannot be discussed without reference to perception. Aside from the fact that it is impossible to draw a dividing line between the perceptual system and the production system, all experiments on time production neces-

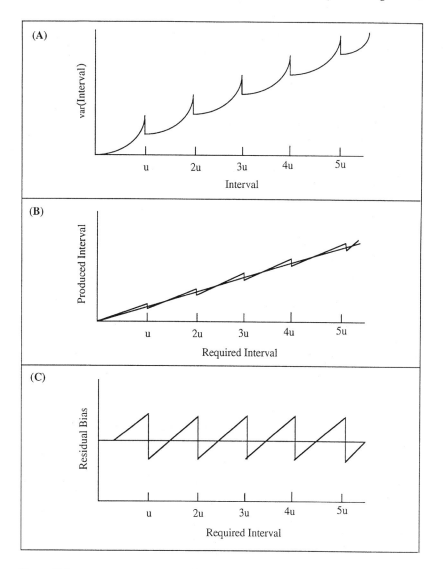

Figure 10.6
Broadcast theory's prediction of special intervals: (A) how interval variance should vary with interval size; (B) how produced intervals should vary with required intervals; (C) how deviations from the straight line relating produced intervals to required intervals should depend on required intervals. *u* denotes the time for a signal to pass through a unit.

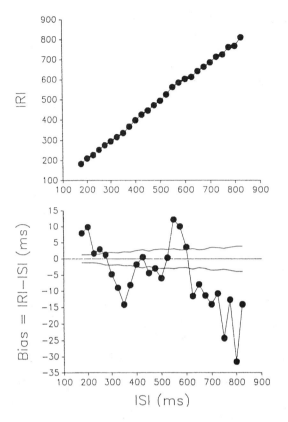

Figure 10.7
Data reported by Collyer, Broadbent, and Church (1992). (Top) Produced inter-reponse intervals as a function of inter-stimulus interval (ISI). (Bottom) Bias data, defined as the deviation of each point from the best-fitting straight line for the produced intervals. Reprinted from Collyer, Broadbent, and Church (1992). Reprinted with permission.

sarily engage perception. For example, the tapping studies of Wing and Kristofferson (1973) used an induction phase in which subjects heard series of tones that defined the rhythm to be manually reproduced.

Broadcast theory provides insights into the perception of time. Consider figure 10.8, which shows how the system can recognize delays. A single input unit, I, receives repeated inputs every t msec (figure 10.8A). The first time I receives an input, it broadcasts a signal. Suppose that J is tuned to I and that K is tuned both to J and I. Suppose as well that the distances $\lambda(I \rightarrow J)$, $\lambda(J \rightarrow K)$, and $\lambda(I \rightarrow K)$ are such that K receives roughly simultaneous inputs from I and J beginning with the second activation of I. By virtue of where K is located, it signifies a particular delay

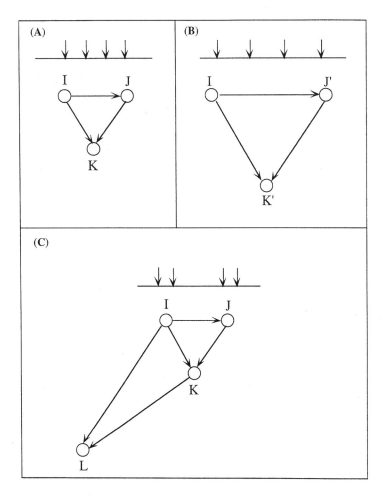

Figure 10.8
Timing of inputs. (A) Timing of regularly delivered inputs received by unit *I*, registered by unit *K*. (B) Timing of more slowly delivered inputs received by unit *I*, registered by unit *K'*. (C) Timing of a rhythmic pattern received by unit *I*, registered by unit *L*. The time scale of the input events (vertical lines descending onto a time line) is arbitrary.

between activations of I. Other delays can be similarly recognized. For example, as seen in figure 10.8B, a unit K' can signal the receipt of inputs to input I every $t + x$ msec.

More complex rhythms can also be recognized, as shown in figure 10.8C. Here, in addition to units I, J, and K, a unit L occupies a position where it receives simultaneous inputs from I and K. L can indicate the more complex short-long alternating pattern shown in figure 10.8C. Other complex patterns, and more complex patterns, can be recognized in a similar fashion. More complex patterns can be recognized by having higher-order units. The likelihood of recognizing a complex pattern should diminish the more complex the pattern is because the number of connections, and so the variance of common arrival times at a candidate recognition unit, should increase with pattern complexity.

10.6 Common Timing for Perception and Production

Broadcast theory provides a way of understanding the relation between production and perception. Previous research has indicated that timing of perceived events and timing of produced events (responses) rely on the same mechanism (Ivry and Hazeltine, 1995; Rosenbaum and Patashnik, 1980). Within the context of broadcast theory, it would be desirable to use the same units for perception and production. That is, if a set of units encoded perceived intervals, it would be economical to have that same set of units underlie production of the same intervals. The theory easily allows for such an arrangement. As shown in figure 10.9, if the signal directions used to perceive an interval (panel A) are reversed (panel B), the interval that is perceived can also be generated.

An interesting problem arises. One might think that signals could run in both directions between the same units to achieve perception and production simultaneously, as shown in figure 10.9C; however, this leads to a breakdown. Desired timing relations fall apart, and the signaling goes on forever. A way to address this problem is to have an architecture like the one shown in figure 10.9D, where the production side is the mirror image of the perception side. Thus, the same type of mechanism is used for perceptual timing and motor timing, but the functional linkages on the production side are the opposite of those on the perception side.

10.7 Final Remarks

In this chapter, I have pursued the simple idea that the nervous system relies on distances between units to regulate timing. A theory based on this idea has several interesting properties. Among them are the capacity to model changes in the timing of successive responses, the inability to

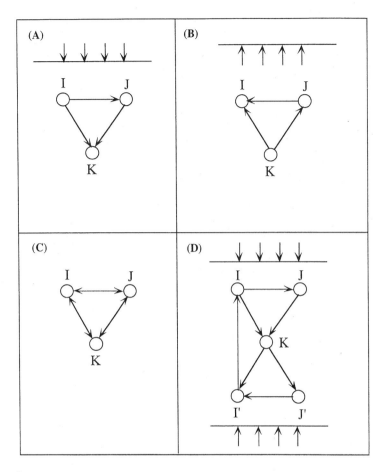

Figure 10.9
Perceptual-motor coupling. (A) Timing of inputs received by unit *I*. (B) Equal timing of outputs generated from unit *I*, triggered from *K*. (C) Bidirectional connections among units *I*, *J*, and *K*. (D) Mirror-image arrangement that enables timing of outputs generated from *I'* to correspond to timing of inputs recevied from *I*. The time scale of the input events (vertical lines descending onto a time line) and output events (vertical lines ascending onto a time line) is arbitrary.

produce all timing relations with equal ease, the ability to perceive temporal patterns, and the ability to understand how perceptual timing and motor timing can rely on the same mechanism. Some issues remain, however:

1. The modeling described here used units in a 2-dimensional space. It remains to be seen what will happen when the space is extended to 3 dimensions.

2. No mechanism has been included for the dissipation of energy. Such a mechanism might be reuired to halt the passing of signals.

3. More details need to be worked out concerning the development of tuning relations between or among units. Having a homunculus who decides which connections should be formed is inadequate. Presumably, relying on correlations between activations of units, as in Hebbian learning, would be a way to address this point.

4. One wonders whether a more elegant method might be possible to achieve common timing of perceptual and motor events. It would be nice only to change the directionality of signaling with the same units, and not to invoke mirror-image architectures.

These points aside, broadcast theory has some attractive features. The most important is that it relies on dependencies between distance and signal speed to impose strong constraints on the regulation of timing. Recent evidence indicates that neural delays may be far more important than previously recognized because the timing of neural events may provide a basis for perceiving *what* has happened, not just *when* things have happened (Singer, 1993). Insofar as the synchronous activity of neurons is mediated by neural delays, it may be that a system like the one suggested here is used even for tasks where timing per se has not been traditionally seen as crucial.

Acknowledgments

This work was supported by grant SBR-94-96290 from the National Science Foundation, a Research Scientist Development Award (KO2 MH00977-03A1) from the National Institute of Mental Health, and a grant from the Research and Graduate Studies Office, College of the Liberal Arts, Pennsylvania State University. The theory was first conceived at the Netherlands Institute for Advanced Study (1989–1990). A preliminary presentation of the theory appeared in a technical report, *Five College Cognitive Science Paper*, #90-2 (University of Massachusetts, Amherst), and was presented at the 31st annual meeting of the Psychonomic Society (New Orleans, Lousiana, November 16–18, 1990) as well as at NEST 1 (Amherst, Massachusetts, January 10, 1991). I thank Russell Church and Charles Collyer for helpful comments.

References

Braitenberg, V., & Atwood, R. P. (1958). Morphological observations on the cerebellar cortex. *Journal of Comparative Neurology, 109*, 1–34.

Church, R., & Broadbent, H. (1990). Alternative representations of time, number, and rate. *Cognition, 37*, 55–81.

Church, R., & Gibbon, J. (1982). Temporal generalization. *Journal of Experimental Psychology: Animal behavior processes, 8*, 165–186.

Cohen, A. H., Rossignol, S., & Grillner, S. (eds.). (1988). *Neural control of rhythmic movements in vertebrates*. New York: John Wiley & Sons.

Collins, A., & Loftus, E. (1975). A spreading activation theory of semantic processing. *Psychological Review, 5*, 85–88.

Collyer, C. E., Broadbent, H. A., & Church, R. M. (1992). Categorical time production: Evidence for discrete timing in motor control. *Perception & Psychophysics, 51*, 134–144.

Collyer, C. E., Broadbent, H. A., & Church, R. M. (1994). Preferred rates of repetitive tapping and categorical time production. *Perception & Psychophysics, 55*, 443–453.

Hays, W. L. (1988). *Statistics* (4th ed.). New York: Holt, Rinehart and Winston.

Helmholtz, H. von. (1850/1948). On the rate of transmission of the nerve impulse. In W. Dennis (ed.), *Readings in the history of psychology* (pp. 197–198). New York: Appleton Century Crofts.

Holst, E. von (1939). Die relative Koordiatnion als Phänomenon und als Methode zentralnervöse Funktionsanalyze. *Erg. Physiol., 42*, 228–306. [English translation in Holst, E. von. (1973). Relative coordination as a phenomenon and as a method of analysis of central nervous functions. In *The behavioural physiology of animal and man: The collected papers of Erich von Holst* (Vol. 1), R. Martin (trans.)]. London: Methuen.

Ivry, R. B., & Hazeltine, R. E. (1995). Perception and production of temporal intervals across a range of durations: Evidence for a common timing mechanism. *Journal of Experimental Psychology: Human Perception and Performance, 21*, 3–18.

MacKay, D. G. (1987). *The organization of perception and action: A theory for language and other cognitive skills?* New York: Springer-Verlag.

Pavlov, I. P. (1928). *Lectures on conditioned reflexes*. New York: International Publishers.

Restle, F. (1970). Theory of serial pattern learning: Structural trees. *Psychological Review, 77*, 481–495.

Rosenbaum, D. A., Kenny, S., & Derr, M. A. (1983). Hierarchical control of rapid movement sequences. *Journal of Experimental Psychology: Human Perception and Performance, 9*, 86–102.

Rosenbaum, D. A., & Patashnik, O. (1980). A mental clock-setting process revealed by reaction times. In G. E. Stelmach & J. Requin (eds.), *Tutorials in motor behavior* (pp. 487–499). Amsterdam: North-Holland.

Simon, H. A. (1972). Complexity and the representation of patterned sequences of symbols. *Psychological Review, 79*, 369–382.

Singer, W. (1993). Synchronization of cortical activity and its putative role in information processing and learning. *Annual Review of Physiology, 55*, 349–374.

Swinnen, S. P., Heuer, H., & Casaer, P. (eds.). (1994). *Interlimb coordination: Neural, dynamical, and cognitive constraints*. San Diego: Academic Press.

Wing, A. M. (1980). The long and short of timing in response sequences. In G. E. Stelmach & J. Requin (eds.), *Tutorials in motor behavior* (pp. 469–486). Amsterdam: North-Holland.

Wing, A. M., Church, R., M., & Gentner, D. R. (1989). Variability in the timing of responses during repetitive tapping with alternate hands. *Psychological Research, 51*, 28–37.

Wing, A. M., & Kristofferson, A. B. (1973). Response delays and the timing of discrete motor responses. *Perception & Psychophysics, 14*, 5–12.

Yaminishi, J., Kawato, M., & Suzuki, R. (1980) Two coupled oscillators as a model for the coordinated finger tapping by both hands. *Biological Cybernetics, 37*, 219.

Chapter 11

Dynamics of Human Intersegmental Coordination: Theory and Research

Polemnia G. Amazeen, Eric L. Amazeen, and Michael T. Turvey

Abstract

A dynamical approach to human intersegmental coordination is presented that has as its historical foundation the physiological theories of Bernstein and von Holst. Mathematically formalized, this dynamical model makes predictions regarding stable patterns of coordination as a function of both competition and cooperation between the component limb segments. A survey of major results provides both confirmation of the model's predictions and directions for expansion, including the integration of traditionally psychological phenomena such as handedness, attention, and learning. The future of the dynamical approach is considered in the light of symmetry group theory and the processes operating at the level of the coordinative subsystems.

11.1 Introduction

The success of any line of research relies on the appropriateness of the description given to the phenomenon being studied. In the present chapter, a dynamical approach to human intersegmental coordination is presented that takes as its roots observations made by two physiologists, Nikolai Bernstein and Erich von Holst. The approach was formalized mathematically with dynamical concepts originally developed for the description of self-sustained oscillations in nonbiological phenomena. Characteristic of the dynamical model is its ability to describe coordination with concepts that are indifferent to the particular substrate (e.g., neural, physiological, psychological, computational, social) supporting the movement (Kelso, 1995; Kugler and Turvey, 1987). The advantage of such a description is that the same laws can be shown to hold across superficially different phenomena, lending credence to the notion that dynamics makes possible the integration of neural, computational, and psychological influences on human intersegmental coordination.

11.2 Historical Antecedents: Bernstein and von Holst

Although the mathematical tools necessary for a dynamical approach to motor control were not fully developed until the latter part of this century, the theoretical tenets of the approach stretch back several decades to the work of Russian physiologist Nikolai Bernstein. Bernstein observed that the production of a given movement required the coordination of a large number of multiply nested musculoskeletal subsystems. When the number of possible states of each subsystem is taken into account, the problem that has come to be identified as Bernstein's (1967) "degrees of freedom problem" becomes clear: there are too many degrees of freedom in a given movement to make executive control of each independently possible. Therefore, Bernstein proposed that, during the performance of any given act, the very many relevant subsystems are grouped into functional units or synergies. Bernstein's division of motor control into synergies laid the groundwork for consideration of laws that were written over the temporarily assembled, *functional* properties of the system rather than over the substructural units (e.g., Kugler, Kelso, and Turvey, 1982).

Although synergies offer a solution to the degrees of freedom problem, Bernstein (1996) claimed that there are levels of control both below and above the level of synergies that are equally important. Together, the levels form a hierarchy for the control of action and are identified by letters (A–D). Coordinated movements at the level of *synergies* (Level B) are made against a background of particular muscle states that reside at the lower level of (muscle) *tone* (Bernstein's Level A). In turn, organization of synergies is subservient to control at the higher levels of *space* and *action* (Bernstein's Levels C and D, respectively). Perceptual control of movement occurs at the level of space, where movement parameters are linked to the states of affairs of the environment. Intentional control of movement occurs at the still higher level of action, where individual movement-links are chained together to produce meaningful, goal-directed actions. The role of intention in Bernstein's hierarchical structure is similar to our experience of intentional control—instead of guiding each individual muscle unit, at the level of tone, we have intentional control of our movements at the more global level of action. The functional distinctions among Bernstein's levels highlight the importance of identifying solutions to motor problems at the level appropriate to the phenomenon. The dynamical model to be presented in the next section is a model at the level of synergies that also allows for the principled integration of control at the other levels (i.e., tone, space, and action).

Like Bernstein, von Holst (1973) acknowledged the need to understand coordination as a function of temporary assemblages of multiple underlying subsystems. Von Holst exploited his observation that the fins of the fish *Labrus* each exhibit a unique preferred frequency of oscillation in isolation yet oscillate at a common frequency while swimming. Careful study revealed that the cooperative pattern retained the stamp of the individual preferred frequencies through the superimposition of individual wave forms. von Holst called the tendency for each fin to oscillate at its own preferred frequency the "maintenance tendency" and the tendency for each fin to be attracted to the other fin's frequency the "magnet effect." Coordination, therefore, is a combination of maintenance tendency and magnet effect, of both competition and cooperation between individual fins.

Although von Holst first observed the competitive and cooperative components of coordination at the level of the fins, like Bernstein, he acknowledged the existence of similar principles at multiple levels of analysis. The fin of the *Labrus* is composed of fin rays, each of which can oscillate at its own preferred frequency (von Holst, 1973). Just as swimming requires the coordination of many fins, the motion of each fin requires the coordination of many fin rays. The maintenance tendency and magnet effect observed at the level of the fin can be observed at the level of the fin ray, opening up the possibility that the same principles of coordination may not be specific to any particular degrees of freedom but rather may be generalizable to all length scales.

11.3 Mathematical Formalisms

Development of dynamical systems theory has allowed for the operationalization of much of Bernstein's and von Holst's legacy. Simply, a dynamical system is one that evolves in time; dynamics are relevant, therefore, to the description of any behavior that changes over time. Formally, a dynamical system can be represented by the flow of a vector field detailing the temporal evolution of one or more observables (Abraham and Shaw, 1992). In the present section, a dynamical model of coordination is developed, from the identification of relevant higher order observables (relative phase) to the formulation of a motion equation in these observables in which the competition and cooperation between components of the coordination are adequately represented.

Symmetric Coordination at the Level of Synergies

In general, coordination refers to a situation in which two or more limb segments exhibit some collective behavior. The collective state of any two limb segments in rhythmic motion can be indexed by the relative phase of the two oscillators ($\phi = \theta_2 - \theta_1$), where θ_i is the phase angle of the individual oscillator. In Bernstein's terms, ϕ is a higher order observable at the level of synergies; that is, it describes a state of organization across units (see Turvey and Carello, 1996). In dynamical terms, ϕ is called an order parameter (Haken, 1977). Changes in ϕ over time ($d\phi/dt$, or $\dot{\phi}$) describe the system's collective behavior and can be expressed as a function of both ϕ and relevant control parameters κ (to be identified) that bring about changes in ϕ:

$$\dot{\phi} = F(\phi, \kappa). \tag{11.1}$$

Equation 11.1 is the equation of a *gradient system*, meaning that it can be put into the form

$$\dot{\phi} = -dV/d\phi, \tag{11.2}$$

where $V = V(\phi, \kappa)$ is a potential function that can be differentiated with respect to ϕ (Gilmore, 1981; Haken, 1977; Jackson, 1989). A function such as V is termed "potential" because it attains a minimum when $\dot{\phi} = 0$ (Hale and Kocak, 1991). In other words, the system will follow a trajectory of states toward the most stable, or least variable, state.

Because the minima of V correspond to observable stable states, empirical investigations of interlimb rhythmic coordination suggest the form of V. The two prototypical patterns witnessed in $1:1$ frequency locking are in-phase ($\phi = 0$) and anti-phase ($\phi = \pi$). Experiments have revealed that the two patterns are not equivalent: $\phi = 0$ is more persistent over frequency scaling than $\phi = \pi$. In one of the earliest experiments, Kelso (1984) asked participants to oscillate their two index fingers (or two hands) at the coupled frequency, ω_c, specified by a metronome. With increasing ω_c, a person's fingers "prepared" anti-phase switched suddenly to in-phase. The direction of the transition (from anti-phase to in-phase) was not reversed by a reduction in ω_c, however, or by initially preparing the fingers in-phase. Based on these results, Haken, Kelso, and Bunz (1985) attempted to determine the form of V. They postulated that: (i) V was periodic, that is, $V(\phi + 2\pi) = V(\phi)$, (ii) the roles of the two limb segments were symmetrical, meaning that $V(\phi) = V(-\phi)$, and (iii) given these postulates, V could be developed as the Fourier series in even (cosine) terms. The coexistence of stable states at $\phi = 0$ and $\phi = \pi$ and the inequality of their attractiveness meant that the series had to include, minimally, the first three even terms [$n \cos(n\phi)$, where $n = 0, 1, 2$], weighted by coefficients a and b. Hence,

$$V = -a\cos(\phi) - b\cos(2\phi). \tag{11.3}$$

Figure 11.1 (left panels) depicts equation 11.3 as a function of variations in the ratio of the parameters b and a. When b/a is large (e.g., 1.5), equation 11.3 has minima at both $\phi = 0$ and $\phi = \pi$. The deeper valley, or global minimum, at $\phi = 0$ indicates that it is more stable than $\phi = \pi$. As b/a decreases (e.g., 0.75, middle left panel), the relative depth of the mini-

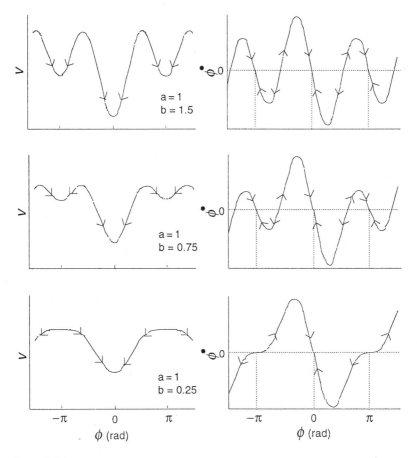

Figure 11.1
The (left panels) potential function (equation 11.3) and (right panels) corresponding motion equation (equation 11.4) change as a function of variations in the ratio of parameters b and a. Arrows indicate that the system will travel toward stable equilibria (attractors) and away from unstable equilibria (repellors). Attractors can be determined by numerically solving for the minima of the potential function and the negative zero crossings of the motion equation. When b/a is large ($b/a = 1.5$, top), stable phase relations exist at both $\phi = 0$ and $\phi = \pi$. As b/a decreases ($b/a = 0.75$, middle), $\phi = \pi$ becomes less stable until it becomes a repellor at $b/a = 0.25$ (bottom).

mum at $\phi = \pi$ decreases. The minimum at $\phi = \pi$ disappears completely, and ceases to be a stable state, at $b/a = 0.25$. At $b/a = 0.25$, the system can only be stable at $\phi = 0$. It is apparent that reversing b/a would cause the minimum at $\phi = \pi$ to reappear but would not change the status of $\phi = 0$ as the global minimum and, therefore, would not dislodge the system from $\phi = 0$. Likewise, preparation in $\phi = 0$ would not change to $\phi = \pi$ as b/a decreased. Returning to the results of Kelso (1984), an equivalence is seen between the empirical effects of ω_c and the computed effects of b/a. Scaling ω_c in the laboratory produces changes in the coordinative patterns of synergies that can be modeled by the inverse scaling of b/a in equation 11.3.

By equation 11.2, the form of the motion equation, equation 11.1, can now be derived from the potential function V (Haken, Kelso, and Bunz, 1985):

$$\dot{\phi} = -a \sin(\phi) - 2b \sin(2\phi). \tag{11.4}$$

This motion equation can be referred to as the deterministic part of the *symmetric coordination law*, also called the elementary coordination dynamics (Kelso, 1994). It applies to rhythmic coordination between segments that assume identical roles in the coordination. Depicted in figure 11.1 (right panels), equation 11.4 allows for the determination of the equilibria of the coordination for any given parameter values by solving numerically for $\dot{\phi} = 0$, that is, by finding the equation's zero crossings.

Two types of equilibrium points exist: stable equilibria (attractors) and unstable equilibria (repellors). They are, respectively, negative and positive zero crossings of the motion equation for given parameters of a and b (see figure 11.1, right panels). Determination of the type of equilibrium point is accomplished mathematically by calculating the slope at the zero crossing, that is, by taking the derivative of $\dot{\phi}$ with respect to ϕ evaluated at ϕ_0. The resulting value, λ, is called the *characteristic value* of the equilibrium or the *Lyapunov exponent* for the region near equilibrium (e.g., Abraham and Shaw, 1992; Haken, 1977; Hilborn, 1994). In general, $\lambda < 0$ for an attractor and $\lambda > 0$ for a repellor. The "attractiveness" of an equilibrium point is determined by the magnitude of $\lambda < 0$. With respect to figure 11.1 (left), λ is an index of the rate of descent to, or the steepness of, a potential well.

A Stochastic Force

Bernstein (1996) made the observation that collective behavior at the level of synergies takes place against a background of interactions at the lower level of muscle tone. By definition, dynamics at the higher level of synergies are going to·exist at longer length and time scales than the processes that are occurring at the lower level of tone. The multiplicity of subsystem interactions causes fluctuations in the collective behavior of the system that appear as stochastic noise in the collective measure ϕ. The deterministic motion equation identified in equations 11.1 and 11.4 must be rewritten to account for the effects of these stochastic processes. Noise welling up from lower levels of the coordination can be identified with ζ_t, a Gaussian white noise component of strength $Q > 0$ (Schöner, Haken, and Kelso, 1986). The elaboration of the symmetric coordination law, equation 11.4, to include this essential random element now appears as:

$$\dot{\phi} = -a\sin(\phi) - 2b\sin(2\phi) + \sqrt{Q}\zeta_t. \tag{11.5}$$

The effect of this stochastic force on the behavior of ϕ will depend on the magnitude of λ. Turning again to figure 11.1 (left), the presence of noise means that ϕ is displaced continuously from the bottom of a potential well by a random sequence of kicks. The consequence will be a distribution of ϕ values concentrated at the value coinciding with the well's minimum and shaped by the well's concavity. The stationary probability distribution function $P(\phi; b/a)$ characterizing the momentary behavior of ϕ is derivable from the potential function (e.g., Gilmore, 1981)

$$P(\phi; b/a) = Ne^{-(a\cos\phi - b\cos 2\phi)/Q}, \tag{11.6}$$

where N is an appropriate normalization constant. The standard deviation of ϕ(SDϕ) around a stable equilibrium point can be determined through equation 11.6 and $|\lambda|$ of the equilibrium point (e.g., Gilmore, 1981):

$$\text{SD}\phi = \sqrt{\frac{Q}{2\lambda}}. \tag{11.7}$$

In sum, a steeper negative slope at a zero crossing of equation 11.5 means a larger λ, a smaller variance in ϕ, and an equilibrium point that is more readily retained against perturbations of strength Q.

Symmetry Breaking Through Frequency Competition
The classical observation of von Holst (1973) concerning the coordination among fins of different sizes and, therefore, different preferred frequencies is readily demonstrated in human coordination (e.g., coordination between the right index finger and left leg). In fact, for the more general case, two segments are not physically identical and so do not contribute identically to interlimb rhythmic coordination. Physical differences introduce competition to the system and break the symmetry of the coordination dynamics. To accommodate this broken symmetry, a detuning term must be introduced to equation 11.5. $\Delta\omega$ is a detuning term that can be equated with the difference $(\omega_2 - \omega_1)$ between the uncoupled frequencies

(e.g., Cohen, Holmes, and Rand, 1982; Kelso, Delcolle, and Schöner, 1990; Kelso and Jeka, 1992; Kopell, 1988; Rand, Cohen, and Holmes, 1988; Sternad, Turvey, and Schmidt, 1992). Hence, equation 11.5 is further elaborated, giving

$$\dot{\phi} = \Delta\omega - a\sin(\phi) - 2b\sin(2\phi) + \sqrt{Q}\zeta_t. \qquad (11.8)$$

Equation 11.8 puts into formal terms the observation made by von Holst that coordination is a combination of competitive ($\Delta\omega$) and cooperative processes (b/a). At the same time, it makes predictions about aspects of intersegmental coordination beyond those on which the equation was originally founded. The following are predictions from the formal dynamical model regarding the displacement of equilibria ϕ_{stable} from an intended phase ψ of either 0 or π and fluctuations ($SD\phi \propto \lambda^{-1}$) of interlimb 1:1 frequency locking (see figure 11.2):

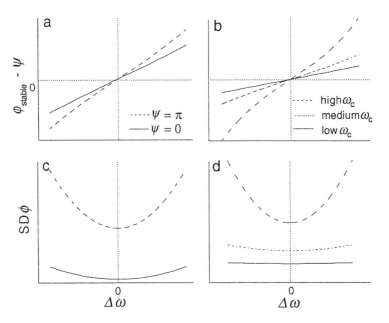

Figure 11.2
Manipulations of frequency competition between individual pendulums, $\Delta\omega$, and the coupling strength, $b/a(\propto\omega_c^{-1})$ in equation 11.8 produce shifts in both the (top) equilibria, or fixed points, measured as the deviation of stable relative phase, ϕ_{stable}, from required phase of $\psi = 0$ or $\psi = \pi$, and (bottom) fluctuations, measured as $SD\phi$. Depicted are predictions for (left) $\psi = 0$ and $\psi = \pi$ when $b/a = 1.5$ and (right) $\psi = 0$ when $b/a = 1.5$ (small ω_c), $b/a = 0.75$ (medium ω_c), and $b/a = 0.50$ (large ω_c). It should be noted that although curvature of the $SD\phi$ effect decreases at lower values of ω_c, it never completely disappears.

1. When $\Delta\omega = 0$, $\phi_{\text{stable}} = \psi$ (figure 11.2a, b).
2. When $\Delta\omega < 0$, $\phi_{\text{stable}} - \psi < 0$; when $\Delta\omega > 0$, $\phi_{\text{stable}} - \psi > 0$ (figure 11.2a, b).
3. When $\Delta\omega \neq 0$, $|\phi_{\text{stable}} - \psi|$ is greater for $\psi = \pi$ than for $\psi = 0$ (figure 11.2a).
4. For a constant ω_c, $|\phi_{\text{stable}} - \psi|$ is larger for larger values of $|\Delta\omega|$ (figure 11.2a).
5. For any $\Delta\omega$ except $\Delta\omega = 0$, $|\phi_{\text{stable}} - \psi|$ is larger for larger values of ω_c (figure 11.2b).
6. SDϕ is larger for $\psi = \pi$ than for $\psi = 0$ (figure 11.2c).
7. For a constant ω_c, SDϕ is larger for larger values of $|\Delta\omega|$ (figure 11.2c).
8. For any $\Delta\omega$ including $\Delta\omega = 0$, SDϕ is larger for larger values of ω_c (figure 11.2d).

Predictions 1 through 8 have been confirmed through experiments that manipulated ψ, $\Delta\omega$, and ω_c (see summaries in Kelso, 1994; Schmidt and Turvey, 1995; Turvey, 1994). Some of these experiments are presented in the following section.

11.4 Empirical Discoveries

In a number of experiments, ψ, $\Delta\omega$, and ω_c have been manipulated using the procedure of Kugler and Turvey (1987) whereby a seated individual oscillates two hand-held pendulums parallel to the sagittal plane. Each pendulum is oscillated about an axis in the wrist (with other joints fixed) (see figure 11.3a). The pendulums can vary in length and mass. The eigenfrequency, or preferred frequency, of such a "hand-held pendulum system" can be estimated as the eigenfrequency of the equivalent simple gravitational pendulum, $\omega = (g/L)^{1/2}$, where L is the *simple pendulum length* (dependent on both the length and mass of the specific pendulum) and g is the constant acceleration due to gravity. Longer, heavier pendulums have a lower preferred frequency than shorter, lighter ones. $\Delta\omega$ is controlled through differences in the simple pendulum lengths of the left and right pendulums, and ω_c is either freely chosen by the subject (comfort frequency) or specified by an auditory metronome.

Controlling the Interaction of Coupling Strength and Frequency Competition
Von Holst (1973) observed that coordination results from the interaction of the maintenance tendency ($\Delta\omega$) and magnet effect (a and b). The ratio b/a and $\Delta\omega$ are usually considered to be independent in terms of their influences on ϕ_{stable}, but it is not unreasonable to assume that an individual might regulate the frequency of oscillation, $\omega_c (\propto (b/a)^{-1})$, as a function of

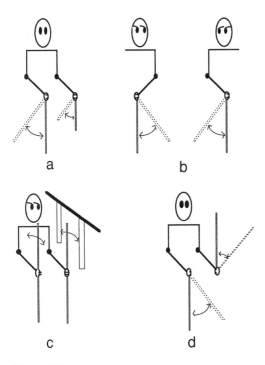

Figure 11.3
The Kugler and Turvey (1987) experimental procedure can be used to investigate the dynamics of human intersegmental coordination. Characteristics of the pendulums are manipulated (a) in order to introduce frequency competition, $\Delta\omega$, and a metronome is used to pace participants at the desired coupled frequency, ω_c. Participants are asked to synchronize the movements of their pendulums to establish a phase relation of either $\psi = 0$ (depicted) or $\psi = \pi$. Interlimb coordination can be studied both within a person and (b) between persons. To test whether handedness effects can be produced by varying attention, participants are instructed to hit targets that are positioned above either their left (c) or their right hand. Symmetry group belongingness can be studied by having participants coordinate the movements of an inverted pendulum and an ordinary pendulum (d). Although the two pendulums are temporally identical, reflectional symmetry is broken through differences in spatial orientation.

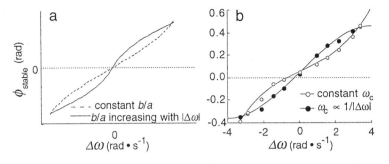

Figure 11.4
Predictions from equation 11.8, (a) and supporting results (b) regarding the influence on ϕ_{stable} of a constant frequency ($\omega_c \propto (b/a)^{-1}$) or frequency inversely scaled to $|\Delta\omega|$.

the increased task demands provided by larger $|\Delta\omega|$. Predictions from equation 11.8 for constant and changing b/a as a function of $\Delta\omega$ are presented in figure 11.4a. Constant b/a produces an increase in the rate at which ϕ_{stable} shifts from ψ at greater values of $|\Delta\omega|$ while increasing b/a with increasing $|\Delta\omega|$ produces a leveling-off of the same function. Confirmation of these predictions was provided in an experiment in which ω_c was held constant or ω_c was lowered with increasing $|\Delta\omega|$ (see figure 11.4b) (Amazeen, Sternad, and Turvey, 1996). These results demonstrate the adequacy of experimental means for controlling b/a and $\Delta\omega$ and underscore the status of equation 11.8 as a basic law of biological rhythmic coordination (Kelso, 1994).

Generalizability
Von Holst (1973) set a precedent for examining the possibility of similarity across levels of coordination that is independent of the properties of the individual subsystems. If equation 11.8 is a basic law of coordination in and between biological movement systems, then one should expect it to apply to both coordination within a single organism, where the coupling between oscillators is achieved through haptic perception, and coordination between organisms, where the coupling is primarily visual. The generalizability of equation 11.8 was first demonstrated in a phase transition task in which two people, seated side by side, coordinated the oscillations of their lower legs by watching each other (Schmidt, Carello, and Turvey, 1990). In support of Kelso (1984), a phase transition, with amplification of SDϕ prior to the transition, was witnessed from $\phi = \pi$ to $\phi = 0$ but not from $\phi = 0$ to $\phi = \pi$.

The hand-held pendulums paradigm was used to test more thoroughly the hypothesis that equation 11.8 could be applied to coordination between people (Amazeen, Schmidt, and Turvey, 1995; Schmidt and

Turvey, 1994). Each member of an experimental pair coordinated the movements of a hand-held pendulum with a pendulum held and oscillated by their partner (see figure 11.3b). Manipulations of ψ, $\Delta\omega$, and ω_c produced results that supported predictions 1, 2, 4, 5, 6, 7, and 8 (Amazeen, Schmidt, and Turvey, 1995). Therefore, the principles governing intersegmental coordination, as revealed in equation 11.8, are general and not specific to any particular anatomical substrate. These results support the claim that equation 11.8 is a basic coordination law of the sort that von Holst was seeking (see Kelso, 1994, 1995).

Expansion of Equation 11.8
Although predictions 1 through 8 have been verified, recent experiments have shown that equation 11.8 fails to accommodate all results. Elaboration of equation 11.8 has been necessary in order to account for more recent observations of bimanual coordination dynamics. Expansion of the dynamical model follows the principle that the accommodation of additional patterns should not negate any prior predictions. This is in keeping with the casual observation that when an organism learns a new coordinative pattern, it does not lose the ability to perform the patterns that it already has in its repertoire. The addition of sinusoidal terms that are similar in kind to the original terms in equation 11.8 allows for the superimposition of new required (or learned) coordination pattern upon the old without loss of the original pattern (see Schöner and Kelso, 1988).

Handedness   Handedness produces systematic effects on interlimb coordination that contradict prediction 1 (Treffner and Turvey, 1995, 1996). Specifically, when $\Delta\omega = 0$, $\phi_{stable} - \psi < 0$ for right-handed individuals and $\phi_{stable} - \psi > 0$ for left-handed individuals. Equation 11.8, from which prediction 1 was made, was based on Haken, Kelso, and Bunz's (1985) postulate (ii) that there is a symmetry in the role of the two limb segments, $V(\phi) = V(-\phi)$. The deviation of ϕ_{stable} from ψ at $\Delta\omega = 0$ implied that the role of the two limb segments was asymmetric and that postulate (ii) was incorrect, that is, $V(\phi) \neq V(-\phi)$. Elaboration of equation 11.8 was required to accommodate this asymmetric component.

In general, asymmetry of V can be handled through the addition of at least two ($n = 0, 1$) odd (sine) terms in its Fourier expansion (as suggested by investigations of synaptic coupling by Kopell, 1988; Kopell and Ermentrout, 1986). The first three odd terms were required to produce the observed equivalent effects of handedness at $\phi = 0$ and $\phi = \pi$ (Treffner and Turvey, 1995). Differentiation of the potential V yielded the following motion equation:

$$\dot{\phi} = \Delta\omega - [a\sin(\phi) + 2b\sin(2\phi)] - [c\cos(\phi) + 2d\cos(2\phi)] + \sqrt{Q}\zeta_t.$$
$$(11.9)$$

Equation 11.9 possesses both symmetric and asymmetric periodic components. Whereas a and b (symmetric components) determine the relative strengths of the fundamental in-phase and anti-phase equilibria, small values of c and d (asymmetric components) break the symmetry of the elementary coordination dynamics while leaving their essential characteristics unaltered. Equation 11.9 produces the requisite patterns of equilibria shift and variability observed by Treffner and Turvey (1995) when $d = 0.05$ for right-handed participants and $d = -0.08$ for left-handed participants (relative to settings of a and b greater than 0.5, and $c = 0$). At the same time, it goes beyond the original observations to make predictions regarding the increase in the relative contribution of d when the value of b/a is decreased (controlled experimentally by an increase in ω_c) The prediction, as shown in figure 11.5a, is that handedness differences will be magnified. Confirmation of this prediction provided further support for the inclusion of the asymmetric coupling terms c and d in equation 11.9 (Treffner and Turvey, 1996). To date, variations in d alone capture the asymmetric effects of handedness (Treffner and Turvey, 1995, 1996).

Attention   An hypothesis has been offered that handedness asymmetries in motor control result from more attention being directed to the preferred hand, thus allowing it to lead the nonpreferred hand during the course of the coordination (Peters, 1981, 1989, 1994). Given this hypothesis, the effects of variations in attention can be captured by variations in the parameter d in equation 11.9; specifically, attending right adds to d while attending left subtracts from d (see figure 11.5b). Figure 11.3c depicts an adaptation of the hand-held pendulums procedure in which direction of attention is manipulated by having participants tap paper targets that hang over either their right or left (depicted) pendulum (Amazeen et al., 1997). In replication of previous results (Treffner and Turvey, 1995, 1996), with $\Delta\omega = 0$, $\phi_{\text{stable}} - \psi < 0$ for right-handed participants and $\phi_{\text{stable}} - \psi > 0$ for left-handed participants. In support of the attention hypothesis and confirming the predictions depicted in figure 11.5b, $|\phi_{\text{stable}} - \psi|$ increased when attention was directed to the preferred hand and decreased when attention was directed to the nonpreferred hand.

Under ordinary circumstances, larger deviations of ϕ_{stable} from ψ are accompanied by greater variability (see predictions 4 and 7 from equation 11.8). In contradiction, results supported the prediction from equation 11.9 that when attention is directed to the preferred hand, greater equilibrium shift should be accompanied by lower variability (compare figure 11.5b and c). Further experiments have shown that the attention effect increases with increasing ω_c (Riley et al., 1997), replicating Treffner and Turvey (1996; predictions in figure 11.5a) and lending credibility to the notion that handedness and attentional effects on coordination are inextricably linked. The role of attention in handedness demonstrates the

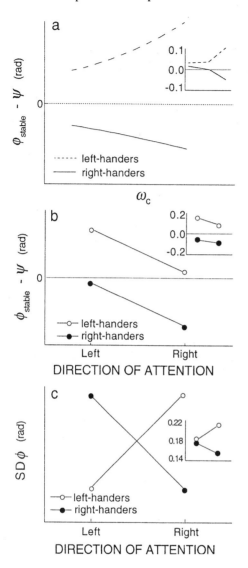

Figure 11.5
Predictions are made from equation 11.9 regarding the following handedness effects, where $d = 0.05$ for right-handed individuals and $d = -0.08$ for left-handed individuals: (a) When $d > 0$, $\phi_{stable} - \psi < 0$ and when $d < 0$, $\phi_{stable} - \psi > 0$; a magnification of this handedness effect is predicted as a function of increases in $\omega_c (\propto (b/a)^{-1}$ in equation 11.9). (b) For both right-handers and left-handers, it is predicted that direction of attention to the right hand makes ϕ_{stable} more negative, while direction of attention to the left hand makes ϕ_{stable} more positive. (c) An interaction is expected between handedness and direction of attention, where variability, measured by $SD\phi$, is expected to be greatest when attention is directed to the nonpreferred hand. In comparison with (b), this last prediction is somewhat paradoxical, because larger deviations of ϕ_{stable} from ψ are usually accompanied by greater variability. Results that confirm these predictions are presented as insets in (a) through (c).

applicability of dynamics to processes traditionally regarded as psychological and strictly under cognitive control.

Multifrequency Coordination   Equation 11.8 was originally formulated to accommodate 1:1 frequency locked coordination. Researchers have recently considered the elaboration of equation 11.8 to accommodate multifrequency coordination, in which the frequencies of the two limb segments form a rational ratio $n : m$, where n and m are the frequencies of the faster and slower moving limbs, respectively (Haken et al., 1996; Sternad, 1995). In order to apply the observables ϕ and $\Delta\omega$ to multifrequency coordination, they were redefined as $\phi = m\theta_{slow} - n\theta_{fast}$ and $\Delta\omega = m\omega_{slow} - n\omega_{fast}$ (Sternad, 1995; see also Keith and Rand, 1984; Rand, Cohen, and Holmes, 1988). When the limb segments are oscillated at the same frequency, $n : m = 1 : 1$, both ϕ and $\Delta\omega$ remain unchanged from their original formulation in equation 11.8. When the movement frequencies of the coupled oscillators are nonidentical, then ϕ and $\Delta\omega$ change to reflect the dynamics of a multifrequency system. In keeping with the principle that new patterns should be superimposed upon the old, equation 11.8 was generalized in the following manner (adapted from Sternad, 1995):

$$\dot{\phi}_{n:m} = \Delta\omega_{n:m} - [a\sin(\phi_{1:1}) + 2b\sin(2\phi_{1:1})] - \cdots$$
$$- [a'\sin(\phi_{n:m}) + 2b'\sin(2\phi_{n:m})] + \sqrt{Q}\zeta_t, \qquad (11.10)$$

where the relative strength of each $n : m$ component of the multifrequency coordination is indicated by the strength of its particular a and b coefficients.

When a dynamical model is able to accommodate multiple multifrequency patterns, predictions can be made regarding transitions between those patterns (e.g., Peper, Beek, and Van Wieringen, 1995; Treffner and Turvey, 1993). Haken et al. (1996) investigated the transitions between multifrequency ratios 5:2, 3:2, and 2:1 as a function of frequency scaling during a bimanual tapping task. Just as frequency scaling produces phase transitions from $\phi = \pi$ to $\phi = 0$, it similarly produces transitions from more complex to less complex ratios during multifrequency tasks. Haken et al. (1996) found that the particular transition routes were fairly individualized, so that intermediate ratios might not necessarily be visited during the transition. Haken et al.'s final model (based on the level of the individual oscillator) bears a close resemblance to equation 11.10. More complex (higher order) multifrequency ratios are represented by coupling terms of increasing power. As ω_c is increased, the coefficients of the higher order terms decrease in value in proportion to the coefficients of the lower order terms, allowing a phase transition to take place. When stability of a higher order state is lost, the stiffness of the individual oscillators is changed until a new frequency locked state is achieved.

Learning   Just as individuals can learn to produce multifrequency coordinative patterns, they can also manipulate the dynamics of 1 : 1 frequency
locking to produce phase relations other than 0 and π. Zanone and Kelso
(1992) demonstrated learning of a $\pi/2$ phase relation using a finger oscillation task in which participants tracked visual metronomes that specified
a 1/4 cycle difference between the fingers. A probe of all phase relations
between 0 and π produced an empirically-obtained approximation to the
potential $V(\phi)$ of the evolving dynamics: only attractors at 0 and at π
were present at the beginning but a third attractor had appeared at $\pi/2$
by the end of the experiment. The addition to equation 11.8 of a sine
term, $-e\sin(\phi - \psi)$, produces an equilibrium point at $\pi/2$ (see Schöner and
Kelso, 1988) when e is sufficiently large. To date, the learning coefficient e
has not been operationalized in the literature, however, it is considered by
the authors of the present chapter to increase in magnitude as a function
of time or practice. Predictions made from this particular expansion of
equation 11.8 with regards to learned phase relations stand in contrast to
predictions made from equation 11.8 regarding the dynamics of 0 and π:
Due to the extremely large magnitude of e required to produce a fixed
point at $\pi/2$, there should be no variability once $\pi/2$ is achieved, and
$\phi_{stable} - \psi = 0$ for all values of $\Delta\omega$ and ω_c.
   Contrary to these predictions, acquisition of the new dynamic appears
to be more similar to the dynamics of 0 and π than dissimilar, suggesting
a simple shifting by $\pi/2$ of the established dynamical regime to include
cosine terms rather than sine terms (Amazeen, 1996). This type of solution suggests that learning is a harnessing of known dynamics to produce
solutions to new problems. The most important finding is that participants who learned to produce $-\pi/2$ under very limiting circumstances
(when $\Delta\omega$ and ω_c were held constant) could subsequently produce the
entire dynamic when $\Delta\omega$ and ω_c were manipulated. It can be argued that
dynamics allows for generalizability because knowing the dynamics of
a learned pattern gives other patterns "for free". In contrast to motor
schema theory (e.g., R. A. Schmidt, 1982a, 1982b), where practice must
occur under varied conditions to produce varied outcomes, participants
were demonstrating that merely tapping into a dynamical regime allows
for production of the required movement under varying circumstances.
The implication is that even if the production of coordinative patterns
is computationally driven, as with Schmidt's motor schema theory,
then the computational driver of the coordination must abide by these
dynamics.

Expansion of the Detuning Term   It has been noted repeatedly that in 1 : 1
frequency locking, a difference in the uncoupled frequencies of the individual oscillators ($\Delta\omega$) causes fixed point shift, with the magnitude of the

shift dependent on the magnitude of $\Delta\omega$ (see predictions 2 and 4 from equation 11.8). It has been shown, however, that this detuning of the fixed point depends on the composition of the detuning term, $\Delta\omega$ (Collins, Sternad, and Turvey, 1996; Sternad, Collins, and Turvey, 1995). When variations in $\Delta\omega$ were brought about by different uncoupled frequencies that always formed a constant ratio Ω, fixed point shift was inversely related to $\Delta\omega$, as opposed to the positive relation expected from prediction 2 (Sternad, Collins, and Turvey, 1995). Further, and in contrast to prediction 7, SDϕ varied with $\Delta\omega$ as a function of the magnitude of Ω constraining the uncoupled frequencies composing $\Delta\omega$. A more direct evaluation of the detuning term was conducted by fixing $\Delta\omega$ and varying Ω—that is, by creating different versions of the same magnitude of $\Delta\omega$. It was confirmed that the detuning of stable relative phase is a function of both absolute ($\Delta\omega$) and relative differences (Ω) in the uncoupled frequencies (Collins, Sternad, and Turvey, 1996). Future research should reveal the precise composition of the expanded detuning term to be used in equations 11.8 through 11.10.

11.5 Implications and Future Directions

Although the dynamical model presented in this chapter is able to accommodate much of the complexity witnessed in human intersegmental coordination, the lesson from those who have considered expansions of the model is that the model in its current form may someday encounter the limits of its explanatory ability. In this section, we present two issues facing the dynamical model as it currently stands, one regarding questions of symmetry and another modeling the dynamics of the individual oscillator. It will become clear that neither issue necessarily requires abandonment of the original model, but rather each allows for a deeper understanding of the structure of the dynamics of intersegmental coordination.

Symmetry Group Belongingness

The research presented in this chapter has investigated the suitability of equation 11.8 as an elementary coordination dynamic with experiments in which oscillators may have been different in preferred timing but were identical in spatial orientation. A hypothesis has been offered that the applicability of equation 11.8 to the coordination of differently-oriented oscillators (e.g., figure 11.3d) may depend on the belongingness of these different systems to the same symmetry group (Amazeen, Amazeen, and Turvey, in press). A symmetry group is defined by the transformations that leave the system unchanged. For example, whenever oscillators that are temporally identical ($\Delta\omega = \omega_{\text{left}} - \omega_{\text{right}} = 0$) are held in the left and right hands, performing a reflectional transformation, or left-right exchange ($\Delta\omega = \omega_{right} - \omega_{left} = 0$), leaves the coordinative system unaltered. Such a system belongs to the reflectional symmetry group. Reflectional symmetric systems produce reflectionally symmetric solutions ($\phi_{stable} = \psi$) (see prediction 1 from equation 11.8); that is, $\phi_{stable} = \theta_{left} - \theta_{right} = \theta_{right} - \theta_{left} = \psi$. When the oscillators are temporally different ($\Delta\omega \neq 0$), reflectional symmetry is broken because left-right exchange of the oscillators changes the physical configuration of the system. The behavior of reflectionally asymmetric systems is likewise altered, and fixed point shift, or deviation from symmetric solutions, is witnessed (see prediction 2 from equation 11.8).

The importance of symmetry group theory lies in the way in which seemingly different systems are shown to relate to each other. Whenever reflectional symmetry is broken (whether it is the system or its behavior), the resulting states are related to each other by reflection (Stewart and Golubitsky, 1992). In figure 11.2, ($\phi_{stable} - \psi$) is equal in magnitude but opposite in direction for equal but opposite values of $\Delta\omega \neq 0$. The significance of this phenomenon is that whenever symmetry is broken by a single state of the system (e.g., $\Delta\omega = 1$), it is preserved via its redistribution across multiple states of the system ($\Delta\omega = \pm 1$). Preservation of the system's symmetry in this manner indicates that it has maintained its belongingness to the reflectional symmetry group.

Predictions and results demonstrate the reflectional relatedness of systems in which reflectional symmetry has been broken through differences in timing ($\Delta\omega$) alone; an identical pattern of results has been shown for systems of oscillators that are spatially identical, that is, that are either both ordinary (downward-oriented) pendulums or both inverted (upward-oriented) pendulums (Amazeen, Amazeen, and Turvey, in press). Reflectional symmetry is no longer preserved when the oscillators of a given coordination are oriented differently, that is, when one is an ordinary pendulum and one is an inverted pendulum (see figure 11.3d). Left-right exchange alters the physical configuration of the pendulum system even when the oscillators are temporally identical ($\Delta\omega = 0$) and results in the prediction that symmetric solutions should not be produced. This hypothesis stands in contrast to prediction 1 from equation 11.8, but was empirically confirmed by the demonstration that differently-oriented pendulums produce a pattern of results that is distinct from identically-oriented pendulums. Results for reflectionally related pairs of differently-oriented pendulums were reflectionally related (see figure 11.6), confirming their belongingness to the reflectional symmetry group. The implication is that although equation 11.8 in its current form may not accommodate spatial symmetry breaking, reflectional symmetry breaking through differ-

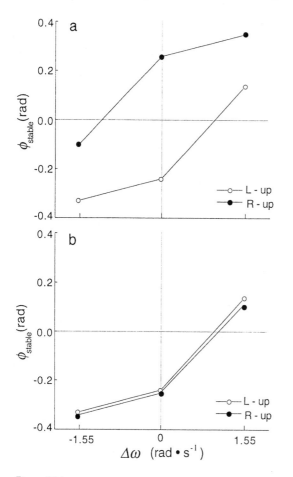

Figure 11.6
A system of one inverted and one ordinary pendulum can be assembled by placing the inverted pendulum in either the left hand (L-up, depicted in figure 11.3d) or the right hand (R-up). Fixed point shift for these two configurations is identical when a reflectional transformation is performed (b), lending support to the hypothesis that a system of differently oriented pendulums belongs to the reflectional symmetry group.

ences in both timing and spatial orientation belongs to a single elementary coordination dynamic.

Behavior of the Individual Oscillator

The approach presented in this chapter addresses coordination dynamics at the level of synergies, defined across the coordination's component oscillators. Another dynamical approach, not antithetical to this one, concentrates on the order parameter dynamics governing Bernstein's level of tone by analyzing the neuromuscular composition of the individual oscillator via the W-method (development of the W-method is demonstrated in Beek and Beek, 1988; and Beek et al., 1995). By considering the oscillating limb segment a self-sustained oscillator, one can investigate the mechanisms responsible for injecting (spring, or elastic forces) and extracting (dissipative, or friction forces) energy from the system in order to produce perfect harmonic oscillations. The W-method empirically determines the relative contribution of such elastic (e.g., Duffing) and friction (e.g., Rayleigh and van der Pol) functions by quantifying the deviation of the individual oscillator from perfect harmonic motion (Beek et al., 1995). Muscular torque, and, therefore, the contribution of the individual functions, was found to change as a function of the eigenfrequency, ω, of the hand-held pendulum, the deviation of ω_c from ω, and the deviation of the required amplitude from the pendulum's preferred amplitude. The success of the W-method in empirically determining the order parameter dynamics at the level of the individual oscillator makes it clear that dynamics serves as an appropriate descriptor for intersegmental coordination at multiple levels.

11.6 Conclusion

A dynamical approach to human intersegmental coordination offers the advantage that the modeling of the behavior is independent of the particular substrate supporting the movement. The empirical work presented in this chapter has concentrated on describing the behavior of coordinated limb segments without relying on their specific anatomical characteristics. As von Holst originally suggested, the use of general principles allows for their application to many different levels. These principles have been shown to extend beyond coordination at the level of synergies to encompass specific muscular influences, the computational processes involved in learning, and other classically psychological phenomena, such as attention, handedness, and social coordination. In each case, their influences are actualized through the resulting parameterization of the dynamics. Because the same dynamics holds in each case, it becomes possible to use this model to integrate such diverse phenomena.

Acknowledgments

The writing of this chapter was supported by National Science Foundation Grant SBR 94–22650 awarded to M. T. Turvey, who is also at Haskins Laboratories in New Haven, CT.

References

Abraham, R. H., & Shaw, C. D. (1992). *Dynamics: The geometry of behavior*. Redwood City, CA: Addison-Wesley.

Amazeen, E. L., Amazeen, P. G., Treffner, P. J., & Turvey, M. T. (1997). Attention and handedness in bimanual coordination dynamics. *Journal of Experimental Psychology: Human Perception and Performance, 23*, 1552–1560.

Amazeen, E. L., Sternad, D., & Turvey, M. T. (1996). Predicting the nonlinear shift of stable equilibria in interlimb rhythmic coordination. *Human Movement Science, 15*, 521–542.

Amazeen, P. G. (1996). Learning a bimanual rhythmic coordination: Schemas as dynamics. Doctoral dissertation. University of Connecticut, Storrs.

Amazeen, P. G., Amazeen, E. L., & Turvey, M. T. (in press). Breaking the reflectional symmetry of interlimb coordination dynamics. *Journal of Motor Behavior*.

Amazeen, P. G., Schmidt, R. C., & Turvey, M. T. (1995). Frequency detuning of the phase entrainment dynamics of visually coupled rhythmic movements. *Biological Cybernetics, 72*, 511–518.

Beek, P. J., & Beek, W. J. (1988). Tools for constructing dynamical models of rhythmic movement. *Human Movement Science, 7*, 301–342.

Beek, P. J., Schmidt, R. C., Morris, A. W., Sim, M-Y., & Turvey, M. T. (1995). Linear and nonlinear stiffness and friction in biological rhythmic movements. *Biological Cybernetics, 73*, 499–507.

Bernstein, N. (1967). *The coordination and regulation of movement*. London: Pergamon Press.

Bernstein, N. A. (1996). Dexterity and its development. In M. Latash & M. T. Turvey (eds.), *Dexterity and its development* (pp. 9–244). Mahwah, NJ: Lawrence Erlbaum Associates.

Cohen, A. H., Holmes, J., and Rand, R. H. (1982). The nature of the coupling between segmental oscillators of the lamprey spinal generator for locomotion: A mathematical model. *Journal of Mathematical Biology, 13*, 345–369.

Collins, D., Sternad, D., & Turvey, M. T. (1996). An experimental note on defining frequency competition in intersegmental coordination dynamics. *Journal of Motor Behavior, 28*, 299–303.

Gilmore, R. (1981). *Catastrophe theory for scientists and engineers*. New York: Wiley.

Haken, H. (1977). *Synergetics*. Berlin: Springer-Verlag.

Haken, H., Kelso, J. A. S., & Bunz, H. (1985). A theoretical model of phase transitions in human hand movements. *Biological Cybernetics, 51*, 347–356.

Haken, H., Peper, C. E., Beek, P. J., & Daffertshofer, A. (1996). A model for phase transitions in human hand movements during multifrequency tapping. *Physica D, 90*, 179–196; *92*, 260 (Erratum).

Hale, J., & Kocak, H. (1991). *Dynamics and bifurcations*. New York: Springer Verlag.

Hilborn, R. C. (1994). *Chaos and nonlinear dynamics: An introduction for scientists and engineers*. New York: Oxford University Press.

Holst, E. von (1973). Relative coordination as a phenomenon and as a method of analysis of central nervous system function. In: R. Martin (ed. and trans.), *The collected papers of Erich von Holst*, vol. 1. *The behavioral physiology of animal and man* (pp. 33–135). Coral Gables: University of Miami Press (original work published 1939).

Jackson, E. A. (1989). *Perspectives of nonlinear dynamics.* Cambridge, UK: Cambridge University Press.

Keith, W. L., & Rand, R. H. (1984). 1:1 and 2:1 phase entrainment in a system of two coupled limit cycle oscillators. *Journal of Mathematical Biology, 20,* 133–152.

Kelso, J. A. S. (1984). Phase transitions and critical behavior in human bimanual coordination. *American Journal of Physiology: Regulatory, Integrative and Comparative, 246,* R1000–R1004.

Kelso, J. A. S. (1994). Elementary coordination dynamics. In S. P. Swinnen, J. H. Massion, H. Heuer, & P. Casaer (eds.), *Interlimb coordination: Neural, dynamical, and cognitive constraints,* pp. 301–318). San Diego: Academic Press.

Kelso, J. A. S. (1995). *Dynamic Patterns.* Cambridge, MA: MIT Press.

Kelso, J. A. S., Delcolle, J. D., & Schöner, G. (1990). Action-perception as a pattern formation process. In M. Jeannerod (ed.), *Attention and performance XIII* (pp. 139–169). Hillsdale, NJ: Lawrence Erlbaum Associates.

Kelso, J. A. S., & Jeka, J. J. (1992). Symmetry breaking dynamics of human multilimb coordination. *Journal of Experimental Psychology: Human Perception and Performance, 18,* 645–668.

Kopell, N. (1988). Toward a theory of modeling central pattern generators. In A. H. Cohen, S. Rossignol, & S. Grillner (eds.), *Neural control of rhythmic movements in vertebrates* (pp. 369–413). New York: Wiley.

Kopell, N., & Ermentrout, G. B. (1986). Symmetry and phase-locking in chains of weakly coupled oscillators. *Commentaries on Pure and Applied Mathematics, 39,* 623–660.

Kugler, P. N., Kelso, J. A. S., & Turvey, M. T. (1982). On the control and coordination of naturally developing systems. In J. A. S. Kelso & J. E. Clarke (eds.), *The development of movement control and coordination* (pp. 5–78). Chichester, UK: Wiley.

Kugler, P. N., & Turvey, M. T. (1987). *Information, natural law, and the self-assembly of rhythmic movement.* Hillsdale, NJ: Lawrence Erlbaum Associates.

Peper, C. E., Beek, P. J., & Van Wieringen, P. C. W. (1995). Frequency induced transitions in bimanual tapping. *Biological Cybernetics, 73,* 301–309.

Peters, M. (1981). Attentional asymmetries during concurrent bimanual performance. *Quarterly Journal of Psychology, 33A,* 95–103.

Peters, M. (1989). Do feedback processing, output variability, and spatial complexity account for manual asymmetries? *Journal of Motor Behavior, 21,* 151–156.

Peters, M. (1994). Does handedness play a role in the coordination of bimanual movement? In S. P. Swinnen, J. H. Massion, H. Heuer, & P. Casaer (eds.), *Interlimb coordination: Neural, dynamical, and cognitive constraints* (pp. 595–612). San Diego: Academic Press.

Rand, R. H., Cohen, A. H., & Holmes, P. J. (1988). Systems of coupled oscillators as models of central pattern generators. In A. H. Cohen, S. Rossignol, & S. Grillner (eds.), *Neural control of rhythmic movements in vertebrates* (pp. 333–367). New York: Wiley.

Riley, M., Amazeen, E. L., Amazeen, P. G., Treffner, P. J., & Turvey, M. T. (1997). Effects of temporal scaling and attention on the asymmetric dynamics of bimanual coordination. *Motor Control, 1,* 263–283.

Schmidt, R. A. (1982a). More on motor programs. In J. A. S. Kelso (ed.), *Human motor behavior: An introduction* (pp. 187–217). Hillsdale, NJ: Lawrence Erlbaum Associates.

Schmidt, R. A. (1982b). The schema concept. In J. A. S. Kelso (ed.), *Human motor behavior: An introduction* (pp. 219–235). Hillsdale, NJ: Lawrence Erlbaum Associates.

Schmidt, R. C., Carello, C., & Turvey, M. T. (1990). Phase transitions and critical fluctuations in the visual coordination of rhythmic movements between people. *Journal of Experimental Psychology: Human Perception and Performance, 16,* 227–247.

Schmidt, R. C., & Turvey, M. T. (1994). Phase-entrainment dynamics of visually coupled rhythmic movements. *Biological Cybernetics, 70,* 369–376.

Schmidt, R. C., & Turvey, M. T. (1995). Models of interlimb coordination: Equilibria, local analyses, and spectral patterning. *Journal of Experimental Psychology: Human Perception and Performance, 21*, 432–443.

Schöner, G., Haken, H., & Kelso, J. A. S. (1986). A stochastic theory of phase transitions in human hand movement. *Biological Cybernetics, 53*, 442–452.

Schöner, G., & Kelso, J. A. S. (1988). A synergetic theory of environmentally-specified and learned patterns of movement coordination. *Biological Cybernetics, 58*, 71–80.

Sternad, D. (1995). Dynamics of 1:2 coordination in rhythmic interlimb movement. Doctoral dissertation, University of Connecticut, Storrs.

Sternad, D., Collins, D., & Turvey, M. T. (1995). The detuning factor in the dynamics of interlimb rhythmic coordination. *Biological Cybernetics, 73*, 27–35.

Sternad, D., Turvey M. T., & Schmidt, R. C. (1992). Average phase difference theory and 1:1 phase entrainment in interlimb coordination. *Biological Cybernetics, 67*, 223–231.

Stewart, I. N., & Golubitsky, M. (1992). *Fearful symmetry: Is God a geometer?* Cambridge, MA: Blackwell.

Treffner, P. J., & Turvey, M. T. (1993). Resonance constraints on rhythmic movement. *Journal of Experimental Psychology: Human Perception and Performance, 19*, 1221–37.

Treffner, P. J., & Turvey, M. T. (1995). Handedness and the asymmetric dynamics of bimanual rhythmic coordination. *Journal of Experimental Psychology: Human Perception and Performance, 21*, 318–333.

Treffner, P. J., & Turvey, M. T. (1996). Symmetry, broken symmetry, and handedness in bimanual coordination dynamics. *Experimental Brain Research, 107*, 463–478.

Turvey, M. T. (1994). From Borelli (1680) and Bell (1826) to the dynamics of action and perception. *Journal of Sport & Exercise Psychology, 16*, S128–S157.

Turvey, M. T., & Carello, C. (1996). Dynamics of Bernstein's level of synergies. In M. Latash & M. T. Turvey (eds.), *Dexterity and its development* (pp. 339–376). Hillsdale, NJ: Lawrence Erlbaum Associates.

Zanone, P. G., & Kelso, J. A. S. (1992). Evolution of behavioral attractors with learning: Nonequilibrium phase transitions. *Journal of Experimental Psychology: Human Perception and Performance, 18*, 403–421.

Chapter 12

Constraints in the Emergence of Preferred Locomotory Patterns

Kenneth G. Holt

Abstract

The emergence of preferred dynamic locomotory sequencing and timing patterns is proposed as an outcome of multiple levels of constraints and their interrelationships. Constraints may be broadly classified as those arising from the nature of the task, the performer's action capabilities, and those that emerge from the action capabilities of the individual performing the task. Linear and nonlinear dynamic, and thermodynamic laws provide the principled means by which the self-organization of gait can be discovered. Investigation of the relations between mechanical, dynamic, and thermodynamic constraints, optimality principles, task constraints and the performer's action capabilities reveal the reasons for differences in coordination patterns between individuals and tasks. The emergence of movement patterns from constraints allows for minimal reliance on executive control as an unanalyzable residual.

12.1 Introduction

To what principles must scientists adhere in devising theories of human motor control and coordination? What are the underlying problems of control and coordination that we wish to understand? In this chapter the answers to these questions serve as the initial guidelines by which data-supported ideas about control and coordination are presented that have their foundation in dynamical systems. I present evidence that supports the notion that coordination parameters arise from constraints specific to the task, the individual, and their interrelationships. I pay particular attention to our research on the gait parameters that arise from the constraints of linear oscillatory and thermodynamic properties of the human body, and the tendency for humans to self-optimize behavior according to task requirements and individual action capabilities. I discuss these findings in relation to other coordinations that arise from nonlinear oscillatory and mechanical constraints.

12.2 Degrees of Freedom and Context-Conditioned Variability

There are an almost infinite number of ways that the neuromuscular apparatuses may be combined to produce movement that is appropriately sequenced and timed. It is possible to locomote by crawling, creeping, running, walking, hopping, or bounding, with knees flexed in a "Groucho" gait pattern, with or without temporal or spatial symmetry between limbs. Yet healthy adult humans and animals normally adopt only two patterns—walking and running. Within each gait the kinematic patterns are also quite limited. It is easy to identify "silly walks" in which the normal timing of segmental motions is deliberately disrupted or when limited or excessive amounts of segmental motion are allowed. The sequencing and timing of gait does change, however, in accord with changes in the task. For example, climbing up stairs is associated with greater knee and hip range of motion that moves the body center of mass more anteriorly—patterns that would appear extraordinary if performed on level ground. Changes in the environment significantly alter the gait pattern. The most convincing example is found in the gait of astronauts in the reduced gravitation of the moon, in which a bounding pattern becomes a major locomotory method. More generally, any change in orientation of body parts with respect to gravity will influence the observed pattern. Raising a limb against gravity requires muscle actions quite different from those used when the same movement is performed with gravity. To perform in a consistent manner independent of the environmental influences, a change in muscular actions will be required. Furthermore, a simple change in limb position can significantly alter the moment arm of the muscle, and hence the muscular requirements for consistent movement patterns. Garnering the many potential degrees of freedom of the neuromuscular system to produce a few recognizable preferred movement patterns and accommodating the context-conditioned variability due to the environment and the current state of the neuromuscular apparatus are core problems for control and coordination of movement within a dynamical systems approach (for review, see Turvey, 1990).

12.3 Guidelines for a Solution

From a dynamical systems perspective the solution, must follow certain philosophical guidelines. Motor control literature prior to the early 1980s is peppered with terms (higher centers, executor, executive intelligence, control center) that reflect a reliance on the brain as a knowing entity that solves control problems faced by the neuromuscular apparatus. A classic example lies in the literature that treats the brain as a serial, digital computer. Motor programs have often been given responsibility for the correct sequencing and timing of motor patterns (see Stelmach, 1976, for examples). To carry the computer metaphor to its logical conclusion, a motor program requires a programmer, an entity that makes intelligent decisions about how to coordinate the body for a particular task. Yet earlier theory is lacking in attempts to understand this intelligence.

The philosophical issue is one of infinite regress; the problems that are to be solved are assigned to an intelligence that itself requires explanation (Dennett, 1978). The problem has long been recognized by philosophers (Koestler, 1967), and contemporary motor program theorists have made efforts to address this issue (e.g. Rosenbaum, 1991). Nevertheless, the problem still occurs, though in more subtle forms. For example, modern equivalents of the motor programming approach are the neural network models that require weighting and initial connections of nodes by the programmer. Although the end result may be successful completion of a task and even learning (e.g. Bullock and Grossberg 1988), there is often no principled way that initial weighting and connections are set up by the programmer. More recent versions of network models use principled ways to set up the network parameters, however. For example, cost functions have been used to build network models (Bruwer and Cruse, 1990). The first principle that must be heeded in devising control and coordination theory is that executive intelligence cannot be an "unanalyzable residual" (Kugler, Kelso, and Turvey, 1980).

The second guideline is also in reference to machine and model simulations. Machines and models have been used as metaphors for motor control theory. The motor program (for review, see Stelmach, 1976), mechanical models (Holt, Hamill, and Andres, 1990a; Kugler and Turvey, 1987), neural network models (Bullock and Grossberg, 1988), and coupled oscillator models (Kelso and Schöner, 1988) have all been used to describe coordination. Although a machine or model may mimic the behavior that we seek to explain, it cannot be claimed that this is the way in which the entity operates. While a conveyer can move objects from one place to another, it has very little use as a model of human portage capabilities. A model capable of predicting novel behaviors is the most powerful, but one that can explain, without special or extensive manipulations, most known coordinations is worthy of consideration. The second principle to be adhered to in devising and assessing theory is that care should be taken to differentiate explanation from description.

12.4 The Concept and a Taxonomy of Constraints

Human anatomical structure allows limited amounts of motion in joints. Knees do not extend beyond 180 degrees, hips do not extend beyond about 200 degrees. The limitations may be due to soft tissues or bony structures. Anatomical structure is a mechanical constraint on the degrees of freedom of human action capabilities. Anatomical structure also allows movement within limits, and so sets boundary conditions for possible coordination patterns. Nevertheless, this example serves to illustrate the concept of constraint. A constraint is any factor that serves to decrease the number of degrees of freedom to be controlled. A constraint is not imposed on the system by a knowing brain, but evolves from the nature of the task, and the action capabilities of the individual.

Constraints may be broadly categorized as those inherent to the task, and those inherent to the individual performing the task. A *task constraint* is one that is inherent to the task regardless of the individual performing it. An *individual constraint* characterizes the differences and similarities between individuals. Task constraints may be extrinsically imposed, as might be exemplified by an experimental paradigm requiring 2:1 phase locking between limbs, or the requirement for great accuracy or speed on the production line in a factory. There may also be constraints that result from requirements inherent to the performance of the task. For example, some tasks may be metabolically very expensive (e.g., walking and running), while others may be potentially injurious (e.g., jumping from a building). There is a cost function intrinsic to the task that will influence the way in which the task is performed. One useful way to identify intrinsic constraints and relate them to an individual has been through the concept of self-optimization—the tendency to perform in ways that lead to a minimization of some cost to the system (Holt, Hamill and Andres, 1991; Holt et al., 1995; Wilke 1977, and for summary of minimization criteria in limb movements, see Latash and Ansen, 1996). Extrinsic and intrinsic constraints will determine the way in which the task is performed. Intrinsic task constraints would potentially include anatomic, metabolic, mechanical, dynamic, and thermodynamic variables. Extrinsic constraints might include speed, accuracy, and coordination patterns that are not intrinsic to the system. Note that extrinsic constraints may violate the constraints inherent to the individual. For example, the graceful movement patterns seen in ballet require motions and coordinations of limbs that often violate functional anatomic constraints and could potentially lead to injury.

Preferred movement patterns also emerge from constraints unique to an individual. Examples abound of constraints that determine differences in the ways individuals perform the same task. Differences in anthropometry, strength, metabolic capability, maturation and aging, disease processes, and skill will all influence the observed sequencing and timing. For example differences in leg length determine differences in stride length and frequency of walking (Holt, Hamill, and Andres, 1990); lack of strength in the legs results in the absence of a reciprocal gait pattern in infancy (Thelen, Fisher, and Ridley-Johnson, 1984); and weakness and pain due to disease can lead to gait asymmetries (Inman, Ralston, and Todd, 1981).

From this perspective, the task for the scientist is to understand the constraints that are operational for a particular task and individual, and how the pertinent constraints influence coordination patterns without recourse to executive intelligence. The influence of multiple constraints on observed coordinations is not simple. Each constraint may influence others in quite complex ways. The remainder of this chapter is committed to reviewing the underlying metabolic, mechanical, dynamic, and thermodynamic task and individual constraints that determine the form of locomotion that emerges in nondisabled and disease states. Our research has been influenced largely by dynamical systems philosophy and method, but here an attempt is made to put it into the broader context that is captured by the constraints perspective.

12.5 Constraints in Locomotion

The primary task in locomotion is not walking or running or hopping or crawling or any other specific locomotory form. The emergence of a *form* of gait is itself in part the result of a functional task constraint. If the task is catching a bus, the constraint is likely to be related to the time it takes to get to the bus before it leaves the stop. Walking and running are alternative solutions. The emergence of one (or neither) will be determined in part by the time constraint. The task sets the boundary conditions through which a particular gait pattern emerges. Walking may simply not be an option if the the bus departure is imminent, and in some cases neither walking nor running may be an option. But time alone is not the sole determinant of the form of gait. Running may not be an option for an individual who has an injury. While one individual may be able to walk fast enough to catch the bus, another may not. The action capabilities of the individual must be considered.

Once a form of gait has been established, the constraints that determine its kinetic and kinematic details must be considered. Speed, frequency, stride length, and phasing (sequencing and timing) of limb segment motions are the kinematic variables of interest, while muscle forcing, the body moment of inertia and elastic energy return from soft tissues are the kinetic variables of interest. My hypothesis is that the underlying linear and nonlinear dynamics and related optimality constraints will determine all the kinematic details.

12.6 Dynamic Constraints on Gait

One of the major claims of the dynamical approach is that self-organization is an emergent property of underlying dynamic and thermodynamic processes. The cornerstone of the theory is in the oscillatory or rhythmical nature of movement, and it is in the physics of oscillatory processes that self-organization is hypothesized to emerge. The major emphasis and claim has been that biological systems are nonlinear and that self-organization emerges from nonlinear processes (see Kelso, 1995 for review). Two main experimental paradigms have been used to study the emergence of coordination patterns based on the dynamic behaviors of coupled nonlinear oscillators as they relate to the process of self-organization.

Dynamic pattern theory is based on the study of the dynamics of phase transitions in physical systems (see Kelso, 1995 for review). Transitions from 180° phase to 0° phase in coupled finger oscillations show many of the features of transitions that occur in physical systems, although transitions from walking to running in humans do not show these features (Lin, 1993). Minimally, the analysis of phase transitions in human gait must consider *thermodynamic* laws (Turvey et al., 1996; Diedrich and Warren, 1995). Triggers for transitions in gait may also be task dependent. For example, gait transitions in horses are triggered by metabolic constraints as speed increases (Hoyt and Taylor, 1981). When the horse is carrying weight, however, transitions occur earlier than the metabolic criterion would predict. The transitions between gaits are triggered by critical force levels (Farley and Taylor, 1991).

The second approach, also based on synergetics (Haken et al., 1985), has been to use the mathematics of coupled linear and nonlinear oscillators to provide a dynamical account of the emergence of coordination in bilateral wrist-hammer swinging (Turvey et al., 1988), complex rhythms such as 1:2 phase relations between the hands (Sternad, 1995), handedness (Treffner and Turvey, 1995), and coordination of limbs between individuals (Schmidt, Carello, and Turvey, 1990). The mathematics of coupled nonlinear oscillators has also been used to describe animal locomotion (Collins and Stewart, 1993; Haken, 1985; Rand, Cohen, and Holmes, 1988; Kopell, 1988).

Oscillators can demonstrate a broad range of behaviors that can be described as random, chaotic, nonlinear, linear, and critically damped so as to be apparently nonoscillatory. In our research, the underlying premise is that certain constraints on movement arise from nonlinear features, while others result from linear features. To anticipate, I will argue that basic gait parameters namely, speed, stride length, and frequency, emerge from linear dynamics while the coordination patterns arise from nonlinear coupling of the limb oscillators. My colleagues have pursued the notion that although biological oscillators are inherently nonlinear, they demonstrate linear behaviors within certain boundaries (Kugler and Turvey, 1987) and that those behaviors can be predicted by linear equations of motion. In the research conducted at Boston University we have used the equation of motion for a force-driven, harmonic, hybrid pendulum, and spring as a means to understand and relate a number of constraints that appear to be relevant to preferred gait patterns.

12.7 The Force-Driven Hybrid (Pendulum and Spring) Model of Locomotion

Research in biomechanics of gait has emphasized the pendular motion of the body in conserving potential and kinetic energy during walking gait. Running has been likened to a bouncing ball in which potential energy is stored in the soft tissues, and released as potential and kinetic energy (McMahon, 1984; Cavagna, Heglund, and Taylor, 1977). In walking, energy is conserved primarily through the pendular actions of the body, while in running energy is primarily conserved through the spring action of the body. It has been recognized, however, that both gaits use both conservation methods to a greater or lesser extent. Modeling has been performed in which both gaits are represented by a hybrid model that has both inertial (pendular) and elastic (spring) components (Holt, Hamill, and Andres, 1990, 1991; Holt, Slavin, and Hamill, 1990; Holt, Jeng, and Fetters, 1991; Holt, Jeng, Ratcliffe, and Hamill, 1995; Kugler and Turvey, 1987; Obusek, Holt, and Rosenstein, 1995; Turvey et al., 1988). The inertial component is determined by the body or limb mass (m), the distance of the body or limb center of mass from the rotational axis (L_e), and acceleration due to gravity (g). The spring component is determined by the stiffness (k) of the soft tissues (figure 12.1).

In walking, the maximum transfer of potential to kinetic energy of the center of mass is about 68%, while in running there is a minimal conservation through pendular-like transfers (McMahon, 1984). In running, energy is conserved by elastic storage and return to give the body potential and kinetic energies that are in phase. In both gaits there are losses of energy during transfers from one form to another (potential to kinetic and vice versa, potential to elastic and vice versa), and viscous damping in soft tissues would cause the oscillations to damp out. In order to continue locomoting with a steady amplitude (stride length), energy must be injected during each locomotory cycle. In human walking about two-thirds of this force-providing energy is from the gastrocnemius-soleus group (Winter, 1983) during the push-off phase of gait.

To summarize the model components, the forced hybrid mass-spring pendulum consists of a periodic forcing function that is required of the muscles to overcome dissipative (damping) losses across gait cycles, and two conservative forces, one due to the body's inertia in the gravitational field and the other due to the spring energy return from the muscles and soft tissues.

My colleagues and I first used this model to try to understand an intriguing fact of locomotion. When individuals are asked to locomote at their preferred rate and stride length of walking or running at any speed, the combination results in a minimal metabolic cost (Zarrugh and Radcliff, 1978). When walking at any imposed stride rate and length for a

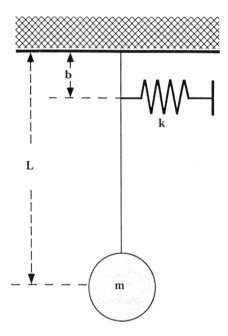

Figure 12.1
Schematic representation of a frictionless, hybrid mass-spring pendulum model, where $m =$ mass of the pendulum, $L =$ simple pendulum equivalent length, $b =$ distance from the axis of rotation to the spring attachment, and $k =$ composite global stiffness.

particular speed, oxygen consumption rises exponentially (figure 12.2). The finding is an example of how biological systems self-optimize. One possible explanation for this phenomenon is that an individual randomly selects a particular stride length and frequency (SL-F), practices in that mode and becomes metabolically economical through a form of specificity training. Alternatively, it might be argued that an individual discovers and operates at a natural (resonant) frequency, based on the inertial and spring characteristics of the musculoskeletal system. The stride length and frequency are emergent properties of a linear oscillator in the resonant mode.

Resonance in a damped oscillator refers to the frequency at which a fixed force produces maximal amplitude, or the frequency at which a minimal force produces a fixed amplitude. At resonance, the amount of forcing by gastrocnemius-soleus group (the largest contributor to the propelling force in locomotion) would be minimized for any particular stride length. Because muscular contractions are made at a metabolic cost, oxygen consumption should be minimized at resonance. Thus, although

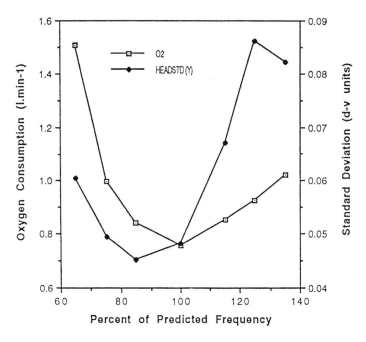

Figure 12.2
Metabolic cost and variability of head trajectory as a function of the walking frequency at a fixed treadmill speed. Predicted frequency is calculated from equation 12.3 in text. Skewed curves suggest that the optimal frequency is constrained by both variables (adapted from Holt, et al., 1995).

the constraint is oscillatory, the result is optimality. From the dynamical systems perspective and its philosophical underpinnings, the dynamically-driven stride length-frequency is more attractive than a brain-mediated choice. Stride frequency is an emergent property of a physical constraint. The brain makes no choice of frequency or stride length—the values are simply emergent behaviors of a system operating in its resonant mode. Nor does the brain need (nor have access to) metabolic feedback to inform it of an optimal SL-F configuration.

It is possible to distinguish between the brain as an agent of choice in the selection of stride length and frequency (SL-F) or the emergence of these parameters as consequences of their own dynamics. In the latter case a lawful relationship between the properties of the individual (mass, length) and stride frequency would be predicted. In the former there is no expectation of a principled way to predict SL-F. Any SL-F combination would suffice, and if practiced sufficiently that SL-F combination would result in a metabolically optimal gait. Our initial test of this prediction was to experimentally manipulate the formula for resonance of the hybrid oscillator by increasing the inertial load by adding weights to the ankle during walking (Holt, Hamill, and Andres, 1990). If frequency is driven by the dynamics it would change according to the solution to the resonance equation for each new inertial condition:

$$\tau = 2\pi(mL_e^2/(mL_eg + kb^2))^{1/2}, \tag{12.1}$$

where, τ is the resonant period, mL_e^2 is the moment of inertia of the leg, mL_eg is the restoring moment due to gravity, and kb^2 is the restoring moment due to stretch on soft tissues, in which k is the global stiffness of the system, and b is the perpendicular distance of the global spring from the axis of rotation (see Obusek, Holt, and Rosenstein, 1995 for full derivation of the model).

Because mL_eg and kb^2 have a common dimensionality (ML^2T^{-2}), one can be expressed in terms of the other (Turvey et al., 1988). For example, an equality in the two conservative moments (Kugler and Turvey, 1987),

$$kb^2 = mL_eg \tag{12.2}$$

allows for substitution so that equation 12.1 can be written as:

$$\tau = 2\pi(L_e/2g))^{1/2}. \tag{12.3}$$

Equation 12.3 successfully predicts the preferred walking frequency of a number of quadrupeds of varying leg length and masses (Kugler and Turvey, 1987). In the unloaded walking condition of adults and nine-year-olds who were not allowed to practice under a new inertial condition, equation 12.3 predicted the preferred walking periods of human adults and children (Holt, Hamill, and Andres, 1990; Holt, Jeng, and Fetters, 1991). Together these findings suggest that the underlying organizing principle across species for walking gait is to be found in the resonance equation of the hybrid oscillator.

The addition of load to the ankle effects changes in resonance by increasing the simple pendulum equivalent length (L_e) in equation 12.3. As loads were added to the ankle, there was an increasing divergence of the predicted from the preferred frequency. If the model is correct, the only other variable that could be manipulated according to equation 12.1 would be the stiffness, k. Evidence in the motor control literature suggests that stiffness is a controllable parameter (for review see Latash, 1993). Is it possible that as the inertial load is increased there is a concomitant increase in the stiffness?

In a recent experiment, we tested the hypothesis that limb stiffness is increased linearly with increases in load when a person freely swings one leg at the hip (Obusek et al., 1995). The inertial values (mLe) can be obtained from the leg anthropometry. Stiffness can be calculated by

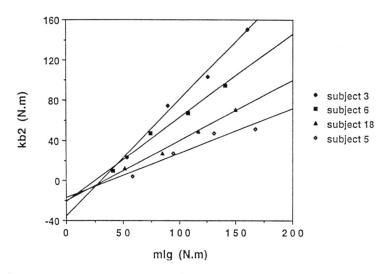

Figure 12.3
Individual subject regressions of stiffness on inertia for increasing ankle loads in preferred leg swinging (adapted from Obusek, Holt, and Rosenstein, 1995).

demonstrating resonance under each load and then rearranging equation 12.1:

$$kb^2 = (mL_e^2/(\tau/2\pi)^2) - mL_e g. \tag{12.4}$$

Because the values for τ and $mL_e g$ are empirically determined, the correlation of kb^2 on $mL_e g$ is not simply a result of the how the quantities are defined. As predicted, the regression of kb^2 on $mL_e g$ was highly linear (figure 12.3). The emergent oscillatory frequency was governed by the dynamics of the limbs as linear hybrid oscillators. The linearity of increases in kb^2 with $mL_e g$ may also be informative about the control variables involved in adjustments made to a changing environment. Orientation of a body part to the gravitational field, and addition of load to a limb if noncompensated, will influence the effect of a particular muscle action on the kinematics through changes in inertia. A scalar increase in stiffness with inertia provides a simple control mechanism. Changes in orientation to gravity or the addition of loads to a limb that would result in inertial changes in a limb would be matched by limb stiffness changes in a linear fashion. The finding of Obusek, Holt, and Rosenstein (1995) suggests a relatively simple mechanism for accommodating the context-conditioned variability due to gravitational orientation and load.

To verify the claim that the resonant frequency resulted in minimal metabolic costs through reduced muscular forcing, we performed an experiment in which adult subjects were asked to walk at the predicted resonant frequency (equation 12.3) at their preferred speed, and at metronome-driven frequencies that were $\pm 15\%$, $\pm 25\%$, $\pm 35\%$ of the predicted. Metabolic cost was measured through steady-state oxygen consumption. Although no direct or indirect measure of muscle force was obtained, a strongly quadratic U-shaped curve of oxygen plotted against frequency was found with a minimum at the predicted frequency (figure 12.2) (Holt et al., 1995).

To summarize so far, evidence suggests that preferred walking can be modeled using the resonance formula for a hybrid pendulum and spring system. This finding can be interpreted as a physically driven solution to the emergence of at least one gait parameter, the preferred walking frequency at the preferred speed. The model suggests that self-optimization of the metabolic cost of walking is an a posteriori fact of a linear system oscillating at resonance. Neither self-optimization nor walking frequency appear to be brain mediated events, although they potentially could be. The leg swinging data suggest that stiffness is a controllable parameter and that it is scaled to the inertial properties of the limb. Furthermore, in the preferred walking mode $mL_e g = kb^2$, and this unifying physical principle carries across species.

12.8 Optimality Constraints and the Hybrid Model

Self-optimization is the tendency to coordinate mechanical and physio-logical variables in order to produce proficient action at a minimal cost to the system. It has been claimed that this principle underlies the coordi-nated activity of many biological processes (Wilke, 1977). Certainly pre-ferred walking gait is associated with a minimal metabolic cost (Holt, Hamill, and Andres, 1991), although our interpretation has been that this is an a posteriori fact of a system at resonance. Do other potential opti-mality criteria emerge from the resonance feature of gait? There are a number of potential constraints on walking gait, including maximizing stability, and shock absorption, minimizing mechanical work or maxi-mizing mechanical energy transfers that might also constrain preferred gait patterns. Do they fall out of the physics in the same way metabolic costs appear to?

Stability has been shown to be an important determinant in coordina-tion dynamics. Studies in non-linear dynamics have shown the attractive-ness of stable solutions in preferred coordination patterns. For example, in oscillating the index fingers there are only two stable states, in-phase and anti-phase, regimes into which the coupled oscillators quickly settle (Kelso et al., 1986). In juggling, however, the claim has been made that stability must be tempered by flexibility in coordination patterns. Thus, expert jugglers hover around but are not rigidly phase locked in the movements of their hands and the balls (Beek, 1989). The question for walking, therefore, is to ask a priori which body systems need stability or flexibility. Following the rationale of Berthoz and colleagues (Pozzo, Berthoz, and Lefort, 1990, Pozzo et al., 1991), my colleagues and I argued that head stability is critical to successful performance in any task requiring accurate visual and vestibular information (Holt et al., 1995). In order to achieve head stabilization, perturbations that occur on ground contact (e.g. variable terrain) must be damped out before reaching the head. This could be accomplished only by considerable variability in the limb and trunk coordination patterns. One has only to look at the actions of a skilled mogul skier to observe this phenomenon. Although there is a great deal of variability in the coordination patterns of the limbs as the skier negotiates the variable terrain, the head appears almost stationary. It was predicted, therefore, that limb trajectories would demonstrate rather large variability, while the head would maintain a stable trajectory

In our experiments on stability, we borrowed phase-plane and time-series methods from nonlinear dynamics (Kay, Saltzman, and Kelso, 1991) to measure stability of the head and joints under predicted and forced walking conditions (Holt et al., 1995). Head stability was measured using variability of the velocity-displacement trajectory across repeated cycles. Joint stability was measured as the relative timing of lower limb joints. To compare head and joint stability, spectral power analysis was computed for the time series data. Results indicated that head and joint stability were maximized at the predicted frequency, and head stability was greater than the stability of any of the joints. Thus, while the limbs showed a great deal of flexibility and complexity in their motions, the motions served to reduce the variability of the head trajectory. One means by which this was achieved was to reduce the amount of shock experienced at the head compared to that experienced in the foot (Ratcliffe and Holt, 1997). Is head and joint stability a constraint on walking frequency, or an emergent property of a system at resonance? By definition a linear system at resonance demonstrates a minimal variability in spectral frequency suggesting that this may be related to the maximization of head and joint stability at the predicted walking frequency.

Stability and minimal metabolic cost are optimality criteria in gait, but the role of mechanical work variables as a constraint is less clear. In walking, pelvic tilt and rotation, and knee flexion serve to minimize the mechanical work performed in raising and lowering the body center of mass (CM) (Inman, Ralston, and Todd, 1979). Specifically, these anatomical functions limit the amplitude of the potential energy curve of the body CM. In our gait studies we wished to identify mechanical constraints that potentially might determine the preferred frequency and stride length.

Two measures were used. In the first, the total mechanical work performed was measured by changes in the potential and kinetic energy of the body and its segments (Holt, Hamill, and Andres, 1991; Pierrynowski, Winter, and Norman, 1980). The experiment used the same protocol as those used for metabolic measures. Individuals were allowed to choose their own speed-frequency-stride length combination and they were metronome driven at frequencies higher and lower than the preferred but at the preferred speed. Potential and kinetic energies were obtained from videotaped data and a motion analysis system. Results showed that the total mechanical work remained constant across all SL-F conditions.

The second measure was justified on the argument that the critical variable was not mechanical work per se, but the mechanical energy that was *conserved*. We performed an experiment to determine the mechanical energy conservation across the SL-F conditions (Holt et al., 1995). Conservation of mechanical energy was measured by the transfers of potential and kinetic energy between and within body segments. As in the case of mechanical work, mechanical energy conservation did not change across conditions. There are problems with the methods of mechanical work and conservation, particularly the lack of account of elastic energy storage and return in soft tissues. Nevertheless, these findings suggest that these mechanical variables do not appear to act as constraints on the preferred SL-F of locomotion.

Mechanical energy conservation may act as a constraint on the *preferred speed* of walking. It has been shown that the preferred speed of walking is about 1.3 ms^{-1}, and at about that speed the oxygen consumption per unit distance is minimized (Turvey et al., 1996). McMahon (1984) showed that transfers between potential and kinetic energy of the body CM was maximal at that speed. These findings exemplify the notion that different parameters and patterns of the gait cycle may be constrained by different optimality criteria. Although walking at a preferred *frequency* is constrained by metabolic and stability criteria, preferred walking *speed* is constrained by metabolic, stability and mechanical criteria. The importance of mechanical and metabolic constraints in preferred speed-stride length-frequency and our studies on gait transitions to be discussed later hint at the possibility that a major constraint on locomotion can be found in the relationships between metabolic regulatory processes and mechanical output.

It remains unclear whether optimality criteria are the principal means by which gait patterns are constrained, or whether they are emergent properties of a system at resonance. Resonance could potentially be discovered as the solution to the drive to optimality. The emergence of optimality from dynamic constraints would be the more likely choice of the dynamical systems protagonist, because resonance is the natural mode for a physical system.

12.9 Generalizability of the Hybrid Model

The resonance model has been a powerful predictor of preferred walking parameters such as SL-F, and preferred walking speed appears to be additionally constrained by mechanical energy conservation. Another issue for the hybrid model is its applicability in nonpreferred gait speeds. At each walking and running speed there is a unique SL-F that gives a minimal metabolic cost. Can the resonance model be expanded to include locomotory speeds that are higher or lower than the preferred speed? The need to walk faster or slower is precipitated by some task constraints such as in the example of the need to catch a bus. Increased speed is accompanied by linear increases in stride length and frequency (Obusek and Holt, in preparation). Do changes in frequency at higher or lower speed walking indicate that the system is no longer at resonance?

According to equation 12.1, if the system remains at resonance, an increase or decrease in frequency must be mediated by changes in stiffness. In addition, if walking is more pendular and running more spring-like, equation 12.1 would suggest that inertia should play a lesser role in determining frequency than stiffness, that is, $kb^2 > mL_eg$. Results of running experiments performed on running bipeds (Kugler and Turvey, 1987) and humans (Holt, Slavin, and Hamill, 1990) support this possibility. In both animals and humans the resonance equation that best predicts the preferred running period turns out to be:

$$\tau = 2\pi(L_e/5g))^{1/2}. \tag{12.5}$$

The rationale for equation 12.2 indicates that the constant under the root reflects the ratio of stiffness to forcing. The empirical relationship in equation 12.5 implies that stiffness has a four times greater influence on period than the inertial component in running.

The first step in determining the usefulness of the model in mediating speed changes in gait is to confirm that the system is operating at resonance at any speed. Furthermore, and consonant with attempting to minimize the degrees of freedom and context conditioned variability problems, it seems reasonable to ask if there are invariances that arise from lawful relationships between the kinetic variables of gait as speed is increased— muscle forcing, elastic energy storage in soft tissues, and inertia.

In recent developments led by a doctoral student, Jack Obusek (1995), we have attempted to refine the model to more accurately reflect the gait cycle and to address these questions. The model developed by Obusek diverges from the resonance model used in our previous studies of an ordinary pendulum that is frictionless, thereby requiring no forcing. In reality, it is the body CM that is being moved over its base of support at the foot. A more accurate representation is that of a *double inverted*

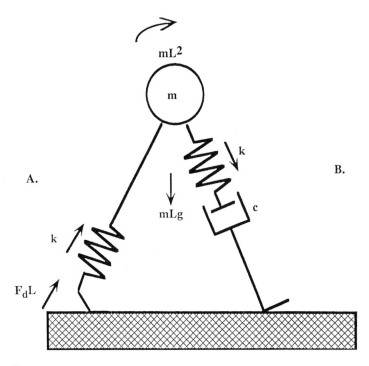

Figure 12.4
Schematic representation of double pendulum and spring in walking gait. *A* represents push off by muscle forcing (F_dL), and release of stored elastic energy in soft tissues (k). *B* represents weight acceptance with energy absorption in muscle and soft tissues (k), and damping due to losses of energy in transfer (c). Limb functions are reversed on next step.

pendulum with spring and inertial components (figure 12.4). Furthermore, there is energy lost on each cycle through two mechanisms. First the viscous damping due to soft tissue has a damping effect, though this is small. Second, major energy loss is due to inefficient energy transfers from one support limb or limb oscillator to the next. Although the model (figure 12.5) consists of only one oscillator, in reality two oscillators are involved. Each step in the gait cycle constitutes a half-cycle. At the end of the half cycle, energy is passed onto the next oscillating unit (the other limb) with some losses that occur in the transfer stage. A forcing function is required to replace energy losses due to these dissipative processes.

The *inverted* pendulum equation of motion for the forced hybrid model (figure 12.5) can be written as

$$mL^2(\ddot{\theta}) = F_dL \cos \theta + mLg \sin \theta - kb \sin \theta b \cos \theta - c(\dot{\theta})b \cos \theta,$$

$$(12.6)$$

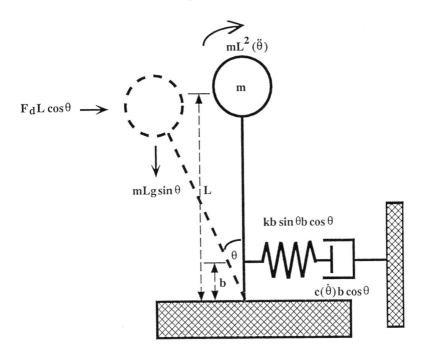

Figure 12.5
Schematic of a single, forced inverted hybrid model of the gait cycle as a simplification of model presented in figure 12.4 (see text for details).

where $mL^2(\ddot{\theta})$ is the net moment of the center of mass, $F_d L \cos \theta$ is the driving moment produced by active muscle contraction, $mL_g \sin \theta$ is the moment produced by gravity on the center of mass, $kb \sin \theta b \cos \theta$ is the moment produced by stretch on soft tissues, and $c(\dot{\theta})b \cos \theta$ is the moment produced by viscous properties of soft tissues and energy absorption in the opposite limb during foot contact and weight acceptance (in which c represents a damping term).

From this basic equation it is possible to derive proportional estimates of each of the energy sources that contributes to the continued oscillations of the body. At resonance, stiffness is related to period (frequency) by equation 12.4. Functions $mL^2(\ddot{\theta})$ and $mLg \sin \theta$ can be measured from kinematic data. Because damping is a velocity-dependent constant, a proportional estimate of forcing $f_d L \cos \theta$ can be obtained. A number of relationships between the energy sources can also be predicted. These include linear relationships between the forcing $F_d L \cos \theta$ and stiffness $kb \sin \theta b \cos \theta$ terms, and between stiffness and the inertia $mLg \sin \theta$. A steady-state oscillatory solution also requires that the stiffness be equal to, or greater than the inertia, $kb \sin \theta b \cos \theta > mLg \sin \theta$.

A walking experiment was conducted to determine if resonance can be shown in each of five walking speeds, and to determine whether the linear relationships between the energy variables holds as predicted (Obusek, Holt, and Rosenstein, 1995). Resonance can be demonstrated if most of the spectral energy is concentrated at the stride frequency. Step frequency power is also included when side to side symmetries are assumed. In all the speed conditions, 99% of the total spectral power was concentrated at the step and stride frequencies, indicating resonance in each condition. As predicted by the model, the linear relationships among forcing, stiffness, and inertia were also observed. The exception to these findings was that in a number of subjects walking at the slowest speed, a steady-state oscillatory solution was not possible because the stiffness term was less than the inertial term. When this occurs, the inertial component causes the oscillator to fall out of the stable cycle. Results of the experiment also showed linearity between the forcing function and oxygen consumption.

In a resonant hybrid system, forcing is linearly related to amplitude (stride length), and stiffness is linearly related to stride frequency. Sufficient force is necessary only to overcome dissipative losses, and stiffness must be great enough to match the body's inertia for oscillations to continue. The stride frequencies and stride lengths observed at any speed are emergent gait parameters that arise as a consequence of a linear dynamical system operating in the resonant mode. Frequency and amplitude are "customized" to the individual's anthropometry (L_e and m), and the gravitational environment (g). Essentially, it is the requirements of resonance in the dynamics that drive the observed kinematics. Although the dynamics of coupled nonlinear oscillators may be informative of the control and order parameters relevant to a particular coordinative structure, the control parameters (speed, frequency) that govern the order parameters are themselves the result of dynamic constraints.

There are advantages to an individual working within linear ranges of an oscillatory system. Of potential importance in control are the linear relationships between forcing, inertia, and stiffness that are properties of a linear hybrid oscillator in its resonant mode. Changes in locomotor speed can be accomplished simply by scalar increases in stiffness and force (figure 12.6), thereby reducing the number of individual variables to be independently controlled (degrees of freedom). In the walking experiment, there were a number of subjects for whom the behaviors became nonlinear at the highest (2.2 ms^{-1}) or lowest (.56 ms^{-1}) walking speed. These extreme experimental speeds are lower and higher than normally assumed walking speeds. Similarly, in an accompanying experiment in which the SL-F were manipulated at a constant speed, nonlinearities were observed in some subjects at the extreme conditions. These results suggest that the

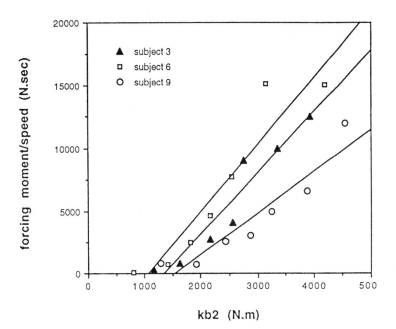

Figure 12.6
Linear regression of forcing on stiffness during walking at increasing speeds. (adapted from Obusek, 1995).

upper and lower bound on preferred walking speeds and SL-F combinations may be related to the advantages of working in linear ranges. In order to minimize the task complexity, walking is normally constrained to speeds and SL-F ranges in which linear relationships can be maintained according to an individual's dynamic capabilities. Planned studies are designed to determine the role of linearity as a constraint on the boundaries of preferred gaits.

In summary, from the studies on the inverted pendulum conducted to this point it is possible to conclude that individuals walk at their resonant frequency regardless of the speed of walking. The general equation of motion governing the behavior of hybrid pendulum and spring oscillators applies to human walking. Thus, linear relationships between muscle forcing and soft tissue stiffness are predicted and observed in the experimental data. Walking speeds appear to be bounded by the linearity constraint. Simply put, by obeying the constraints imposed by Newtonian laws of motion, an individual is constrained to walk at certain speeds, has fewer *dynamic* degrees of freedom to control, and optimizes performance from a metabolic and muscular perspective.

12.10 Individual Constraints and the Hybrid Model

Our work on individual constraints in locomotion has emphasized constraints on the dynamics that are the result of disease processes, particularly those due to cerebral palsy (CP) (Holt, 1993, 1996; Jeng, Holt, and Fetters, 1993; Jeng et al., 1996). Cerebral palsy is an upper motor neuron disease typified by a number of changes in the neuromuscular apparatus. Of particular interest are (1) increases in limb stiffness due to changes in the morphology of soft tissues (Dietz and Berger, 1983) and cocontraction of antagonist muscle groups (Berger, Quintern, and Dietz, 1982), and (2) weakness in the power-producing gastrocnemius-soleus group (Olney, MacPhail, and Hedden, 1990). We sought to determine if the individual constraints could account for gait differences between hemiplegic CP and nondisabled children, matched on the basis of anthropometrical considerations.

Children with hemiplegic (one-sided involvement) CP walk more slowly, at a higher stride frequency, and with shorter stride length than their nondisabled peers (Jeng, Holt, and Fetters, 1993). There is limb asymmetry both in spatial and temporal patterns of motion. In diplegic (bilateral involvement) CP, the walking gait often has the appearance of running, characterized by a lack of energy exchanges between potential energy (PE) and kinetic energy (KE) (Olney, MacPhail, and Hedden, 1990), by inphase flexion of the hip, knee, and ankle (Bruin et al., 1982; Gage, 1990; Strotzky, 1983; Leonard, Hirschfeld, and Forssberg, 1991), and by increased vertical displacement of the center of mass (Strotzky, 1983). A plantar flexed foot on ground contact (equinus foot) is a common characteristic of CP gait. Using the dynamic requirements for continued oscillations of a hybrid pendulum and spring we sought to understand the relationship between the muscular and stiffness constraints, and the kinematic differences found between CP and nondisabled children.

The conservative inertial and elastic properties of the hybrid oscillator, and a forcing function ensure its continued oscillations. According to equation 12.6, the individual contributions that give the body CM a net moment (and hence continued oscillations) can be variable. At resonance, amplitude is effected by forcing and frequency by stiffness. Model predictions for a locomotor system that has decreased forcing and increased stiffness are a decrease in the stride length and an increase in stride frequency. In earlier research, the model predictions held. Stride length and stride frequency changes were in the predicted direction (Jeng et al., 1996). Thus, stride frequency and length appear to be constrained by the dynamics of the task, (modeled as a hybrid pendulum and spring) and by the dynamics that are available to the individual. No estimates of the relative contributions of forcing, stiffness, and inertia to the continued oscillations were made by Jeng and colleagues (1996), and no attempt was made to show resonance. Current research is designed to address these issues.

The lack of certain action capabilities in disordered gait raises a number of interesting questions. Are the gait pattern seen in diplegic and hemiplegic CP a reflection of the availability or lack of sources of energy (conservative and forcing)? Are some of the symptoms of CP adaptations that allow for gait in the absence of other factors? A number of researchers are now beginning to argue that the movement patterns in neuronal diseases are not symptoms of the disease, but adaptations to the disease (Holt, 1996; Latash and Ansen, 1996). For example, morphological changes in soft tissues, cocontraction, and a plantar flexed foot may be adaptations that allow greater elastic energy storage and return. From this perspective, one of the challenges for rehabilitation will be to differentiate between causes and adaptations. Treatment of the cause may obviate the need for the adaptation. For example, it has been shown that artificially increasing forcing in the gastrocnemius-soleus (G-S) in CP by electrical stimulation during the push-off phase improves the gait pattern. Of particular interest is the paradoxical finding that the foot plantar flexion that prevents normal heel strike in CP disappeared following electrical stimulation, contrary to what might be expected by stimulation of the G-S group (Carmick, 1993). Electrical stimulation obviates the need for adaptations (plantar flexed foot, morphological changes, cocontraction) that allow for increased use of elastic energy to maintain oscillations in the absence of adequate forcing.

In sum, the action capabilities that the individual brings to the task act as constraints on the types of movement patterns that are observed. Observed coordination patterns arise from the dynamic requirements of the task *and* the dynamic action capabilities of the individual to accommodate these requirements. Adaptations may be viewed as alternative solutions to the dynamic task of maintaining the oscillations in locomotion.

12.11 Thermodynamic Constraints as a Basis for Gait Transitions

A consistent theme in this chapter has been the importance of metabolic processes to emergent kinetic and kinematic gait properties. Loss of energy due to dissipative processes requires periodic muscle forcing derived from the chemical energy stored in muscle, which in turn is derived from other metabolic sources. The dynamics of locomotion are but one aspect of the capture-degrade and dissipative processes of a thermodynamic system. It may be in thermodynamic law that metabolic and dynamic constraints are unified.

One way to understand self-organization in coordination patterns has been to use experimental paradigms that investigate changes from one pattern to another. For example, transition experiments are the core support for synergetic (dynamic pattern) theory (Kelso et al., 1986). Other experimenters have used transition experiments to determine if there are dynamic (Lin 1993), mechanical (Farley and Taylor 1991), kinematic (Hreljac 1995), or metabolic (Hoyt and Taylor, 1981; Hreljac,1993) "triggers" for gait transitions. The underlying rationale for this type of experiment is based on the notion that once a pattern becomes costly for an animal, a transition to a less costly pattern will occur. Neither synergetic constraints nor triggers have satisfactorily accounted for transitions from walking to running in humans, with the exception, perhaps of Diedrich and Warren (chapter 14), who nevertheless used metabolic arguments to support synergetic claims.

One feature of thermodynamic systems is the property of adiabatic invariance, where certain quantities are left unchanged by transformations. One adiabatic invariant, proposed by Ehrenfest, that may have applicability to human locomotion and its transitions is the linearity between the kinetic energy (E_{KE}) and frequency ($f(s^{-1})$) of a conservative periodic system where change in frequency is brought about infinitely slowly. Kugler and Turvey (1987) proposed that the adiabatic hypothesis might be applied to nonconservative behaviors such as locomotion, in which energy is lost (and replaced) by metabolic sources. They proposed an adiabatic invariant that consisted of the sum of the conservative (E_{KE}) and non-conservative (metabolic) energy forms per frequency. Turvey and colleagues argued that in locomotion it is the *changes* in rotational and translational kinetic energy (ΔE_{KE}) interconverted with other sources (chemical potential in muscle, gravitational potential, and elastic potential in muscle and tendon) per stride that is a more relevant measure of the E_{KE} term. Similarly, the appropriate frequency term is the stride frequency of a gait cycle (Turvey et al., 1996). One indicator that the hypothesis is correct is the demonstration of linearity in the plot of ΔE_{KE} vs $f(s^1)$ as running speed increases, with a negative ΔE_{KE} intercept reflecting nonconservative metabolic energy losses (E_t). As part of a larger project an experiment was conducted in which running speed was increased from $7\,kh^{-1}$ to $13\,kh^{-1}$. In (unreported) data from that experiment the group and individual plots of $\Delta E_{KE} x f(s^{-1})$ show the predicted relationship (figure 12.7). This finding provided initial support that the application of Ehrenfest's hypothesis to locomotion is fundamentally viable.

In a hybrid pendulum and spring oscillator, the ratio of conservative (inertia and elasticity) and nonconservative (friction) forces is termed the Q factor. In a locomotory system operating at resonance the required muscular forces overcome only the dissipative losses, and are reflected in

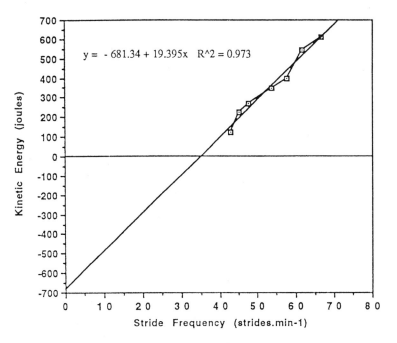

Figure 12.7
Regression of kinetic energy changes on frequency changes as running speed is increased.

the metabolic cost (Obusek, Holt, and Rosenstein, 1995). Q, from the linear hybrid model and from the nonconservative adiabatic hypothesis of Kugler and Turvey (1987), can be defined as $Q = E_{KE}/Et$ (Turvey et al., 1996). The Q factor may be the critical variable that defines and differentiates walking and running gaits. When $Q = 1$, the muscles supply exactly the E_{KE} for the oscillations of the body segments. At $Q < 1$, there is greater muscle activity than is produced in the E_{KE}. At $Q > 1$, muscular forces do not account for all of the E_{KE}. At $Q > 1$ energy sources other than those supplied from concentric muscle activity are utilized. In running, this energy is supplied by reactive forces facilitated by elastic energy return in the soft tissues. In walking, particularly at lower speeds when there cannot be a steady state oscillatory solution, some of the muscular force is required to overcome the body inertia, and is not seen in body motion E_{KE}.

A number of hypotheses that arise from this thermodynamic model were supported in a walking and running experiment (Turvey et al., 1996). One major prediction was that the boundary between walking and running occurs at $Q = 1$, with walking constrained to $Q \leq 1$ and running constrained to $Q > 1$. The speed for gait transitions from walking to run-

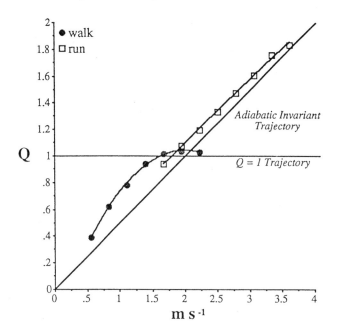

Figure 12.8
Data and prediction of gait transitions (intersection of $Q = 1$ and the adiabatic invariant trajectory) based on thermodynamic constraints (adapted from Turvey, et al., 1996)

ning is about $2\,ms^{-1}$. The experimental data showed that the boundary between walking and running did indeed occur at $Q = 1$ at a mean predicted speed of $2.02\ ms^{-1}$ (figure 12.8). The model is in the early stages of development and further research is needed (and underway) to determine the model's potential to predict gait transitions for individuals based on their individual energy curves. Nevertheless, the adiabatic hypothesis has the potential to provide a way to understand the relationship between metabolic and mechanical constraints on locomotor transitions.

12.12 Summary

Locomotion is an example of a complex, skilled activity, stably and flexibly organized, that would, if its organization were the sole responsibility of the brain, require a great deal of computational power. It would be difficult to walk and do just about anything else at the same time! The central theme of this chapter has been to demonstrate the self-organization that underlies the parameters of locomotion as an alternative to the philosophical and practical problems of assigning the responsibility to executive intelligence. Self-organization arises from multiple constraints that may be characterized as those due to the relationship between the task and the individual's action capabilities (personal), linear and nonlinear dynamics, and thermodynamics. Constraints that arise from the tendency for biological organisms to self-optimize must also be taken into account. The emphasis in our research has been to discover the constraints that arise from oscillatory processes that can be approximated by the linear dynamics of a pendulum and spring and to relate this mechanical model to observable self-optimizing features.

At this point I will attempt to present a framework for understanding the control and coordination involved in human locomotion that is a preface to a general theory of constraints in human motion. By way of example, assume again the task of catching a bus. The emergence of gait form may be based on the relation between the task requirement (e.g., "enough" speed), and the action capability of the individual (the capability to produce enough speed). The relationship may perhaps be captured by a parameter such as time-to-contact that encompasses the two variables. In order to achieve a certain speed, the individual must be capable of producing sufficient force (amplitude) and stiffness (frequency). Walking and running gaits are defined by the extent to which the individual has available the dynamic resources to achieve a given speed. If high speed is required, the only solution may be a gait that uses high forces and significant elastic energy return (running). The flexibility of the relationship between forcing and elastic energy as sources of energy may result in a running gait at lower speeds. This possibility is demonstrated by our work that suggests increasing stiffness and decreasing force in individuals with weakness in the major forcing muscles (Jeng et al., 1996). Children with some forms of spastic cerebral palsy locomote by a gait that is quantitatively describable as running, even at low speeds. Thus, as a first stage, I would claim that the relationship between the task and individual constraints serve as information for emergence of a particular gait form.

This interpretation of the empirical observations is consonant with a general theory of Action Systems (Reed, 1982), elaborated upon by Kugler and Turvey (1987) for the locomotory system. The fundamental features of an action are described as follows: "An action is (a) not a thing but a relation (among properties distributed over the acting animal and the surround) ... (b) not a particular aggregation of elemental anatomical mechanisms but a specific mode of resource use...; and (c) not categorized by reference to the anatomy that it involves but by reference to the function that it performs, that is, it is functionally specific, not anatomically specific" (Kugler and Turvey, 1987, p 407).

The equations of motion for a forced hybrid model provide a formal description of the relations of properties (mass, length, elasticity, gravity, damping) of the animal locomoting in the gravitational field. Walking and running as actions in the locomotory system are specific modes of resource use. Resources refer to the gravitational potential, tissue elastic potential, and muscle chemical potential. The units of action for a loco-moting system are the coupled limb and trunk oscillators. In locomotion it makes little sense to talk of actions in reference to gross anatomy because the same muscles and limb segments are involved in running and walking. Nevertheless, it is important to understand the relationship between re-sources, the availability of resources and the mechanisms of resource use. Our research suggests that the individual exploits the available energy resources through the dynamics by exploring different coordinative pat-terns that may eventually lead to changes in anatomical structures (mor-phological adaptation) in order to fulfill the functional requirements of the task (catch a bus, find food).

Once form of gait has been established (walk, run, no action), stride length and frequency are constrained by the resonance of the linear pen-dulum and spring. The actual inter- and intra-limb coordination patterns (that may be described by relative phase or some other timing measure) could potentially emerge from two types of constraints. Consonant with dynamic pattern theory (Kelso, 1995), which treats limbs and segments as coupled nonlinear oscillators, the frequency that falls out of resonance and the linear equations of motion may serve as a control parameter for the emergence of stable coordination patterns (order parameter). There is, as yet, no evidence to support this intriguing possibility. Alternatively, an interlimb coordination pattern may reflect the optimal configuration for transmission of energy from the force producing muscles of the leg to the body center of mass as the oscillating mass of an inverted pendulum. Further research is also needed to support this hypothesis.

The above-outlined scheme cannot account for a number of facts of gait. The major problem to be addressed is that humans and animals can walk more quickly and run more slowly than would normally be observed. The simple relationship between task requirements and action capabilities outlined above is insufficient to account for gait form and transitions. What is missing? Locomotion is metabolically expensive. One possibility is that animals and humans change gaits when the new gait becomes less metabolically expensive. Horses change from a trot to a gallop under this constraint (Hoyt and Taylor, 1981). Humans walk at a frequency that minimizes metabolic cost for any locomotor speed, and human gait tran-sitions from walking to running occur at about $2ms^{-1}$, even though it is metabolically more expensive to run at that speed (figure 12.9). This implies that gait form and transformations are related to metabolic costs, but not in a simple manner. Our work on thermodynamic constraints implies that form and transitions may be governed by the relationships

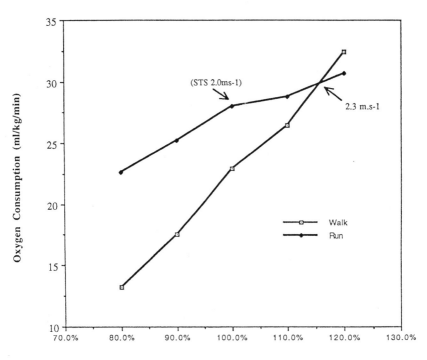

Figure 12.9
Forced walking and running around the spontaneous transition speed (STS) indicates that running becomes metabolically less expensive than running at a higher speed than the actual transition speed (2.3 ms^{-1}).

between mechanical output, and metabolic input, between the gains and losses in energy and matter (Nicolis, 1989; Turvey, 1990).

There are other interesting facts of locomotion that cannot be readily accounted for by an oscillator dynamic or thermodynamic account. When loads are added to a horse, transitions are triggered when a critical force level occurs (Farley and Taylor, 1991). When people walk down stairs more knee flexion is observed on foot contact, but in walking over ground knee flexion is small. In level walking, however, increases in knee flexion of the magnitude that might be seen in downhill walking (through a Groucho-like gait) cause large increases in metabolic cost (McMahon, Valiant, and Frederick, 1987). A compliant walk of this form is usually not adopted. This outcome suggests that walking down stairs is metabolically expensive, but that it serves to minimize shock to the body. Furthermore, animals will not adopt a gait pattern that causes the stresses on joints and bones to exceed 2/3 of their yield stress (Rubin and Lanyon, 1984). These findings show that a change in gait pattern is precipitated by changes in the locomotory task (loaded vs. unloaded gait). The data suggest that the intrinsic task constraint, as it relates to the actor, changes from metabolic economy to injury prevention. These examples serve to demonstrate that gait patterns are constrained not only by the dynamics, but in rather complex ways related to self-optimization. The cost factors may include minimization of metabolic cost (through resonance constraints of the hybrid oscillator), injury avoidance (through mechanical parameters such as shock absorption), maximizing head stability (as governed by the principles of non-linear dynamics). Other research has shown other cost factors that may constrain movement patterns including minimization of jerk, minimization of torque, minimization of "effort" and maximization of "comfort" (see Latash, 1993, for review).

Gait patterns may also be governed by quasi-static postural equilibrium constraints. For example, a marked change in gait pattern occurs when there is weakness in the gluteus medius (GM) muscle. Under normal circumstances, during the single support phase of gait the gluteus medius on the weight-bearing side prevents the contralateral hip from dropping down by its attachment between the hip and pelvis. If there is GM weakness due to disease, the individual moves the center of mass closer to the hip axis by moving the trunk toward the weight-bearing hip on the stance limb, thereby reducing the moment arm due to the body weight. The so-called "gluteus medius lurch" or Trendelenberg gait prevents dropping of the contralateral hip, and in so doing produces profound changes and interlimb asymmetries in the coordination pattern. Although it may be argued that GM weakness is a constraint on the oscillatory dynamics by virtue of its role in *preventing* rotatory motion around the hip, full invocation of dynamic models is not critical to understanding the coordination pattern that emerges.

There is much work to be done to understand the relevant constraints on the emergence of gait patterns, and I suspect on the emergence of any functional task. Minimally, the intrinsic and extrinsic task constraints must be accommodated, as must those related to the individual and the relationship between task and individual. It is an oversimplification to believe that the self-organizing capability of the individual for most tasks can be explained solely by linear, nonlinear, or thermodynamic constraints of oscillatory processes. As I hope this chapter has shown, however, the constraints perspective provides a useful starting point for a complete account of locomotory control, and a conceptual basis for investigation of many other skilled activities.

References

Beek, P. (1989). Timing and phase locking in cascade juggling. *Ecological Psychology, 1*, 55–96.

Berger, W., Quintern, J., & Dietz, V. 1982. Pathophysiology of gait in children with cerebral palsy. *Electroencephalography and Clinical Neurology, 53*, 538–548.

Bruin, D. D., Eng, P., Russell, J., Latter J. E., & Sadler, J. T. S. (1982). Angle-angle diagrams in monitoring and quantifications for children with cerebral palsy. *American Journal of Physical Medicine, 61*, 176–192.

Bruwer, M., & Cruse, H. (1990). A network model for the control of movement of a redundant manipulator. *Biological Cybernetics, 62*, 549–555.

Bullock, D., & Grossberg, S. (1988). Neural dynamics of planned arm movements: Emergent invariants and speed-accuracy properties during trajectory formation. *Psychological Review, 95*, 49–90.

Carmick, J. 1993. Clinical use of neuromuscular electrical stimulation in children with cerebral palsy. *Physical Therapy, 73*, 505–513.

Cavagna G. A., Heglund N. C., & Taylor C. R. (1977). Mechanical work in terrestrial locomotion: two basic mechanisms for minimizing energy expenditure. *American Journal of Physiology, 233*, R243–R261.

Collins J. J., & Stewart L. (1993). Hexapodal gaits and coupled nonlinear oscillator models. *Biological Cybernetics, 68*, 287–298

Dennett, D. C. (1978). *Brainstorms: Philosophical Essays on Mind and Psychology.* Montgomery, VT: Bradford Books.

Diedrich, F. J., & Warren W. H., (1995). Why change gaits? Dynamics of the walk-run transition. *Journal of Experimental Psychology: Human Performance and Perception, 21*, 183–202.

Dietz, V., & Berger, W. (1983). Normal and impaired regulation of muscle stiffness in gait: a new hypothesis about muscle hypertonia. *Experimental Neurology, 79*, 680–687.

Farley, C. T., & Taylor, C. R. (1991). A mechanical trigger for the trot-gallop transition in horses. *Science, 253*, 306–308.

Gage, J. R. (1990). Surgical treatment of knee dysfunction in cerebral palsy. *Clinical Orthopedic Research, 253*, 45–54.

Haken, H., Kelso, J. A. S., & Bunz, H. (1985). A theoretical model of phase transitions in human hand movements. *Biological Cybernetics, 51*, 347–356.

Holt, K. G. (1993). Towards general principles for research and rehabilitation of disabled populations. *Physical Theory Practice, 2*, 1–18.

Holt, K. G. (1996). 'Constraint' versus 'choice' in preferred movement patterns. *Brain and Behavioral Sciences, 19*, 76–77.

Holt, K. G., Hamill, J., & Andres R. O., (1990). The force-driven harmonic oscillator as a model for human locomotion. *Human Movement Science, 9*, 55–68.

Holt, K. G., Hamill, J., & Andres R. O., (1991). Predicting the minimal energy costs of human walking. *Medicine and Science in Sports and Exercise, 23*, 491–498.

Holt, K. G., Jeng, S. F., & Fetters, L. (1991). Walking cadence of 9-year olds is predictable as the resonant frequency of a force-driven harmonic oscillator. *Pediatric Exercise Science, 3*, 121–128.

Holt, K. G., Jeng, S. F., Ratcliffe, R., & Hamill, J. (1995). Energetic cost and stability in preferred human walking. *Journal of Motor Behavior, 27*, 164–179.

Holt, K. G., Slavin, M. M., & Hamill, J. (1990). Running at resonance: Is it a learned phenomenon? Proceedings of the Canadian Society for Biomechanics, Quebec: Organizing Committee, CSB.

Hoyt, D. F., & Taylor, C. R. (1981). Gait and the energetics of locomotion in horses. *Nature, 292*, 239–240.

Hreljac, A. (1993). Preferred and energetically optimal transition speeds in human locomotion. *Medicine and Science in Sports and Exercise, 25,* 1158–1162.

Hreljac, A. (1995). Determinants of the gait transition speed during human locomoiton: Kinematic factors. *Journal of Biomechanics, 28,* 669–677.

Inman, V. T., Ralston, H. J., & Todd, F. (1979). *Human Walking.* Baltimore: Williams & Wilkins.

Jeng, S. F., Holt, K. G., Fetters, L., & Certo, C. (1996). Self-optimization of walking in non-disabled children and children with spastic hemiplegic cerebral palsy. *Journal of Motor Behavior, 28,* 15–27.

Kay, B. A., Saltzman, E. L., & Kelso, J. A. S. (1991). Steady state and perturbed rhythmical movements: A dynamical analysis. *Journal of Experimental Psychology: Human Perception and Performance, 17,* 183–197.

Kelso, J. A. S. (1995). *Dynamic Patterns: The Self-Organization of Brain and Behavior.* Cambridge: MIT Press.

Kelso, J. A. S., Scholtz, J. P., & Schoner, G. (1986). Non-equilibrium phase transitions in coordinated biological motion: Critical Fluctuations. *Physical Letters, 118,* 279–284.

Kelso, J. A. S., & Schöner, G. S. (1988). Self-organization of coordinative movement patterns. *Human Movement Science, 7,* 27–46.

Koestler, A. (1967). *The ghost in the machine.* New York: Macmillan.

Kopell, N. (1988). Toward a theory of modelling central pattern generators. In Cohen AH, Rossignol S, Grillner S (eds.). *Neural Control of Rhythmic Movements in Vertebrates,* (369–413). New York: Wiley.

Kugler, P. N., Kelso, J. A. S., & Turvey, M. T. (1980). On the concept of coordinative structures as dissipative structures. Theoretical lines of convergence. In G. E. Stelmach & J. Requin (eds.) *Tutorials in Motor Behavior,* Amsterdam: North Holland.

Kugler, P. N., and Turvey, M. T. (1987). *Information, natural law, and the self-assembly of rhythmic movement* (pp. 3–70). Hillsdale, NJ: Erlbaum.

Latash, M. L. 1993. *Control of Human Movement.* Champaign, IL: Human Kinetics.

Latash, M. L., and Anson, J. G. (1996). What are "normal movements" in atypical population? *Behavioral and Brain Sciences, 19,* 55–68.

Leonard, C. T., Hirschfeld, H., and Forssberg, H. (1991). The development of independent walking in children with cerebral palsy. *Developmental Medicine and Child Neurology, 33,* 567–577.

Lin, C. C. (1993). What triggers human gait transitions? Masters thesis, Boston University, Boston.

McMahon, T. A. (1984). *Muscles, Reflexes, and Locomotion.* Princeton, NJ: Princeton University Press.

McMahon, T. A., Valiant, G., & Frederick, E. C. (1987). Groucho Running. *Journal of Applied Physiology, 62,* 2326–2337.

Nicolis, G. (1989). Physics of far-from-equilibrium systems and self-organization. In P. Davis (ed.). *The New Physics* (pp. 316–347). Cambridge, UK: Cambridge University Press.

Obusek, J. (1995). The force-driven hybrid oscillator model in the control of human walking speed and stride frequency. Doctoral dissertation, Boston University, Boston.

Obusek, J., Holt, K. G., & Rosenstein, R. (1995). The hybrid mass-spring pendulum model of leg swinging: Stiffness in the control of cycle period. *Biological Cybernetics, 73,* 139–147.

Olney, S. J., Costigan, P. A., & Hedden. D. M. (1987). Mechanical energy patterns in gait of cerebral palsied children with hemiplegia. *Physical Therapy, 67,* 1348–1354.

Olney, S. J., MacPhail, H. A., & Hedden, D. M. (1990). Work and power in hemiplegic cerebral palsy. *Physical Therapy, 70,* 431–438.

Pierrynowski, M. R., Winter, D. A., & Norman, R. W. (1980). Transfers of mechanical energy within the total body and mechanical efficiency during treadmill walking. *Ergonomics, 23,* 147–156.

Pozzo, T., Berthoz, A., & Lefort, L. (1990). Head stabilization during various locomotor tasks in humans: Normal subjects. *Experimental Brain Research, 82,* 97–106.

Pozzo, T., Berthoz, A., Lefort, L., & Vitte, E. (1991). Head stabilization during various loco-motor tasks in humans. Patients with bilateral vestibular deficits. *Experimental Brain Research, 85,* 208–217.

Rand R. H., Cohen A. H., & Holmes P. J. (1988). Systems of coupled oscillators as models of central pattern generators. In A. H. Cohen, S. Rossignol, & S. Grillner (eds.), (pp. 333–367) *Neural Control of Rhythmic Movements in Vertebrates.* New York: Wiley.

Ratcliffe, R., and Holt, K. G. (1997). Low Frequency shock absorption in human walking. *Gait and Posture, 5,* 93–100.

Reed, E. S. (1982). An outline of a theory of action systems. *Journal of Motor Behavior, 14,* 98–114.

Rosenbaum, D. A. (1991). Programs for Movement Sequences. In D. J. Napoli, and J. A. Kegl (eds.), *Bridges Between Psychology and Linguistics: A Swathmore Festschrift for Lila Gleit-man* (pp. 19–31). Hillsdale, NJ: Erlbaum.

Rubin, C. T., and Lanyon, L. E. (1984). Dynamic strain similarity in vertebrates: An alter-native to allometric limb bone scaling. *Journal of Theoretical Biology, 107,* 321–327.

Schmidt, R. C., Carello, C., and Turvey, M. T. (1990). Phase transitions and critical fluctua-tions in the visual coordination of rhythmic movements between people. *Journal of Experimental Psychology: Human Perception and Performance, 16,* 227–247.

Stelmach, G. E. (1976). *Motor control: Issues and trends.* New York: Academic Press.

Sternad, D. (1995). *Dynamics Of 1:2 Coordination In Rhythmic Interlimb Movement.* Doctoral dissertation, University of Connecticut, Storrs.

Strotzky, K. (1983). Gait analysis in cerebral palsied and nonhandicapped children. *Archives of Physical Medicine and Rehabilitation, 64,* 291–295.

Thelen, E., Fisher, D. M., and Ridley-Johnson, R. (1984). The relationship between physical growth and a newborn reflex. *Infant Behavior Development. 7,* 479–493.

Treffner, P. J., and Turvey, M. T. (1995). Handedness and the asymmetric dynamics of bimanual rhythmic coordination. *Journal of Experimental Psychology: Human Perception and Performance, 21,* 318–333.

Turvey, M. T. 1990. Coordination. *American Psychologist, 45,* 938–953.

Turvey, M. T., Holt, K. G., Obusek, J. P., Salo, A., & Kugler, P. N. (1996). Adiabatic trans-formability hypothesis of human locomotion. *Biological Cybernetics, 74,* 107–115.

Turvey, M. T., Schmidt, R. C., Rosenblum, L. D., and Kugler, P. N. (1988). On the time allometry of co-ordinated rhythmic movements. *Journal of Theoretical Biology, 130,* 285–325.

Wilke, J. T. (1977). Ulradian biological periodicities in the integration of behavior. *Interna-tional Journal of Neuroscience, 7,* 125–143.

Winter, D. A. (1983). Biomechanical motor patterns in nondisabled walking. *Journal of Motor Behavior, 15,* 302–330.

Zarrugh, M. Y., & Radcliff, C. W. (1978). Predicting metabolic cost of level walking. *European Journal of Applied Physiology, 38,* 215–223.

Chapter 13

A Dynamical Model of the Coupling between Posture and Gait

Bruce A. Kay and William H. Warren, Jr.

Abstract

Walking requires the coordination of several tasks, including making forward progress (by producing a gait) and maintaining upright posture. In this chapter we discuss how a dynamical model of this coordination can be constructed. Experimentally, subjects walked on a treadmill while viewing large-field visual displays of an oscillating hallway. In our modeling, we focus on two features of the data, mode-locking between posture and gait (in which N cycles of postural sway were produced for M gait cycles) and the amplitude response (as a function of frequency) of the postural component. We discuss how to characterize dynamically posture and gait and their coupling, detailing a coupled-oscillator model of these and other coordination features. Although the model does not capture several other features of posture-gait coordination, we discuss how such a modeling effort can inform theories of how stable walking behavior is produced.

13.1 Introduction

Walking is one of the most ubiquitous activities performed by humans. It is an act that requires the timing and sequencing of many components for a walker to effectively navigate through the environment. Although there are many ways to analyze this complex action, a good starting point for looking at this coordination is to break it down into its component tasks. First, the walker makes forward progress through the world, or locomotes. Second, while doing so, the walker must maintain balance using an upright posture. Given that a biped's base of support is constantly changing and the center of mass is never directly above the stance foot, this involves a complex balancing act. Third, the walker must navigate through the normally cluttered natural environment, steering through openings such as doors and around obstacles such as parked cars—some of which may be moving. Finally, actors often perform other activities while walking (e.g., thinking, talking, gum-chewing), which implies that walking is a stable act, going along by itself if not greatly perturbed. That is, its essential components are robustly sequenced and timed.

In our laboratory, we have been looking at how three of the main component tasks of walking—locomoting, maintaining balance, and steering

—are coordinated. In this chapter, we describe the nature of the coordination between two of these components, posture and locomotion, as revealed by changes in postural sway and gait when probed with visual stimulation. We also describe a dynamical systems model of this behavior, going into the details of the modeling endeavor and showing that such modeling can make definite contributions to a theory of how humans walk. Our working hypothesis is that each component of walking can be understood as a component dynamical system having it own properties, and that the behavior of the walking system as a whole can be understood as the complex interaction—or coupling—of the component dynamics. In short, our first goal is to characterize each component's dynamics, and the second is to understand how the components' dynamics interact to produce the behavior of the entire walking system. Our overall aim in this modeling effort is to produce something "sufficiently definite" that can lead to constructive insights about this task.

Before going on, we should clarify what we mean by dynamical systems and dynamical models. A dynamical system is a system whose state at any instant of time can be characterized, at least in principle, by a set of scalar observables (Thompson and Stewart, 1986). The evolutionary history of the system is given by the time-series of these observables. Any system that evolves in time can be considered a dynamical system. The importance of a dynamical systems analysis for a theory of how a system works comes in the detailed specification of the dynamics of the system. The two main questions asked in a dynamical systems analysis are (1) what is the set of scalar observables that characterize the system, and (2) what are the dynamical laws that give rise to the patterns seen in the observables' time-series? The latter take the form of relationships among the observables, that is, expressions of how the observables interact. Having answers to these two questions can take us a long way toward understanding how a system operates.

For a simple system, such as a planar pendulum, we can identify the relevant observables ahead of time, for example, its angular displacement from the straight-down position and its angular velocity. The dynamical laws can be written down, based on a physical analysis of the forces present in the system, and any structural parameters present (e.g., the length of the pendulum and the force of gravity). These laws often take the form of differential equations, because in many situations they can be stated as functions that relate the rates of change of the various observables. Dynamical systems theory is used to describe the evolution of the system's state over time from a variety of starting conditions, both qualitatively and quantitatively, given the applicable laws. For a pendulum, the theory describes how the bob will move given its initial displacement and velocity (the starting conditions) and the parameterized pendulum equation (the law for this situation), in terms of both the qualitative and the exact time-series behavior of the observables (see, e.g., Thompson and Stewart, 1986).

In principle, walking can be considered a dynamical system because there is presumably a set of time-varying observables that can completely characterize its state. A detailed biomechanical-neural list of all the observables and the laws expressing their evolution over time could be worked out, but the sheer complexity of such a list is mind-boggling (e.g., Hatze, 1980). It is conceivable that from such a set of laws specific predictions could be made about global features such as the coordination of posture and locomotion, but the road to those predictions appears to us to be extremely long and arduous. Very little is known about the behavior of dynamical systems having so many observables (e.g., Guckenheimer and Holmes, 1983). In any attempt to understand such a system, then, we must simplify the system and choose a much smaller set of observables to try to understand. We do not know ahead of time which of the many possible observables are crucial for understanding the behavior we are interested in, so the choices we make are arbitrary, but we must start somewhere. Having chosen a small subset of the entire observable set, we must also make hypotheses about what the laws of interaction for the small subset are, because we can no longer rely on detailed analysis of how the observables in the full set interact.

Therefore, our approach, which is complementary to a detailed biomechanical-neural one, is to choose for study some simple observables that reflect global walking behavior, such as the sway associated with a point on the body or the angle between two leg segments. Recording the time-series of these observables, we look for patterns in the time-series, and try to reproduce these patterns with a candidate dynamical model.

Dynamical systems modeling is dynamical systems theory in reverse— an attempt to determine what kinds of laws relating the chosen observables could have produced similar behavior. From generic properties of known dynamical systems, we choose candidate laws relating our observables, then analyze and simulate these systems to evaluate the parallel between the candidate model and the observed behavior. If there are close parallels, such that the model produces time-series similar to the observed behavior, we say that we have a good model, and proceed to generate more predictions that can be tested experimentally. We can also say that the operation of the model—how the observables are functionally related in the laws—must be similar to the actual system in some manner, and if we understand the model, we have thereby achieved some understanding of the system. If there are distinct dissimilarities between the model and the real data, we keep trying, and hopefully will have learned something, at least what kind of dynamics our behavior is not. In dynamical system modeling, understanding of a complex task like walking is proportional to how well the dynamical models mimic the observed behavior, and how well we understand the way the laws in the model produce the mimesis.

Again, our hypothesis is that we can do such modeling at the level of the components of the walking task, with separate models for the separate components, and then synthesize the components into a larger model for walking as a whole, choosing the appropriate dynamical laws that couple the components. Before proceeding from the components to the aggregate, a component model must pass the test of similarity to its component's real behavior. Let us now try to characterize in dynamical terms the component systems of posture and gait.

13.2 The Postural System

The task of the postural system during both quiet stance and walking is to maintain an upright balance. While standing in place, this task is to maintain the body's center of gravity (cg) over the base of support, which can be thought of as an area on the ground bordered by the feet. The phase space for posture—the space of all the observables of the postural state—can be simplified to the fore-aft/left-right coordinates of the cg with respect to the base of support. For postural stability, only a restricted region of this space is thus allowed. If at any time the cg is above a point outside this area, balance will be lost if no corrective measures (e.g., moving the feet, throwing one's arms out) are available to the actor. Thus, the cg must be kept within a restricted region of postural phase space, and if perturbed away from this region, the postural system's task is to bring it back using various effectors, based primarily upon visual and somatosensory information.

In the language of dynamical systems theory, this restricted region in postural space can be described as an *attractor*, although of a somewhat peculiar kind. The standard dynamical attractor that is its closest analog is the *point attractor*—that is, a preferred single state (consisting of the position, velocity,... of the system), which is returned to following arbitrary perturbations (figure 13.1). The postural attractor, on the other hand, is not a single point in phase space, but a whole set of points in a restricted region of the phase space. The salient feature of the postural task from the dynamical systems perspective is that the observables return to a restricted region of phase space following perturbation. Within that subset of phase space, the motion of the cg over the base of support may be periodic, chaotic, or stochastic (Chow and Collins, 1995), as long as upright posture is maintained.

As a first simplification, then, we can try modeling the postural attractor as a point attractor. A simple dynamical system that exhibits a point

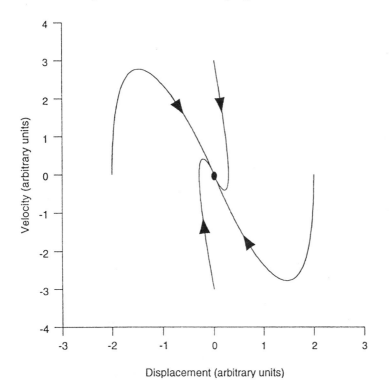

Figure 13.1
Point-attractor dynamics on the phase plane (position versus velocity). Following perturbation, all trajectories are attracted back to the point-attractor. The damped mass-spring used in the model is used here as the example system.

attractor is the following ordinary differential equation, which describes a damped linear mass-spring system:

$$m_p x'' + b x' + k_p x = 0. \tag{13.1}$$

This is an ordinary second-order differential equation that states the law relating the time-varying behaviors of the system's observables. The observables are the displacement x of the mass from its rest or equilibrium position (i.e., when $x = 0$, the spring is neither stretched nor compressed) at any time, and its velocity and acceleration x' and x'' respectively, using the prime notation to denote differentiation with respect to the final observable, time. Time is implicitly present in the time-derivatives of displacement, and is the independent variable in the equation, the other observables being dynamic variables, that is, dependent on time. The equation has three parameters that do not change over time, the mass m_p, the amount of damping b, and the stiffness of the spring k_P (the subscript "P" denotes "Posture").[1] This equation states that the three observables are linearly related to each other, and given this relationship, the mass exhibits point attractor behavior: from any initial starting point (some definite values of x and x' at some start time), or equivalently, after being perturbed away from the equilibrium position, the mass will return to the equilibrium point after some transient motion (figure 13.1).

The behavior of the linear damped mass-spring system is well understood (French, 1971; Thomson, 1981). In particular, it is well known what will happen if a sinusoidal external force is applied to the mass. This additional force is added to the right side of equation 13.1:

$$m_P x'' + bx' + k_P x = F \cos(2\pi f_D t) \qquad (13.2)$$

and introduces an explicit relationship between time and the rest of the system's observables. In this equation, F is the amplitude and f_D is the frequency (in Hz, or cycles per second) of the forcing function (the subscript "D" denotes Driver). After an initial transient, the mass oscillates at the same frequency as the external driver, with a fixed amplitude and phase relationship with respect to the driver. Thus the mass exhibits $1:1$ mode-locking with the driver, that is, one cycle of forcing produces one cycle of response.[2] The amplitude and phase of the response, which are functions of all the parameters of the equation, is termed the *frequency response* of the system (Thomson, 1981). If an unknown mass-spring system is forced with an oscillating driver at various frequencies (f_D), the damping and stiffness coefficients b and k_P can be recovered from the observed amplitude-frequency and phase-frequency plots (given a known mass). In particular, for light damping, a peak occurs in the amplitude response near the natural frequency of the mass-spring (determined by the ratio of stiffness to mass). The mass-spring is said to "resonate" to the driver at this frequency, and so this is called a resonance peak (figure 13.2, solid curve). For heavy damping the amplitude response is a monotically decreasing function of the driver frequency (figure 13.2, dashed curve). This is termed "low-pass" behavior, as the mass-spring-damper acts as a filter that allows only the lower driver frequencies to "pass through" in the mass's motion relatively unattenuated (Oppenheim and Schafer, 1975). The amount of damping is measured relative to the values of the other parameters in the equation; for higher values of mass or stiffness, higher values of b are required for the same relative amount of damping to be present.

Applying this methodology to standing posture, several researchers (e.g., Andersen and Dyre, 1989; van Asten, Gielen, and van der Gon, 1988; Yoneda and Tokumasu, 1986) have found that when the postural system is visually driven by a sinusoidally oscillating display over a range

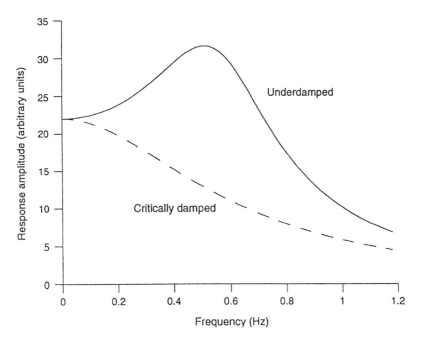

Figure 13.2
Amplitude response functions for an underdamped (solid line) and critically damped (dashed line) linear mass-spring system of figure 13.1.

of frequencies, it exhibits low-pass behavior. That is, the body sways at the same frequency as the visual driver (and so exhibits 1:1 mode-locking with the visual driver), and the amplitude of its response drops monotonically and very rapidly as the frequency of the visual driver is increased. Both of these facts are consistent with the dynamical system of equation 13.2. There is no resonance peak in the amplitude response function; thus the damping coefficient must be large compared with the other coefficients.

Whereas the results just presented pertain to standing, the postural response to visual oscillation during walking is quite different. In our experiments, participants walked on a treadmill, gazing at a large-screen display of a simulated 3-D hallway (subtended visual angles 110° × 95°, horizontal × vertical, figure 13.3), which oscillated sinusoidally in the lateral direction at 14 different frequencies (0.075 Hz to 1.025 Hz, amplitude = 34 cm peak-to-peak) so as to simulate side-to-side translation of the entire hallway.[3] This oscillation was superimposed on a basic radial flow component simulating forward progression down the hallway. Subjects were instructed to follow the side-to-side motions of the hallway so as to remain in the middle of the hallway, using body sway, side-to-side step-

Figure 13.3
Static depiction of the visual hallway (black/white reversed due to printing limitations). The scene was presented on a large rear-projection screen 1 m from the subject.

ping, or whatever motion they felt was appropriate to perform the task. While the subjects walked (during four 40-sec trials at each of the driver frequencies), we recorded their lateral sway using an infrared motion analysis system to record the 3D positions of reflective markers on the side of the neck and the leg (figure 13.4). Four subjects swayed at the same frequency as the visual driver at all 14 frequencies; the other four did so only at the lower frequencies (below about 0.3 Hz). We report data of the former subjects here, although after discussing the model we will return to the latter subjects' behavior.

As in standing posture, we observed 1:1 mode-locking between sway and driver during walking, which is a characteristic of the forced linear system of equation 13.2 (figure 13.5). As can be seen in figure 13.6, however, the amplitude response for postural sway during walking not only has a low-pass characteristic like that for stance, but also a second peak around 0.8 Hz, which is close to the preferred stride frequency of 0.9 Hz observed on control trials with no display oscillation. This second peak

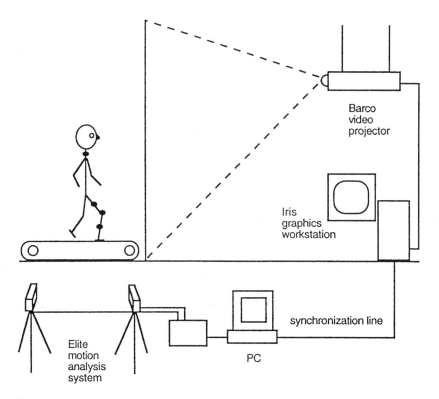

Figure 13.4
A schematic depiction of the experimental setup, showing the location of the passive reflective markers, whose 3D positions are recorded directly to disk by the Elite motion analysis system.

cannot be explained by equation 13.2, which predicts at most a single peak, with reduced sway amplitudes on either side. Also, the second peak is rather broad, such that the sway amplitude is affected at a range of frequencies, not just one.

So, it appears that gait has some influence on postural sway, particularly near the subject's preferred stride frequency. In our dynamical model, this influence takes a particular form of coupling between the two systems. Before turning to that issue, however, we must discuss how to characterize the second task of walking, locomotion, in dynamical terms.

13.3 The Locomotor System

In order to locomote over the ground, evolution has provided bipeds with a gait system in which two legs alternately swing back and forth, so

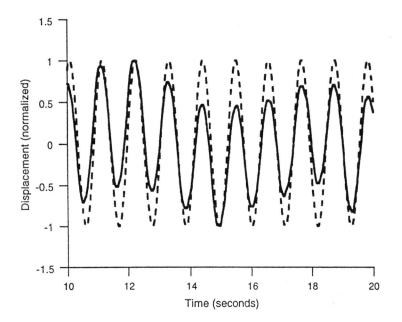

Figure 13.5
A 10-second example time-series of side-to-side sway when visually driven at a frequency of
0.925 Hz (solid line), and a time-shifted version of the sinusoidal driver (the best fit to the
data time-series, dotted line). The displacements of the two time-series have been normalized
to the interval $[-1, 1]$ for plotting purposes. The correlation between sway and driver was
0.921 for the entire 40-second trial.

that the feet are placed on the ground at the appropriate times and places.
Dynamically, one of the most salient features of this behavior is the oscillatory component of gait. Walkers typically choose a preferred frequency
and amplitude of leg motion, and if interrupted (by having to step over or
around an obstacle, for example), they return to roughly these same two
parameters of walking (Belanger and Patla, 1987). The closest dynamical
analog is the *limit-cycle* attractor, an oscillation that has stable frequency,
amplitude, and waveform in the face of perturbation. The reason this is
called a limit-cycle can be shown by representing such a stable oscillation
on the phase plane, a plot of the instantaneous position and velocity of
the oscillating element. On the phase plane, there is one path that is stable
for the limit-cycle, and this is a closed orbit. Following an arbitrary initial
condition (again, x and x' at start time) or any arbitrary perturbation away
from the limit-cycle, the system will evolve back to the limit-cycle during
a transient process (figure 13.7).

The gait system's behavior is not quite a limit-cycle attractor. There is
not a single closed cycle in any phase space representing the system's

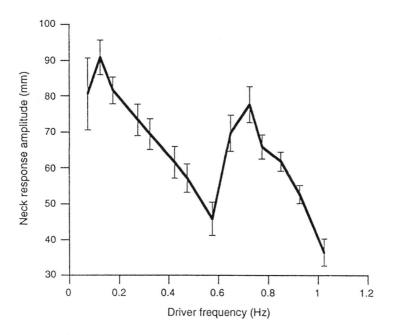

Figure 13.6
Amplitude response of body sway in response to visual oscillation during walking, for our successful walkers, with standard error bars at each driver frequency. Note the basic low-pass characteristic plus a broad peak around 0.8 Hz.

state, but rather a collection of such cycles into a band of attraction (Kay, 1988). Not exactly the same amplitude or frequency is used in each stride cycle, so the same states are not visited again and again, because gait is modulated slightly to maintain balance and adapt to environmental conditions. For now we will simplify and assume that we can model the salient oscillatory nature of gait as a limit-cycle attractor, for the same reasons that we simplified our model of the postural attractor.

A simple dynamical equation that exhibits a limit-cycle attractor is the van der Pol oscillator:

$$m_L y'' + \varepsilon(y^2 - 1)y' + k_L y = 0 \tag{13.3}$$

(Jordan and Smith, 1977; Nayfeh and Mook, 1979; Thompson and Stewart, 1986). Here, y represents the motion of the oscillating component away from the rest position ($y = 0$) and m_L is the component's mass (the subscript "L" denotes Locomotion). The van der Pol oscillator has a nonlinear damping term (the middle term), so the system observables are *nonlinearly* related. This nonlinearity allows the presence of a limit-cycle attractor. Roughly, it causes the oscillator's energy losses and gains to be

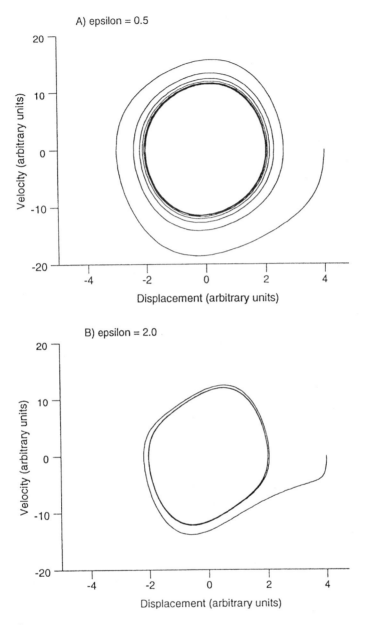

Figure 13.7
Phase-plane plots of the behavior of a van der Pol oscillator. *A*, with nonlinearity (ε) set to 0.5 and *B*, ε set to 2.0. Notice that it takes several cycles for the oscillation to settle down to its limit cycle in *A* following the start, whereas the settling time is much shorter in *B*. On the other hand, the oscillation is much more sinusoidal in *A* than in *B*, since the limit cycle is much more circular in the former.

exactly balanced on the limit cycle. The size of the parameter ε relative to the other parameters is a measure of how nonlinear it is; with larger ε's, return to the limit-cycle is faster than with smaller values, and the oscillations on the limit-cycle are less sinusoidal (figure 13.7).

We assume that the oscillatory gait component can be estimated by measuring any of the leg's motions that oscillate stably over time, such as the angle of the knee, which also happens to be rather easy to measure and analyze. In this case, we are not concerned about modeling either the amplitude of knee oscillation or how it changes over walking frequencies; in any event, this change is small (Diedrich and Warren, 1995). Because it is a salient feature of gait, however, we do want to incorporate a preferred frequency into our model. For fixed parameters, equation 13.3 has a fixed frequency of oscillation, which is approximately the square root of $(k_L/m)/(2\pi)$ for small ε. When not forced by some other term, the van der Pol will oscillate at this frequency regardless of the initial conditions or perturbations.

To anticipate, visually induced oscillations in the postural component appear to have an effect on the limit cycle of the locomotory component. To model this influence, we might try forcing the van der Pol oscillator (Nayfeh and Mook, 1979; Thompson and Stewart, 1986):

$$m_L y'' + \varepsilon(y^2 - 1)y' + k_L y = F\cos(2\pi f_D t). \tag{13.4}$$

This dynamical system exhibits very complex behavior. Unlike the linear point attractor dynamic, the forced van der Pol will oscillate at the same frequency as the external driver only under a restricted set of circumstances. The stability of the van der Pol's intrinsic oscillation means that its observed frequency usually deviates only slightly from its preferred frequency when forced. Thus, the oscillator (M) does not usually exhibit $1:1$ mode-locking with the external driver (N). Either $N:M$ mode-locking, where N and M are (small) integers, occurs (such as $1:1$, $2:3$, $1:2$, etc.), or the two frequencies are unrelated, or chaotic behavior ensues, all depending on the parameter values used in equation 13.4, especially the amplitude of forcing F and the frequency of forcing f_D (Hayashi, 1964; Jordan and Smith, 1977; Nayfeh and Mook, 1979; Thompson and Stewart, 1986). Holding F fixed and decreasing f_D, one observes a particular integer mode-locking for an interval of f_D values, followed by a usually larger interval of unrelated behavior between the two oscillations, followed by a smaller interval of mode-locking, and so forth.

In our experiments we observed both $1:1$ and $N:M$ mode-locking between postural sway and the stride cycle when our walkers were swaying $1:1$ with the hallway. Because postural sway oscillated at the same frequency as the display on all trials, we computed the frequency ratio between the visual driver (N) and the stride cycle (M, as estimated by the

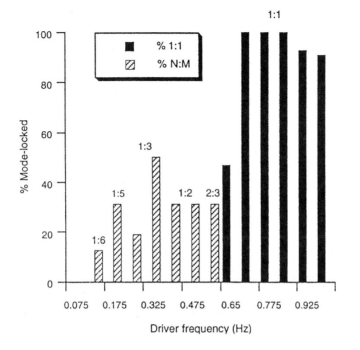

Figure 13.8
Percentages of trials that exhibited mode-locking between the visual display and the knee angle motion (out of 28 trials at each frequency), for the walkers who successfully swayed in synchrony with the visual display. Where no mode-locking occurred, the knees and display had incommensurate frequencies to the resolution of a trial. For visual clarity, the 1:1 mode-locks are indicated by solid bars, the others by striped bars.

knee angle), using several measures of inter-oscillator phase to confirm mode-locking for an entire 40 s trial. Figure 13.8 depicts the percentage of trials in which integer mode-locking was observed at each visual driver frequency. Note that 1:1 mode-locking—in which each cycle of visual oscillation was accompanied by one cycle of knee motion, over an entire trial of 40 seconds—occurred for all trials at or near the preferred stride frequency. The range of driver frequencies for which this mode is stable extends from 0.725 Hz to 1.025 Hz, the highest driver frequency studied. Other $N:M$ modes, such as 2:3 (i.e., two cycles of visual oscillation were accompanied by three cycles of knee motion), 1:2, and 1:3, occurred for lower visual driver frequencies, although less often, with many trials showing no stable integer mode-locking between posture and locomotion.[4] The ranges of driver frequencies over which these modes are stable are much smaller than the range for 1:1 mode-locking. Apparently, the locomotory component exhibits some of the same qualitative features as the van der Pol oscillator when sinusoidally forced.

13.4 Parameterizing the Component Dynamics

We have described two component dynamical systems to serve as candidate models for the postural and locomotor tasks. As described so far, we have a fairly generic form for each of them, with the *qualitative* properties of model and task being made to be in good correspondence. We would like to see if more *quantitative* properties of our observables can be mimicked by the models, which means that we would like to pick reasonable values of the parameters in the candidate laws (equations 13.2 and 13.4). After all, the forms of the models may be correct, but if there are systematic differences between the models and the data, we want to know about it and make corrections if possible. Only by choosing specific values for the parameters can we take this next step. We take each component in turn again.

The postural point attractor dynamic of equation 13.2 can be used to model the low-pass portion of the amplitude response curve we obtained (figure 13.6), ignoring the broad peak around the stride frequency. For simplicity, in the remaining we assume the mass of both the postural and locomotory components to be equal to 1.0 (see note 1). Assuming that the system is critically damped, that is, there is just enough damping to eliminate oscillations in any unforced transient and produce a monotonic amplitude response, the only remaining free parameter is the stiffness k_P. A value of $k_P = 14.21$ closely mimics the shape of the amplitude response, which implies a natural frequency of $f_0 = \mathrm{sqrt}(k_P)/(2\pi) = 0.6$ Hz, and a damping of $b = 2m\omega_0 = (2)(1)(2\pi f_0) = 7.54$. To scale it to the actual amplitudes (in mm) we observed, the forcing term is $F = 312.61$.

For the gait component, there are only two parameters to set, stiffness k_L and nonlinearity ε (having set the mass to 1.0). We can determine k_L from the preferred stride frequency we observed in our subjects when they are not being forced by a visual oscillation. The average stride frequency was 0.9 Hz, which corresponds to a $k_L = 31.98 = (2\pi^* 0.9)^2$. We chose ε to be 0.5, as this gives moderately fast return to the limit-cycle while still producing fairly sinusoidal oscillations, both of which make for a much simpler analysis and simulation effort.

13.5 Coupling the Postural and Locomotor Systems

We have now identified two separate dynamical models for two components of walking: a linear point attractor dynamic for posture, and a nonlinear limit-cycle attractor dynamic for gait. How do these two components interact? We made some initial hypotheses about what the coupling might be like, and then observed the total model's behavior via numerical simulation. Validation of the model comes in judging how well the simulation maps onto the observed behavior of our subjects.

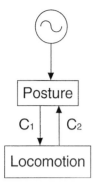

Figure 13.9
Schematic depiction of what is coupled to what in our walking situation, as we see it. C_1 and C_2 refer to the coupling terms of equation 13.5.

The first set of hypotheses is about the overall structure of the situation (figure 13.9). First, suppose that the visual driver has a direct influence on the postural system as in equation 13.2, such that the driver is coupled unidirectionally to the postural system, but postural sway does not reciprocally influence the visual driver. This was the situation in our experiment because we used open-loop displays, so the perspective in the display on the screen was not updated on the basis of the observer's head position, but this is distinctly not the case in natural situations, where the view of a hallway, for example, changes with every move of the head. Second, suppose that some form of coupling is present between posture and gait. Our data suggest that this coupling is bidirectional, for not only does gait affect postural sway, but also vice versa. The peak in the postural amplitude response near the preferred stride frequency indicates that posture is affected by gait. Conversely, the mode-locking behavior indicates that the visual driver acts to modulate the frequency of the stride cycle. Given the assumption that the visual driver is directly influencing only the postural component, gait must be influenced indirectly by the visual driver through the postural component.

Now, what is the exact form of these couplings? That is, given the parameterized system:

$$x'' + 7.54x' + 14.21x = 312.61\cos(2\pi f_D t) + C_1 \tag{13.5a}$$

$$y'' + 0.5(y^2 - 1)y' + 31.98y = C_2, \tag{13.5b}$$

what are the coupling functions C_1 and C_2? One of the simplest forms the coupling functions C_1 and C_2 could take is linear functions of the other component's observables; for example,

$$C_1 = a_1 y + b_1 y' \tag{13.6a}$$

$$C_2 = a_2 x + b_2 x', \tag{13.6b}$$

where the as and bs are constants.

Consider first the coupling function C_2, from posture to gait. Suppose coefficient a_2 is set to some nonzero value, with all the rest of the coefficients set to zero. With these settings, the postural component's displacement directly affects the motion of the gait component, but gait has no effect back on posture. In this case, the visual oscillation would drive the postural component at the driver frequency (but with an amplitude and phase depending on its frequency response), and the postural component would in turn drive the locomotor component sinusoidally. This would also be the case if coefficient b_2 were set to a nonzero value, so that the velocity of the postural component would be coupled to the gait component (with all other coefficients in equation 13.6 equal to zero). Either of these coupling functions might mimic the mode-locking behavior we observed, since a sinusoidally driven van der Pol exhibits mode-locking.

The sinusoidally forced van der Pol and similar oscillators exhibit exceedingly narrow mode-locking regions for the case where $N < M$, that is, when the driver frequency (N) is lower than the natural frequency of the van der Pol (M) (Hayashi, 1964; Nayfeh and Mook, 1979). This frequency relationship, which is the one we found in our experiment, is called *superharmonic entrainment*, because the response is at a higher frequency than the driver. In the forced van der Pol, much broader mode-locking regions exist for *subharmonic entrainment*, where the response is at a lower frequency than the driver. The superharmonic mode-locking regions for this way of forcing the oscillator are so narrow that it ought to have been very difficult for us to find them in our experiments. In other words, no mode-locking occurs at all for nearly any value of a_2 with driving frequencies below the natural frequency of the van der Pol, yet we observed some form of mode-locking at almost all driving frequencies we tested (figure 13.8). Putting it another way, this way of forcing the van der Pol oscillator is structurally unstable for superharmonic mode-locks, in that very slight variations in parameter values lead to very large changes in the behavior of the system (Thompson and Stewart, 1986). Consequently, this way of coupling from posture to gait doesn't predict the observed behavior.

Larger superharmonic mode-locking regions, observable over a wider range of frequencies, are produced by exciting the van der Pol in a very different way. Rather than directly forcing the van der Pol's observable state variables (y, y', y''), the driver varies one of its parameters, stiffness

k_L, which was previously held constant:

$$y'' + 0.5(y^2 - 1)y' + (31.98 + \beta x')y = 0. \tag{13.7}$$

Here, the coefficient of y is the sum of two terms, but can still be considered as the stiffness of the van der Pol. Thus, its stiffness is now continuously affected by the velocity x' of the postural component. The equation can be rewritten algebraically to show that $C_2 = -\beta x'y$, so another way to describe this is that this coupling function introduces a nonlinear relationship among the observables of the two components. This type of coupling—called *parametric excitation* (Cartmell, 1990; Nayfeh and Mook, 1979)—continuously modulates the original relationship among the van der Pol's observables themselves. In the case where there is no coupling back to the postural component, x' is a sinusoid and thus excites the van der Pol's stiffness sinusoidally. That is, the van der Pol's stiffness is now a function of time: $k'_P = k_P + \beta V \cos(2\pi f_D t)$, where V is the peak velocity of the postural component, which depends on the driver frequency according to the postural component's amplitude response.

In addition to the wider frequency ranges that exhibit superharmonic mode-locking, this type of mode-locking exists for much larger ranges of values of β (the amount of coupling from the postural component to the locomotory component) than it did for the linear coupling parameters a_2 and b_2 in equation 13.6b. The presence of wide regions of stable superharmonic mode-locking indicates that such mode-locking is now structurally stable. We have numerically computed these regions of stability in the two-dimensional parameter space of driver frequency and amplitude for the parametrically forced van der Pol in equation 13.7, and they appear in figure 13.10. The tongue-like shape of the stable $1:1$ parameter region is apparent; that is, the range of frequencies that exhibit this mode-locking increases as the forcing amplitude is increased from the tongue's "tip" to its "blade." In this regard these regions are similar to the *Arnold tongues* observed in some closely related dynamical systems (named for the Russian mathematician V. I. Arnold; Thompson and Stewart, 1986). Note also that some minimum amount of forcing is required for mode-locking at any forcing frequency, below which the two oscillations are unrelated. In rough form, then, we have some idea of how to couple the postural component to the gait component.

Now consider the reciprocal coupling function C_1 back from gait to posture. What we want to account for is an increase in postural sway around the stride frequency. As it turns out, direct forcing of the postural state produces this effect, once the parametric excitation from the postural component to the gait component has been introduced. Specifically, we set b_1 in equation 13.6a to a nonzero value; the greater its value, the

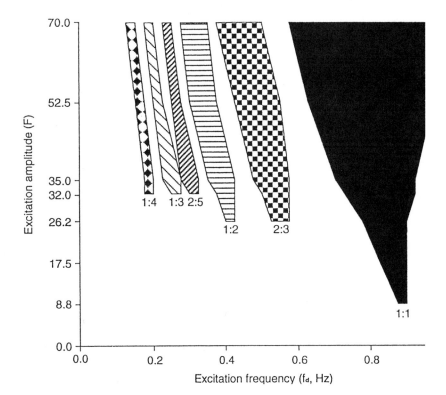

Figure 13.10
Mode-locking regions for the parametrically excited van der Pol oscillator, with the parameters of equation 13.7, except that the term bx' is replaced by $F\cos(2\pi f_d t)$, where F is the excitation amplitude and f_d is the excitation frequency. Inside the shaded regions of this parameter space, the variously labeled mode-locks ($N : M = \#$ excitation cycles : $\#$ observed oscillator cycles) are stable and easily observed; outside, the relationship between the excitation and the van der Pol is quasiperiodic (N and M are not rationally related), that is, no mode-locking occurs there. This figure summarizes the results of simulations at 630 combinations of the two parameters, that is, at seven excitation amplitudes (see ordinate for the values) and 90 excitation frequencies (from 0.10 to 1.00 Hz in 0.01 Hz steps).

stronger the coupling from gait to posture and the larger the resonance peak.

Concerning exact values for β and b_1, we chose β so that the width of the $1:1$ mode-locking regime was equal to what we observed in our data, that is, from 0.725 Hz to 0.925 Hz, when b_1 was set to zero; β turned out to be 1.0. Then, we increased b_1 until a large resonance peak appeared around the gait frequency; somewhat arbitrarily, we settled on $b_1 = 10.0$. We note that the $1:1$ mode-locking regime maintained the same width, as did the other modes depicted in figure 13.10, when the C_1 coupling from gait to posture was added to the model.

13.6 The Complete Model and Its Successes

We now have a detailed, if preliminary, dynamical model of the interaction of posture and gait in our experimental setting:

$$x'' + 7.54x' + 14.21x = 312.61\cos(2\pi f_D t) + 10.0y' \tag{13.8a}$$

$$y'' + 0.5(y^2 - 1)y' + (31.98 + 1.0x')y = 0 \tag{13.8b}$$

Let us summarize how the terms in these equations correspond to the two components, and how the model operates. A sinusoidal visual driver directly forces the postural component, which has a linear point-attractor dynamic. In turn, the postural component parametrically excites the stiffness of the gait component, which has a nonlinear limit-cycle dynamic; reciprocally, the gait component directly forces the postural component's state. Thus, the two components are coupled bidirectionally but in two fundamentally different ways, using parametric coupling in one case and direct coupling in the other. Reflecting the open-loop conditions in our experiments, the visual display is only unidirectionally coupled to the walker's dynamics, although we will soon close the loop in our apparatus and extend the model to this case. To simulate the system's response to different frequency drivers, the only parameter that is changed is the driver frequency (f_d), while the structure of the equations and all the remaining parameters are held constant.

The model successfully reproduces key features of the behavior we observed in our subjects. The first two features were built into the model, and so we will review them briefly, but the remaining three features were discovered after the whole model was constructed.

First, the amplitude response of the postural component is very similar to that of the neck marker, with a low-pass region below about 0.6 Hz and a resonance peak around the preferred locomotor frequency (figure 13.11, solid curve). The low-pass feature is due to the intrinsic dynamics of the model's postural component (dashed curve), and the resonance peak

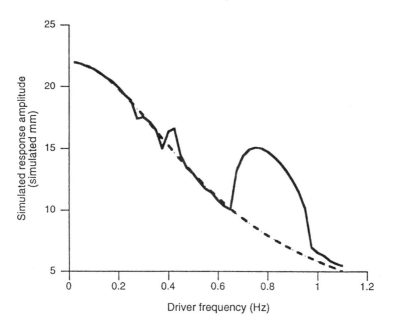

Figure 13.11
Amplitude response of the complete model (solid line) and the amplitude response of the forced linear mass-spring without the coupling from the locomotory component (dashed line).

is due to the combination of parametric coupling from the postural component to the gait component and the direct coupling in the opposite direction. Without both, no such resonance peak occurs. The model postural component also locks to the visual driver in the 1:1 mode across all driver frequencies used in the experiment. Second, there are a number of regions in the parameter space of the model where observable superharmonic mode-locking occurs between its two dynamical components (figure 13.10), similar to the observed walking behavior. In fact, the widths of the superharmonic regions decrease for the higher $N:M$ modes, as does the percentage of mode-locked trials in our data (compare figure 13.8). In the model, the width of the 1:2 region is one-quarter that of the 1:1 region, which compares closely to the relative frequencies of occurrence of the two modes in walking. This feature of the model's behavior is due to the parametric coupling from the postural to the gait component.

Third, and unexpectedly, no stable mode-locks between the visual driver and the gait component occur in the model much above the locomotor frequency (0.9 Hz). That is, the model appears to have very narrow subharmonic entrainment regions (and so in a sense is the opposite of a directly driven system). Nor was the model's postural component able to track the visual driver at these frequencies. Similarly, the postural sway in our subjects failed to lock to any driver faster than about 1.0 Hz. In the model, the gait component appears to dominate the behavior of the postural component at the higher frequencies.

Fourth, the model may be able to account for individual differences among our subjects. Recall that some subjects swayed 1:1 with the driver at all frequencies, whereas others only tracked the display at frequencies below about 0.3 Hz. With the preceding parameter settings, the model mimics the former subjects' amplitude response and mode-locking behavior rather closely. Interestingly, the unsuccessful subjects' behavior can be qualitatively mimicked by changing one parameter in the model—the coupling strength between the visual driver and the postural component, F. If F is reduced from 312.61 to 50.0, say, the postural response is dominated by the gait component at a much lower frequency, resulting in a 1:1 mode-locking region that extends out to about 0.3 Hz (figure 13.12).

Finally, when the visual driver is turned off, which corresponds to $F = 0.0$ in model, the gait component causes the postural component to oscillate at the stride frequency, as we observe in control trials that had no display oscillation.

13.7 The Model's Failures

The model is not a complete success, however. Simulations behave differently from the observed behavior when we turn from the rather gross features of mode-locking and amplitude resonance to finer time-series details. In particular, there are two important differences between the actual and modeled kinematics of the knee. First, the amplitude of knee oscillation remains rather constant from cycle to cycle in the real walkers, but does not in the model. For example, in the 1:2 mode the simulated knee amplitude varies systematically, being large on one cycle, small in the next, in a strictly alternating pattern (figure 13.13b, middle waveforms). Amplitude modulation of the model's "knee" is even more apparent when mode-locking is absent, whereas there is very little cycle-by-cycle knee variation in amplitude in the walking data (compare figure 13.13a and b, bottom waveforms). Second, the timing of the model's peak displacements at 1:2 has the same alternating pattern, first a long, then a short cycle in time, whereas the observed knee timings do not vary in this systematic manner. In real walking, it appears that the overall stride frequency has been altered to match the postural oscillations, but that individual cycles are not modified in order to do so. In the model, on the other hand, the continuous modulation of the gait stiffness parameter produces cycle-by-cycle changes in the oscillator's frequency. We shall return to this point later.

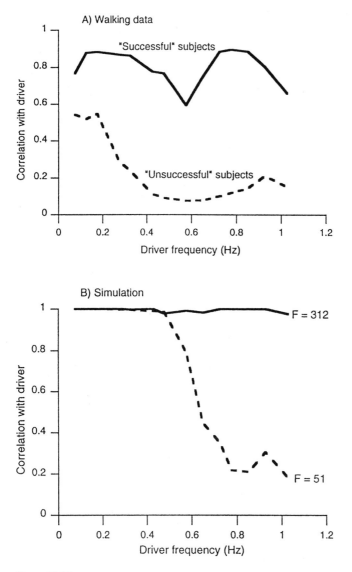

Figure 13.12
A) Mean correlation between the visual display and the neck marker motion for successful (solid line) and unsuccessful (dashed line) subjects. B) Correlation between the visual driver and the locomotory component of the model for $F = 312.61$ (solid line) and $F = 51.0$ (dashed line). For $1:1$ mode-locking between the driver and locomotion, the correlation should be near 1.0.

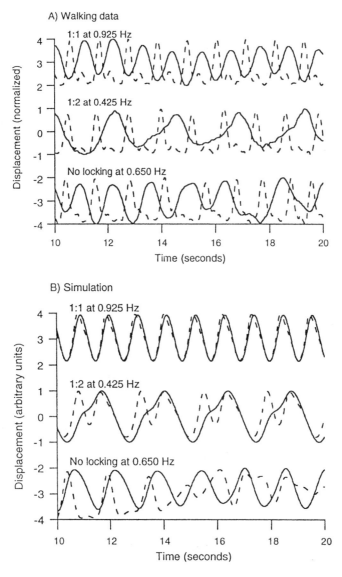

Figure 13.13
Ten-second example time-series of lateral sway motion (solid lines) and knee angle motion (dashed lines) in A) the walking data and B) numerical simulations of the model. From top to bottom in each sub-plot the visual driver was at 0.925, 0.425, and 0.650 Hz.

Besides the preceding kinematic details, the model is unsuccessful in duplicating an aspect of postural sway behavior we observed in another experiment, in which we used sum-of-sines displays. An important distinguishing feature of nonlinear systems is that they lack linear superposition, that is, the response to a sum of input sinusoids, for example, is not equal to the sum of the responses to the sinusoids when input individually. To test whether the postural component is nonlinear, we created a set of composite waveforms, each consisting of the sum of four sinusoids from the same set of fourteen frequencies that were used one at a time in the single-sine experiment discussed previously. In order to make the analysis easier, the four frequencies that were summed in any one trial were incommensurate to the base sampling rate of a trial. This produced waveforms with overall patterns that repeated only once every 40 seconds (the duration of a trial), and appeared very random and unpredictable to the walkers. We then measured the amplitude response of the neck sway at each of the four frequencies in each trial. Across the set of composite waveforms we thus had a measure of the response at each of the fourteen original frequencies, which we then compared to the response when each frequency was presented individually. In the sum-of-sines response, we found the same low-pass characteristic and the resonance peak around the preferred locomotor frequency as we obtained for single-sine displays, but in addition we found a second peak between the low-pass and locomotor peak, at around 0.5 Hz (figure 13.14, solid curve). Some type of nonlinearity in visually-induced postural sway is signaled by this difference.

On the other hand, our model is patently nonlinear, due to the van der Pol's damping term and the parametric excitation term, so we were hopeful that it might produce this result. However, when we forced the model (equation 13.8) with the same sum-of-sines waveforms as we used in the experiment (i.e., by replacing the right side of equation 13.8a with the sums of four cosine terms we used in the experiment), we obtained a fairly flat low-pass amplitude response (figure 13.14, dashed curve). Although there is a difference between the single- and sum-of-sines responses of the model, which reflects its nonlinearity, the form of the difference is not the same as what we observed in our walkers. One possibility is that the model's sum-of-sines response depends upon the precise frequency combinations used, and so slightly different frequency combinations may result in a frequency response that more closely mimics the form of the observed data. Even if that were true, it would imply that the frequency response function is not robust in the face of such changes, and so would not be a good model of this rather consistent finding, which was observed in a number of subjects.

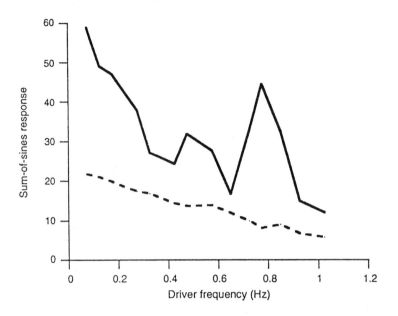

Figure 13.14
Amplitude response function for walking, when sum-of-sines waveforms were used in each trial (solid line), and the corresponding response of the dynamical model to sum-of-sines drivers (dashed line). Compare with figures 13.5 and 13.9.

13.8 What Have We Learned?

As we have shown, our model of the interaction between posture and gait is more successful in some respects and less so in others. It could be argued that some of the model's successes are due to our having built them into the model; some of its failures, as a consequence, are things we did not choose to include. But there are also some fundamental differences between the observed walking data and the model's behavior at the level of the cycle-by-cycle time series, and in the fundamental nature of its nonlinearity as revealed by the sum-of-sines displays. Consequently, the model must be modified or replaced to capture more accurately the interaction between posture and gait in walking.

Nevertheless, both the successes and the failures of the model inform us about the nature of that interaction, and allow us to draw some general conclusions.

A. Posture and Gait Are (Probably) Bidirectionally Coupled. This is not so trivial a point as it may at first appear. When we first looked at the knee data, we were puzzled to find many trials in which it appeared that the postural oscillations had no effect on the locomotor motions of the knee.

In fact, in only about 30% of the low-frequency trials (that is, well away from the preferred stride frequency) did we observe mode-locking. The remaining trials showed an independence of the two oscillations. Thus, our first idea was that at many postural frequencies, the two components act independently of each other for all intents and purposes. Even with fixed parameters, however, the model also shows independence at the level of its observed kinematics. Except in the mode-locking regions, the two components oscillate relatively independently of one another. The model's behavior thus also looks as though the two components are uncoupled at some driving frequencies, yet the coupling terms are always present, and the two components are therefore always influencing each other. The lesson to be learned, then, is that posture and gait may be bidirectionally *coupled* at all times, though the coupling may not produce tightly-coupled *behavior* in all circumstances.

B. *The Coupling Between Posture and Gait Is in Terms Not Only of the Components' Observables but also in terms of the Components' Parameters.* As we have shown, the observed mode-locking behavior can be modeled using parametric, and not direct, coupling, from the postural to the locomotor component. This tells us that the overall system involves not only interactions in observables, but also interactions at the level of parameters.

C. *The Interaction of Posture and Gait may be at an Altogether Different Level of Dynamics than that Described in Our Model.* Although the model can produce superharmonic mode-locking behavior similar to what we observed in our data, we noted above that the details of how that behavior is produced differ drastically between model and data, with small cycle-by-cycle variation in both amplitude and timing in the real knee behavior, but systematic cycle-by-cycle amplitude and timing variations in the modeled knee.

Apparently, mode-locking in actual walking is accomplished in a very different manner from how it is accomplished in the model. Parametric excitation—the basis of the coupling from the postural component to the locomotor component in the model—is a form of coupling that entails continuous variations in one component's parameters (gait stiffness). By virtue of that modulation, gait stiffness has effectively become another time-varying observable, evolving in time at the same rate as the other observables in the model (i.e., it evolves at exactly the same rate as the velocity of the postural component), rather than being a fixed parameter (Farmer, 1990; Saltzman and Munhall, 1992). At each moment in time, then, stiffness takes on a new value, thus changing the observed frequency of the oscillator.

Thus, this continuous variation of gait stiffness in the model says that this crucial locomotor parameter is adjusted continuously, which does not seem to be a reasonable biological solution to the problem. It may make more sense for a walker to reset the value of his or her locomotor stiffness to a new value in order to mode-lock with the postural oscillations, and then stick with that new value for as long as the postural oscillations are required. This calls for a completely different coupling scheme, in which both the postural and locomotory components' parameters are adjusted by some other process (Dijkstra et al., 1994), rather than by virtue of couplings that are invariant across visual driver frequency, as in the current model. This new way of modulating the locomotor component has the virtue of retaining parameters as parameters, that is, gait stiffness would be re-set by the other process and left there, and so would be constant in time, not evolving at the same rate as the observables. This would also produce the observed phenomenon of fixed cycle-by-cycle knee frequency and amplitude.

The main drawback of the latter approach is that the interaction is taken to a very different dynamical level. It implies the presence of some other process that occurs at a time scale very different from that of the evolution of the two components' observables. Furthermore, it would no longer be the case that it is the dynamics of the interaction of these two components' observables that provides the mode-locking phenomena. It is hard to see how the limited mode-locking regions we observe in both the present data and model would be generated in such an approach. If the locomotor frequency could be adjusted to any frequency, we might expect that some stable form of mode-locking would be present for any driver frequency, because some small-integer frequency ratio could be chosen for any arbitrary driver frequency. The interaction between these two components could not then serve as an explanation of how the preferred mode-lockings arise. As stated, this approach does not have all the answers either.

13.9 In Sum

We have outlined a dynamical model of the interaction of posture and gait when the postural component of walking is required to follow a visual oscillation. The model has some strong points as well as some shortcomings. Despite the model's limitations, we have shown that such a modeling effort can lead to some interesting and definite questions about how two important components of a complex task interact. For example, we have tried to ask (and answer), how do we characterize the individual components dynamically? And how are they linked? In other task settings, such as a more natural closed-loop situation in which the subject's movement influences the visual display, we may be able to answer the question, how is vision coupled to the rest of the system? Such questions, we think, are best answered when definite hypotheses of how the couplings work can be stated, and our choice is to state those hypotheses in the language of dynamical systems.

Acknowledgments

We thank David Rosenbaum and an anonymous reviewer for their very helpful comments on an earlier draft of this chapter. We take full responsibility for any remaining obfuscation. The work reported herein was supported by NIH Grant EY10923.

Notes

1. Because the type of analysis we are pursuing is a solely kinematic one, where motions and not forces are being analyzed, strictly speaking mass should not be in this equation or the following ones. In terms of a dynamical analysis, this is of little importance, since mass plays the role of just another parameter, a linear weight on the acceleration in the present equation. As we discuss later, we arbitrarily set mass to 1.0, but could be altered for modeling purposes if necessary.
2. We have chosen the term "mode-locking" as opposed to frequency- or phase-locking because of its generality. Both frequency- and phase-locking imply that the two oscillations are operating at the same frequency, so that the phase between them is constant. Although this does apply to the case of a 1:1 frequency ratio between driver and response in our experiments, it does not apply to the case of $N:M$ frequency ratios where N and M are unequal.
3. Thus the amount of oscillation with respect to the retina varied as a function of location in the scene, with minimal motion at the center of the screen, that is, for "far" portions of the hallway, and maximal motion at the screen edges, where the hallway was "close" to the walker. For more details on the experimental apparatus, setup, and data analysis, see Warren, Kay, and Yilmaz, 1996.
4. Even chaos may be present in our walking data, but it is extremely difficult to demonstrate in systems as noisy as biological ones, so we will not try here.

References

Andersen, G. J., & Dyre, B. P. (1989). Spatial orientation from optic flow in the central visual field. *Perception & Psychophysics, 45,* 453–458.

Belanger, M., & Patla, A. E. (1987). Phase-dependent compensatory responses to perturbation applied during walking in humans. *Journal of Motor Behavior, 19,* 434–453.

Cartmell, M. (1990). *Introduction to linear, parametric and nonlinear vibrations.* London: Chapman and Hall.

Chow, C. C., & Collins, J. J. (1995). Pinned polymer model of posture control. *Physical Review E, 52,* 907–912.

Diedrich, F., & Warren, W. H. (1995). Why change gaits? Dynamics of the walk-run transition. *Journal of Experimental Psychology: Human Perception and Performance, 21,* 183–202.

Dijkstra, T. M. H., Schöner, G., Giese, M. A., & Gielen, C. C. A. M. (1994). Frequency dependence of the action-perception cycle for postural control in a moving visual environment: relative phase dynamics. *Biological Cybernetics, 71,* 489–501.

Farmer, J. D. (1990). A Rosetta stone for connectionism. *Physica D, 42,* 153–187.

French, A. P. (1971). *Vibrations and Waves.* New York: Norton.

Guckenheimer, J., & Holmes, P. (1983). *Nonlinear oscillations, dynamical systems, and bifurcations of vector fields.* New York: Springer-Verlag.

Hatze, H. (1980). Neuromusculoskeletal control systems modeling—a critical survey of recent developments. *IEEE Transactions on Automatic Control, AC-25,* 375–385.

Hayashi, C. (1964). *Nonlinear oscillations in physical systems.* New York: McGraw-Hill.

Jordan, D. W., & Smith, P. (1977). *Nonlinear ordinary differential equations.* Oxford, UK: Clarendon.

Kay, B. A. (1988). The dimensionality of movement trajectories and the degrees of freedom problem: A tutorial. *Human Movement Science, 7,* 343–364.

Nayfeh, A. H., & Mook, D. T. (1979). *Nonlinear Oscillations.* New York: Wiley-Interscience.

Oppenheim, A. V., & Schafer, R. W. (1975). *Digital Signal Processing.* Englewood Cliffs, NJ: Prentice-Hall.

Saltzman, E. L., & Munhall, K. G. (1992). Skill acquisition and development: The roles of state-, parameter-, and graph-dynamics. *Journal of Motor Behavior, 24,* 49–57.

Thompson, J. M. T., & Stewart, H. B. (1986). *Nonlinear dynamics and chaos: Geometrical methods for engineers and scientists.* New York: Wiley.

Thomson, W. T. (1981). *Theory of Vibrations with Applications, 2d ed.* Englewood Cliffs, NJ: Prentice-Hall.

van Asten, W. N. J. C., Gielen, C. C. A. M., & van der Gon, J. J. D. (1988). Postural movements induced by rotation of visual scenes. *Journal of the Optical Society of America, A, 5,* 1781–1789.

Warren, W. H., Kay, B. A., & Yilmaz, E. H. (1996). Visual control of posture during walking: Functional specificity. *Journal of Experiment Psychology: Human Perception and Performance, 22,* 818–838.

Yoneda, S., & Tokumasu, K. (1986). Frequency analysis of body sway in the upright posture: Statistical study in cases of peripheral vestibular disease. *Acta Otolaryngolica* (Stockholm), *102,* 87–92.

Chapter 14

Dynamics of Human Gait Transitions

Frederick J. Diedrich and William H. Warren, Jr.

Abstract

What is responsible for the organization of complex actions? In this chapter, we address this question by focusing on the transition from walking to running in humans. First, we consider the concept of a motor program as a source of the organization seen in human gait. We then present evidence consistent with a dynamic theory of the shift between gaits. Results from our studies indicate that preferred gaits are attractors that exhibit stable phase relationships between the leg segments, whereas gait transitions are bifurcations characterized by a loss of stability. We conclude that complex behaviors such as locomotion likely emerge from the dynamics of the motor system and task constraints, and that they are not imposed on the system by a motor program.

14.1 Introduction

Complex actions require a large number of degrees of freedom to be coordinated in a precise manner (Bernstein, 1967). For instance, during bipedal locomotion the legs move 180° out-of-phase with each other, and the segments within each leg exhibit specific phase relationships (Diedrich and Warren, 1995b). What is responsible for these complex sequences of limb movements? In this paper, we approach this question by considering the walk-run transition in humans. First, we consider motor programs as a possible source of the organization seen in human gait. We then discuss a dynamic theory of human gait and present supporting evidence from several recent experiments. We conclude that actions such as gait likely emerge from the dynamics of the action system and task constraints.

14.2 The Origin of Organization

It is often assumed that the organization and timing of movements is due to the prior organization of some entity in the motor system. An example from psychology is the motor program, typically defined as a hierarchical memory structure that specifies many aspects of a movement, beginning with the order, phasing, and relative force of its components, and ending with a sequence of specific muscle contractions (Keele, 1982; Schmidt, 1988). A related example from neuroscience is the central pattern generator (CPG), classically conceived as a neural circuit in the spinal cord that produces a specific pattern of motor neuron activity (Grillner, 1975). According to this view, the organization of behavior is prescribed by a previously organized internal structure, with different modes of movement attributable to different structures. This implies that transitions between movements occur via switching between these internal entities. In the case of human gait, for example, Shapiro and colleagues (1981) proposed that the walk-run transition results from the selection of different motor programs for walking and running.

Although the concept of a motor program addresses the sequencing and timing of limb movements, it leaves a number of questions unanswered. First, the problem of the origin of organization is simply relocated from observable movements to unobservable structures in the nervous system. Even if we grant the existence of motor programs or CPGs, how did they come to be so structured, and why do they have the particular organization they do? This leads us to look to the constraints on movement for a deeper explanation, including the behavioral function or task (e.g. forward progression), the mechanics of the task (e.g., coupled, springy multilink pendula and ground surface characteristics), and the dynamics of self-organization (e.g. the spontaneous behavior of coupled oscillators). Indeed, as currently conceived, CPGs themselves look less like hard-wired structures and more like self-organizing dynamical systems, for interactions among a small network of neurons and neuromodulators can flexibly generate a variety of patterns, and conversely, the same pattern can be produced by different neural networks (Marder, 1988; Harris-Warwick and Johnson, 1989). We will have to appeal to more general principles to account for the organization not only of movements, but also of the CPGs purported to control them, for the answer is unlikely to be found in the neural structure alone.

A second problem with the motor program concept concerns behavioral transitions. The mechanism responsible for selecting appropriate motor programs or CPGs is unclear. The act of switching between programs or CPGs implies the existence of a central controller, with all its attendant problems (Carello et al., 1984). Further, simply claiming that behavioral transitions are due to the switching of motor programs begs the question of why such transitions occur, that is, why certain action modes are preferred over others under particular conditions.

One way of addressing the question of why behavioral transitions occur when they do is to ask what variables are optimized by the transition. Many optimization criteria have been proposed in the biomechanics literature, including overall energy expenditure and mechanical stresses (e.g., Margaria, 1976; Farley and Taylor, 1991). Although this literature does not address the underlying control processes, the optimization of particular costs can be made consistent with a motor programming perspective if one assumes that the controller is appraised of the cost variable and knows how to evaluate it in order to switch programs. A system can also optimize a cost variable and exhibit stable values as the outcome of a dynamical process, without that variable being explicitly used by a central controller (see later discussion; Kugler and Turvey, 1987).

14.3 Gait Transitions

What optimization criteria can account for the transition between walking and running? A first type of explanation proposes that the shift between gaits occurs to minimize mechanical stresses, thereby avoiding injury. For instance, loaded and unloaded horses make the trot-gallop transition at different speeds, but in both cases the transition reduces the peak vertical ground reaction force below a critical level (Farley and Taylor, 1991). In contrast, Hreljac (1993a) measured several kinetic variables in human locomotion (maximum loading rate, braking and propulsive impulses, and braking and propulsive force peaks), and found that none of these measures predicted the walk-run transition. Instead, he proposed that the switch is made to prevent the overexertion of the ankle dorsi-flexors by redistributing the work load to larger muscles in the upper legs (Hreljac, 1995). This analysis does not, however, predict the run-to-walk transition, as this transition likely increases the exertion of the ankle dorsi-flexors.

A second type of explanation proposes that gait transitions occur in order to minimize energy-related costs, such as overall metabolic cost (e.g., Margaria, 1976; Mercier et al., 1994), or mechanical work (Alexander, 1992). Although appealing, these approaches have not been able to predict the transition speed with sufficient accuracy. For instance, Hreljac (1993b) reported that during treadmill locomotion the energetically optimal transition speed (2.24 m/s) is significantly higher than the preferred transition speed (2.06 m/s), and that energy expenditure actually increases from a walk to a run at the transition. These data seem to be inconsistent with the hypothesis of a simple "energetic trigger" for gait transitions, where a trigger is defined as a mechanism that detects when a variable reaches a critical value and initiates a transition. A recent treadmill study did in fact report evidence of a decrease in metabolic cost at the transition (Mercier et al., 1994), but the authors only studied the transition from walking to running, and not the reverse, thus failing to take hysteresis effects into account (see later discussion). This limitation raises the possibility that their estimated transition speed may be too high.

In contrast to these results, measurements of overground locomotion reveal that there are speed jumps at the transition from walking to running (Minetti, Ardigo, and Saibene, 1994), an effect that cannot be observed on a speed-controlled treadmill. Importantly, the metabolic cost at the running speed adopted after the transition is actually lower than the cost would be if walking continued at that speed. This result indicates that energetic costs are minimized by the transition during overground locomotion, despite the small difference between the preferred and energetically optimal transition speeds on the treadmill. Such a minimization of energetic costs is consistent with the dynamic view presented in subsequent sections of this paper, although energetics are not considered to be the proximal cause of the transition.

Finally, one alternative to these optimization criteria is that the walk-to-run transition simply occurs at the mechanical limit of the walking gait. Alexander (1984) predicted this maximum possible walking speed to be about 3.0 m/s. The observed transition speed is significantly lower, however, around 2.1 m/s (Beuter and Lalonde, 1989; Diedrich and Warren, 1995a, 1995b; Hreljac, 1993b; Thorstensson and Roberthson, 1987). Furthermore, participants can maintain a walk at a faster speed than the preferred transition point (e.g., Diedrich and Warren, 1995b, 1998). In addition, this approach does not make a clear prediction for the run-to-walk transition.

In sum, there is little evidence that gait transitions occur in order to explicitly optimize a cost variable or that they occur at the mechanical limit of a gait. Therefore, we turn to an additional class of explanations.

14.4 A Dynamical Approach

The dynamical systems approach to action views behavior as a consequence of the dynamics of the action system within task constraints (e.g., Kelso, 1995; Kugler and Turvey, 1987). In contrast to a motor program imposing organization on the system, the dynamical view seeks to account for stable coordinative patterns and transitions between them as arising from the self-organizing dynamics of the action system. Such principles of self-organization have been observed in a variety of physical systems, as well as in nonlinear mathematical systems (e.g., Haken, 1983; Prigogene and Stengers, 1984), and are increasingly being applied to biological systems. Thus, much of the organization in behavior may come for "free," rather than assuming prior organization in the nervous system.

As an example, consider the well-studied case of phase transitions in bimanual coordination (Kelso and Schöner, 1988). In these experiments, participants are asked to oscillate their fingers in an out-of-phase mode and to slowly increase the frequency of oscillation. At a critical frequency, the fingers exhibit a new behavioral pattern, switching to an in-phase mode. According to a dynamical model, this behavioral transition emerges as the system bifurcates from one attractor state (out-of-phase) to another attractor state (in-phase) when frequency reaches a critical level (Haken, Kelso, and Bunz, 1985; Schöner, Haken, and Kelso, 1986). In this case, the relative phase of the fingers is considered to be the order parameter of the system, a low-dimensional collective variable that describes the organizational state of the system and that indexes its stability (Haken, 1983). The control parameter is the frequency of oscillation, a nonspecific parameter that scales the system through the critical value at which a bifurcation between attractor states is observed. An attractor is defined as a subset of the space of possible states the system can occupy, toward which the system evolves as time goes to infinity (Kelso, Ding, and Schöner, 1992). A bifurcation is a sudden jump from one attractor to another that occurs due to a loss of stability.

Could the organization of an ecologically important action such as gait likewise emerge from the self-organizing dynamics of the motor system? An early clue to this question came from work on decerebrated cats (Shik and Orlovskii, 1976; Shik, Severin, and Orlovskii, 1966). In these experiments, a cat was suspended above a motor-driven treadmill after the brain stem and spinal cord were isolated from higher brain centers. At low treadmill speeds, and at low levels of stimulation of particular regions in the brain stem, the cat began to walk. Then, as the speed of the treadmill increased, and as the stimulation increased, the cat began to trot and ultimately to gallop. Surprisingly, these data indicate that a cortical control mechanism that switches between motor programs is not necessary for an animal to switch gaits. Instead, gaits and gait transitions may emerge from the action of coupled oscillators in the spinal cord or brain stem that spontaneously exhibit different patterns of firing when a control parameter is varied (see, e.g., Collins and Stewart, 1993; Taga, Yamaguchi, and Shimizu, 1991; Schöner, Jiang, and Kelso, 1990). This class of explanations therefore views preferred gaits and gait transitions as manifestations of the dynamics of the motor system within a specific context of constraint (see also Diedrich and Warren, 1995a, 1998; Higgins et al., 1995; Thelen and Ulrich, 1991; Turvey et al., 1996; Taga, 1995a,b; Wagenaar and van Emmerik, 1994).

We argue, then, that gait transitions occur as one mode of behavior becomes unstable and the system switches to a new stable mode of behavior (Diedrich and Warren, 1995b). According to this model, the relative phase of the segments within one leg is the order parameter of the system; that is, the relationships between the extensions and flexions of the various leg segments during the gait cycle. Speed of locomotion is considered to be the control parameter of the system. Because speed is the product of stride frequency and stride length, there are actually two control parameters for human locomotion that can be expressed together as speed. It is important to be clear that this theory does not suppose the existence of a "stability trigger" in the sense of a control mechanism that explicitly senses stability and uses it to regulate the transition. Rather, the transition emerges from the dynamics of the system when the control parameter is scaled past a critical value.

The dynamics of the walk-run transition can be represented by the following potential function (see Tuller et al., 1994), where x is the order parameter and k is the control parameter, as illustrated in figure 14.1.

$$V(x) = kx - x^2/2 + x^4/4. \tag{14.1}$$

Equation 14.1 is simply the generic form of a potential function that can have two co-existing fixed point attractors and that illustrates transitions between these attractor states (see Kelso, Ding, and Schöner, 1992). Following this model, a phase transition should have the following properties (Kelso and Schoner, 1988). First, there should be a sudden and qualitative reorganization of the system at the transition. Second, the system should show a loss of stability in the transition region. When the system is in a transitory state (i.e., the participants are allowed to switch gaits), stability may be assessed by measuring critical fluctuations and critical slowing down. Critical fluctuations arise near the transition due to a loss of stability that occurs as the potential function $V(x)$ deforms, allowing the system to occupy a greater number states given a constant level of noise. The presence of critical fluctuations is noted by increases in the standard deviation of the relative phase of the limb segments. Critical slowing down is indicated by an increase in the time it takes for the system to recover from a perturbation (relaxation time) in the transition region, due to the shallower gradients of the potential function. An increase in relaxation time is indicative of the loss of stability that underlies the transition. Alternatively, stability may be assessed during steady states (Schmidt, Carello, and Turvey, 1990; Schmidt and Turvey, 1995), in which the system is held in one mode (i.e., one gait). Once again, stability can be measured via fluctuations of phase or responses to perturbations, with larger fluctuations and longer relaxation times indicating lower stability. Third, there should be a tendency for the system to remain in the current basin of attraction as the control parameter moves the system through the transition region, resulting in hysteresis, which is, for gait, the tendency for the walk-to-run transition to occur at a higher speed than the run-to-walk transition.

Diedrich and Warren (1995b) reported evidence consistent with this dynamic theory. First, the transition is sudden and is characterized by a qualitative reorganization of the relative phase of the segments within a

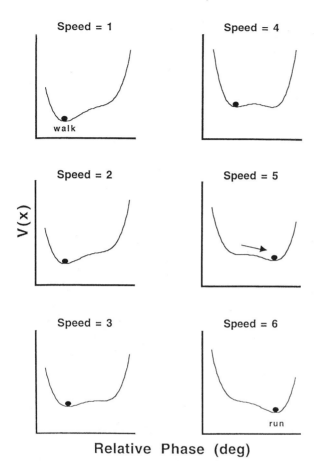

Figure 14.1
Hypothetical potential function for the walk-run transition. As speed increases, the system moves from a stable walking attractor (speed 1) into a bistable region (speed 4), and then jumps to a stable running attractor (speed 6).

leg. Figure 14.2 shows the ankle-knee phase relationship and the ankle-hip phase relationship during a typical transition trial (speed increases with time along the X-axis). The peak extensions of the joints near the end of the stance phase (near toe-off) were used in the calculation of point estimates of relative phase. During walking, the ankle-hip phase is about 45° and the ankle-knee phase is about 85°. In contrast, both phase relationships are close to 0° for running. These results indicate that the ankle extends after both the knee and hip during walking (more out-of-phase), but that the joints extend together during running (more in-phase). Furthermore, this plot shows that the switch between gaits occurs rapidly

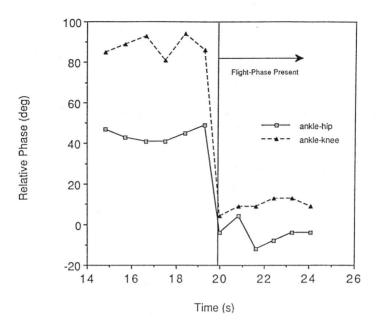

Figure 14.2
The relative phases of the leg segments during a sample walk-to-run transition trial. From "Why change gaits? Dynamics of the walk-run transition," by F. J. Diedrich and W. H. Warren, 1995, *Journal of Experimental Psychology: Human Perception and Performance, 21,* 183–202. Copyright 1995 by the American Psychological Association. Reprinted with permission.

within one stride, consistent with the presence of a bifurcation between attractors, each with its own characteristic phase relationship. Note that the change in phase coincides with the presence of a flight phase, which is the traditional indication of a running gait.

We also measured stability during steady-state trials in which the participants performed particular gaits at a variety of speeds below, at, and beyond the transition (Diedrich and Warren, 1995b, 1996). Using this method, we observed that fluctuations of the relative phases of the leg segments are enhanced in both gaits when speed is scaled away from preferred values, and that in general, these fluctuations begin to increase in the typical transition region for both gaits. In particular, figure 14.3 indicates that for both phase relationships, the SD of phase is a U-shaped function of speed for walking, and a declining exponential for running. Note that the SD of phase is plotted as a function of Froude number $\mathbf{F}$, where v is speed, L is the leg length, and g is the acceleration due to gravity (Alexander and Jayes, 1983):

$$\mathbf{F} = v^2/L^*g. \tag{14.2}$$

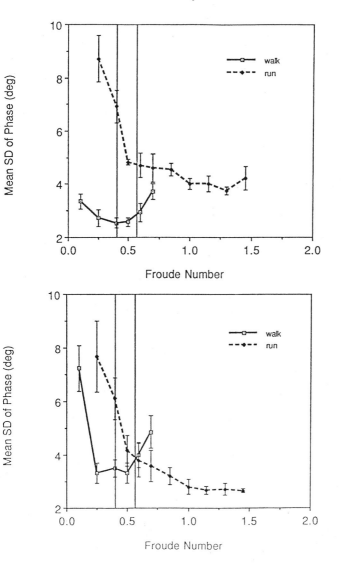

Figure 14.3
Mean within-trial standard deviation of phase by Froude number (speed). Top: Ankle-hip. Bottom: Ankle-knee. Vertical lines show transition region. Error bars show standard error. From "Why change gaits? Dynamics of the walk-run transition," by F. J. Diedrich and W. H. Warren, 1995, *Journal of Experimental Psychology: Human Perception and Performance, 21,* 183–202. Copyright 1995 by the American Psychological Association. Reprinted with permission.

By normalizing speed to leg length, we can average data across participants (or animals) of different sizes. Thus, although the absolute speeds at which particular activities occur across participants may be different, they are the same relative to the participants' anthropometric characteristics. Because speed increases as Froude number increases, for simplicity we can consider Froude number to be speed.

In sum, these data on phase fluctuations demonstrate that the control parameter (speed) weakens the dynamics as it is scaled, consistent with the claim that relative phase indexes different attractor states for walking and running. Furthermore, because there is a sudden, nonlinear change in relative phase at the transition from values that define a walk to values that define a run (figure 14.2), we have evidence that the transition behaves as a bifurcation between two relative phase attractors caused by a loss of stability. Formal measurements of critical fluctuations and critical slowing down are planned for future work.

In general there is also evidence for the presence of hysteresis, as the walk-to-run transition speed is often higher than the run-to-walk transition speed, although this effect depends on the rate at which the control parameter (speed) is scaled (Beuter and Lalonde, 1989; Diedrich and Warren 1995a, 1995b, 1998; Hreljac, 1993b; Thorstensson and Roberthson, 1987). Diedrich and Warren (1995a) tested for the presence of hysteresis using trials in which speed was changed "continuously" (in a smooth manner), in steps of 0.083 m/s each lasting 10 s, or in steps of 0.083 m/s each lasting 20 s. Significant hysteresis was found only in the continuous condition, with a hysteresis trend in the 10-s condition, and a reverse hysteresis trend in the 20-s condition (figure 14.4). Reverse hysteresis, or enhanced contrast, means that the run-to-walk transition actually occurred at a higher speed than the walk-to-run transition. Such a dependence of hysteresis on the scaling of the control parameter can be anticipated from the dynamic theory (Kelso, 1995). Near the transition the system is not deterministic as there is a bistable region (speed 4 in figure 14.1) characterized by the presence of multiple attractors and noise. Significant hysteresis is observed in the continuous condition because the system is moved through this bistable region quickly enough that it remains in its current basin of attraction until the attractor actually disappears. In contrast, for long plateaus in the transition region, it is likely that one will see spontaneous shifts between gaits due to random fluctuations, reflecting a decrease in the system's equilibration time (see, Kelso, Ding, and Schöner, 1992; Schmidt, Carello, and Turvey, 1990). Such spontaneous shifts would eliminate any strong hysteresis effects. It is interesting to note that the degree and amount of hysteresis also depends on the individual participants, although the hysteresis pattern is predominant (Diedrich and Warren, 1995a, 1995b, 1998). Some participants do show significant re-

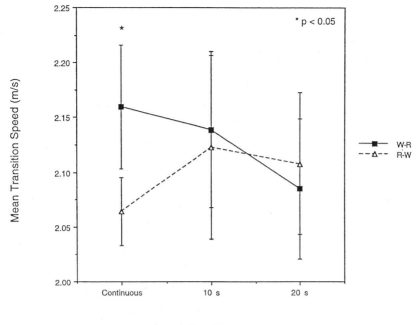

Figure 14.4
Mean walk-to-run (W-R) and run-to-walk (R-W) transition speeds, for various speed manipulations (continuous, steps of 10 s, or 20 s). Error bars show the standard error.

verse hysteresis, which is further evidence for a bistable transition region, because both gaits are possible over a range of speeds (Tuller et al., 1994). At this time, however, the specific reasons for these individual differences remain unclear.

Although these data suggest that speed is a control parameter for gait because speed is the product of stride frequency and stride length, in theory either stride frequency, stride length, or speed (their combination) could act as the actual control parameter. To empirically identify the control parameter, Diedrich and Warren (1995b) dissociated these variables by pacing participants with a metronome. This pacing caused participants to use different combinations of stride frequency and length at equivalent speeds. When the treadmill was accelerated or decelerated, the participants made the transition at a constant speed, while allowing stride frequency and length to vary. This indicates that speed likely acts as the control parameter for locomotion when on a flat treadmill, because it reflects a tightly coupled relationship between stride frequency and stride length. Under other circumstances, however, these variables can be decoupled, such as when wearing ankle weights (see later description; Diedrich and Warren, 1998). Therefore, one should always consider the dual actions of stride frequency and length when considering different locomotor tasks.

In summary, there is evidence for a dynamic interpretation of the transition from walking to running in humans. The evidence is consistent with a change in the relative phase of the leg segments at the transition, accompanied by a loss of stability and the presence of hysteresis.

14.5 Energetics of Locomotion

In addition to the results reported previously, an additional step in the analysis of the dynamics of human locomotion is to ask more about the nature of the attractors for each gait. For instance, how do the attractors reflect the costs of locomotion? In an initial attempt to address this question, Diedrich and Warren (1995b) suggested that increases in total metabolic energy expenditure roughly reflect the costs of driving the locomotor system away from its attractor or resonant states, along with other metabolic factors. To understand this idea, recall that a linear oscillator requires a minimal amount of force to sustain oscillation when driven at its natural frequency (see Holt, Hamill, and Andres, 1990; Kugler and Turvey, 1987). As the driving frequency moves away from the natural frequency, more force is required to sustain oscillation, leading to increases in energy costs. If these costs are specified by proprioceptive information and the system follows the information gradient back toward the natural frequency, then the natural frequency can be considered an attractor (Bingham, 1995; Hatsopoulos and Warren, 1996; Kugler and Turvey, 1987). Consistent with this claim, it has been shown that the walk-run transition reduces the internal mechanical work that reflects the costs of accelerating the limb segments (Minetti, Ardigo, and Saibene, 1994). Also, it is clear that proprioceptive information could play a role as perceived exertion is minimized by the transition, although it is unclear what variables influence this perceived exertion (Hreljac, 1993b; Noble et al., 1973). These results illustrate that the dynamics are inherently informational (Kelso, 1995).

Following this logic, it is informative to take a closer look at the energetics of human locomotion (figure 14.5; see Diedrich and Warren, 1995b, for notes on the calculations and previous data used to construct this figure, following Molen, Rozendal, and Boon, 1972a, 1972b). For walking there is a preferred combination of stride frequency and length (a speed) at which energy expenditure per unit distance is minimized at approximately 0.79 cal/kg/m (smallest circle, figure 14.5). Any change in stride frequency or length away from this preferred combination results in in-

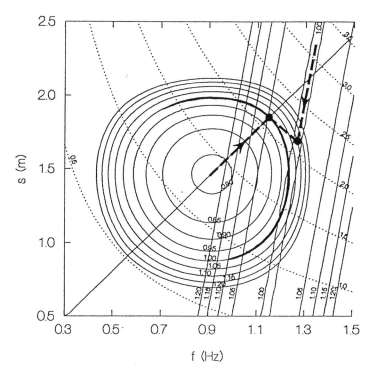

Figure 14.5
Contour plot of energy expenditure per unit distance (cal/kg/m) as a function of stride length (s in m) and stride frequency (f in Hz) for walking (concentric circles) and running (parallel lines). The dotted lines are iso-speed contours, the bold line is the equal-energy separatrix, and the bold dashed line is the minimum energy route. From "Why change gaits? Dynamics of the walk-run transition," by F. J. Diedrich and W. H. Warren, 1995, *Journal of Experimental Psychology: Human Perception and Performance, 21,* 183–202. Copyright 1995 by the American Psychological Association. Reprinted with permission.

creases in energy expenditure (larger circles, figure 14.5). In contrast, for running there is no single speed that minimizes energetic costs, as energy expenditure per unit distance is constant at approximately 1.0 cal/kg/m across a wide range of running speeds (inner set of parallel lines, figure 14.5). Nevertheless, at any given speed a departure from the preferred combination of stride frequency and stride length results in increases in energy expenditure (outer sets of parallel lines, figure 14.5). These data suggest that there is a round "basin" of attraction for walking (concentric circles in figure 14.5) and an elongated "valley" of attraction for running (parallel lines in figure 14.5) in stride frequency-stride length space. There is also evidence for an equal-energy separatrix (a boundary at which the system is pulled toward either walking or running) between the attractors (bold curve in figure 14.5), which corresponds to those stride frequency-stride length combinations for walking that have a cost of 1.0 cal/kg/m that matches the cost of a preferred run at any given speed. In total, these data suggest that the dynamics of human locomotion can be described in a four dimensional space, with stride frequency (f) and stride length (s) as control parameters, relative phase as the order parameter, and a potential function $V(x)$. This space consists of a set of curves like those in figure 14.1, with one curve placed at each stride frequency-stride length combination in figure 14.5. The height of a ball rolling on the potential function roughly reflects energy expenditure per unit distance.

Consistent with these claims, Diedrich and Warren (1995b) showed that for walking there is a minimum in the U-shaped function that relates speed to the standard deviation of the relative phase of the leg segments (figure 14.3). This U-shaped function is predicted by the basin of attraction shown by the data for metabolic cost, and suggests that for walking there is an attractor characterized by minimal energy expenditure and by low fluctuations of relative phase. For running, fluctuations of phase increase in the transition region, but are low across a wide range of speeds that correspond to the bottom of the running valley suggested by the energetic data. The transition occurs quite close to the equal-energy separatrix at a speed of approximately 2.1 to 2.2 m/s. In addition, the transition is characterized by changes in stride frequency and stride length that are consistent with the minimization of energetic costs (see the dashed, bold line in figure 14.5).

14.6 Task Dynamics

Evidence consistent with a link between stability and energetics also comes from experiments that manipulated the properties of the attractors by investigating the effects of changes in the task dynamics (Diedrich and Warren, 1998). These experiments tested the prediction that movement of the attractors will result in corresponding changes in the transition. For example, if both of the attractors shift down in speed, then the system will lose stability at a lower speed, and as a result, the walk-run transition will occur at a lower speed. Specifically, because any movement along a speed axis implies some combination of changes in stride frequency and stride length, the dynamic theory predicts that movement of the attractors to new stride frequency-stride length combinations will result in a corresponding shift of the transition.

One way to manipulate the task dynamics, and thereby shift the attractors, is to manipulate the grade of the treadmill. From previous data, we know that the walking speed at which energy expenditure per unit distance is minimized decreases from 1.30 m/s on a 0% grade to 1.26 m/s on a 10% grade, and that the speed at which the equal-energy separatrix is located drops from 2.32 m/s to 1.90 m/s (fits on Margaria's 1938 data using equations developed by Inman, Ralston, and Todd, 1981). Therefore, given the link between energetics and stability, it is likely that these changes in metabolic cost reflect changes in the location of the attractor states. In fact, as predicted by the dynamic theory, a change in the inclination of the treadmill does act to move the attractors and the transition (Diedrich and Warren, 1998). Consistent with the energetic data, an increase in grade affects both the stable walking attractor and the transition by moving them down along a speed axis, as measured by the ankle-hip phase relationship (figure 14.6, top, see arrows). These data, along with the observation of changes in the preferred stride frequency-stride length combinations used at any given walking speed (crossing lines in figure 14.6, top), suggest that the attractor layout rotates in stride length-stride frequency space when going uphill, leading to corresponding changes at the walk-run transition (figure 14.6, top).

A second way to manipulate the location of the attractors is to load the participants' legs with ankle weights (Diedrich and Warren, 1998). Previous data indicate that there are increases in energy expenditure when participants wear loads on their ankles or feet (e.g., Claremont and Hall, 1988; Inman, Ralston, and Todd, 1981). Although data are not available that assess directional shifts in energy expenditure, the preferred walking frequency drops when loads are added to the ankles (Holt, Hamill, and Andres, 1990). As predicted, the addition of load does in fact reduce both the most stable walking speed and the transition speed through reductions in stride frequency, with no significant changes in stride length (figure 14.6, bottom, see arrows). These results indicate that the attractor layout translates down along a frequency axis in stride length-stride frequency space when load is added to the ankles (figure 14.6, bottom), as predicted by a drop in the natural frequencies of each gait (Diedrich and Warren, 1998; see also Holt, Hamill, and Andres 1990).

As predicted by the dynamic theory, these data are generally consistent with the claim that movement of the attractors is accompanied by corresponding changes at the walk-run transition. Importantly, these experiments make it clear that the precise nature of the attractors is a product of the dynamics of the task, which includes support surface characteristics and external loads, as well as the state of the motor system itself. Given these results, it is also clear that there are strong links between measures of stability and energetics. In many ways, overall metabolic cost per unit distance and measures of stability closely correspond to each other. For both gaits the overall metabolic cost predicts the patterns of changes in stability that occur with speed manipulation, and these energetic measures

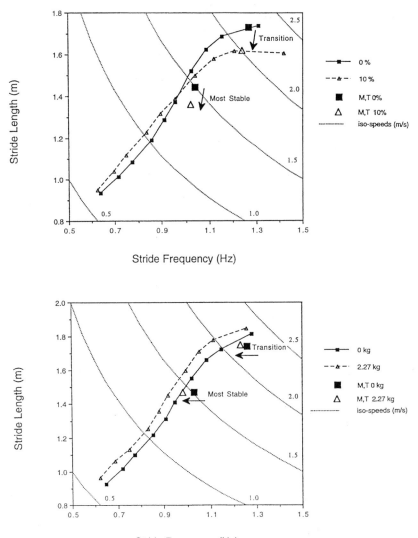

Figure 14.6
(Top) Stride length-stride frequency combinations for the 0% (squares) and 10% grade (triangles) conditions. (Bottom) Stride length-stride frequency combinations for the unloaded (squares) and loaded (triangles) conditions. Large symbols show the most stable (M) and mean transition points (T), arrows show the direction of shifts, small symbols show preferred walking combinations, and dotted lines are iso-speed contours. (Adapted from "The dynamics of gait transitions: Effects of grade and load," by F. J. Diedrich and W. H. Warren, 1998, Journal of Motor Behavior, 30, 60–78. Copyright 1998 by Heldref Publications. Reprinted with permission.)

also correspond to the directional shifts seen for the grade manipulation. It is also clear that the measures of the most stable speed (1.65 m/s; Diedrich and Warren, 1998) do not exactly match the energetically optimal speed (1.3 m/s; Margaria, 1938), although direct comparisons between the experiments cannot be made due to unspecified differences in the participants' leg lengths. In addition, recall that when on a treadmill the optimal energy transition speed is slightly different than the actual transition speed (Hreljac, 1993b). Thus, the energy and stability measures closely, but not exactly, correspond to each other. This relationship between stability and energetics needs to be explored more fully by using the same participants to measure both stability and energy expenditure across the whole space shown in figure 14.5. These relationships have already been explored for participants walking along a single frequency axis at a constant speed (Holt et al., 1995). As expected, the ankle-knee phase relationship accurately predicted the energetic minimum, but the minimum for the ankle-hip phase relationship was slightly different. This experiment indicates that there is still a need to fully explore the attractor space using multiple stability measures as well as energetic measures. Nevertheless, the general pattern of results is consistent with the idea that overall changes in total metabolic cost roughly reflect the costs of driving the system away from its attractor states.

14.7 Conclusions

What is responsible for the complex coordinative patterns that comprise actions such as gait? Evidence from a wide range of motor tasks suggests that, rather than motor programs imposing organization, stable patterns of behavior and transitions between them arise from the self-organizing dynamics of the motor system and task constraints (e.g., Kelso, 1995). Apparently, as reviewed here, the walk-run transition in humans also behaves as a bifurcation between attractors (Diedrich and Warren, 1995a, 1995b, 1998). The transition is characterized by a sudden and qualitative reorganization of the relative phase of the segments within a leg, by a loss of stability, by increases in energetic costs, and by hysteresis. Furthermore, as predicted by the dynamic theory, movement of the attractors is accompanied by corresponding movement of the transition, indicating that the attractor layout is a product of the dynamics of the task. Although it is unclear if a theory of motor programming could account for the full range of results presented in this paper, motor programming theories have been proposed for some phase transition phenomena (e.g., Rosenbaum, 1991). Dynamic systems theory offers the advantage that it can account for pattern formation across a wide range of systems and tasks without assuming prior organization in the nervous system.

Although these experiments have provided substantial evidence in support of the dynamic theory, several aspects of gait remain to be tested. First, all of the experiments conducted so far on the dynamics of locomotion have been performed on a motorized treadmill. Although it is likely that most aspects of overground locomotion are similar to those observed for treadmill locomotion (e.g., Arsenault, Winter, and Marteniuk, 1986; Elliot and Blanksby, 1976), it is necessary to see how the present results generalize to overground locomotion given small differences reported for behavior at the transition (Minetti, Ardigo, and Saibene, 1994).

Second, it is necessary to further evaluate the stability of gait by exploring the prediction of critical slowing down. It should take longer for the system to recover from a perturbation when in the transition region due to a loss of stability. Such experiments could be accomplished through the use of mechanical perturbations and would enable us to determine whether external perturbations influence the internal rhythm of the system, thus providing information about the coupling between the central oscillator and the limbs (Kay, Saltzman, and Kelso, 1991).

A third investigation will focus on independent changes in stride frequency and stride length. Under normal circumstances, increases in speed derive from simultaneous increases in stride frequency and length. The dynamic theory predicts that independent variation of these variables away from their preferred values will also lead to a loss of stability and ultimately to a transition. Consistent with this idea, there are changes in stability when stride frequency is varied at one speed during walking (Holt et al., 1995). Yet, stability has not been measured across the complete variety of stride frequencies and stride lengths in both gaits (figure 14.5), and the predicted transitions have yet to be explored.

Finally, there is still some question as to whether we have in fact identified "the" order parameter. Our measures reveal a change in relative phase and a loss of stability at the transition. In brief, the ankle extends after the knee and hip during walking, and the joints extend simultaneously during running. These changes in phase may, however, simply reflect the movement of the center of mass of the body, as they are consistent with an inverted pendulum model for walking and a bouncing ball model for running (e.g., Margaria, 1976; McMahon, 1984). During walking, the center of mass of the body rotates over the support foot acting to extend the hip and knee prior to the push-off at the ankle. In contrast, during running, the joints accept (flex) and release weight (extend) together, much like a bouncing ball. This distinction is important, as the potential and kinetic energy cycles are out-of-phase during walking (inverted pendulum), but in-phase during running (bouncing ball). Phase thought of in this way could act as the order parameter, and should be investigated with respect to changes in stability.

In conclusion, the experiments that have been conducted so far provide evidence in support of a dynamical interpretation of human locomotion. Although many questions remain to be asked, these experiments lend further support to the claim that much of the organization of behavior arises from the dynamics of the action system and task constraints.

Acknowledgments

This research was supported by Grants R01 AG05223 and R01 EY10923 from the National Institutes of Health, both awarded to William H. Warren. We thank David Rosenbaum and an anonymous reviewer for helpful comments.

References

Alexander, R. M. (1984). Walking and running. *American Scientist, 72*, 348–354.

Alexander, R. M. (1992). A model of bipedal locomotion on compliant legs. *Philosophical Transactions of the Royal Society of London B., 338*, 189–198.

Alexander, R. M., & Jayes, A. S. (1983). A dynamic similarity hypothesis for the gaits of quadrupedal mammals. *Journal of Zoology (London), 201*, 135–152.

Arsenault, A. B., Winter, D. A., & Marteniuk, R. G. (1986). Treadmill versus walkway locomotion in humans: An EMG study. *Ergonomics, 29*, 665–676.

Bernstein, N. (1967). *The coordination and regulation of movements.* London: Pergamon.

Beuter, A., & Lalonde, F. (1989). Analysis of a phase transition in human locomotion using singularity theory. *Neuroscience Research Communications, 3*, 127–132.

Bingham, G. P. (1995). The role of perception in timing: Feedback control in motor programming and task dynamics. In E. Covey, H. Hawkins, T. McMullen, & R. Port, (eds.), *Neural representation of temporal patterns* (pp. 129–158). New York: Plenum.

Carello, C., Turvey, M. T., Kugler, P. N., & Shaw, R. E. (1984). Inadequacies of the computer metaphor. In M. S. Gazzaniga (ed.), *Handbook of cognitive neuroscience* (pp. 229–248). New York: Plenum Press.

Claremont, A. D., & Hall, S. J. (1988). Effects of extremity loading upon energy expenditure and running mechanics. *Medicine and Science in Sports and Exercise, 20*, 167–171.

Collins, J. J., & Stewart, I. N. (1993). Coupled nonlinear oscillators and the symmetries of animal gaits. *Journal of Nonlinear Science, 3*, 349–392.

Diedrich, F. J., & Warren, W. H. (1995a). The dynamics of human locomotion: Hysteresis at the walk-run transition. Poster presented at the 25th annual meeting of the Society for Neuroscience, San Diego.

Diedrich, F. J., & Warren, W. H. (1995b). Why change gaits? Dynamics of the walk-run transition. *Journal of Experimental Psychology: Human Perception and Performance, 21*, 183–202.

Diedrich, F. J., & Warren, W. H. (1998). The dynamics of gait transitions: Effects of grade and load. *Journal of Motor Behavior, 30*, 60–78.

Elliot, B. C., & Blanksby, B. A. (1976). A cinematographic analysis of overground and treadmill running by males and females. *Medicine and Science in Sports, 8*, 84–87.

Farley, C. T., & Taylor, C. R. (1991). A mechanical trigger for the trot-gallop transition in horses. *Science, 253*, 306–308.

Grillner, S. (1975). Locomotion in vertebrates: Central mechanisms and reflex interaction. *Physiological Reviews, 55*, 247–304.

Haken, H. (1983). *Synergetics: An introduction* (3d ed.). Berlin: Springer.

Haken, H., Kelso, J. A. S., & Bunz, H. (1985). A theoretical model of phase transitions in human hand movements. *Biological Cybernetics, 51,* 347–356.

Harris-Warwick, R. M., & Johnson, G. (1989). Motor pattern networks. Flexible foundations for rhythmic pattern production. In T. J. Carew & D. B. Kelley (eds.), *Perspectives in neural systems and behavior* (pp. 51–71). New York: Alan R. Liss.

Hatsopoulos, N. G., & Warren, W. H. (1996). Resonance tuning in arm swinging. *Journal of Motor Behavior, 28,* 3–14.

Higgins, J. R., Bennett, B. C., Doyle, J. W., & Higgins, S. (1995). Walking as influenced by dimensional changes in environmental obstacles. Poster presented at the 25th Annual Meeting of the Society for Neuroscience, San Diego.

Holt, K. G., Hamill, J., & Andres, R. O. (1990). The force-driven harmonic oscillator as a model for human locomotion. *Human Movement Science, 9,* 55–68.

Holt, K. G., Jeng, S. F., Ratcliffe, R., & Hamill, J. (1995). Energetic cost and stability during human walking at the preferred stride frequency. *Journal of Motor Behavior, 27,* 164–179.

Hreljac, A. (1993a). Determinants of the gait transition speed during human locomotion. *Gait & Posture, 1,* 217–223.

Hreljac, A. (1993b). Preferred and energetically optimal gait transition speeds in human locomotion. *Medicine and Science in Sports and Exercise, 25,* 1158–1162.

Hreljac, A. (1995). Determinants of the gait transition speed during human locomotion: Kinematic factors. *Journal of Biomechanics, 28,* 669–677.

Inman, V. T., Ralston, H. J., & Todd, F. (1981). *Human walking.* Baltimore: Williams and Wilkins.

Kay, B. A., Saltzman, E. L., & Kelso, J. A. S. (1991). Steady-state and perturbed rhythmical movements: A dynamical analysis. *Journal of Experimental Psychology: Human Perception and Performance, 17,* 183–197.

Keele, S. W. (1982). Learning and control of coordinated motor patterns: The programming perspective. In J. A. S. Kelso (ed.), *Human motor behavior: An introduction* (pp. 161–186). Hillsdale, NJ: Erlbaum.

Kelso, J. A. S. (1995). *Dynamic patterns: The self-organization of brain and behavior.* Cambridge: MIT Press.

Kelso, J. A. S., Ding, M., & Schöner, G. (1992). Dynamic pattern formation: A primer. In J. Mittenthal & A. Baskin (eds.), *Principles of organization in organisms, SFI studies in the sciences of complexity, Proceedings Vol. 13* (pp. 397–439). Reading, MA: Addison-Wesley.

Kelso, J. A. S., & Schöner, G. (1988). Self-organization of coordinative movement patterns. *Human Movement Science, 7,* 27–46.

Kugler, P. N., & Turvey, M. T. (1987). *Information, natural law, and the self-assembly of rhythmic movement.* Hillsdale, NJ: Erlbaum.

Marder, E. (1988). Modulating a neuronal network. *Nature, 335,* 296–297.

Margaria, R. (1938). Sulla fisiologia, e specialmente sul consumo energetico, della marcia e della corsa a varie velocita ed inclinazioni del terreno. *Atti Accad. Naz. Lincei Memorie, Serie VI, 7,* 299–368.

Margaria, R. (1976). *Biomechanics and energetics of muscular exercise.* Oxford: Clarendon Press.

McMahon, T. A. (1984). *Muscles, reflexes, and locomotion.* Princeton: Princeton University Press.

Mercier, J., Gallais, D., Durand, M., Goudal, C., Micallef, J. P., & Prefaut, C. (1994). Energy expenditure and cardiorespiratory responses at the transition between walking and running. *European Journal of Applied Physiology, 69,* 525–529.

Minetti, A. E., Ardigo, L. P., & Saibene, F. (1994). The transition between walking and running in humans: Metabolic and mechanical aspects at different gradients. *Acta Physiologia Scandinavica, 150,* 315–323.

Molen, N. H., Rozendal, R. H., & Boon, W. (1972a). Fundamental characteristics of human gait in relation to sex and locomotion. *Proceedings Koninklijke Nederlandse Academie van Wetenschappen, C-75.* 215–223.

Molen, N. H., Rozendal, R. H., & Boon, W. (1972b). Graphic representation of the relationship between oxygen-consumption and characteristics of normal gait of the human male. *Proceedings Koninklijke Nederlandse Academie van Wetenschappen, C-75,* 305–314.

Noble, B. J., Metz, K. F., Pandolf, K. B., Bell, C. W., Cafarelli, E., & Sime, W. E. (1973). Perceived exertion during walking and running—II. *Medicine and Science in Sports, 5,* 116–120.

Prigogene, I., & Stengers, I. (1984). *Order out of chaos: Man's new dialogue with nature.* New York: Bantam Books.

Rosenbaum, D. A. (1991). *Human motor control.* New York: Academic Press.

Schmidt, R. A. (1988). *Motor control and learning.* Champaign, IL: Human Kinetics.

Schmidt, R. C., Carello, C., & Turvey, M. T. (1990). Phase transitions and critical fluctuations in the visual coordination of rhythmic movements between people. *Journal of Experimental Psychology? Human Perception and Performance, 16,* 227–247.

Schmidt, R. C., & Turvey, M. T. (1995). Models of interlimb coordination—Equilibria, local analyses, and spectral patterning: Comment on Fuchs and Kelso (1994). *Journal of Experimental Psychology: Human Perception and Performance, 21,* 432–443.

Schöner, G., Haken, H., & Kelso, J. A. S. (1986). A stochastic theory of phase transitions in human hand movement. *Biological Cybernetics, 53,* 247–258.

Schöner, G., Jiang, W. Y., & Kelso, J.A.S. (1990). A synergetic theory of quadrupedal gaits and gait transitions. *Journal of Theoretical Biology, 142,* 359–391.

Shapiro, D. C., Zernicke, R. F., Gregor, R. J., & Diestel, J. D. (1981). Evidence for generalized motor programs using gait pattern analysis. *Journal of Motor Behavior, 13,* 33–47.

Shik, M. L., & Orlovskii, G. N. (1976). Neurophysiology of a locomotor automatism. *Physiological Reviews, 56,* 465–501.

Shik, M. L., Severin, F. V., & Orlovskii, G. N. (1966). Control of walking and running by means of electrical stimulation of the mid-brain. *Biophysics, 11,* 756–765.

Taga, G. (1995a). A model of the neuro-musculo-skeletal system for human locomotion: I. Emergence of basic gait. *Biological Cybernetics, 73,* 97–111.

Taga, G. (1995b). A model of the neuro-musculo-skeletal system for human locomotion: II. Real-time adaptability under various constraints. *Biological Cybernetics, 73,* 113–121.

Taga, G., Yamaguchi, Y., & Shimizu, H. (1991). Self-organized control of bipedal locomotion by neural oscillators in unpredictable environment. *Biological Cybernetics, 65,* 147–159.

Thelen, E., & Ulrich, B. D. (1991). Hidden skills: A dynamic systems analysis of treadmill stepping during the first year. *Monographs of the Society for Research in Child Development, 56* (1, Serial No. 223).

Thorstensson, A., & Roberthson, H. (1987). Adaptations to changing speed in human locomotion. Speed of transition between walking and running. *Acta Physiologia Scandinavia, 131,* 211–214.

Turvey, M. T., Holt, K. G., Obusek, J., Salo, A., & Kugler, P. N. (1996). Adiabatic transformability hypothesis of human locomotion. *Biological Cybernetics, 74,* 107–115.

Tuller, B., Case, P., Ding, M., & Kelso, J. A. S. (1994). The nonlinear dynamics of speech categorization. *Journal of Experimental Psychology: Human Perception and Performance, 20,* 3–16.

Wagenaar, R. C., & van Emmerik, R. E. A. (1994). Dynamics of pathological gait. *Human Movement Science, 13,* 441–471.

Chapter 15

A Computational Model for Repetitive Motion

Kjeldy A. Haugsjaa, Kamal Souccar, Christopher I. Connolly, and Roderic A. Grupen

Abstract

One of the central issues in the control of articulated limbs is the specification of dynamically feasible trajectories for motion planning. We provide an introduction to discrete configuration space representations and discuss numerical relaxation techniques for computing harmonic potential surfaces in these grids. The properties exhibited by harmonic functions that make them well suited to the kind of motion control problems posed in nature are reviewed. Then, an energy-referenced controller that makes use of the harmonic potential is formulated to generate and control repetitive motion plans for an articulated mechanism. A possible role for the basal ganglia as a potential-based motor planning mechanism is introduced. Finally, the energy-referenced control scheme is applied to dynamic simulations of the human leg to produce feedback compensated walking gaits. The gaits produced are similar to those derived from human subjects. These preliminary results postulate a simple mechanism for regulating the energy in a biomechanical oscillator in order to produce periodic motor plans.

15.1 Introduction

One of the central issues in the control of articulated limbs is the specification of trajectories from one posture to another within constraints imposed by the task. The contexts in which these systems operate vary dramatically. In some cases, collisions with objects in the world must never occur, or joint range limits must not be violated, or at times the quality (kinematic conditioning, actuator load, path smoothness) of the trajectory is critical. This variety of objectives often motivates computational optimization techniques that use models of the task to search for trajectories that meet task specifications. These approaches are typically expensive, however, and rely on the existence of complex models that are both complete and correct. As a result, trajectory search may lead to brittle strategies that fail in ways that cannot be fully anticipated beforehand, often from seemingly minor deficiencies in the task model. Even if the motion plan is acceptable, it must be compiled into a strategy for driving the actuators so as to track the desired trajectory precisely. The problem is further complicated in dynamical systems, where motion strategies must be feasible in light of the forces and inertias of the limb. This complication is especially relevant in periodic or orbital motion control, a very important class of motion control applications in natural and robot systems. A theory is required for motion control that incorporates generic constraints, is dynamically consistent with the articulated structure, and constitutes a feedback control policy for executing the motion.

In contrast to search techniques, we show how potential fields can be used to formulate "total energy" methods for planning motion. The use of a constant total energy constraint for control has been explored for hopping and juggling robots (Raibert, 1986; Koditschek and Bühler, 1991; Ostrowski and Burdick, 1993). Similarly, the approach described here converges to approximately constant energy orbits when released from an initial state. This "energy reference" concept is likewise an attempt to control the system such that the system's total energy is kept constant. The treatment described in this chapter relies on an artificial potential (in the same sense as in (Koditschek, 1991a)). We show how the regulation of constant energy orbits can be achieved by using an energy-referenced feedback loop based on an artificial total energy function (sometimes called a Hamiltonian function) for the system.

In this chapter, a harmonic potential field is employed for generating motor plans. Harmonic potentials can be computed with resistive networks, and are "programmable" in the sense that minimum and maximum points only occur at prespecified locations. This means that goal points and orbit centers can be preprogrammed into the potential with the guarantee that they will be the only such points in the potential. Obstacles or bounds on the motion are also preprogrammed as maximum points. It is shown how this can be used to construct convergent (i.e., goal-directed) and repetitive motion plans for a manipulator. In addition, control derived from harmonic potential fields results in bounded torques to the joints, and produces compliant, collision-free dynamic behavior. A brief discussion of a recent neurophysiological model (Connolly and Burns, 1993a, 1993b) that postulates a role for the basal ganglia as a potential-based motor planning mechanism is presented. The work described here offers a possible extension of this biological model into the realm of continuous and repetitive motion. The ultimate goal of this work is to incorporate energy and task constraints in a common framework, and to support general classes of kinodynamic planning and control. Kinodynamic planning incorporates both geometric and dynamic aspects of the motion. As an example of the generation of repetitive motions, the energy-referenced control scheme is presented for a simulated human leg executing a walking gait.

15.2 Discrete Configuration Space Representation

The configuration variables, representing independently controllable degrees of freedom in an articulated mechanism, form a natural representation for expressing motion plans. In this chapter, we discuss robot manipulators and dynamic simulations of the human leg. For these types of mechanisms, the configuration variables are the relative angles between adjacent links, $(\theta_1, \theta_2, \ldots, \theta_n)$. The configuration space reflects the range of allowable values on these angles. By using these angles, the manipulator can be mapped from a three-dimensional volume to a single point in its configuration space (Lozano-Perez, 1981). Likewise, a single coordinate in configuration space corresponds to the entire volume in Cartesian space occupied by the manipulator.

In addition to the manipulator, obstacles and goals must also be mapped into the configuration space. Each configuration variable is divided into a number of bins, yielding a discrete configuration space grid or bitmap that describes the entire work space of the limb in terms of its joint angles. Each node in this grid is labeled as either an obstacle, a goal, or accessible free-space. Obstacles typically correspond to geometric constraints for the limb, including other objects in the workspace, joint range limits, or self collision constraints, but in general may represent any constraint on the accessibility of configuration states. If any subset of the Cartesian volume subtended by the mechanism contains an obstacle constraint, then the corresponding configuration space coordinate is labeled inaccessible. Once a configuration space grid has been constructed which contains information about the obstacles and goals, the path planning problem can be posed as determining an obstacle-avoiding path from a start point to a goal point within the accessible configuration space.

Figure 15.1 shows the result of a complete mapping for a simple robot workcell. A rectangular object is illustrated inside the workspace of a 2-degrees-of-freedom planar manipulator. Because this manipulator has no joint limits, the configuration space for this problem wraps around at the boundaries. Notice that there are multiple goal configurations and there are inaccessible goal configurations embedded within obstacles.

15.3 Harmonic Potentials

The hardware and software required to execute a trajectory comprise the controller for that trajectory. Important properties of controllers, such as stability, convergence, and the existence of spurious equilibria, can be established by examining properties of an underlying potential function. If the potential surface can be shown to have certain properties, then control can be realized as a gradient descent of this surface. This approach leads

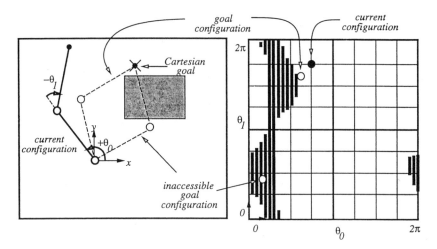

Figure 15.1
Configuration space for a 2-degrees-of-freedom, planar arm.

to robust, closed-loop motor plans that are responsive to variations in the world. In this section, we review these properties as they apply to harmonic potentials to justify the application of harmonic potentials to generic motion control tasks. We also introduce a simple numerical method for computing harmonic potentials. In subsequent sections, motor plans are generated for both robot and biological systems that employ harmonic potentials, including periodic motions such as those employed in the human walking gait.

Definition and Properties
A potential field is simply a single-valued function whose gradient is a force applied to the system. An example of a natural potential field is the gravitational potential (mgh), whose gradient, with respect to configuration variable, h (height), is the gravitational force (mg). Gradient descent on artificial potentials in configuration space is often used in robotics as a means of generating torques on the joints of an articulated structure, and yielding responsive, sensor-based robot path plans (Khatib, 1985; Krogh, 1984; Newman and Hogan, 1986; Lyons, 1986; Arkin, 1987; Myers, 1985; Koditschek, 1987). The way this works is analogous to a marble rolling through a surface of hills and valleys. Unfortunately, the usual formulations of potential fields for path planning do not preclude the spontaneous creation of minima other than the goal. The robot can therefore fall into these minima and achieve a stable configuration short of the goal

(Khatib, 1985; Arkin, 1987; Lozano-Perez, 1982; Canny and Lin, 1990; Barraquand and Latombe, 1991).

Koditschek (1987b) introduced the formal notion of an admissible potential function for robot path planning. A series of papers (Koditschek, 1989, 1991a, 1991b) established a framework for using artificial potentials to plan and control the trajectories of a mechanical system (e.g., a robot manipulator). Using a total energy formulation, as discussed earlier, "safe" (bounded-torque) controllers can be derived as long as the artificial potential satisfies certain constraints.

Connolly, Burns, and Weiss (1990), and independently Akishita, Kawamura, and Hayashi (1990) described the application of harmonic functions to the path-planning problem. Harmonic functions are, by definition, solutions to Laplace's equation,

$$\nabla^2 \phi = \frac{\partial^2 \phi}{\partial q_0^2} + \frac{\partial^2 \phi}{\partial q_1^2} + \cdots + \frac{\partial^2 \phi}{\partial q_n^2} = 0, \tag{15.1}$$

where ϕ is a single-valued function of n independent configuration variables, $\{q_0, q_1, \ldots, q_n\}$. Potential functions that satisfy Laplace's equation are "harmonic potentials." Such potentials generally satisfy the constraints of an admissible potential function, as established by Koditschek, and they exhibit several additional useful properties that make them well suited to motion control applications (Connolly and Grupen, 1993):

1. *Correctness.* Harmonic potentials take on their minimum and maximum values only at goals and obstacles, so a marble rolling on the surface will always reach a goal as long as one is accessible,

2. *Completeness.* If a path exists, it will be found up to the resolution of the configuration space grid.

3. *Robustness.* Control derived from the harmonic potential responds well to imprecise and/or newly observed constraints, and gradient descent of the harmonic potential minimizes the probability of collisions (Connolly, 1994).

4. *Responsiveness.* There is the potential for analog or parallel digital implementations that are capable of forming motion plans very quickly (McCann and Wilts, 1949; Tarassenko and Blake, 1991; Stan et al., 1994).

Harmonic potentials can be computed over arbitrary, discretized environments such as our configuration space grid, by very fast relaxation techniques. From a biological standpoint, harmonic potentials are useful because they serve as mathematical models for a variety of natural phenomena, including voltages in an electrical network.

Numerical Technique

As detailed in section 15.2, the configuration space grid is a discrete (bitmap) representation of the limb workspace. In the most straightforward implementation of a harmonic function motor planning mechanism, obstacles are set to a fixed maximum potential ($\phi_{obs} = 1$), and goals are grounded ($\phi_{goal} = 0$). The harmonic potential over the remaining free space can be computed using a variety of simple algorithms, most of which can be thought of as forms of repeated averaging or "smoothing" of the function (Burden, Faires, and Reynolds, 1978).

An example of such an algorithm is Jacobi iteration. The Jacobi iteration for harmonic functions replaces every nonboundary grid point, $u(x_i, y_j)$, with the average of its neighbors' values simultaneously. In two dimensions, this scheme can be written as

$$u^{(k+1)}(x_i, y_j) = \tfrac{1}{4}(u^k(x_{i+1}, y_j) + u^k(x_{i-1}, y_j)$$
$$+ u^k(x_i, y_{j+1}) + u^k(x_i, y_{j-1})), \qquad (15.2)$$

where k is the iteration number. In general, Jacobi iteration replaces the current value with the average of neighboring values. With a parallel array of simple processing elements, an iteration over the grid can be accomplished in one parallel step using only one solution variable per processing element, so Jacobi iteration is very efficient on parallel architectures. Even on sequential computers, relaxation for harmonic potentials is computed very quickly for moderately sized problems. Relaxation times for the examples presented in this chapter are typically 15 ms. Figure 15.2

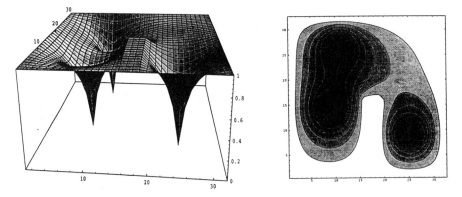

Figure 15.2
Left: Converged plot of a harmonic potential function with three goals; Right: level sets of harmonic potential, where white is the obstacle potential ($\Phi_{obs} = 1$) and black is the goal potential ($\Phi_{goal} = 0$).

provides an example of a 32 × 32 configuration space grid with geometric obstacles and three goals. Two views of the resulting potential surface are presented; the left panel shows a surface plot and the right panel illustrates the level curves of the surface when viewed from above. Even though the configuration space representation is discrete, we are left with a continuous, smooth surface for control, by interpolating in the space between samples.

15.4 Energy-Referenced Control

Up to this point, we have introduced harmonic potentials for motion control and reviewed an algorithm for computing them. In this section, we describe a controller in which joint torque commands are obtained from the gradient of a harmonic potential. This control paradigm is illustrated by the generation of repetitive orbital motion. Additionally, the precision with which an industrial-grade robot tracks a reference energy using this paradigm is measured and presented. A role for the basal ganglia in influencing motor control is also suggested.

If we assume we have a perfect dynamic model of the system, that is, we know the masses of the links and the viscosity and friction at the joints, then each degree of freedom in the system can be compensated. Compensation allows us to treat the system as a unit mass; in this case, there is no difference between torque and acceleration. This greatly simplifies the required computation. Such a controller is referred to as a model-based controller, which computes and sends torque commands to the joint motors of the robot. Under these conditions, we can imagine the system to be a marble of unit mass rolling across the harmonic potential surface. The total energy H in this system is the sum of kinetic and potential energies:

$$H(q, p) = \tfrac{1}{2}p^2 + \phi(q), \tag{15.3}$$

where the potential energy is the harmonic potential $\Phi(q)$, q is the configuration, and p is the magnitude of the momentum of the particle. Because the mass is 1, the momentum $p = |mv|$ is simply velocity, and $(1/2)p^2$ is the kinetic energy of the compensated system. In this formulation, total energy is conserved, that is, $H(q; p)$ ideally stays constant. Hamilton's equations describe the tradeoff between potential and kinetic energy, in terms of position and momentum:

$$\dot{q} = \frac{\partial H}{\partial p} = p$$

$$\dot{p} = -\frac{\partial H}{\partial q} = -\nabla\phi \tag{15.4}$$

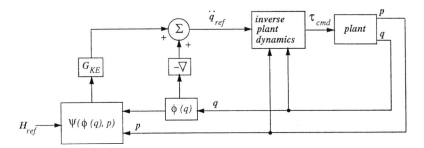

Figure 15.3
Energy-referenced controller.

These equations describe the motion of a system whose total energy remains constant (a conservative system). By these equations, the constant
energy constraint requires a reference acceleration for the mechanism, $\dot{p}$,
that is equal to the negative gradient of the potential ϕ.

In real mechanisms (robotic and biological), energy is dissipated in joint
bearings or in tissue deformation. One might expect the dynamic relation
expressed in equation 15.4 to slowly "run down" due to these losses in
the system. Our solution to this property which is inherent in all
real systems is to actively regulate the total energy by adjusting kinetic
energy. That is, the desired total energy, H, is regulated by introducing
or removing kinetic energy—accelerating when energy is too low and
decelerating when energy is too high. It will be shown how this energy-
referenced control scheme can be used to dissipate energy during convergent motion ($H = 0$), or can be used to overcome dissipation during
orbital motion ($H = E_0$). In this chapter, we are mainly interested in the
repetitive motions achieved when total desired energy is positive.

Figure 15.3 shows the proposed control system. We use closed-loop
feedback regulation of the system in which harmonic potential and kinetic
energy influence control. Ideally, the total energy of the system should
remain at a reference energy:

$$H_{ref} = \tfrac{1}{2}(p + \Delta p)^2 + \phi(q), \tag{15.5}$$

where p is the change of momentum required to satisfy the constant
energy constraint.

$$\Delta p = [2(H_{ref} - \phi(q))]^{1/2} - p. \tag{15.6}$$

For a given reference energy, H_{ref} in figure 15.3, a compensator,
$\Psi(\phi(q), p)$, is defined as follows:

$$\Psi(\phi(q), p) = [2H_{ref} - \phi(q))]^{1/2} - p, \quad \text{if } (H_{ref} - \phi(q)) > 0$$

$$= -p \quad \text{otherwise.} \tag{15.7}$$

In the first case, $H_{ref} > \phi(q)$, and enough energy is introduced in the form of momentum to make up for the system energy deficit. That is, the system's speed (kinetic energy) will have to be increased to keep H_{ref} at its original value. In the second case, however, the system has moved into a region where potentials are too high with respect to the reference, so the system will be braked (the speed lowered), again to keep the total energy constant. In other words, the kinetic energy compensation must behave as a damper to dissipate momentum. In the examples presented, kinetic energy is added or removed only along the current trajectory.

Under these conditions, the reference acceleration of the system is:

$$\ddot{q}_{ref} = -\nabla\phi + G_{KE}[\Psi(\phi(q), p)], \tag{15.8}$$

where G_{KE} is the derivative feedback gain that weighs the relative influence of kinetic and potential energy in the system.

As mentioned earlier, obstacle potentials are fixed at a uniform value, $\phi_{obs} = 1$, which is the maximum potential energy in the system. Under the energy-referenced control scheme, the system energy is never allowed to exceed this obstacle potential. If errors in the energy-referenced controller are neglected, then as long as $H_{ref} < \phi_{obs}$, the system cannot encounter a configuration space obstacle with non-zero velocity. In general, level sets of ϕ at $\phi = H_{ref}$ bound the motion of the system. The right panel of figure 15.2 illustrates the level sets of ϕ for that motion planning problem. As the reference energy H_{ref} is set to smaller values, the system becomes constrained by smaller areas surrounding the goal configurations.

Tracking Precision
Just as in classical feedback compensators, the precision and settling time of the system as it seeks the reference energy are functions of the control gains for proportional and derivative feedback. To provide a data point regarding the stability and tracking performance in a real system, the energy-referenced control scheme was implemented on a GE-P50 robot arm. The shoulder and the elbow of this robot were controlled forming a 2-degrees-of-freedom planar arm. The P50 is a relatively massive industrial robot for which only coarse feedforward dynamic compensators are available. This is a common deficiency in most real systems (and perhaps biological systems as well), the effect of which is to introduce unmodeled disturbances. Figure 15.4 shows an example trajectory derived from this system. The left panel depicts the configuration space of the

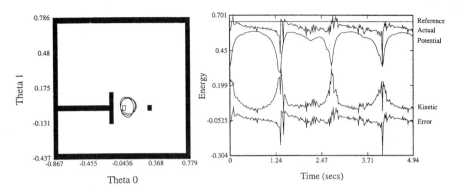

Figure 15.4
GE-P50 constant-energy orbit. Left: configuration space; Right: energy levels.

robot where the open square again represents the goal ($\phi_{goal} = 0$) and dark filled squares represent obstacles ($\phi_{obs=1}$). The right panel shows the energy levels measured during the motion sequence. The example is typical of real systems and illustrates that relatively small tracking errors are possible for suitable control parameters.

Orbital Motion
When H_{ref} is set to 0, the system configuration reaches one of the available goal configurations (where the potential energy is 0) and stops (kinetic energy is 0). Because $\Phi_{goal} = 0$, this represents a kind of goal-directed (or convergent) motion. Orbital motion is achieved by setting H_{ref} to some value between ϕ_{goal} and ϕ_{obs}. This results in an approximately constant energy trajectory that is bounded by the corresponding equipotential set of ϕ. The system becomes trapped within the basin of attraction of a goal. In other words, if we try to keep H_{ref} at a constant, positive value, the system will tend to orbit the goal (minimum) points of ϕ, the harmonic potential. Figure 15.4 depicts such an orbit in the motion sequence derived from our P50 robot arm. The balance of kinetic and potential energy maintains the elliptical motion illustrated. This representation can be used to "plan" simple repetitive motions such as turning a crank or stepping in a legged system, as we shall see in section 15.5.

Speculations on Neural Substrates
The motion planning approach described in the preceding sections relies on a harmonic potential to guide and restrict the movement of a limb. Harmonic (or nearly harmonic) potentials arise in a variety of physical phenomena, such as diffusion, electrostatics, fluid flow, and especially resistive networks. In particular, we can replace the grid of parallel processors

described in section 15.2 with a grid of resistors, and still obtain a harmonic potential. It seems natural to ask whether it is plausible for some neural process to exploit these phenomena for motor planning.

Some recent speculations on the function of the basal ganglia (Houk, Davis, and Beiser, 1995) suggest that these nuclei are involved in context-driven generation of motor plans, that is, they associate sensory cues and environmental context with an appropriate action or goal. One relevant feature of the basal ganglia is that they are topographically organized. In primates, the striatum (the "input" area for the basal ganglia) appears to be subdivided into regions corresponding to the face and limbs (Alexander and Crutcher, 1990). Basal ganglia involvement in motor planning seems likely given the symptoms of Parkinson's (e.g., festination, rigidity) and Huntington's diseases (e.g., chorea, involuntary twitching), both of which severely affect the basal ganglia. One view of basal ganglia function, then, is that they receive sensory information (context) from the cortex, and help select appropriate actions and goals based on that context.

A recent theory of striatum function (Connolly and Burns, 1993a; Connolly and Burns, 1995) suggests that a resistive network can serve as a model for the motor-planning role of the striatum. An additional motivation for this suggestion is recent evidence of dye coupling (Onn and Grace, 1994; Cepeda et al., 1989) and gap junctions (Kita, Kosaka, and Heizmann, 1990) among cells in the striatum. Dye-coupling and the presence of gap junctions suggest that striatal neurons could have direct cell-to-cell connections—probably at the dendrites—through which small molecules, cytoplasm, and electrical current can flow. This allows the network of cells in the striatum to be thought of as a resistive network. Even when they are not firing, striatal cells are known to exhibit fluctuations in their membrane potentials (so-called "subthreshold activity" (Houk, Davis, and Beiser, 1995)). Striatal projection neurons (which comprise about 95% of the striatum) are usually quiet. A large amount of cortical excitation drives striatal neurons into an "up" state, which is at a membrane potential just below the firing threshold. These neurons are also known to exhibit a "down" state. For motor planning, it is possible that these two states represent information about obstacle and goal configurations (the task context), in which case resistive coupling among these cells would rapidly give rise to a harmonic potential expressed as the membrane potentials of cells in a limb-related region of striatal tissue. This in turn could be used as part of the motor planning process for that limb.

As stated, the theory (Connolly and Burns, 1993a) represents pure path planning. That is, motion is planned as a gradient descent on a harmonic potential, without considering the dynamics of the limb. A natural extension to this theory would incorporate the results described in this chapter, using the physical properties of the limb (e.g., mass, joint viscosity) in the motion planning process. One consequence of this theoretical treatment is an explanation for festination (the "running-down" seen in Parkinson's patients), The inability to maintain potentials in the striatum during repetitive motion (e.g., walking or handwriting) results in progressively smaller orbits, until the motion ceases altogether. This effect can be achieved in a robotic system by allowing the goal potential to "float upward," until it reaches the same value as the obstacle potential. With a positive reference energy H_{ref}, this results in progressively smaller orbits, until the motion ceases altogether, at which point the system is rigid. The rigidity observed in a robotic system at this point is analogous to rigidity seen in Parkinson's patients. The limb is plastic, and upon being moved to a different configuration, will stay there.

15.5 Simulation of the Human Leg

Human locomotion is naturally expressed as an orbital gait pattern. We postulate that natural walking gaits consist of a synergy between constraint satisfaction and a dynamically feasible motor plan. The constraints, in this case, require that the trajectory not exceed joint limits and that the total system energy be regulated so as to further restrict the set of achievable configurations. This section introduces a simple kinematic and dynamic model of the human leg and generates a periodic gait pattern using the energy-referenced control scheme. The performance of the controller is compared to data derived from a human subject.

Terminology
The term "gait pattern" is used here to refer to the periodic leg trajectory generated when people move forward over smooth terrain. More specifically, this chapter focuses on patterns of walking gaits. Figure 15.5 illustrates a common cycle in a walking gait. In the biomechanics literature, this diagram is referred to as an "angle-angle" diagram (Enoka, Miller, and Burgess 1982), and is essentially equivalent to a trajectory through configuration space. The time history of the hip and knee configuration characterizes the gait pattern, so angle-angle diagrams are helpful in evaluating and comparing gaits. Knee and ankle diagrams are also often used. The usefulness of angle-angle diagrams for therapeutic purposes are noted by (Rosenbaum, 1991). They will be used in this paper to evaluate and compare our simulated monoped gait to that of a real human.

Figure 15.5 identifies critical events in a walking gait pattern. Knee flexion is indicated by downward motion and knee extension is indicated by upward motion in the angle-angle plots. Likewise, hip rotation forward is to the right and backward rotation is to the left. Toe-Off (TO) is the

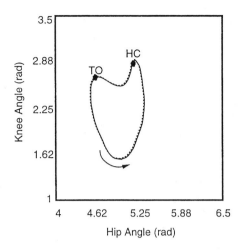

Figure 15.5
Typical angle-angle diagram of a walking gait.

point when a given foot leaves the ground at one of the relatively extreme knee extensions. After TO, the leg is in the swing phase until heel contact (HC), where the knee angle is almost fully extended. At this point, the leg enters the stance phase of the cycle where it remains until TO again. The stance phase is the part of the orbit between HC and TO, seen by the "dip" at the top of the cycle in the angle-angle diagrams. One complete walking stride is defined as the period between successive TOs. Thus, a stride is one orbit in the counterclockwise direction from TO to TO. The range of motion of both joints is indicated by the total area covered by the cycle.

Mechanics of the Human Leg
We use a three degree-of-freedom, planar mechanism to approximate the human leg as illustrated in figure 15.6. The thigh, shank, and foot, links 0, 1, and 2 respectively, are all modeled, and the motion of the leg is restricted to the sagittal plane (xy plane). Each of the three links is characterized by a point mass located at the center of mass and a rotational moment of inertia. The dynamic parameters are defined as those of the subject used in the walking trial example found in (Winter, 1990). The mass moments of inertia were calculated using the data for the average radii of gyration specified in (Winter, 1990). The values associated with the inertial parameters are summarized in table 15.1.

The simulation also models the passive elasticity in each joint as this is known to play a significant role in managing the motion of the skeleton

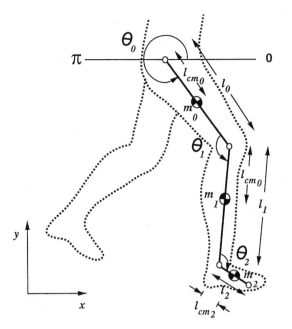

Figure 15.6
Geometry of the simulated human leg.

Table 15.1
Kinematic and dynamic parameters of the human subject

Link	Length (m)	Center of Mass (kg)	Mass (m)	Moment of Inertia (kg * m²)
Thigh (0)	0.36	0.16	5.67	0.079
Shank (1)	0.39	0.17	2.34	0.032
Foot (2)	0.24	0.12	0.82	0.010

Note that values for the location of the center of mass are lengths from the proximal end of each segment.

(Winter, 1990). The complex interconnection of limb segments in a human body involves many muscles, ligaments, tendons, and skin crossing each joint. A passive joint moment arises from the deformation of all these tissues. Elastic moments about the hip and the knee were modeled from measurements of such moments in vivo (Yoon and Mansour, 1982; Mansour and Audu, 1986). Exponential functions were fitted to these experimental data for joint flexion and extension, and a linear function was used in the midrange joint values, when the elastic moment is near 0. A similar elasticity function was determined for the ankle joint. These functions represent the relationship between the passive hip, knee, and ankle moment and the respective joint angles, as shown in figure 15.7. Clearly as a joint nears its limit, the passive elastic moment increases greatly. The elastic moment of the hip is strongly dependent on the position of both knee and hip (it should be noticeably more difficult to rotate your hip forward as your knee is further extended). As a result we use one of three functions, indexed by knee angle, to model the elastic moments of the hip.

Dynamics of the Human Leg
The dynamic model employed by our simulated monoped is given by the following equation:

$$\tau = M(\theta)\ddot{\theta} + C(\theta, \dot{\theta}) + G(\theta) + E(\theta). \tag{15.9}$$

M ( ) is the 3×3 inertia tensor for the leg, $C(;\_)$ expresses Coriolis and centrifugal loads, $G( )$ represents the gravity loads, and $E( )$ is a vector which accounts for moments from the natural elasticity of tissues surrounding the joints of a human leg. Equation 15.9 transforms the state of motion, $(;\_)$, and the desired acceleration in the mechanism, into the torque load o at each joint in the mechanism. Likewise, the state of motion $(;\_)$ and the applied torque yield the acceleration in the leg,

$$\ddot{\theta} = M^{-1}[\tau - C(\theta, \dot{\theta}) - G(\theta) - E(\theta). \tag{15.10}$$

The Newton-Euler method was used to obtain the dynamic equation of motion. The parameters of the equation of motion are given in appendix 15.A.

Energy-Referenced Control
Figure 15.8 shows an example of an orbit generated by the energy-referenced controller driving the simulated leg. The dark regions again represent obstacles assigned a potential of $\phi_{obs} = 1$. These boundary obstacles represent the joint angle limits of the leg. The open squares represent goals assigned a potential of $\phi_{goal} = 0$. The energy reference, H_{ref}, is defined to be $0:8$. The energy-referenced controller manages the hip, θ_o, and

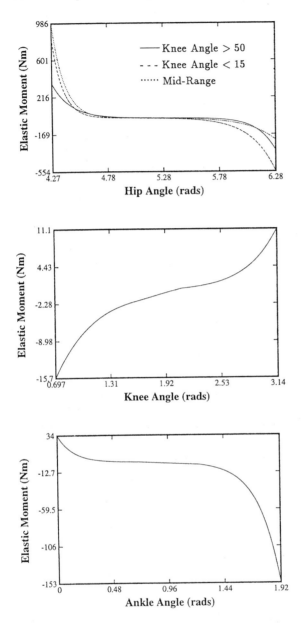

Figure 15.7
Elastic moment about the hip, knee, and ankle joints. (Adapted from Yoon and Mansour, 1982; Mansour and Audu, 1986.)

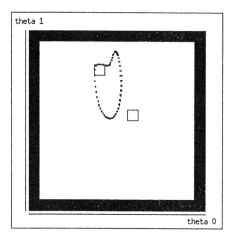

Figure 15.8
Monoped constant-energy orbit in configuration space.

the knee, θ_1, while the ankle is subject to the passive elastic moments exclusively. The results presented here are derived from 10 full simulated strides of the monoped.

Figure 15.9 presents a comparison with a walking stride derived from the human subject reported in Winter, (1990) and the energy-referenced controller acting on the dynamic simulation of Winter's subject. The two angle-angle plots give the general impression that they share a similar pattern of motion. Both execute a stable, cyclic motion pattern with the characteristic dip during the stance phase, and both orbits cover a similar area.

15.6 Summary and Discussion

In this chapter, we introduced the configuration space representation and motivated a procedure for mapping task geometry to accessibility constraints for articulated limbs. A procedure for transforming geometric motion constraints into the harmonic potential was presented. As result of the properties of harmonic potential functions, we formulated an energy-referenced controller capable of sustaining periodic, orbital motion and demonstrated such orbital motion in robot systems. A role for the basal ganglia in biological motor control was postulated. We then introduced a kinematic and dynamic model of the human leg and applied the energy-referenced control paradigm to this system. We demonstrated that this approach yields qualitatively similar behavior to that observed in the human walking gait. The results lend credibility to the notion that motion

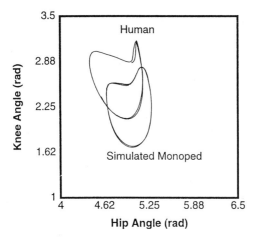

Figure 15.9
Comparison of the angle-angle diagram for the human subject and the dynamically equivalent leg simulation.

plans should deal with external constraints in a manner consistent with the underlying dynamics of physical systems.

Underlying this work is the presumption that human motor control has evolved to optimize energetic efficiency and so has exploited the dynamics of the "plant" (arm, leg, etc). Our objective has been to apply engineering principles to implement a controller that can generate convergent and periodic motions while responding to systems of dynamic constraints. In a sense, we have formulated a natural oscillator in the configuration of the leg, constrained initially by intrinsic kinematics, and subsequently "shaped" by the placement of task specific constraints (goals and obstacles) and control parameters (H_{ref}) .

In robot control applications, it is prudent to treat joint angle limits as obstacles and thus to guarantee that the trajectory plan will not violate them. Moreover, full knee extension is a kinematic singularity implying that impact at ground strike with an extended knee transmits large forces into the joints. Both circumstances lead to expensive failures in robot applications. Walking gaits in humans clearly emphasize energetic efficiency rather than joint limits or kinematic singularities. During the stance phase, the knee is very nearly fully extended. This makes sense in that during the load-carrying phase of the stride, this posture effectively transfers the load from the musculature into the skeleton, but only at the expense of knee and hip joints. In recent work, we have begun to formulate adaptive mechanisms for optimizing performance by modulating the shape of the harmonic potential (Coelho, Sitaraman, and Grupen, 1996). We propose these mechanisms as a means of acquiring skillful and efficient motor policies in a manner consistent with intrinsic kinematic and dynamic properties.

Although there are many overall similarities in the gait patterns presented here, if we turn up the microscope, so to speak, there are noteworthy variations. As figure 15.9 illustrates, the simulated knee does not extend as much as the actual human knee, and it flexes too much. This is possibly due to an aversion of our controller to joint limits, as described in the previous paragraph. As for the hip angle, it is rotated forward slightly for the entire stride—rotating forward excessively before HC and then not rotating backward quite enough for TO. Also, the "dip" at the top of each angle-angle diagram, which represents the stance (or load carrying) phase, is fairly different in shape. It is possible that this difference is the result of ground reaction forces experienced by human subjects, but not modeled in the simulator. The effect of a periodic external perturbation on the orbit can be a primary influence on the shape of the kinodynamic orbit. Moreover, the shape of this periodic forcing function, a property that depends on the shape of the foot, is likewise, potentially critical. The simulated leg does not experience these loads. This could account for many of the differences observed. Specifically, the tendency of the orbit to be skewed forward might be due to the lack of a backward directed friction force during the support phase.

From a technical perspective, several important questions regarding the application of energy-referenced controllers remain open. For instance, kinetic energy is currently added or removed from the system along the current trajectory, but there are other alternatives. It may be possible to address phase space constraints, that is, maintenance of a particular phase relationship between joint velocities, or to excite fundamental oscillatory modes of the device. These methods may provide a means for strategically shaping the orbit for a task.

Finally, although it is premature to draw any strong conclusions with respect to the proposed role of the basal ganglia in motor control, we have shown that dynamic oscillators driven by conservative potentials form a compelling basis for periodic, kinodynamic behavior. The value of harmonic potentials in robot systems is manifold, from their computational characteristics, collision avoidance properties, robustness with respect to cumulative information, their ability to incorporate generic constraints, and the absence of local minima. Moreover, the variety of natural processes captured by Laplace's equation and the potential to exploit massive parallelism when computing harmonic potentials offers evidence (albeit circumstantial) that this process could reside in the basal ganglia. One advantage to the scheme discussed in this chapter is that it does not directly specify positions or velocities for a limb. Instead, it relies on delivering torques to the joints to influence movement in a compliant way (that is, the limb can yield to external forces if necessary). This is consistent with observations of force-related responses in striatal neurons (Wickens, 1993), which offers further support for the view that the mechanisms for motor control we have discussed map onto the mechanisms embodied in the basal ganglia.

Appendix 15.A

Equation of Motion
The following is the dynamic equation of motion for the three link manipulator.

$$\tau = M(\theta)(\ddot{\theta}) + C(\theta, \dot{\theta}) + G(\theta) + E(\theta)$$

where:

$$M(\theta) = \begin{bmatrix} M_{00} & M_{01} & M_{02} \\ M_{10} & M_{11} & M_{12} \\ M_{20} & M_{21} & M_{22} \end{bmatrix} \quad C(\theta, \dot{\theta}) = \begin{bmatrix} C_0 \\ C_1 \\ C_2 \end{bmatrix} \quad G(\theta) = \begin{bmatrix} G_0 \\ G_1 \\ G_2 \end{bmatrix}$$

$$E(\theta) = \begin{bmatrix} E_0 \\ E_1 \\ E_2 \end{bmatrix}$$

$$M_{22} = I_2 + I_{cm2}$$
$$M_{21} = M_{22} + l_1 l_{cm2} m_2 c_2$$
$$M_{20} = M_{21} + l_0 l_{cm2} m_2 c_{12}$$
$$M_{12} = M_{21}$$
$$M_{11} = M_{12} + I_1 + I_{cm1} + l_1^2 m_2 + l_1 l_{cm2} m_2 c_2$$
$$M_{10} = M_{11} + (l_0 l_{cm1} m_1 + l_0 l_1 m_2) c_1 + l_0 l_{cm2} m_2 c_{12}$$
$$M_{02} = M_{20}$$
$$M_{01} = M_{10}$$
$$M_{00} = M_{01} + I_0 + I_{cm0} + l_0^2 (m_1 + m_2) + (l_0 l_{cm1} m_1 + l_0 l_1 m_2) c_1$$
$$\qquad + l_0 l_{cm2} m_2 c_{12}$$
$$C_2 = l_1 l_{cm2} m_2 s_2 (\dot{\theta}_0^2 + 2\dot{\theta}_0 \dot{\theta}_1 + \dot{\theta}_1^2) + l_0 l_{cm2} m_2 s_{12} \dot{\theta}_0^2$$
$$C_1 = (l_0 l_{cm1} m_1 + l_1 m_2) s_1 \dot{\theta}_0^2 - l_1 l_{cm2} m_2 s_2 (2\dot{\theta}_0 \dot{\theta}_2 + 2\dot{\theta}_1 \dot{\theta}_2 + \dot{\theta}_2^2)$$
$$\qquad + l_0 l_{cm2} m_2 s_{12} \dot{\theta}_0^2$$
$$C_0 = -(l_0 l_{cm1} m_1 + l_1 m_2) s_1 (2\dot{\theta}_0 \dot{\theta}_1 + \dot{\theta}_1^2) - l_1 l_{cm2} m_2 s_2 (2\dot{\theta}_0 \dot{\theta}_2 + 2\dot{\theta}_1 \dot{\theta}_2 + \dot{\theta}_2^2)$$
$$\qquad - l_0 l_{cm2} m_2 s_{12} (2\dot{\theta}_0 \theta_0 \theta_1 + 2\dot{\theta}_0 + 2\dot{\theta}_2 + 2\dot{\theta}_1 \dot{\theta}_2 + \dot{\theta}_1^2) + \dot{\theta}_2^2)$$
$$G_2 = g l_{cm2} m_2 s_{012}$$
$$G_1 = G_2 + g(l_{cm1} + l_1 m_2)_{s_{01}}$$

$$G_0 = G_1 + g(l_{cm0}m_0 + l_0 m_1 + l_0 m_2)_{s_0}$$

E_2 = Refer to bottom panel of figure 7.

E_1 = Refer to middle panel of figure 7.

E_0 = Refer to top panel of figure 7.

and in general:

$$s_{ijk} = \sin(\theta_i + \theta_j + \theta_k)$$

$$c_{ijk} = \cos(\theta_i + \theta_j + \theta_k).$$

Acknowledgments

This work was supported by the National Science Foundation under grants CDA-8922572, IRI-9116297, and IRI-9208920.

References

Akishita, S., Kawamura, S., & Hayashi, K. (1990). Laplace potential for moving obstacle avoidance & approach of a mobile robot. In *1990 Japan-USA symposium on flexible automation, a pacific rim conference*, (pp. 139–142) American Society of Mechanical Engineers.

Alexander, G. E., & Crutcher, M. D. (1990). Functional architecture of basal ganglia circuits: neural substrates of parallel processing. *Trends in Neurosciences, 13(7)*, 266–271.

Arkin, R. C. (1987). Towards cosmopolitan robots: Intelligent navigation in extended man-made environments. *Technical Report 87–80*, Amherst: COINS Department, University of Massachusetts.

Barraquand, J., & Latombe, J.-C. (1991). Robot motion planning: A distributed representation approach. *International Journal of Robotics Research, 10*, 628–649.

Burden, R. L., Faires, J. D., & Reynolds, A. C. (1978). *Numerical Analysis*. Boston: Prindle, Weber and Schmidt.

Canny, J. F., & Lin, M. C. (1990). An opportunistic global path planner. In *Proceedings of the 1990 IEEE international conference on robotics and automation* (pp. 1554–1559) IEEE Robotics and Automation Society.

Cepeda, C., Walsh, J. P., Hull, C. D., Howard, S. G., Buchwald, N. A., & Levine, M. S. (1989). Dye-coupling in the neostriatum of the rat: I. modulation by dopamine-depleting lesions. *Synapse, 4*, 229–237.

Coelho, J. A., Sitaraman, R. K., & Grupen, R. A. (1996). Parallel optimization of motion controllers via policy iteration. In M. C. Mozer, M. I. Jordan, & T. Petsche (eds.), *Proceedings of the 1996 advances in neural information processing systems* (pp. 996–1002).

Connolly, C. I. (1994). Harmonic functions & collision probabilities. *International Journal of Robotics. Research, 16*, 497–507.

Connolly, C. I., & Burns, J. B. (1993a). A model for the functioning of the striatum. *Biological Cybernetics, 68(6)*, 535–544.

Connolly, C. I., & Burns, J. B. (1993b). A new striatal model & its relationship to basal ganglia diseases. *Neuroscience Research, 16*, 271–274.

Connolly, C., & Burns, J. B. (1995). A state-space striatal model. In J. Houk, J. Davis, & D. Beiser, (eds.), *Models of information processing in the basal ganglia.* (pp. 163–177). Cambridge, MA: MIT Press.

Connolly, C. I., Burns, J. B., & Weiss, R. (1990). Path planning using Laplace's Equation. In *Proceedings of the 1990 IEEE international conference on robotics and automation* (pp. 2102–2106). IEEE Robotics and Automation Society.

Connolly, C. I., & Grupen, R. (1992). Applications of harmonic functions to robotics. *Technical Report 92–12*. Amherst: COINS Department, University of Massachusetts.

Connolly, C. I., & Grupen, R. A. (1993). The applications of harmonic functions to robotics. *Journal of Robotic Systems, 10*, 931–946.

Enoka, R. M., Miller, D. I., & Burgess, E. M. (1982). Below-knee amputee running gait. *American Journal of Physical Medicine, 61*, 66–84.

Houk, J., Davis, J., & Beiser, D., (eds.) (1995). *Models of information processing in the basal ganglia*. Cambridge, MA: MIT Press.

Khatib, O. (1985). Real-time obstacle avoidance for manipulators and mobile robots. In *Proceedings of the 1985 IEEE International Conference on Robotics and Automation* (pp. 500–505). IEEE Robotics and Automation Society.

Kita, H., Kosaka, T., & Heizmann, C. W. (1990). Parvalbumin-immunoreactive neurons in the rat neostriatum: A light and electon microscope study. *Brain Research, 536*, 1–15.

Koditschek, D. E. (1987). Exact robot navigation by means of potential functions: Some topological considerations. In *Proceedings of the 1987 IEEE international conference on robotics and automation* (pp. 1–6). IEEE Robotics and Automation Society.

Koditschek, D. E. (1989). The application of total energy as a lyapunov function for mechanical control systems. In J. E. Marsden, P. S. Krishnaprasad, & J. C. Simo (eds.), *Dynamics and control of multibody systems*, Vol. 97, *Contemporary mathematics* (pp. 131–157). American Mathematical Society.

Koditschek, D. E. (1991a). The control of natural motion in mechanical systems. *Journal of Dynamic Systems, Measurement, and Control, 113*, 547–551.

Koditschek, D. E. (1991b). Some applications of natural motion control. *Journal of Dynamic Systems, Measurement, and Control, 113*, 552–557.

Koditschek, D. E. & Bühler, M. (1991). Analysis of a simplified hopping robot. *International Journal of Robotics Research, 10(6)*, 587–605.

Krogh, B. H. (1984). A generalized potential field approach to obstacle avoidance control. In *robotics research: The next five years and beyond* (no. MS84–484). Society of Manufacturing Engineers.

Lozano-Perez, T. (1981). Automatic planning of manipulator transfer movements. *IEEE Transactions on Systems, Man, and Cybernetics, SMC-11(10)*, 681–698.

Lozano-Perez, T. (1982). Robotics (correspondent's report). *Artificial Intelligence, 19(2)*, 137–143.

Lyons, D. (1986). Tagged potential fields: An approach to specification of complex manipulator configurations. In *Proceedings of the 1986 IEEE international conference on robotics and automation* (pp. 1749–1754). IEEE Robotics and Automation Society.

Mansour, J. M., & Audu, M. L. (1986). The passive elastic moment at the knee and its influence on human gait. *Journal of Biomechanics, 19(5)*, 369–373.

McCann, G. D., & Wilts, C. H. (1949). Application of electric-analog computers to heat-transfer and fluid-flow problems. *Journal of Applied Mechanics, 16(3)*, 247–258.

Myers, J. K. (1985). Multiarm collision avoidance using the potential field approach. In W. C. Chiou (ed.), *Space station automation* (pp. 78–87). Bellingham, WA: SPIE.

Newman, W. S., & Hogan, N. (1986). High speed robot control and obstacle avoidance using dynamic potential functions. *Technical Report TR-86-042*. Philips Laboratories.

Onn, S.-P., & Grace, A. A. (1994). Dye coupling between rat striatal neurons recorded in vivo: Compartmental organization and modulation by dopamine. *Journal of Neurophysiology, 71*, 1917–1934.

Ostrowski, J. P., & Burdick, J. W. (1993). Designing feedback algorithms for controlling the periodic motions of legged robots. In *Proceedings of the 1993 IEEE international conference on robotics and automation* (pp. 254–260). IEEE Robotics and Automation Society.

Raibert, M. H. (1986). *Legged robots that balance.* Cambridge, MA: MIT Press.

Rosenbaum, D. A. (1991). *Human motor control.* San Diego: Academic Press.

Stan, M. R., Burleson, W. P., Connolly, C. I., & Grupen, R. A. (1994). Analog vlsi for robot path planning. *Journal of VLSI Signal Processing, 8(1)*, 61–73.

Tarassenko, L., & Blake, A. (1991). Analogue computation of collision-free paths. In *Proceedings of the 1991 IEEE international conference on robotics and automation* (pp. 540–545). IEEE.

Wickens, J. (1993). *A theory of the striatum,* Vol. 7, Pergamon studies in neuroscience. New York: Pergamon Press.

Winter, D. A. (1990). *Biomechanics and motor control of human movement.* New York: John Wiley & Son, New York.

Yoon, Y. S., & Mansour, J. M. (1982). The passive elastic moment at the hip. *Journal of Biomechanics, 15*, 905–910.

Contributors

Lorraine G. Allan
Psychology Department
McMaster University
Hamilton, Ontario, Canada

Eric Amezeen
Faculty of Human Movement
Sciences
Vrije Universiteit
Amsterdam, The Netherlands

Polemnia Amezeen
Faculty of Human Movement
Sciences
Vrije Universiteit
Amsterdam, The Netherlands

Heather Jane Barnes
Department of Psychology
University of North Carolina,
Greensboro
Greensboro, North Carolina

Steven Boker
Department of Psychology
University of Notre Dame
Notre Dame, Indiana

Darlene H. Brunzell
Department of Psychology
University of Massachusetts
Amherst, Massachusetts

June-Seek Choi
Department of Psychology
University of Massachusetts
Amherst, Massachusetts

Russell Church
Department of Psychology
Brown University
Providence, Rhode Island

Charles E. Collyer
Department of Psychology
University of Rhode Island
Kingston, Rhode Island

Christopher Connolly
SRI International
Menlo Park, California

Frederick J. Diedrich
Department of Psychology
Indiana University
Bloomington, Indiana

John Gibbon
Biopsychology
New York State Psychiatric
Institute
New York, New York

Roderic A. Grupen
Laboratory for Perceptual Robotics
Computer Science Department
University of Massachusetts
Amherst, Massachusetts

Kathleen Y. Haaland
Department of Veterans Affairs
Medical Center
Albuquerque, New Mexico

Deborah L. Harrington
Department of Veterans Affairs
Medical Center
Albuquerque, New Mexico

Kjeldy A. Haugsjaa
Laboratory For Perceptual Robotics
Computer Science Department
University of Massachusetts
Amherst, Massachusetts

Kenneth G. Holt
Department of Physical Therapy
Boston University
Boston, Massachusetts

John Jeka
Department of Kinesiology
College of Health and Human
Performance
University of Maryland
College Park, Maryland

Bruce A. Kay
Department of Cognitive &
Linguistic Sciences
Brown University
Providence, Rhode Island

Michael Kubovy
Psychology Department
University of Virginia
Charlottesville, Virginia

Tiffany Mattson
Department of Psychology
Hamilton College
Clinton, New York

Warren Meck
Department of Psychology:
Experimental
Duke University
Durham, North Carolina

John Moore
Department of Psychology
University of Massachusetts
Amherst, Massachusetts

Trevor Penney
Max Planck Institute of Cognitive
Neuroscience
Leipzig, Germany

Bruno H. Repp
Haskins Laboratories
New Haven, Connecticut

David A. Rosenbaum
Department of Psychology
Pennsylvania State University
University Park, Pennsylvania

Kamal Souccar
Laboratory For Perceptual Robotics
Computer Science Department
University of Massachusetts
Amherst, Massachusetts

Michael T. Turvey
Center for the Ecological Study of
Perception and Action
University of Connecticut
Storrs, Connecticut

Jonathan Vaughan
Department of Psychology
Hamilton College
Clinton, New York

William H. Warren, Jr.
Department of Cognitive &
Linguistic Sciences
Brown University
Providence, Rhode Island

Author Index

Subject Index